the Boatbuilder's Apprentice

The Ins and Outs of Building Lapstrake, Carvel, Stitch-and-Glue,
Strip-Planked, and Other Wooden Boats

greg rössel

International Marine / McGraw-Hill

Camden, Maine ■ New York ■ Chicago ■ San Francisco ■ Lisbon ■ London ■ Madrid ■ Mexico City
Milan ■ New Delhi ■ San Juan ■ Seoul ■ Singapore ■ Sydney ■ Toronto

The McGraw·Hill Companies

3 4 5 6 6 7 8 9 WC*K* WC*K* 0 9

Library of Congress Cataloging-in-Publication Data
Rössel, Greg, 1951-
   The boatbuilder's apprentice : the ins and outs of building lapstrake, carvel, stitch-and-glue, strip-planked, and other wooden boats / Greg Rössel.
        p.   cm.
   Includes index.
   ISBN-13: 978-0-07-14605-5 (hardcover : alk. paper)
   ISBN-10: 0-07-146405-0
   1. Boatbuilding—Handbooks, manuals, etc. 2. Wooden boats—Design and construction—Handbooks, manuals, etc. I. Title.
   VM351.R675 2006
   623.8'184—dc22   2006029380

Questions regarding the content of this book should be addressed to
International Marine
P.O. Box 220
Camden, ME 04843
internationalmarine.com

Questions regarding the ordering of this book should be addressed to
The McGraw-Hill Companies
Customer Service Department
P.O. Box 547
Blacklick, OH 43004
Retail customers: 1-800-262-4729
Bookstores: 1-800-722-4726

A version of Chapter 2 originally appeared in *WoodenBoat*; portions of Chapter 3 originally appeared in *Water Craft*; a portion of Chapter 4 originally appeared in *Water Craft*; Chapter 14 originally appeared in *Water Craft*; Chapter 17 originally appeared in *WoodenBoat*; Chapter 18 originally appeared in *Classic Boat*; parts of Chapter 20 originally appeared in *Maine Boats and Harbors* and *Classic Boat*; Chapter 21 originally appeared in *National Fisherman*; a version of Chapter 22 originally appeared in *WoodenBoat*; a version of Chapter 28 originally appeared in *WoodenBoat*; Chapter 28 originally appeared in *Classic Boat*; Chapter 29 originally appeared in *Water Craft*; Chapter 30 originally appeared in *Water Craft*; Chapter 31 originally appeared in *WoodenBoat*; Chapter 32 originally appeared *WoodenBoat*; Chapter 38 originally appeared in *Classic Boat*.

Photographs and boat plans are by the author unless otherwise noted.

To B.B., Carl, Hap, and Will—master mechanics all—thank you.

Contents

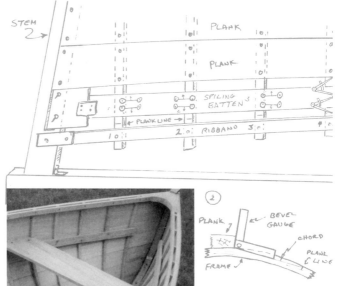

Acknowledgments

Many thanks to good friends, who kindly took the time to proofread and reread, debug, cajole, provide photos and offer gentle suggestions on how to make the text better. Thanks to Will Ansel; John Brooks and Ruth Ann Hill; Ben Fuller; Paul Gartside; Ted Moores; Harry Bryan; Ford Reid; Koji Matano; Adam Green; Joe Youcha; Sam Devlin; Kent Thurston; Andy Fishkind; Matthew P. Murphy; Jason Rucker; John Harris; Emily Herman; Bill Doll; Muriel Short; Pygmy Kayak and Dave Grimmer; Rich Hilsinger; Bob Nutt; Bob Savage; Ellis Rowe; Jim Brown; Alan Kiehle; and David Stimson.

And thanks once again to my most tolerant wife Norma who endured predawn typing, late-night drawing, and mountains of plans, reference books, photos, blueprints and teetering towers of text; and to Bob Holtzman, good friend and editor extraordinaire who was able to assemble this book.

Preface

It's a marvel that anyone even talks about, much less builds, wooden boats any more. After all, there are so many more modern materials that one could build with—aluminum, steel, fiberglass, and exotic composite sandwiches of materials such as kevlar, carbon fiber, and extruded-polypropylene honeycomb cores. All these make great building materials. One would think that wood would be put gracefully out to pasture and that the mechanics that build boats with it would be assigned the same historically interesting status as buggy whip manufacturers and gargoyle carvers.

So, what does wood have going for it?

As for beauty, wood is without peer. No other medium offers the appeal that wood does. Fiberglass boatbuilders know this and incorporate wood trim into their better models and will even go as far as casting faux plank lines into their hulls. From the humblest scow to the grandest of cruisers, the eye has no problem picking up the crispness of lines and fairness of curve that wood affords. A boat of wood often has a classic design that, if well maintained, has an heirloom quality.

Wood is infinitely variable. Indeed, almost any style or shape of boat, be it demanding or simple, can be built from wood, without expensive molds and forms. Traditional wooden boats are repairable—a quality that anyone who has purchased a toaster recently can appreciate. Hulls are built of replaceable components that, if damaged, can be replicated easily. And then there is the sheer practicality of the stuff. The raw materials can be gotten locally at a reasonable cost. Wood is a renewable resource that is accessible, affordable, and in many localities, the most logical alternative.

Wooden boats are a natural for the home builder. They are assembled piece by piece in a logical manner, with low-tech tools. Home boatbuilding offers a way to obtain a top-notch vessel at a bargain price, with the bonus of satisfaction in a job well done. For one-off construction, wood is quite cost-competitive with either fiberglass or aluminum. In short, a home-built wooden boat offers choice.

Not sold yet? Well, how about thinking of wood as a sophisticated, modern structural composite of lightweight cellulose and glue? Wood has high compression strength, in some cases higher in proportion to its weight than steel. Wood is naturally very durable: if not attacked by living organisms, it will last for hundreds or even thousands of years. Wood can have high bending strength. Wood is tough stuff that will resist abrasion much better than fiberglass, and it doesn't rust like steel. It retains its strength despite repeated stress cycles of tension and compression from rough seas, and it doesn't get brittle with age as fiberglass and plastic can. Indeed, with a bit of research, a builder can select and tailor woods with just the right qualities of durability, weight, compression strength, and bending strength necessary for the job.

Introduce modern adhesives and laminated structures and we ratchet wood up the technology scale.

With plywood, and with modern construction methods such as glued lapstrake and glass-covered thin-strip planking, the mechanic can produce hulls that are lighter, very strong, quickly built, and structurally stable—while still maintaining many of the elegant qualities of sawn lumber. Boat design software is able to assure that even the relatively simple shapes of most flat-panel plywood boats are seaworthy and efficient, while Computer Numerical Control (CNC) cutting machines can cut panels and planks with tremendous speed and precision and minimal waste, making the vessel very economical and easy to assemble.

Perhaps the quote that best sums up the argument for building with wood comes from multi-hull designer and builder Jim Brown. Jim is most famous for his Constant Camber wood-and-epoxy laminated boat designs that are in use all over the planet. No neo-Luddite, he is part contrarian, part Buckminster Fuller when it comes to boatbuilding. Says Jim, "Indeed, I think wooden boats must be the most lifelike of all our artifacts—especially the ones that sail. They respond to the environment, and communicate with their maker, more than anything else humans can devise." One can't ask for much more than that.

HOW TO USE THIS BOOK

Over the years of teaching at the WoodenBoat School, I've often been asked by students what sort of boat they should build. This question is more complex than it seems. The smorgasbord of choices in hull styles, techniques, materials; whether to go with oar, sail, or power; kits versus plank-on-frame; and owner preference all tend to muddy the waters and (at least initially) be daunting enough to make one give serious consideration to that used aluminum pontoon party boat offered for sale by the neighbor. But as with most endeavors, just a bit of information can demystify the process and make all the difference in coming to a satisfactory decision.

Such is the intent of this book—to provide an introduction to and survey of the whole range of wooden boat building. We'll explore the pros and cons of different planking schemes and construction styles (such as traditional carvel and lapstrake construction, stitch-and-glue, and strip planking) and their levels of complexity to help the reader understand what he or she is getting into. We'll address the question of whether to build right-side-up or upside down; look at the tools and materials necessary for the various construction methods; and describe the essential techniques associated with each, such as steam bending, cutting a rabbet, scarfing, laminating, and oar and spar making. And since most boats that are not built from kits must be lofted, or drawn out full size prior to beginning construction, there's a detailed discussion of that fascinating and useful procedure.

How to build a boat is only half the question—the other half is what kind of boat one wants to own and use. So we'll also compare some of the attributes of hull shapes—flat-bottomed, round, V-hull, and semi-dory style—and examine why they are used in different situations. Finally, we'll look at and recommend several specific examples of good boat designs for sail, power, oar, and paddle.

This book is organized somewhat as I teach: not with a rigid, formal structure, but by logical associations, interesting digressions, spontaneous application of the facts at hand, and (I hope) a bit of humor. As such, it need not be read in order, from beginning to end—although it can be used in that fashion. Rather, it is designed to be used as a reference in which the reader can access the desired information quickly. Whenever possible, a number of techniques and options are illustrated to address a given situation.

This is the nature of boatbuilding. There is always another way to do the job, and the best choice depends on the situation, the materials to be used, the amounts of time and money available, and the builder's predilections. The knowledge and skills to build a boat (like the shop tools employed in their construction) are best acquired a bit at a time, in manageable amounts, when you need them. And like a good tool, this book is designed to be used, marked up, sawdust-filled, and coffee-stained. Happy building!

Introduction
Selecting a Small Boat to Build

Years ago, before the advent of easy communication, ready transportation, and the widespread ability to commit design lines to paper, every creek, cove, harbor, and bay had its boatbuilders, constructing what they considered the ideal boats for their local waters. It could be said these boats went through a process of natural selection: the best of the lot survived and were nurtured and improved, and the weak ones were left to molder in the weeds or burnt for their fastenings—if they made it back to shore in the first place. The survivors—often the best of the best— were the rich fodder that kept Howard Chapelle and other historians busy taking lines and they are also the ones now gracing the storage barns of maritime museums around the world.

These old-timers exhibit the same kind of exquisite fine-tuning and tweaking that is currently lavished on racecars and aircraft. From Maine came the nimble peapod whose double-ended shape allowed it to work safely around ledges and shallow waters, and whose carrying capacity made it a natural for the lobster industry. The Sea Bright skiff—with its flat bottom that sat upright on the beach and a unique ability to ride the surf over sand bars—made it just the ticket for working the beaches of New Jersey. The swift and stable sharpie could be found working the shallow oyster beds of Long Island Sound and getting the harvest back quickly to market in New Haven, Connecticut, and the swift and able Whitehall-types acted as taxis and pickup trucks serving the schooners in New York Harbor.

These are just a small sampling from the northeast of the United States. They all had one thing in common: they were uniquely developed to serve the needs of their users.

But times change and although the notion of totally standardized and homogenized, one-size-fits-all design never really took off in the marine industry, the constraints imposed by mass production and marketing tended to favor certain kinds of boats. It's more in the salesman's best interest to offer a boat of general appeal that will do okay everywhere, than to try to build a tight campaign around "the hot little model that will blow the doors off the other porgy fishery competitors in Raritan Bay!" The introduction of lightweight and relatively powerful engines and cheap fuel encouraged speed over efficiency. The costs of labor and materials tended to favor simple-to-assemble hulls with a "rounded off" nonidiosyncratic personality. Good for business; not so good for diversity.

Fortunately, as a home-based boatbuilder, you have the opportunity to assemble a purpose-built boat that has nearly all the features you're looking for. Yes, there are some compromises—no design does everything well, and there is probably no such thing as a "general purpose boat." But then, you probably wouldn't expect to haul gravel in a sports car either. The trick is to decide how you are going to use the boat (mostly) and select the design characteristics to match. Start by asking yourself a few questions, such as:

The flat-bottomed sharpie, which evolved as a working boat for shell-fishermen, makes an excellent shallow-water daysailer.

The Whitehall style is swift and seaworthy and lends itself to building in various construction methods. When planked carvel-style, it just oozes grace and tradition.

- Do you fancy rowing, or a small sailing craft? What about an outboard? Usually a design will do one thing better than the others.
- What's your likely boating destination? What sort of waters will the boat be used in? Does it need to stand up to the chop of a lake? Or should it have a shallow draft hull that allows for backwater gunkholing? Maybe you want something more robust for a wide-open bay, or a nimble boat that can dodge rocks on a whitewater river?
- Will it live in the water or on a trailer? Will it require a mooring (and do you have access to one)?
- Should it be fancy or utilitarian? How much time do you have to do maintenance?
- How much time do you have to build—or use it?

While you are pondering, let's take a look at a few samples.

WHAT MOVES YOU?

The type of propulsion you choose is one of the most basic decisions you will have to make. You may already picture yourself sailing, rowing, paddling, or driving something with an engine. But let's look into the implications of these choices.

Oar and Paddle

Maybe your plans involve your family, and you're looking for a true picnic boat—one that's great for rowing, tracks well, is able to handle a bit of chop on a bay or lake, has good carrying capacity, and might look good with a basket, a bottle of wine, and a parasol. A round-bottomed pulling boat may be a good choice (see Chapter 33). These boats aren't great for sailing, as their long keel makes them reluctant to come about, and they would have to be fitted with either a centerboard (which would cut into the usable space) or leeboards (which require a lot of tending, and are much less parasol friendly). On the other hand, these sleek hulls will handle a light outboard motor (especially electric) nicely.

Perhaps instead you wish to venture offshore single-handed. For cruising, touring, island camping, or simply low-cost exploration, the long, efficient, and seaworthy sea kayak is a great choice (see Chapter 34). There is a fine selection of plans and kits available for construction in either plywood or strip planking.

Available as a kit from Chesapeake Light Craft, the Chester Yawl is a round-bottomed pulling boat that looks good and is relatively easy to build. (Photo: Joe Provey, Chesapeake Light Craft)

Kayaks can be built from kits or plans in plywood, strip planking, or skin-on-frame, and by other methods. The lovely lines of this kit-built model should put to rest any qualms about the appearance of a plywood boat. (Photo: Pygmy Boats)

Canoes offer access to remote areas that are inaccessible by any other type of boat. Traditional wood/canvas canoes can be rugged, nimble, and capable of handling whitewater at various levels. (Photo: Peter Wallace, courtesy of Northwoods Canoe Co.)

For simplicity of construction, a feeling of stability in protected waters, or use as a tender to a larger craft, it is hard to beat a flatiron skiff powered by either oar or outboard (see Chapter 33). These boats are also great for bird watching (or hunting), fishing, or as an introductory boat for a young person.

If your plans involve access to remote waters, either by cartopping or by portaging, there is a vast array of canoe styles from which to choose, using almost every available method of construction: traditional wood and canvas, strip planking, stitch-and-glue, and even plank on frame (see Chapter 34). Canoe designs range from open water, moose-carrying varieties to river running sports cars to double-paddled, decked canoes that will float on a hint of water and take you to the back reaches of a wilderness waterway or cypress swamp.

One of the easiest hull types to build by traditional methods, the flatiron skiff offers great stability in protected waters.

Sail

The same sort of variety is available for sail (see Chapter 36). If you have access to deep water and a mooring, you might choose something such as Joel White's elegant Herreshoff-inspired Haven 12½. This round-bottomed, plank-on-frame hull with a combination lead ballast keel and centerboard is an extraordinary daysailer and a head turner in any harbor.

Yearning for a (relatively) low-cost cruiser? Perhaps a hard-chined, 25'7" Sea Bird yawl might be for you (see Chapter 37). This updated plywood-over-sawn-frame version is based on a 1901 design by Thomas Day and C. D. Mower. Built in numbers all over the world, this economic vessel sports a Marconi yawl rig, will accommodate two to four crew overnight, and is even trailerable.

Is the Sea Bird too much boat, too much time to build, or too much money? How about something for sporty sailing conditions—the 12', flat-bottomed, plywood San Francisco Pelican? A bit of a cross between a dory and a sampan and designed as a heavy weather sailer, this little centerboard skiff can be built easily and inexpensively (see Chapter 36).

How about something with a little Scandinavian influence? Iain Oughtred based his 14½' lapstrake, multi-chined double ender, Whilly Boat, on the Shetland ness yoles and sixterns (see Chapter 36). Built with glued lap plywood, and with no lofting necessary, this

A lot of work and skill go into building a Haven 12½, from the board of Joel White. The result is a sweet-sailing beauty that will delight any sailor and complement the docks of any yacht club. (Photo: Rich Hilsinger, WoodenBoat)

rugged little daysailer can be built with either a centerboard or a daggerboard and will easily live on a trailer.

Power

There are also a multitude of options when it comes to powerboats (see Chapter 37). A humble outboard-powered dory or semi-dory, built either traditionally or with plywood, can get you out on the water for a bargain basement price. For fuel economy, Harry Bryan's lapstrake, 16½' V-hulled Rambler will give you 20-miles-per-gallon frugality with an 8-horsepower inboard diesel. For the fisherman and pleasure cruiser, you might consider Sam

Devlin's stitch-and-glue Dipper power cruiser, which takes but 10 to 15 horsepower to push at 8 knots with good range. Or perhaps one of myriad workboat-based hulls that are swift, seaworthy, and economical.

DESIGN CONSIDERATIONS AND COMPROMISES

Transoms, Lines, and Power

Take a look at old-time designs in photographs and lines plans and one thing becomes readily apparent: the hull will be relatively narrow, and the bottom of

The Pelican is surprisingly capable for such a small boat. As a popular class racer on windy San Francisco Bay, it has to be. (Photo: Ellis Rowe)

the transom (if there is one) will minimally touch, or be elevated totally out of, the water. This isn't an antiquarian affection. It is an expression of designing for efficiency during a time when manufacturers simply didn't have access to large engines.

The most efficient waterline shape for a displacement (nonplaning) vessel is one that has a sharp or hollow entrance at the bow and tapers gracefully to the stern. Introduce something that disturbs that flow of water (like a transom), and you create unnecessary drag. The more transom there is in the water, the greater the drag. Compare those broad-butted barges that are passed off as rowboats and often rented at city parks to weekend picnickers with a svelte Whitehall or a Rangeley. The dowdy park craft pokes along with eddies boiling away at the stern and sweat pouring off the brow of the muttering Sunday captain as he toils away at the sweeps. The oarsman in the nicely designed pulling boat of the same length, load, and perhaps oars, experiences none of the consternation of his plodding colleague. The boat tracks easily, rows with little effort, and produces very little wake. (Excessive wake is an indicator of wasted energy.)

On the other hand, if you are considering primarily outboard power instead of oars, a wider transom will provide more buoyancy aft to support the weight of the engine, while less rocker, or curve in the fore and aft direction, will contribute to the boat's directional stability. It's all a matter of the intent of the design.

Designed for dory-lap planking, this semi-dory is a great all-purpose power skiff for work or play.

Gently-curving waterlines at the stern help a boat move smoothly through the water. Even carrying a load, this Whitehall wouldn't submerge the bottom of its transom.

Not all transoms want to stay out of the water. Most outboard-powered boats need a wide flat stern to serve as a planing surface and provide sufficient buoyancy to support the weight of the engine.

At the opposite end of the same Whitehall, the hollow entrance helps part the water easily.

Greater length is desirable—sometimes. With displacement vessels, the laws of physics dictate that the longer the vessel, the faster it will go. Skene's *Elements of Yacht Design* offers the following formula for determining the top speed of displacement craft: The square root of the designed water line times 1.25 equals the speed in knots. Maybe small potatoes—but in a race, or when rowing over a long distance, a little extra speed makes a big difference. On the other hand, length imposes some liabilities, such as slower turning response, and difficulties of transportation and storage.

Keels and Stems

A long keel, as found on a pulling boat, will keep a boat "on the rails," resisting sideways movement from the wind. This quality can be a joy while rowing down a lazy river, cruising across an open lake or bay, or shooting under narrow bridges. It can, however, make changing course a chore as the boat has to be levered around with oar or rudder against the keel's resistance. On the other hand, a near keelless vessel can turn on a dime and will draw less water, but can feel twitchy when crossing open water. A skeg will provide better tracking as long as it's deep enough to remain in the water however the boat is loaded.

Many traditional designs have a perpendicular or plumb stem that meets the keel at a near right angle (the forefoot). This assists the long keel in keeping the boat on track. It also adds resistance that makes turning slower, can make for difficult towing, and is problematic in following seas and surf. A more angled or raked stem with a cut-away or rounded-off forefoot is a better choice when quick maneuvering is a prime concern.

*A plumb stem and a raked
stem, or cutaway forefoot.*

For sail, a full or ballast keel promises stability and "big boat" performance. Generally, this kind of hull will live on a mooring and will need access to deeper waters. For shallower waters and/or boats whose mooring is a trailer, designs with a centerboard, dagger board, or lee boards are a good choice. A grand compromise between the two versions is the aforementioned Haven 12½—an adaptation of the deep-drawing, ballast-keeled Buzzards Bay 12½ where, by modifying the lines slightly and adding a centerboard, the designer was able to reduce the vessel's draft while retaining the displacement, stability, and performance.

Flat bottoms vs. round (vs. hard-chined vs. multi-chined)

Then there is the matter of choosing what shape of hull to build. As always, the choices involve nuance and compromise. Flat-bottomed hulls provide a lot of bang-for-the-buck in shallow water and near-shore operation. They are relatively easy to build and have a lot of initial stability. They can, however, provide a rough ride in a sea. Round-bottomed hulls are considerably more

complex to build, but are elegant, strong, quite efficient under power, and much more comfortable in a chop. They will roll more readily than a flat-bottomed hull, but their ultimate stability (their ability to resist capsize) may be greater. (Think of the difference between getting into a flatiron skiff versus a canoe.)

Hard-chined hulls, with more or less V-shape to the bottom, are popular as power craft, because they plane readily but don't pound like flat-bottomed boats. They are also common choices for sail or oar, as they are (or at least appear to be) less complicated to build than round hulls, and the form is much more accommodating for plywood construction. The hard-chined hull provides more stability than a round one, but it also has more wetted surface, which increases resistance through the water and so requires more power (be it by oar, engine, or sail) to attain the same speed. Multi-chined hulls sound terribly complex and high tech. Actually, this style has been around for ages. Good examples include the old-time Swampscot type dory, the standard-transom semi-dories, and some modern plywood kayaks. The plank lines generate

Harry Bryan's handsome Handy Billy has a V-shaped bottom and hard chines.

facets on the hull, not unlike those produced on a round-bottomed lapstrake (clinker) hull, only there are fewer of them. Thus the hull exhibits many of the characteristics of a truly round hull, but it is much easier and faster to build. Multi-chined hulls are good candidates for plywood plank construction.

Weight and See

Much is made of the relatively light weight of many of today's small craft designs. Less weight certainly can be a boon when single-handedly turning a boat over for painting, loading it onto a vehicle, portaging, or launching at some remote site. That said, some weight is not necessarily a bad thing—if it leads to a more rugged, stable, and seaworthy craft. Once the boat gets moving, the additional weight of a conventionally built hull can work in your favor, as its greater momentum slices through waves that might daunt a lighter hull and allows the boat to "carry" between oar or paddle strokes.

Hey buddy, do you have the time?

It can be tempting to build too big of a boat. Many dream of sailing their boat around the globe like Joshua Slocum, when really what's needed is something to get them out on the lake for an afternoon. There are a lot of pieces that go into a boat. The larger the boat, the more pieces that need to be made, the heavier they will be, and the more they will cost.

Then there is the matter of how much extra time it will take to build and maintain the boat. A completed smaller boat in use is a lot more fun than a dust-covered half-built larger one, neglected and forgotten in the back shed. For all its class and heritage, a traditionally built plank-on-frame boat will take a lot longer to build than one built of plywood, especially in the stitch-and-glue method. So you'd better ask yourself what your primary objective is: to build a boat or to use it? Building is certainly a worthy objective, but it might not be yours.

Storage and Transport

Size and construction method also come into consideration when thinking about storage and over-land travel. An in-the-water mooring is the ideal way to keep some boats. Water is, after all, the boat's natural environment, keeping the hull well supported and at proper moisture content. That said, in-the-water storage can be expensive and hard to come by in many regions. There may be mooring or dockage fees, and maintenance expenses. For many, a better harbor is a trailer in a carport.

Carvel hulls are at their best in the water, since this way they avoid constantly going through shrinking and swelling cycles. They can live on a trailer during the boating season (mine do), but precautions have to be taken.

Lapstrake hulls, both traditional and glued-lap, are certainly happy in the water but also fair much better than carvel as trailer boats. Indeed, before fiberglass hit the scene, the common family trailerable runabout was a lapstrake—think Old Town, Grady-White, and their kin.

Traditional strip-planked hulls like being full-time water dwellers, while glass-and-epoxy-embalmed strip hulls are delighted to be anywhere.

Plywood hulls are much the same. The shrinking and swelling of the natural woods is not a consideration. In many ways (although certainly not all) they can be treated like those other laminated boats—fiberglass.

Which brings us to the matter of transport. Consideration needs to be given to the size of vehicle you have or want to own. Despite the pleas of motor vehicle manufacturers, you do not need a colossal four-wheel drive truck with a Cummins diesel to pull a light boat and trailer. It simply isn't true. But if your boat weighs the equivalent of 20 well-fed Holsteins, you will need some sort of conveyance with commensurate towing capabilities. It is worth checking out the boat's projected weight before building.

Winter storage at a boatyard can be pricy. If possible, the best place for your boat is at home. There

How big a boat can you move? Where will you store it? Will it live on a mooring, or on a trailer? Let logistics influence your choice of a boat to build.

you can keep an eye on it, keep the snow from building up, and remember to do spring maintenance as the old girl is right there to remind you every time you walk out the door. The question is, can you store a 40-foot lobsterboat complete with traditional bait buckets in the back yard, inside a plastic building, without the neighbors sending over the local code enforcement officer?

Maintenance and Reparability

That there are still so many wooden boats around today is a tribute to their ease of repair. Traditional hulls are a compendium of replaceable components. When a part is damaged or wears out, the fastenings can be removed and the defective part can be easily replaced with a newly fashioned one. Longevity is increased by using as many rot-resistant materials as possible and ensuring plenty of ventilation.

New designs use a higher-tech approach. To gain strength and lightness, many are totally glued together and are embalmed in glass and epoxy with fittings and trim bedded in indestructible polyurethane adhesives. It's an approach that works well until something needs fixing—and then it's like having to change a tire on your car and discovering that the manufacturer has welded the lug nuts on. On the other hand, a strong argument in favor of composite boats is the ability to use wood as an engineering material and to put just enough wood in the right place to do the job with the least amount of weight.

As good as these newer methods are, care still needs to be taken to ensure their longevity. Look for designs that offer inspection access and ventilation. If the hull is designed to be totally covered with epoxy, make sure it is totally sealed—especially the end grain to prevent water migration into the wood. All fastenings that penetrate the hull need to be properly sealed. Since any fittings and trim that can possibly be damaged probably will be damaged sometime, they should be bedded in a removable compound. If, however, a hull was not designed to be sealed, do not seal it. If a part was intended to move and breathe, let it.

A complaint often heard about wooden boats is that there is so much springtime maintenance—especially related to applying new finish. Much of this conundrum can be traced to owner/operator-induced varnish syndrome. A glass-slick, multi-coated brightwork finish is a joy to behold. Unfortunately it is very time consuming to apply properly, and it doesn't hold up well under heavy usage. Fortunately there is a cure for this malady: paint. Not only does paint build coats quicker than varnish, but it also resists abrasion better in marine applications. In many ways paint will enhance the lines of a hull better than varnish, as the eye is not distracted by the wood grain. Light paint colors will make a less-than-fair hull look respectable. Saving the varnish for just the trim and spars not only saves maintenance time and headaches but also can make the boat look better.

REGULATIONS

In the United States, home builders of monohull boats less than 20 feet in length are expected to comply with the same safety standards and administrative regulations as professional boat manufacturers and are required to display a U.S. Coast Guard Maximum Capacities label or plate in a location where it is visible to the operator when getting the boat underway. Sailboats, canoes, kayaks, and inflatables are exempt from this rule. Backyard boatbuilders are also required to have a hull identification number (HIN) on their boat. All the rules change above 20 feet.

This is about safety. Overloading small craft is a common occurrence. If a hull sinks without any sort of flotation, it leaves the victims with nothing to cling to except their life preservers (if, on the off

Compliance with Coast Guard and other regulations is a good idea. Even a capacity plate can add a touch of class if it's a nice brass one.

chance, they happen to be wearing them). Gasoline fumes collecting in inadequately ventilated spaces can cause boats to blow up. Running at dark without navigational lights is asking for trouble. Putting too large an engine on a hull can make it handle dangerously. The Coast Guard, part of whose mandate is to rescue recreational boaters in trouble, has established standards for boats—mostly reasonable and easily complied with—intended to keep this part of their job to a minimum.

The regulations are available in a document called the "Boatbuilder's Handbook," available from the Coast Guard at www.uscgboating.org. This handbook has forms, the pertinent Code of Federal Regulations, and most importantly, design guidelines, such as safe loading and display of capacity information, flotation requirements, electrical systems, ventilation, and more. The Coast Guard encourages home boatbuilders to follow the guidelines. The rules are based on common sense and the tests are easy to perform and worthwhile to determine how many people you can safely carry in a design that was drawn before the Age of Litigation. The capacity plate is a simple way to alert everyone on board how many people are considered safe. It doesn't stop overloading, but it does negate the "I didn't know" excuse. Insurance companies like these too.

The individual states administer the federal hull-numbering requirement. The HIN is a handy way for state governments to collect revenues, identify boating scofflaws, and return lost or stolen boats to their owners.

In some states, municipal offices have request forms that can be used to obtain a HIN for a home-built boat. Another option is to go to the National Association of State Boating Law Administrators website: www.nasbla.org. Click on "Boating Law Administrators" at the top, then select your state and look for "Titling and Registration." This should provide you a telephone number for a real person to speak to about obtaining a HIN.

PLANS AND BLUEPRINTS

So where can you get plans? There are a plethora of designs available (see Appendix B). New designs can be purchased directly from the designer. Historic plans, some of them available for little more than the price of reproduction, can be obtained from maritime museums. Check the back pages of magazines such as *WoodenBoat* and *Boatbuilder* for advertisements. The Internet has been a boon for accessing great designers throughout the world. Another place to find functional plans is in boatbuilding books.

What you will generally get with your blueprints is a set of lines and offsets for the hull and a sheet (or sheets) of construction details. The level of detail varies with the plan and the designer. You also get a reasonable assurance that the plans are buildable. With designs from living designers, you often get to speak with the person who drew them. With the historic plans, chances are there are replicas out there that you can see and perhaps even use.

A Case for Lofting

Just the thought of lofting will send many a novice builder forth to the catacombs of catalogs in a near-futile search for the Holy Grail of boat plans: the one with perfect full-size patterns. Alas, all too often, those highly sought blueprints are but a chimera. And if the plan is actually discovered, those full-size patterns are often found to be disturbingly inaccurate. Why inaccuracies in patterns? It could be the print itself. Other than Mylar, plan material (i.e., paper) is dimensionally unstable. Or the pattern plan or part of it may have simply been drawn incorrectly. Without lofting, you really don't know for sure. Unless you are building a stitch-and-glue hull or building from a kit, you will need to loft.

So what is this business of lofting anyway? Think of a set of boat plans as a collection of interlocking topographic maps with lots of information that is

Lofting your boat will give you a comprehensive look at how it will go together.

drawn to a given scale. Lofting is just taking the lines provided on those plans and expanding and drawing them out full size to get the patterns to build the boat. It is through this process that the details and the lines are fully refined and debugged. The lofted plan not only generates the curves of the molds that dictate the final shape of the hull, but also provides full-size templates for the stem, keel and transom, bolt patterns for the backbone, and the exact shape of the centerboards and many other parts. In many ways, lofting allows you to virtually "build" the boat with a pencil on the floor. Most problems in the plans can be found and fixed quickly at this stage with an eraser instead of later with a saw, shims, and glue. By the time you get around to building the boat for real, you already know where and how each piece of wood is installed. A small investment in lofting pays big dividends in savings in time and materials.

Pattern Making

Wooden boatbuilding is more akin to dressmaking and tailoring than to, say, cabinet making. Domestic furniture is most often joined at right angles, plans are typically precise, and you can measure and cut the shape shown in the plans and expect the pieces to fit together if you've done your work carefully. But consider what goes into making a suit or a dress: you develop patterns that allow you to wrap expensive, flexible panels of material around a complex, curvaceous surface. Considerations need to be made for movement of the garment and the structure underneath it, and the more voluptuous and buxom the subject is, the greater the need for patterns. And the better the pattern, the better the product will be, wasting less material and time. So it is with boatbuilding. Hull forms range from simple to complex. The more complex the hull form, the more sophisticated the pattern must be. Indeed, it can be argued that boatbuilding is all about pattern making.

Modifying Designs and Designing Your Own

It can be tempting to eliminate seemingly unnecessary "clutter"—thwart knees, posts, maybe some frames—in an attempt to lighten or simplify a design. This sort of work should only be done with great caution and research. A traditionally built boat is a matrix of parts that depend on one another for strength. That inconvenient bulkhead being nixed to save room could be the moral equivalent to pulling out a bearing wall in your house. What seems to be a good idea at the time can come back to haunt you later.

Material changes can cause problems as well. For example, taking the lines for a traditional plank-on-frame pulling boat and changing it to a modern strip-plank system can lighten the boat by more than half. This is maybe, but not necessarily, a good thing. The boat will float a lot higher, and that can affect how it handles or its stability. The oarlocks may ride higher out of the water than is comfortable. You might end up having to add ballast—concrete blocks or bags of turnips—just to get the boat back to where it performs as expected. Changing a boat that has relatively flat sides from standard planking to plywood sheets can

cause difficulty as well. The hull may have a more complex shape than appears at first, and the sheet plywood may not be able to handle the compound curves the way that the individual planks can.

Then there is the question of that design that would be perfect if only it were bigger. It is true that most designs can be blown up or shrunk by small percentages—up to 10%, perhaps. Much more than that and problems arise. As an analogy, say we have plans for a picnic table that is just about perfect—nice design, easy to build, but not big enough for all our friends. If we made it 50% larger, it would be just right. So be it. When done, it looks like the plans—only bigger! And there is plenty of room for everyone to sit. But . . . the comfortable 16″ high seat is now a foot-dangling 24″ and the tabletop, which had been 29″, is now a chest-high 43.5″—great for shoveling in the chow, I guess. And the new table is as heavy as a bucket of bricks. So it is with expanding the lines for a boat—without a lot of care, you may end up with more than you reckoned for.

How about designing your own first boat? While you can design a hull from scratch, and there are a number of good books on the subject, it begs the question: why bother? Building a boat involves a serious investment in time and materials. Do you really want to incur that expense for an unknown product that may or may not perform the way you want it to? Like buying an automobile, a good argument can be made for building a boat that you've had a chance to road test. Traditional designs went though a process of evolution before they became classics. New boat designers go to a lot of work to predict how a boat will perform. But don't let me influence your decision.

An alternative to designing your own is to take the lines from an existing historic vessel. There are still plenty of great boats out there that have not been measured. Perhaps there was a dynamite sloop you saw in the Bahamas, or a fishing boat in Newfoundland that really struck your eye. The technique isn't difficult (we'll be dealing with that later in the book) and it's a chance to save a bit of history.

Part One

METHODS OF HULL CONSTRUCTION

*P*lanking the hull is the synthesis of appropriate technology, practicality, and elegance.

▪ 1 ▪

Construction Systems

One of the most important and intriguing considerations when deciding on a boat to build is what system to choose for hull construction. There is a vast range of styles to choose from. From the complex, time-and-material-consuming, to the relatively quick-and-easy, each of the systems has something to offer—that's why they were developed in the first place.

Considering boatbuilding historically, the business has always been about innovation, using the best from the past and embracing (albeit, many times begrudgingly) the latest in technology. New fangledness, however, does not necessarily make the method or the product better than the old way. Is a steel warehouse better than a post-and-beam barn? Both do the job they were intended to do.

It's all about using technology that is appropriate for the job. A laminated epoxy composite hull is great, but if you are in a remote locale where there is no way to manufacture the laminates and the glue is prohibitively expensive or impossible to import, building in the older plank-on-frame methods with indigenous materials makes a lot of sense.

There is also the matter of intangibles and philosophy. For many, there is a certain mojo when working with natural wood and time-tested methods. There is a smell and a tactile satisfaction that comes with shaping a cedar plank from raw material that was obviously a tree—bark, knots, and all—not that long ago. For others, building a boat from raw wood is about as up-to-date as gargoyle carving and as practical as deciding to build an automobile starting with iron ore and rubber trees.

Take planking for example. Not every style lends itself to every design. For example, stitch-and-glue is a wonderful innovation, but the technique is restricted by the constraints imposed by the manufactured material (i.e., plywood) used. There aren't many Herreshoff 12½-style boats being built in stitch-and-glue, much less any Friendship sloops. The hull shapes are simply too complex. For those designs, the highly versatile yet somewhat archaic carvel planking is the way to go. On the other hand, the simplicity of stitch-and-glue and the strength of plywood and epoxy make that technique a top choice for building a kayak. You could build a kayak in carvel, but the additional expense, time, weight, and maintenance hardly make it a first choice.

Then there are the versatile hull designs that can be built with a number of different techniques. Take the traditional Whitehall-type pulling boat. A beautiful and reliable hull can be fashioned using carvel, lapstrake (clinker), strip planking (either edge-nailed or glued-strip with fiberglass), glued lap, cold molding, or thoroughly modern, computer carved LapStitch planking.

You'll note that I'm referring to planking methods and construction methods almost interchangeably. In many ways, the two are nearly synonymous. Traditional carvel and lapstrake planking inevitably imply the use of plank-on-frame construction. Strip planking

CHOOSING THE BEST PLANKING OR CONSTRUCTION METHOD

The availability of building materials and where the boat will be used may dictate what type of planking or construction method is best. Strip planking was originally developed to take advantage of economical scraps and edgings from sawmills. In their heyday, the old-time dory builders had access to lumber cut from old forest trees of great girth. Building stock of that caliber is getting harder to come by, but plywood, applied either as sheets or as planks, can easily be substituted. Coastal dwellers who live in humid, temperate climes and can keep their craft in the water full time can take advantage of local woods and traditional lapstrake or carvel construction. On the other hand, people who live in semi-desert environments and keep their "prairie schooners" on a trailer in a hot carport will find that using glue-stabilized-and-embalmed plywood and epoxy/cloth-covered strip planks makes sense.

A range of appropriate options also exists for the construction of the backbone of the vessel. Early vessels used the naturally grown crooks of roots and branches, which were strong and rot-resistant. But the resource dwindled, so shorter and straighter pieces were used, augmented with top-notch joinery and what were, by

then, easily available mechanical fastenings. The next innovation, which was made possible by the introduction of truly waterproof adhesives, was the laminated backbone, built up from many thin strips of wood bound together with resorcinol or epoxy—ironically mimicking the strength of naturally grown crooks, and making fastenings less important. The next step was the "pour-a-keel" technology of lightweight-but-strong epoxy fillets reinforced with fibers and fiberglass cloth.

The same evolution can be seen with fasteners, perhaps starting with cinched-up sinews and moving to wooden trunnels ("tree nails," or wood pegs). Technology then introduced nails and rivets, followed by machined, threaded fasteners, followed by adhesives. Again, which to use depends on the situation. One could imagine a heavily built workboat that employs natural knees for the frames, natural lumber planks scarfed with epoxy to length and fastened to the frames with both trunnels and iron spikes, laminated deck beams held in place with threaded bolts, and a plywood deck fastened to the beams with screws and covered with Dynel cloth and epoxy. The builder probably wouldn't give it a second thought. It all works.

is also known as strip construction, or strip building, and since there's almost no structure to a strip-built hull besides the planks, this makes sense. The same goes for stitch-and-glue: it's a construction method that relies upon stitched-and-glued panels (in place of planks, *per se*).

PLANKING METHODS

Lapstrake

For hundreds of years, mechanics have had access to a plethora of planking methods. One of the oldest is the lapstrake or clinker method where the top edge of each plank is beveled, overlapped by, and fastened to the bottom edge of the next one up. Lapstrake boats are strong, relatively lightweight, and generally easy to keep tight (at least when new) thanks to the overlapping planks. Dory lap is a variation that uses a bevel on both the top and bottom edges of the plank. This is done to reduce the thickness of the lap. The glued plywood

Lapstrake planking.

A Rushton-style lapstrake pulling boat (Photo: Koji Matano)

lapstrake method (or simply "glued lap") was introduced just a few years ago, taking advantage of the benefits of plywood and epoxy to increase the durability of the planking, eliminate leaks, and cut down on the number of frames required.

Lapstrake construction in general is best suited for a hull without a tremendous amount of shape or large changes in girth or circumference in the hull moving fore to aft. For a good-looking job and for easy planking, care must be taken to carefully predetermine, or "line out," the plank locations. Curiously, lapstrake boats are somewhat "noisy" or musical as the moving water chortles past the laps.

Traditional lapstrake fares well out of the water for extended periods—that's why the method was often used for lifeboats.

Carvel Planking

Smooth or carvel planking has the classic look that is often associated with yachts. Any kind of hull can be built with edge-to-edge-fit carvel planking, as each individual plank is patterned and sculpted to shape. Where lapstrake planking is a series of flat planes with a bevel on one edge, the carvel plank is hollowed on the inside, rounded on the outside, and compound-beveled on one edge (occasionally two) to fit tightly against its neighbor. Watertightness comes from both this high-level joinery and a strand of cotton caulking driven into the seam between the planks. The driven cotton also stiffens the hull. Unlike lapstrake, carvel does not have the reinforcement offered by lapping each plank over its neighbor, so the planking

Carvel planking.

must be heavier. With the requirement to not just cut, but also form, each plank in three dimensions, traditional carvel is probably the most complicated of the planking methods.

Access to an electric planer is almost a must. A pattern must be made for each plank, in a process called spiling, and the bevels must be recorded and planed. After the planks are hung, the hull must be caulked with cotton.

Traditional carvel is good looking and very durable if well cared for. It is happiest when it can stay in the water throughout the season. That said, in a moderate climate and with a bit of care, a carvel hull can live happily on a trailer.

Some designs call for batten seam construction, in which a reinforcing hardwood batten runs behind each seam along its full length on the inside of the hull. Often seen on V-hulled power and sail boats, this adds strength and watertightness and a bit more complexity.

Both lapstrake and carvel are demanding of time and materials. Lapstrake planking is a lot more forgiving in the building process than carvel, however. Traditional boat planking is a bit like tailoring a suit, in that a pattern must be made for most pieces. The building

Batten seam construction.

techniques are not difficult, but they must be done. Boatbuilding lumber is a specialty item that can be hard to find, and after finding it, there is a considerable amount of waste material produced—a natural result of cutting curved pieces out of (usually) rectangular ones. That said, the result is worth it. The traditionally built hull is good looking, durable, and flexible, yet ironically, it is the easiest to repair.

Strip Planking

Strip planking is another form of carvel planking. Instead of patterning individual pieces of various widths and shapes, the builder uses long, narrow, flexible strips or battens. In traditional strip planking, the bottom edge of each strip has a compound bevel to match the angles of the previous strip. A later advance involves milling a concave shape into one edge of each strip, and a matching convex shape into the other, for a cove-and-bead arrangement. When put together, the rounded edges conform to one another (sort of like ball joints in a car), eliminating the need for careful beveling. Either way, the strips are edge nailed (and often glued) to one another, which makes for a very strong and tight hull, and the outside is faired smooth. Modern strip planking uses very thin

planking that again relies on cove and bead joinery. By itself, this light planking is rather weak, but it actually forms the core of what can be considered a composite hull. When encased inside and out by glass cloth and epoxy, the result is a light but very strong, watertight hull that needs little in the way of internal reinforcement.

Is there a fly in the ointment of strip planking? Of course. As every boat's girth varies from bow to stern, simply planking with those thin strips will leave you short of the sheer amidships. Various schemes

Traditional strip-planked construction with relatively thick strips.

Modern strip-planked construction with thin strips. This kayak hull will be covered with fiberglass and epoxy for strength.

Modern thin-strip planking will produce a very lightweight hull with an uncluttered interior. You might like this, or you might find the "missing" frames a bit disconcerting.

"Traditional" strip planking with thick strips, while hardly traditional for a Whitehall, still looks great and produces a strong, tight hull.

exist to fill out the shortage, but the look is different from the elegantly tapered shapes of traditional lapstrake or carvel planks, and strip planking can be tricky to repair.

Plywood

Plywood is yet another option—strong, (relatively) easy to find, and waterproof. Early designs usually were slab-sided V-shaped hulls that were conventionally framed, with the plywood basically acting as a replacement for conventional planking. A more modern innovation is the stitch-and-glue technique where the shapes of the plywood panels actually drive the shape of the hull (which is built from the skin inward), and much of the lofting, framing, bulkheads, and setup are eliminated or reduced. Stitch-and-glue designer and builder Sam Devlin likens the concept to peeling a banana, eating the fruit, and then reassembling the peels to create the banana shape again. During construction, the panels are provisionally sewn together into a boat shape with wire ties—much like a tailor would tack together a suit. Epoxy fillets (thickened epoxy radiuses on the interior) are toweled into the wired joints. The fillets replace the longitudinal chine in early plywood designs. Lightweight stitch-and-glue hulls, such as kayaks, are often covered inside and out with fabric and epoxy. The innovative technique is well suited for kit construction, and is one of the easiest ways to build a boat. Many stitch-and-glue boats are designed purely for function, however, and some boaters find their large, flat planes of plywood and boxy lines downright ugly, while others find them perfectly acceptable from a utilitarian aesthetic. It is also possible to create graceful and curvaceous designs for stitch-and-glue. Unfortunately, relatively few designers are developing such boats, and the number of available designs is limited.

A glued plywood lap hull is a near composite hull and therefore much more resistant to changes in weather and humidity. The finished hull is elegant and it makes a great choice for someone who wants the look and heft of the traditionally built hull but still needs to keep the boat on the trailer most of the time.

Cold Molding

Cold Molding is yet another way to go. This is the process of laminating the hull in place with wood veneers and epoxy. Picture a boat-shaped piece of high-quality plywood (or maybe a wooden bias ply tire). When well done, the result is strong, fair, and good looking. The difficulty is getting to that point. A laminated hull built entirely of veneers and epoxy requires a complex, elaborate mold to hold the floppy veneers fair and stable, and the process demands a lot of epoxy, nylon staples, and a vacuum pump. It is a very labor-intensive way to build just one hull, and you really have to like epoxy. (The time spent building the mold can speed the production of additional hulls, however.) Another use of cold molding, usually confined to 20-foot boats or larger, is to first strip plank the hull and then laminate veneers over of the strips.

Stitch-and-glue construction.
(Photo: Chesapeake Light Craft)

Cold molding. (Photo: Emily Herman)

KIT BOATS

The boat in a box is worth serious consideration. Whether it be a kayak, a canoe, a pram, a sharpie, or a pulling boat, the kit boat offers a number of advantages for the home boatbuilder:

These boats are designed to go together with a minimum of fuss, tools, and time.

The kit comes with instructions that are intended to walk the builder through the construction process with little in the way of jig setup and no lofting.

Kit boats, either strip planked or plywood, are designed to be safely stored in nonmarine environments, and they can be easily trailered or strapped to the top of a car and launched leak-free.

The kits generally come with everything to build the entire boat. Strip planking is milled with proper bead-and-cove edges, and plywood is cut to shape by computer-driven cutters. Glues, fastenings, and hardware are all included. Construction time is considerably

less than for conventional methods. Whether you are in Altoona or the Antarctic, there are no worries about having to buy some difficult-to-find, exotic product—at least until you break or lose a component.

The new kit-boat designs look good and hearken back to their traditionally built ancestors. Kits for pulling boats are available for both stitch-and-glue construction and in LapStitch, a proprietary method using L-shaped laps available from Chesapeake Light Craft (see Appendix B). The stitch-and-glue hulls are reminiscent of broad planked salmon wherries, while the LapStitch version (as shown on page 24), looks much like a traditional lapstrake Whitehall.

Kit boats do have a few downsides. There are only a limited number of designs available, you will be restricted to the kinds of planking supplied with the kit, and these boats are designed to be relatively light, which is not the best solution for every situation.

(continued next page)

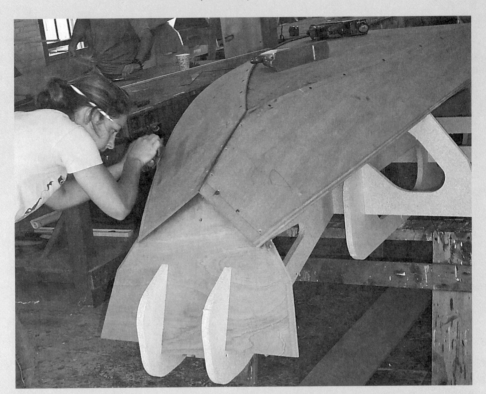

Building a Nutshell Pram from a kit.

The Chester Yawl is available as a kit from Chesapeake Light Craft. CLC's proprietary LapStitch building method is an elaboration on glued-lap construction. (Photo: Joe Provey, Chesapeake Light Craft)

MORE CONSTRUCTION DECISIONS

Depending on hull shape, frames in small craft can be steam bent to shape, sawn, or laminated. Steaming is quick and easy and requires no sophisticated apparatus, and it is usually the method of choice for round-bottomed boats, providing the virtues of light weight and speed of construction. (Steaming can also be used to produce a lightweight bent keel or an elaborate cockpit coaming.) Steamed frames may be installed after the planking is in place on the molds, or longitudinal ribbands may be fastened to the building forms to provide a foundation over which to bend the frames—and then the planks can be fastened directly to the frames.

For hard-chined and multi-chined construction, sawn frames are the most popular way to go. The various sections of the frames are sawn to shape and then assembled with fasteners and often gussets at the joints. A big advantage of sawn frames is that they also serve as the building forms, eliminating a few steps of the construction process.

Laminated frames can be used for round and multi-chined construction. These are built up from multiple layers of very thin wood, glued together, bent around a form, and held there with clamps until the glue sets. This method requires perhaps the lowest level of carpentry skills, but it is by far the messiest.

Sawn frames.

Lastly there is the question of whether to build the boat right-side up or upside down. While it may seem counterintuitive, in most cases upside down has the edge. It's all a matter of accessibility and gravity. It's a lot easier to bend planking down into place than up. The builder spends a lot less time on his or her back on a mechanic's creeper, and there is much less chance of being clobbered by a falling clamp—not a small consideration. (See Chapter 25 for a further discussion of this issue.)

Steamed frames.

COMPARISON SHOPPING

In trying to decide what kind of boat to build and how to build it, consider your needs and make a list of your priorities. For example, you might want your boat to do the following:

- Work well on a lake and a flatwater river.
- Have two rowing stations, so one of the children can assist at the oars.
- Be fast enough to get out to the island easily.
- Take a small outboard.
- Be big and stable enough to do a bit of fishing with the kids, but small enough to trailer easily and manhandle when necessary.
- Look great in the plans and on the water.

Now you might want to do some comparison shopping, considering both the building process and the finished product. Whichever construction method you choose, from ancient to thoroughly modern, will produce a beautiful hull that will get you out on the water in style and elegance.

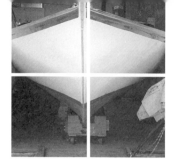

· 2 ·

Carvel Planking

It has been said that almost any kind of a hull can be built in carvel, as the individual planks are actually sculpted to shape. This style of planking is reminiscent of the staves on a wooden barrel, which taper as they approach the barrel heads. Carvel planking is dependent on and fastened to a system of transverse frames that are either sawn or steam bent to shape. Watertightness and interlocking connective strength are gained from a fiber caulk (usually cotton) that is driven into the seams between the planks.

Patterns are made for each plank. On a round hull, to accommodate constantly changing girths and curves, each and every plank will be a different shape from the next. One can expect to see a plethora of

shapes: crescents, lazy S's, and curious planks that resemble handlebar mustaches. As opposed to lapstrake (clinker) planking, which covers a curved hull with flat planks of a single thickness a bit like clapboards on a house, the inside faces of carvel planks are carved—hollowed, actually—to lie tight against the frames. The outside of the planking is also shaped. When the planking thickness is given on a set of plans, it is the finished thickness—after all the shaping has been done. As the planking is coming around a changing curve, we can expect to have to work in a compound bevel on at least one edge of the plank. Oh yes—there is also a caulking bevel planed into one edge as well.

A bit more work? Perhaps, but it's worth it. Here are some positives:

As mentioned, very elaborate and efficient shapes can be built with carvel. If damaged, the hull can be readily repaired, because the hull is made up of many individual components, and only the damaged ones have to be unfastened and replaced. If the hull starts to leak, it is a straightforward task to remove the caulking and replace it with new. You can build with local materials and use standard carpentry tools, and there is little need for drums of glue. Finally, it's hard to beat the classic look of a well-planked carvel hull.

SPILING AND PATTERNS

Wooden boatbuilding is more akin to dressmaking and tailoring than to, say, cabinetmaking. Domestic furniture is most often joined at right angles, plans are typically

A handsome carvel-planked Joel White–designed Flatfish.

precise, and you can measure and cut the shape shown in the plans and expect the pieces to fit together if you've done your work carefully. But consider what goes into making a suit or a dress: you develop patterns that allow you to wrap expensive, flexible panels of material around a complex, curvaceous surface. Considerations need to be made for movement of the garment and the structure underneath it, and the more voluptuous and buxom the subject is, the greater the need is for patterns. And the better the pattern, the better the product will be, wasting less material and time. So it is with boatbuilding. Hull forms range from simple to complex. The more complex the hull form, the more sophisticated the pattern must be. Indeed, it can be argued that boatbuilding is all about pattern making.

Traditional carvel is the most demanding of the planking systems and thus requires the most complicated pattern making. Complicated, but not difficult. It is just a series of simple steps to record the required information. Once you've done one plank, the technique remains the same for all subsequent ones.

Spiling is the process of taking the measurements or otherwise tracing or determining the shape of a plank. For our discussion, let's assume we are spiling a pattern for a round-bottomed dinghy that is being built with steam-bent frames. The first couple of planks are on and the rest of the plank locations have been lined out (predetermined). The plans call for ½" planking. The hood (forward) end of each plank will be fitted into a rabbeted stem.

The place to begin is with the construction of a spiling batten, the purpose of which is to help us capture the shape of the as-yet-unmade plank and record the positions of its upper and lower edges at regular intervals. The batten will also record the shape of the new plank where it hits the stem.

The batten is made up of a number of long pieces of lightweight wood (⅛" plywood works well) that are wide enough to just fit between the plank already in place and the scribed lines on the frames that indicate the other edge of the new plank. The plywood pieces are clamped or tacked to the frames, end to end, on the boat. The pieces should not touch the previous plank or cover the plank edge line drawn on the frames. The pieces should also lie easily against the frames and not be pushed or twisted into location. Next, connect the pieces to one another with gussets. These joints need

to be stout and rugged, as an articulated joint (aka hinge) will cause the batten to give you false information as well as drive you nuts. Use glue and staples, belts and suspenders, or whatever you have to make sure it's secure. With that done, you are ready to record the widths of the plank at regular intervals.

There are a number of methods one can use to record the planking width onto the spiling batten: capturing distances with a ruler, using a scribing block, swinging a compass, or registering points with a divider. Which to use depends on the builder's preference and the degree of accuracy desired. The theory is the same for all methods: use a device to acquire the distances from the existing plank and the scribed new plank lines on the frames and record those measurements onto the batten at regular intervals. Not to worry—we'll go into detail in just a few paragraphs.

Next remove the batten from the boat and place it on top of the planking stock. The first thing you will notice is that the pieced-together spiling batten will have a lot of curve to it. So will the plank that you'll be making. Tack the spiling batten to the stock. Reverse the procedure to bring the acquired information over onto the planking stock. Connect the points with a long, stiff softwood batten to give you a smooth curve that replicates the shape of both the edge of the previous plank and the curve of the other side of the new plank. To say it another way, you'll have not only the curve of the new plank but the changing widths as well—at least on the inside face of the plank; more on this in a moment.

Spiling a Plank

With the theory under our belt, let's start spiling that plank on the round-bottomed dinghy. Our spiling batten is tacked into place and nicely joined. Because this is a complex hull with a lot of changes of shape, let's use the divider method for spiling. Round up a straightedge (the ruler blade of a 12" combination square works well) and, at each location where a bent frame passes under the plywood batten, using the ruler and a pencil, trace one edge of the frame across the face of the spiling batten from one edge to the other. Soon the batten will be covered by a series of vertical lines.

Next, break out your best two-pointed divider—the one that can lock the legs in place so they don't move. Set the divider distance so that if you placed one point

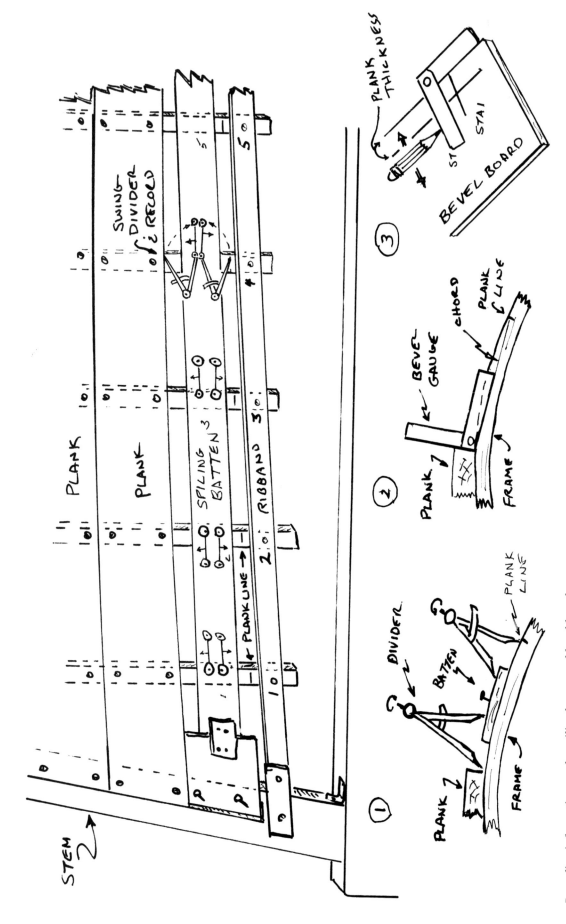

Recording information on the spiling batten and bevel board.

against the edge of the previous plank, the other point would land roughly in the middle of the spiling batten.

Bring the divider to the drawn line that represents one edge of frame #1, as shown in the small drawing #1 in the accompanying illustration. Place one point of the divider on the intersection of the frame and the plank edge, and swing the divider's other leg around to the pencil line. Poke a pinhole into the spiling batten and circle it. You have now recorded the exact distance to the plank edge. For extra insurance, swing the "plank edge" leg around to the batten and poke another hole (and circle it). Connect the two holes with a pencil line and draw an arrow pointing to the plank edge. Label it "frame 1." Isn't that a bit redundant, you say? Yep. But, on the other hand, this is a lot faster than having to make another plank because you have used the wrong points. By recording and connecting the two points you now have on record the proper distance used—even if the divider has been dropped or its spacing otherwise accidentally changed. Also, on that pencil line on the spiling batten you will end up recording two points—one for the top edge of the plank, and another for the bottom. The arrow guarantees that when you later use the circled point to swing your captured distance back onto the planking stock, you use the correct circled point.

Repeat the divider operation to record the points for the opposite edge onto the pencil line. Then move onto the next frame and continue the process, picking up the dimensions for the entire length of the plank. With that done, you are ready to remove the spiling batten—almost. The shape of the hood end still needs to be recorded. While it is possible to spile the shape onto the end of the spiling batten, a more reliable method is to scribe and fit a small piece of plywood that replicates exactly the curve of the rabbet and that touches both the top and bottom edges of the plank-to-be. Tack or staple it temporarily into place and attach it to the rest of the spiling batten with a glued gusset. *Now* it's time to remove the spiling batten and start to make the plank.

PLANK THICKNESS AND BEVELS

At this point, if we were building a hard-chined boat with straight sides, we would be just about done. With the majority of the planks squarely butting up to one another and no hollow to carve, the planking stock could be planed to final thickness. Then the spiling

batten would be tacked or clamped to the planking stock. With a straightedge, you would extend the straight frame lines you drew on the spiling batten out onto the planking stock. Using the dividers, you'd swing the prerecorded distances from the spiling batten to the drawn lines on the planking stock. A flexible batten would be sprung through those points to get fair lines for the top and bottom edges of the plank. Then trace against the batten line onto the stock with with a pencil, saw it out a little oversize, and hand-plane down to the line. Add a small caulking bevel and we'd be in business. But with a round-bottomed boat, you need a little more information.

Plank Thickness

Our next task is to determine the thickness that we have to plane our planking stock to. The planking thickness given on the plans refers to the finished or shaped plank. The curved surfaces (both inside and out) have been hand planed in. If the plans called for $\frac{1}{2}$" stock and we milled our stock to $\frac{1}{2}$", each plank would be too thin when the shaping was done.

So instead we'll inspect the curved frames in the region that will be covered by the new plank and find the ones that have the greatest bend. Take the straight steel rule and place it alongside that frame with one edge connecting the edge of the previous plank and the scribed plank line mark that represents the new plank's opposite edge. The rule will create a chord. (Back in geometry class, you learned that a chord is a straight line segment joining any two points on an arc, curve, or circumference. And you thought you'd never use that information!) Measure from the chord to the greatest height of the curve. Let's say it's $\frac{1}{4}$". Add that figure to the specified plank thickness: in this case, we'll mill the stock to $\frac{3}{4}$" to give us enough meat to cover or back out of its middle.

Beveling the Plank

When we recorded the plank width information on the spiling batten, we developed a very accurate rendition of the inside face of the plank. The problem is that we are coming around a curve, and the planks, before being shaped on the outside face, lie on the hull like facets. If we cut out the planks square on both edges, the planks would only touch on their inside edges. We need to put a compound bevel on one edge of every plank to fill the gap. (The other edge is left square.) To do that, we have to add width to that edge of the plank so that when the bevel is planed in from the outside edge to the inside edge, the inside of the plank returns to the width that we originally spiled. It's not as bad as it sounds.

We need two tools: a bevel gauge and a bevel board. The bevel gauge should be a small one. This can be store-bought, or an equally fine one can be made from two pieces of hacksaw blade riveted together at one end. The bevel board is simply a short piece of scrap wood with a straight edge planed into it. Now we are ready to go.

Picking Up the Bevels

Our hypothetical boat is a fiendishly curvaceous one, so to be on the safe side, we are going to pick up the plank-to-plank bevel at every frame. It is difficult to get a proper bevel reading if we simply put the bevel gauge directly on the bent frame. As the frame curve is constantly changing, where would you hold it anyway? Instead, we'll return to the steel rule and the chord. If we recreate the chord (this time at every frame) with the ruler, we can sit one leg of the bevel gauge on the rule and put the other leg up against the edge of the previous plank, as shown in the small drawing #2 on page 29. When you think of it, this is actually a very accurate way to pick up the bevel, since the inside face of the new plank will be dead flat before we hollow it out–just like the ruler.

Place one leg of the bevel gauge against the straight edge of the bevel board and record the bevel with pencil onto the board and label it (see the small drawing #3 on page 29). Repeat the operation for every frame, since the bevel between the planks will change throughout the length of the boat.

Adding the Distance

Now, draw a line parallel to the straight edge of the bevel board and ½" in from the edge, corresponding with the ½" plank thickness. The edge of the bevel board and the parallel line that you just drew represent the inside and outside faces of the plank, and the area between them represents the beveled edge of the plank.

Take a square and slide it along the straight edge until it hits the intersection of one of the bevel lines and the ½" plank line. Draw a line square from that point to the straight edge. The distance between where the beveled line and the perpendicular line intersect the straight edge is the distance to be added to the spiling point for that frame. Repeat the operation for each bevel.

Laying Out the Plank

With the enhanced bevel distances acquired, its time to lay out the plank. Take the spiling batten and align it on the stock to take advantage of the grain of the wood and to avoid things such as sapwood and knots. Then anchor the batten down so that it doesn't escape. The hood end of the pattern can be traced onto the stock with a pencil. Then use that ruler again to carry those straight lines at each frame location onto the stock. After double-checking the spacing on the dividers, swing the distances from the batten to the lines that you just drew on the planking stock. There will be a lot of marks on the wood, so to avoid confusion, circle the points and label them.

On the nonbeveled edge of the plank, run a batten from the traced hood end through the divider points and trace the line in with a pencil. On the beveled edge, you need to add the extra distance developed on the bevel board to the outside of each one of the divider points on those straight lines. (A divider or tick strip will work.) After doing that, spring a batten through the new points and the hood end and trace in the line just as you did on the nonbeveled edge. Remove the spiling batten from the stock and it's off to the band saw to trim the plank to just outside the lines. After you've cut the plank it can be planed square down to the lines.

Planing In the Bevels

Finally we get to cut in the bevels. As always, there are plenty of ways to do this, but perhaps the easiest is to use the information you have already developed. The lines you have just drawn are on the outside (bigger) face of the plank. Now we are going to take the same bevel distances that we used to make the plank wider on the outside and plot them on the inside face to make that side smaller (or at least bring us back to where we started when we spiled in the first place). This is why boat builders get the big money: value added.

On the "bevel" side of the plank, square over those straight frame lines to the "inside" face of the plank. Measuring down from the planed line, use the bevel

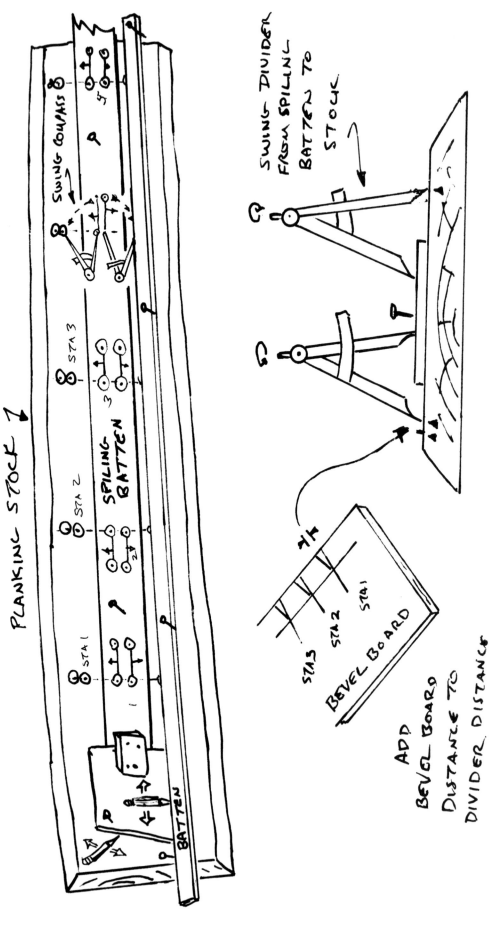

Transferring information from the spiling batten and the bevel board to the plank stock.

distances at each frame location and make a mark. After all the marks have been made on the inside face, working from the stem to the transom, spring a batten through all the points and scribe the line in pencil.

Then, using a block plane, plane in the compound bevel that runs from the enhanced width line on the outside face to the new line on the inside face. The changing bevel automatically develops without you having to measure. But if you wanted to check with your bevel gauge, you'd find the bevel on the plank matches the one on your bevel board at each frame.

A small caulking bevel can be added on the beveled face at this time.

Backing Out the Plank

Now it's time to hollow or back out the inside face of the plank. As with everything else, the depth of the hollow changes through the length of the plank. Patterns have to be made at regular intervals, using either homemade templates with the frame shape scribed onto

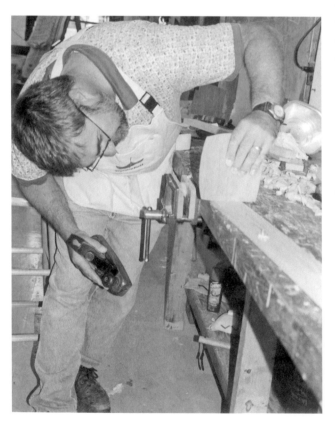

Use a plane with a convex-edged blade to hollow the inside of the plank. A set of templates of varying radius curves can be made from thin plywood, or a sliding-pin gauge can be used to capture the curve from the frame.

them, or one of those ubiquitous "multi-sliding pin" shape gauges from the hardware store. The excess wood is most easily scooped out with a shop-built plane or an old wooden-bodied plane modified for the task.

That's about it. Well, there is a bit of shaping and thinning on the outside of the plank, but with that and a slight bit of care and tuning, the plank will bend easily and snugly to the hull.

Clamping the Planks

Fitting the hood (forward) end of the plank into the cut rabbet in the stem can be irksome. Generally there is a lot of twisting action going on that will necessitate either steaming or boiling. Also, there are almost no good places to clamp onto to draw the recalcitrant thing into place.

What to do? Plan ahead. Assemble your clamps, pads, and other aids and get them ready for fast action. If you have a plank in the steam box, take a moment to do a dry run with a piece of scrap that looks sort of like your plank. Remember that the easiest way to clamp up to the stem is to present the plank directly to the stem as though it were tangent to the curve of the hull at the stem. That way, you won't have to fight the bend and twist. This will require having the other end suspended by a helper, deadman, sling, or some other sort of device. After the stem is secured, the rest of the plank can be sprung into place.

Is there a plank on the other side yet? If not, perhaps your clamp can grab onto the stem. Chances are, however, that due to the angle that your new plank is entering the stem, you won't be able to clamp to the flat of the opposite side of the stem. If you clamp onto the inboard edge of the stem, there won't be much purchase for the clamp and after dinging the wood, the clamp will likely slip off and spring merrily toward you. Consider making a set of stem clamping blocks out of 2" thick stock that have 90° notches cut into them at different angles. These are sort of the analog to the rabbet cut into the stem. Place one of these babies on the inside edge of the stem, and not only will it not rock but it will also allow your clamp to work at right angles to the plank.

If there is a plank on the opposite side, other stratagems will be required. If the stem is deep enough, you still may be able to grab the inside edge with a sliding bar clamp. Alternately, you may be able to pull the plank into place using offset clamping pressure. This can be done by employing a bridging clamp block—simply a bar of wood with two lobes cut into it. One lobe is longer than the other by the thickness of the plank. Put the block in place, with the short lobe contacting the plank and the long one in the rabbet next to the plank. The clamp will be affixed to the bar as close to the new plank as possible while grabbing the other side of the stem. As the clamp is tightened, the bar will act as a lever to push the plank down into place.

If the forward face of the stem has not yet been faired off (i.e., the sides of the stem are still flat and parallel to one another), you may be able to pinch the plank into place by placing a block on the very forward edge of the plank and binding the block and the two opposing faces of the stem with a clamp. Chances are good the situation will hold long enough to get your screws in.

Clamp pads slipping? Try giving them more traction by gluing some sandpaper (sand side out) to them with spray-on sanding disc adhesive. Or you can stick the pad right to the plank with the adhesive. (Don't worry about the finish—the hull has to be sanded anyway.) Is the clamp pad in the way of the screws? Just drill through it and insert a screw.

One last thing about fitting the hood end. Often, after the plank has been all clamped up, it's discovered that the hood end has been set a bit too far from the rabbet. A common fix for this is to simply loosen up all the clamps and lightly tap the butt end of the plank with a wooden mallet to advance the plank into place. This works well if done with caution. One tap too many, however, and the angled hood will contact the angled rabbet and cause the forward end of the plank to move away from the previous plank, resulting in a gapped seam. At best, you have to move the plank back and reclamp. At worst, it won't be noticed until after the plank has been fastened and the formerly tight seam will be big enough to drop coins through.

Installing the Plank

Now it's time to clamp down the rest of the plank. When you think about it, the act of installation and clamping is asking a lot of a piece of long flat wood that is irregularly shaped, beveled, and sculpted. It must not only be hauled around the curve of the boat, but also rolled onto the hull and shifted sideways to mate to the previous plank. Only then can it be properly clamped. The rolling in *and* shifting bit is the rub.

The natural tendency of the new plank is to resist being twisted as it is being wrapped around the hull. If the builder is not paying close attention, and simply uses sideways pressure when mating the plank to the previous one, the result will be a funky fit, with the lower inner edge of the new plank being jammed midway up the contacting edge of the prior plank. This will leave a gap between the frames and the plank, and it will be difficult to caulk. Additionally, since the edge of the plank will be standing proud when it comes time to fair the hull, one side of the plank must be planed to less than the desired thickness.

If one is working right-side up, this misalignment can be easily seen (at least if one is paying attention). Upside-down construction is another matter. It is far too easy to let optimism get the upper hand and just push that plank sideways toward the previous plank until it looks good, and fasten it.

A change in tactics is in order, in which the plank will be pushed (or rolled) down against the frames before it is pushed sideways toward the previous plank. Begin by lightly clamping the plank into place with a C-clamp or bar clamp. Then, use a version of the aforementioned bridging bar/clamp arrangement to put

ABOUT FASTENINGS

Fastenings, whether screws, rivets, or clench nails, are not miniclamps and are only intended to hold the plank where the real clamps have brought it. In this era of high-power screw guns and the ubiquitous Sheetrock screw, this is sometimes forgotten. Which also brings to mind the proper setting of screws. Set the screw only to where it lands into the bored countersink. Push it beyond that point and your screw transmogrifies from a fastener into a splitting wedge as the head presses into the tapered countersunk hole—especially at the hood end of a plank. Screw gun aficionados take note. And of course, don't forget to wax those screws— you'll be glad you did.

downward pressure onto the edge nearest the preceding plank (but not too much pressure—you still want the plank to be able to move sideways).

Next, we are ready to give the plank the proper amount of sideways push. You can use a special two-way clamp, using one of the screws to clamp the device to the frame and the other to edge-set the plank. Absent these nice and hard-to-come-by devices, you can employ a homegrown method using blocks and wedges. Fashion a number of blocks that have sufficient depth to allow a "tunnel" to be cut in them that is the approximate dimension of the frame. These are clamped to the outside face of the frame at a ribband location. The block makes firm contact with both the frame and the ribband, which eliminates rocking or twisting. Next, make up a batch of softwood wedges—the longer the better. Sawn cedar shingles work well. Slip these between the clamped block and the plank, inserting them side-by-side in opposition to one another. Use a pair of small hammers to advance the wedges. As the wedges move in, the plank moves sideways. Long wedges with very low angles work best, as there is greater contact surface between them and less chance of damaging the plank.

Whatever method you use, get in the habit of checking that the plank is lying tight against the ribs by peeking in behind, using a mirror, or just feeling with your fingers. When all looks well, tighten both the C-clamp and the bridge clamp. Now with the planks in proper alignment you can check the fit of the new plank's seam.

The Rest of the Story

Once again, in upright construction whatever you have for fit is on display. Upside down, the fit is concealed. Another way to ascertain what's going on

The special two-way clamp (center) grabs hold of a frame or ribband, and then applies pressure to edge-set the plank against its neighbor. Always use wood pads, as shown, to distribute the pressure and avoid crushing the fibers of the plank.

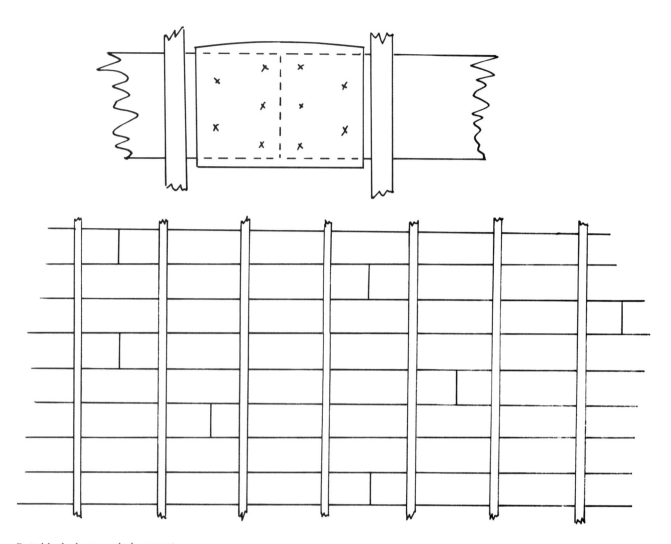

Butt block shape and placement.

(other than sending in a trained baby ape to appraise the situation) is to pass a reflector lamp along the seam on the inside of the inverted hull. Open seams will appear as bright spots when viewed from the outside. Mark any contact points on the plank edge that need to be planed.

Usually it is not necessary to remove the plank completely from the boat for trimming. Simply remove the clamps up forward and leave the aft end of the plank clamped. Spring out the plank and touch up the offending locations with a block plane and put the plank back into place. If all looks well, reclamp the forward section of the plank and release the aft end. Plane and check the fit. Reclamp the plank as before and you are finally ready to fasten that plank down. Don't forget to recheck your fit partway through the fastening process, which could cause some clamps to back off.

TRIMMING THE SHEER

Sheer lines are curious things—while they have little to do with how a boat performs on the water, they have seemingly everything to do with how it looks. A sheer that looked jaunty on the lofting board can look either disceptically flat or "powder-hornish" when slavishly transferred to the three-dimensional hull. In the end, it is the builder's eye that makes a sheer look right. It's a perspective thing. What may look fine in a two-dimensional plan can look odd on the three-dimensional boat. When observed in profile, the sheer at the stem (farther away from the viewer) tends to recede a bit while the sheer at the forward quarter seems optically to grow. Do all plans have this problem? No, but a lot do.

This phenomenon is less noticeable on long and lean boats that have a lot of swoop to the sheer, such as Whitehalls and many launches. Plans that have been

EASY STRIP PLUGGING

There are few tasks as tedious as the manufacture and installation of bungs over fastenings. The time spent toiling away at the drill press seems endless. Then there is the removal of the units from the stock and placing them into a receptacle only to retrieve them a short time later for insertion after dipping into oozing gelatinous glue with the fingers, aligning the grain, and tapping them into place. Finally, there is the trimming off of the little darlings—hoping that they don't break off below the surface—and sanding them smooth with the rest of the hull.

Considering the sheer number of fastenings—roughly two per frame for each plank, times the number of planks on both sides—it would be hard to fault the builder for entertaining an enhanced appreciation for the subtle beauty of hole-filling putty. (Or, alternately, hiring a trained baby ape to make and install the plugs.) While there seems little chance of streamlining the trim and sand portion of the job, Boatbuilder Harry Bryan of St. George, New Brunswick, Canada has passed along a technique that he has long used to speed up the manufacture and gluing end—i.e., the strip bung approach.

The Bryan procedure does away with using the wide face of a board to cut a plethora of random bungs that have to be individually removed. Instead, they are cut into a narrow strip of wood that has been cut with the grain and is just wide enough to allow a single continuous line of plugs to be manufactured. The stock for the bungs should also be thin enough that, when the drill press is set properly, the edges of the cutter bottom out just $1/_{16}$" from the lower side of the wooden strip. What remains is a series of bungs that are interconnected with a slim, flexible sliver of wood that can easily be held in the hand.

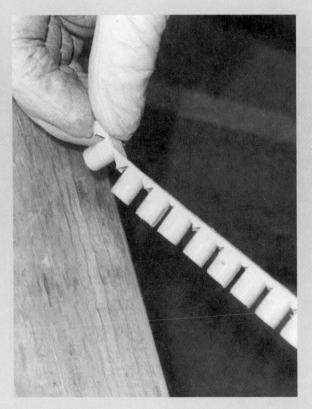

For quick bunging, cut the bungs out of a strip that is just wide enough. You can then dip the end in a pot of glue, set the first bung in its hole, break it off, push it in, and continue, assembly-line fashion.

To use the strip, simply grip the band of bungs in the hand like a handle. Then dip the last bung of the series into the pot of glue, align the strip with the grain of the wood being plugged, push the bung in with your thumb, and break the plug off the strip. If you wish, tap it with a mallet and that's all there is to it. It's clean and easy with a few good breaks.

drawn from preexisting vessels (such as from museum collections) are likely to be fine, as they are documenting boats that have already had their sheers corrected by the builder. Vessels that are suspect are those that are more rotund and that carry that beamy sheer forward and then curve quickly into the stem, such as catboats and pinkies. Boats with subtle or nearly flat sheers are also prone to exhibit this problem, as are those that have a lot of flare forward, such as high-speed powerboats. Why don't designers correct for this? Some do, but many don't.

So what to do? One way is to make an accurate half model of the boat so you can actually see the boat in three dimensions and note if any corrections need to be made. Another, perhaps easier, way is to simply make the correction on the boat before planking.

After the boat has been set up (either right-side up or upside down) connect the sheer marks on the molds (or frames) and those marked on the transom and stem with a flexible batten tacked into place. Stand back and eyeball the line from several different angles. The forward quarter is a common trouble area. Tinker the line up and down in the forward quarter until it looks right, and then scribe it onto the molds and stem in ink. This is a matter of subtlety: we're only looking to ease out unsightly humps or flats in the sheer, not create a Viking ship look. Repeat the exercise on the other side, making sure the lines are symmetrical. Then bring the cut rabbet or bevel up on the stem to meet the new and improved sheer line. Now you're ready to go into the planking business.

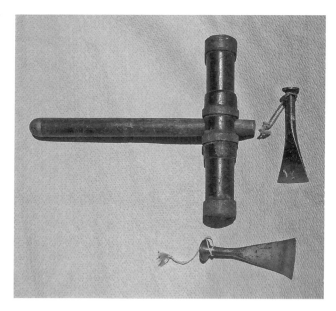

Caulking mallet and irons.

CAULKING

Caulking with fiber not only keeps water from coming in, but it also stiffens and solidifies the sides of the hull into a continuous shell. The driven fiber acts almost like a key, locking the planks together. Carvel planked small craft are caulked with cotton, which is sold in one-pound skeins much like yarn. (Oakum is for the big rigs.) Used alone, modern flexible caulks that are either troweled or gunned in will keep water out but do little to tighten the hull. It's a bit like caulking the hull with rubber bands.

Caulking is perhaps the most opinionated division in the boatbuilding trade. It seems like every practitioner has their own take on which is the best (and perhaps only) way to do the job. It is a specialized trade, and it takes a skilled hand to properly caulk a hardwood-planked hull—enough to tighten it up and not so much that the planks want to spring off when they swell. That said, caulking can be done well by the careful first-time caulker—especially if the planking is of softwood that can compress to accommodate some over-enthusiastic application of cotton with iron and mallet.

The seams between planks are V-shaped for about half their thickness on the outside surface and flush

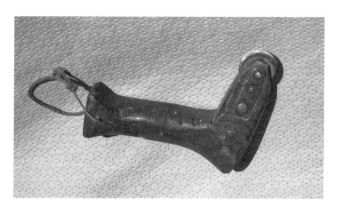

Homemade caulking wheel or roller.

and tight on the inside. This caulking seam is usually formed as a small bevel planed on part of only one plank edge. Caulking is either driven in with a broadbladed caulking iron and mallet or pressed into place with a caulking wheel. Most of a well-planked hull can usually be easily and quickly caulked with a caulking wheel, although the mallet and iron usually come into play for the garboard and rabbet seams. After pressing the cotton into place in the seam, some oil-based paint (not enough to saturate it) is brushed onto the cotton to keep it from "puffing" back out. Then the seams are "payed" or filled with a flexible mastic or compound.

▪3▪

Lapstrake Planking

Lapstrake, or *clinker* in the UK, has long been a preferred method of planking for small craft. It is easy to see why. There is certainly plenty of appeal on the practical side of things. The interconnected, overlapping nature of the planking lends a tremendous amount of almost girder-like strength to the hull. This permits the use of lighter-weight planking than carvel demands. With no caulking in the seams to dry out, a lapstrake boat can sit around on deck or on the beach for long periods and still not leak when launched (or at least not much). And rather than having the planks be individually sculpted to shape like carvel, lapped strakes simply cover the hull as flat planes or facets, permitting the builder to either mill all the plank stock to a uniform thickness, or use plywood. The spiling of the overlapping planks is more forgiving than the tight edge-fits demanded by carvel. Even if the mechanic is off a fraction of an inch, laps will still make the boat tight and strong. This forgiving nature also makes it easier to fashion two mirror-image planks from the same spiling. Additionally, the construction jig is comparatively simple, using relatively few molds and, unlike carvel or strip planking, there is no need to fair the planked hull.

The technique's appeal has been further enhanced with the introduction of high-quality, waterproof adhesives such as epoxy and resorcinol that allow reliable glued-scarf joints to replace cranky mechanical ones. Indeed, on plywood planking, even the plank-to-plank fastenings can be replaced with glue, thus producing a light, leak-proof, almost monocoque hull with

A well lined-out lapstrake hull.

relatively few frames. If high-quality plywood is used, there is no need to sheath the hull with cloth and epoxy.

On the aesthetics side of the equation, the long sweeping lines of well-laid-out lapstrake planking can dignify and add a sense of class to even the humblest working vessel.

LINING THE HULL

Of all the considerations involved with planking, the one that has the least romance is the lining off of the planks. Yet, especially for lapstrake-planked round hulls, it is probably the most important. At best, a poorly lined hull will have a haphazard appearance, and at worst the planks may be so wide that they don't land properly on the adjoining strake. If the hull has a very tight turn to it

DESIGNER PAUL GARTSIDE ON LAPSTRAKE/CLINKER

To me, clinker construction is as close to real boat building as we get in this life. Nothing else looks quite as good as a nicely lined out clinker boat or sounds quite as authentic when we step into it. Years ago I remember Sid Mashford, famous old boat builder in Plymouth, England, remark that he thought a clinker dinghy was one of mankind's finest creations. As I remember, his argument revolved around weight—the fiberglass versions then becoming popular were too light, making them skittish and dangerous to step into, while the heavier carvel punts were tiresome to row and hard to get up the beach. Clinker seemed hit the sweet spot of compromise better than any other method. I suspect there was also an emotional resonance there that had to do with the look of tapered planking and the chuckle of water under the laps, though Sid would have been the last to admit it.

While it might be overstating it to say that if you can build a clinker boat you can build anything, I don't think it is far from the truth. Almost all the challenges of boatbuilding are to be found in a small clinker boat—lofting, laying out rabbets, lining planking, bending frames etc. The beauty of it is that here the scale is small, mistakes can be corrected or thrown out without undue financial stress and since the building cycle is short, it is easy to go round it a few times and become practiced in the art. It is a great place to learn real boatbuilding.

Of all the building methods I have tried, I find none gives as much pleasure as clinker. The materials are of the simplest kind, but the results can be as sophisticated as anything made with wood. It is not hard to do, but it takes a lot of practice to do well. A look at quality examples from the past will reveal the degree to which the small clinker boat has been used as a display of

Skylark sailing dinghy by Paul Gartside.

prowess by builders before us, and just what can be done with hand tools and a good eye. There is a texture to these boats that highlights skill and artistry. The evenness of the plank tapers, the spacing of frames, particularly in the ends of the hull and the alignment of the plank fastenings between them, all tell a story wherever the eye comes to rest. It is rare to find one that's perfect, and in my experience, impossible to create one. But there is great pleasure to be had in the attempt.

One of the first boats I ever built was a clinker pram and I still remember the thrill of seeing that little boat go together, crude as it was, and how, even when stored upside down for the winter, it would give me a buzz just walking by. These can be immensely pleasing boats to build and use and beautiful objects to have in our lives. In the end those are the most important reasons for choosing them.

—Paul Gartside is a boatbuilder and designer in Sidney, British Columbia. (See Appendix B for contact information.)

(as many do at the turn of the bilge) and the new plank is too wide, no amount of beveling of the previous plank will allow the new plank to fit—leaving a large gap right where you don't want it.

What to do? Take the time to establish those plank lines. Begin by milling battens out of clear softwood (spruce works well). A useful technique is to mill the battens to the thickness of the planking and the same

width as the lap (or *land* as it is known in the UK). This information is usually—but alas, not always—given on the plans. You should have as many battens as you have planks per side.

The greatest bugaboo for the first-time builder is deciding where to start. Lining off is more art than science, but there are some rules of thumb for small craft. The important thing is to get the lines on the molds, and then you can tinker them to where you want them. As the boat is symmetrical (or should be), you only have to line off one side of the hull and transfer the marks to the other side. A good place to begin is by roughly dividing the girth of the transom (from sheer to rabbet) equally by the desired number of planks.

Don't forget to allow for the rub rail when laying out the sheerstrake. After the rub rail is affixed it will optically decrease the width of the strake. So if the rail is 1¼″ wide and the sheerstrake is only 2″ wide at the stern, the eye will perceive the plank to be a diminutive ¾″ wide. The easiest way to accommodate this is to mark the bottom of the rub rail on the molds right in the beginning and work from that line rather than the sheer.

After dealing with the transom, repeat the exercise for the stem. This is a bit of a gray area, as there is no sharp end-point at the bottom to measure to as there is on the transom. The best you can do is to select a point for the garboard that is just beyond the turn of the rabbet as the stem starts to sweep upward. Then divide the remaining distance equally. Remember, these points can all be tinkered with later.

Now it's time to divide up the middle of the vessel. It is tempting to once again use equal spacing. This will likely not work (unless the hull is truly round) due to the aforementioned planes-going-around-the-curve phenomenon. One way to go is to first measure the girth of the largest midship mold and divide it by the number of planks to come up with an average plank width.

Then, starting at the garboard (where the hull is the flattest), work toward the turn of the bilge, laying out the plank widths oversize. Around the turn of the bilge, where the curve is greatest, reduce the plank widths from the average. The remaining topside planks can then be roughly divided to the original measurement.

Testing the Marks

Now you are ready to spring battens around the hull, almost. First let's test whether these divined plank marks will actually work. Make a lap-testing gauge by taking a piece of straight stock a bit longer than your widest expected plank width. Near the end of the stick, cut a rectangular notch that is plank-thickness deep and longer than the lap width. This notched straight-edge simulates the inside face of the plank. Take a second piece of stock, which we will call the planking simulator, that is the thickness of the planking and mark the lap line onto it (measured in from the edge).

Now the moment of truth! Hold (or tack) the simulator to the proposed plank line on the widest mold. Then place the gauge so that on one end, the further edge of the cutout notch touches the drawn lap line on the plank simulator. The other side of the gauge should touch the line-off mark for the next plank. If the gauge only touches the lap line on one end and the line-off mark on the other, the proposed plank width will work. If, however, the gauge contacts the curve of the mold and lifts the gauge off of the lap line on the simulator,

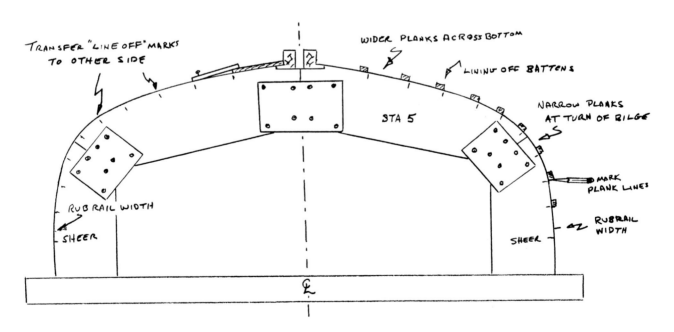

Lining off the hull.

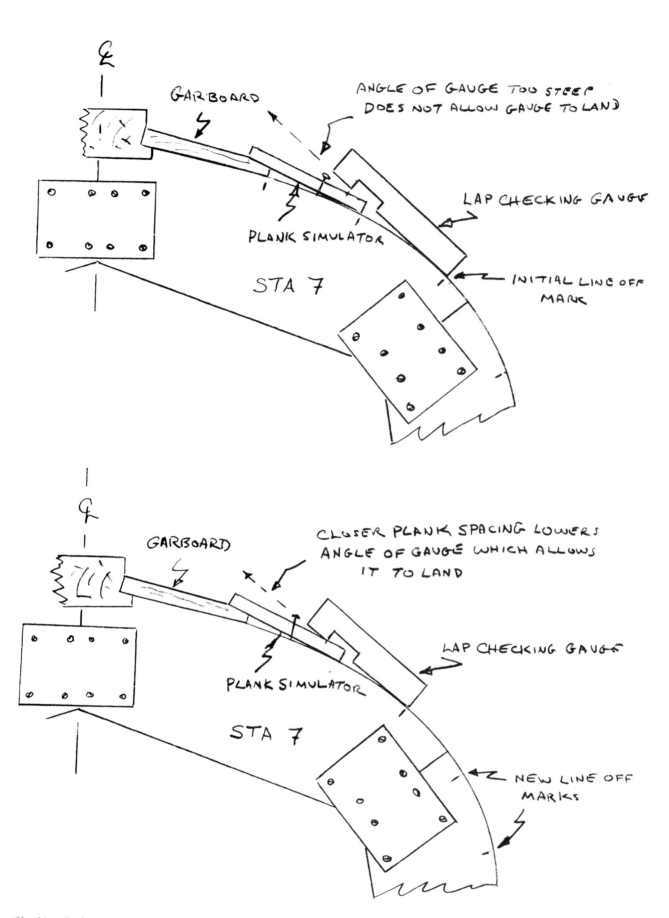

ANGLE OF GAUGE TOO STEEP DOES NOT ALLOW GAUGE TO LAND

GARBOARD

LAP CHECKING GAUGE

PLANK SIMULATOR

STA 7

INITIAL LINE OFF MARK

CLOSER PLANK SPACING LOWERS ANGLE OF GAUGE WHICH ALLOWS IT TO LAND

GARBOARD

LAP CHECKING GAUGE

PLANK SIMULATOR

STA 7

NEW LINE OFF MARKS

Checking the laps.

the plank will be too wide to work in that location and the width should be reduced. Check all the rest of the plank widths on the mold the same way.

Running the Battens

Tack the batten onto the scribed lines at the midship mold and at the transom and stem. Eyeball it for fairness and check the batten at each mold with the gauge. When you've got it where you like it, put a few more nails in to hold it. Proceed to the next plank and repeat the process, checking with the gauge as you go.

Soon the hull will be covered with a set of battens that will give you a pretty good idea how the boat will look when planked up. Any kinks or unfairness in the lines should be corrected. Usually it just involves pulling a few nails and letting the batten fair itself. Any large corrections should be rechecked with the gauge. When it looks right, scribe the lines onto the edges of the molds with a bright pen line to keep them distinct from your earlier pencil marks. Remove the battens and transfer the plank lines to the other side, either by measuring up from the keel rabbet or down from the sheer. (Paper tape or thin wooden battens work well for this exercise.) Pay especially close attention to getting the plank lines on the stem symmetrical. It's a good idea to run the battens through the new marks just to make sure the lines were properly transferred.

One last consideration. Generally speaking, the planking will be too thin to "back out" or hollow to accommodate a curved transom. One easy way to deal with this is to plane flats onto the transom between the lined-off marks. This fine-tuning is best done as the planking proceeds to accommodate any subtle changes in the lining.

SPILING THE PLANKS

Light plywood makes a convenient and stable spiling batten. Either ⅛" or ¼" will work—the choice depends on the shape of the hull, the span between frames or molds, and the amount of twist required.

Spiling a lapstrake plank is similar to spiling a carvel plank—just a matter of using a pencil compass and swinging arcs to transfer fixed distances from the setup boat onto a fixed spiling batten. Indeed, for the garboard, the technique is exactly the same as carvel. The plank is spiled, picking up information from the

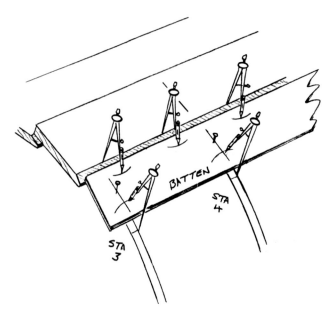

Spiling a clinker plank.

rabbet and the established plank lines. That information is then transferred to the planking stock, the points are connected with a batten, the plank is cut out, and the edges are squared up and fit to the rabbet. The difference comes with the planks that follow the garboard. Instead of recording the outer edge of the previous plank as you would in carvel, with lapstrake you record the lap line that is drawn on the outer face. And with the exception of the rabbet side of the garboard strake, the spiling batten should project onto the bevel of the previous plank. This is very important. If the spiling batten does not land on the beveled lap, but instead is tacked directly to the molds (as you would with carvel), the plank shape developed will be incorrect.

After you cut out the plank, square-edged, there are two more operations to perform before it can be installed: putting the long compound bevel on the lap on the first plank, and tending to the ends of the planks so they come out flush where they fit into the rabbet and against the transom. A good place to begin is the long bevel.

The Bevel Is in the Details

To make the connection between adjacent planks watertight, a bevel must be placed on the top outward edge (the sheer side) of the garboard and all the subsequent planks. Running from the lap line to the edge, this compound bevel must offer full contact between the planks with no leak-producing crowns, gaps, or

The Compass-Arc Spiling Method

Dust off that old high school geometry book that you swore you would never use again. Somewhere in that section with the bisection of angles and Mr. Isosceles' theorem is a notation that, if you take a compass, place it on a starting position, and draw an arc, you can then come back to that spot by placing the point of the compass on any two locations on the arc and drawing arcs back. Where the arcs cross, is the original starting position. That's what happens with the arcs drawn onto the spiling batten tacked to the planking stock. When you draw those two arcs back onto the planking stock, you create a series of accurate X's that

you can then spring a wooden batten through. Trace that line onto the stock to replicate the shape of the plank.

Any drawbacks? Yep. The technique is only accurate if you have a quality compass that will clamp the pencil tightly. If the pencil moves, all bets are off. If the pencil breaks or you sharpen the pencil, error can be introduced. If the radius is changed by the operator during the process, and that change isn't noted, the results will again be flawed. One remedy is to record the arc before starting, stick with that arc for the entire job, and check your compass against your recorded distance often.

hollows. As always, there are a number of approaches to this task.

One method is to record the angle of the bevel at each of the molds onto the clamped-up plank, and then remove the plank, lay it flat on the bench, and plane in the long rolling bevel. (This is similar to the process used for dory-lap planking, described in Chapter 4.) The necessary tools are pretty simple—a block plane (or spokeshave or chisel) and a short straightedge (a ruler or even a short block of wood). Starting at the first mold, use the straightedge to simulate the next plank, putting one edge of it on the line for the other side of the plank and lay the length of the rule against the edge of the plank to be beveled. Shave a bit off the edge and check it with the straightedge. Repeat and check it again, until finally the rule lands at the pencil lap line and lies flush along the shaved bevel.

Repeat the exercise for all the other molds. You can then connect all the spot bevels with a hand plane to create a continuous compound bevel. Use a thin batten on the edge of the plank and draw a guideline to connect the low points of the bevel. Some builders avoid removing the plank by free handing the planing between the notches right on the boat, but care needs to be taken as the long distances between the molds invite scalloping of the bevel.

There is a better way: the old batten and notched-gauge technique. Nail a stiff softwood batten to the molds, stem, and transom along the points lined off for the next plank. Next, make a notched lap gauge. Take a

straight piece of wood, a bit longer than the plank is wide, and draw a line parallel to the edge of the gauge that is the same thickness as the batten. Cut along that line for about half the length of the wood. Then finish the notch by cutting into the first slice from the outside edge.

How does this rig work? Take the gauge to a mold and hold it in place against the new plank with the notched part of the gauge riding on the batten. Using the same technique described for the straightedge method, use a spokeshave to remove stock along the edge of the plank until the gauge lands on the drawn lap line. All the gauge does is permit you to use the straightedge method along the full length of a clamped or fastened plank. By using a sharp block plane, set fine, to cut the bevel and riding the stepped gauge along the length

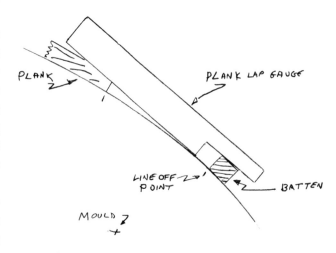

Using a lap gauge.

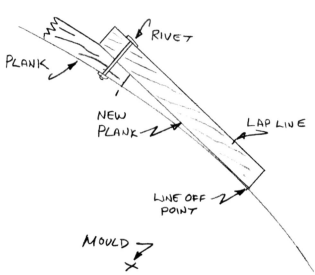

Cross-section of a new plank fastened in and ready for beveling.

A bit more needs to be planed off the bevel here for the lap gauge to lie flat.

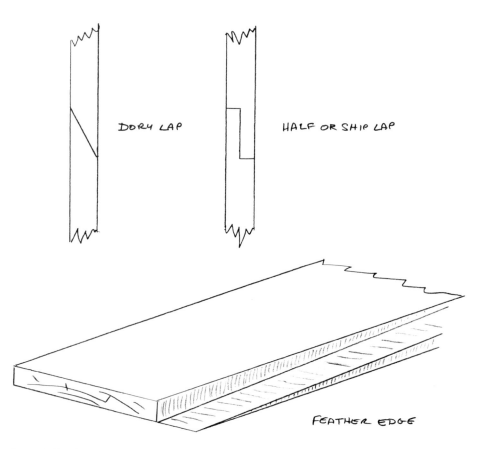

Laps at the stem.

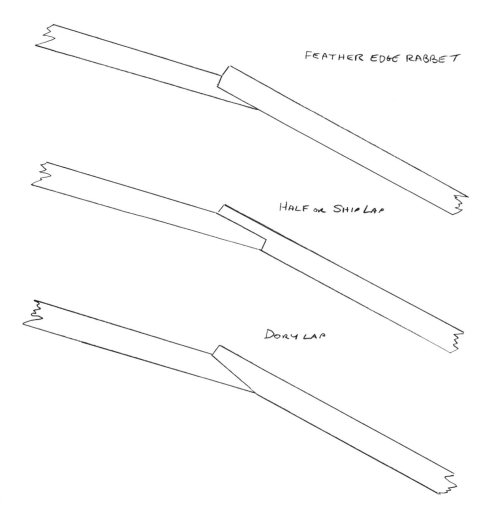

Laps at the transom.

FEATHER EDGE RABBET

HALF or SHIP LAP

DORY LAP

of the batten to check your work, you can quickly develop the correct bevel onto the face of the plank. Eureka! Now it's time to deal with the ends of the laps.

A HAPPY ENDING

The question of how to deal with the end of a lapped plank is enough to make the first-time builder blanch. Those planks that were so straightforwardly overlapped must now (somehow) merge together like carvel planking forward and tightly mate at the transom. There are at least three approaches: ship or half lap, rabbeted to a featheredge, and dory lap. One method is probably as good as the others.

The Half-lap or Ship-lap

One popular approach is to use mating half-laps at the plank ends. They can be cut with a rabbet plane that has an attached fence that can be set to the lap width, or by fastening a batten along the lap line and using it as a fence for the rabbet plane.

Clamp or tack the plank to the bench, and then, starting from 12" or so from the ends, plane a square-sided rabbet (an L-shaped channel) into the lap surface of the plank. At the stem, this rabbet will be a straight, flat ramp starting from the 12" point and cutting down to one half the plank's thickness at the end. At the stem end of the plank, this will be done twice: once on the "under" side that mates with the previous plank, and again on the "outer" side that will accept the next one.

On a rounded transom, a more conservative approach needs to be taken. This is due to the angle at which the next plank will land on the lap. If a half-thickness rabbet is cut both into the underlying plank and the mating (upper plank), when the two are put together the outside edge of the outer plank will lift, producing a vexatious and leak-prone gap. The most sure-fire solution to this problem is the empirical plank sample technique. Make two short sample pieces of plank of appropriate width and plane a half-thickness

Getting the ends of the planks to come together in a line at the stem requires special lapping methods.

lap into them. Put them in place on the transom and measure the amount of gap that develops. This will tell how deep to cut the inner plank's rabbet.

After planing in the rabbets to their desired depth fore and aft, hang the plank, and bevel the lap edge of the plank as described above. Only a small amount of bevel will be needed on the forward rabbet. More will be needed aft. Again, a measured approach is called for. More bevel can be worked in as you fit the adjoining plank.

Spile and get out the next plank and provisionally clamp it in place on the lap line of the previous plank. Trace the edge of the plank beneath onto the bottom of the new plank from inside the hull. Also, mark the point where the new rabbet begins fore and aft. Remove the new plank and plane in the matching rabbets on the bottom side. Mate the planks again, and check the fit.

Featheredge Rabbet

Similar to the half-lap, this traditional method involves cutting a ramp-like rabbet with a rabbet plane that tapers to a featheredge on the lap of the lower plank. Although this technique has a reputation for fragility,

it's quite serviceable as the featheredge is backed up by the rabbet in the stem and by the transom back aft. On the positive side of the ledger, no modifications need to be done to the underside of the overlapping second plank.

To cut your rabbet, start by placing your freshly cut and square-edged plank on the bench, face up. Mark the lap line in pencil. Next, tack down a batten along the lap line as a guide for the rabbet plane. How far back to bring the "ramp" is a matter of preference but 12″ is usually good. Then plane in the square-sided ramp, starting from the top of the plank face at 12″ to a featheredge at the hood end of the plank.

Once again the transom rabbet needs to be dealt with differently to accommodate the lap bevel. Use the sample pieces of plank to divine the amount of rabbet at the transom. This time, however, use full thickness, unrabbeted stock. Mark the minimum rabbet depth (which occurs at the lap line) onto the plank and plane the tapering rabbet to that depth.

Install your plank on the boat and bevel it using the notched gauge. When you reach the rabbets, make a shorter version of the notched gauge (if necessary) and continue the bevel right into the rabbet. With no extra shaping needed on the bottom of the overlapping plank, the next strake can be fit with a minimum of fuss.

The Dory-Lap Option

Instead of matching rabbets, this method uses complementary bevels on the adjoining planks to bring the ends in flush in the bow and tight at the transom. Begin by clamping the plank in place and capturing the bevels along its length. Then take the plank to the bench and plane the entire bevel in with your jack plane. Mark the start of the dory-lap bevel at a constant distance from the ends of the plank, both fore and aft (say 20″). Gradually plane or roll the bevel so that it comes to a featheredge at the far ends of the plank. Then fasten the plank to the boat.

The next plank can then be spiled, gotten out, and planed square at its edges. Clamp this new plank into place along the drawn lap line of the previous strake to check its fit. While it is clamped up, trace the lap line on the inside face of the new plank. Also mark the location of where the dory-lap part of the bevel begins. Take the plank to the bench and on the bow end of the plank, plane a bevel into the marked lap that starts at full plank thickness at the beginning

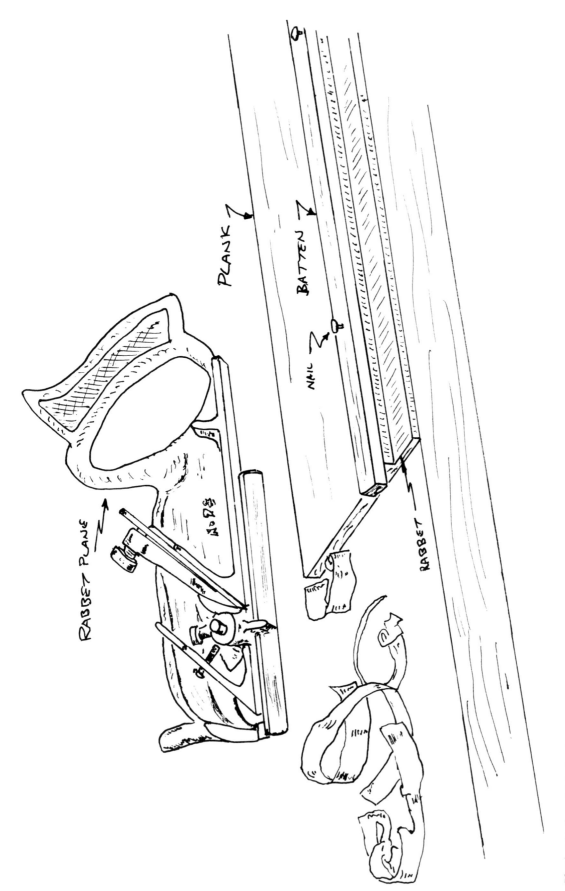

Planing in the rabbeted gain.

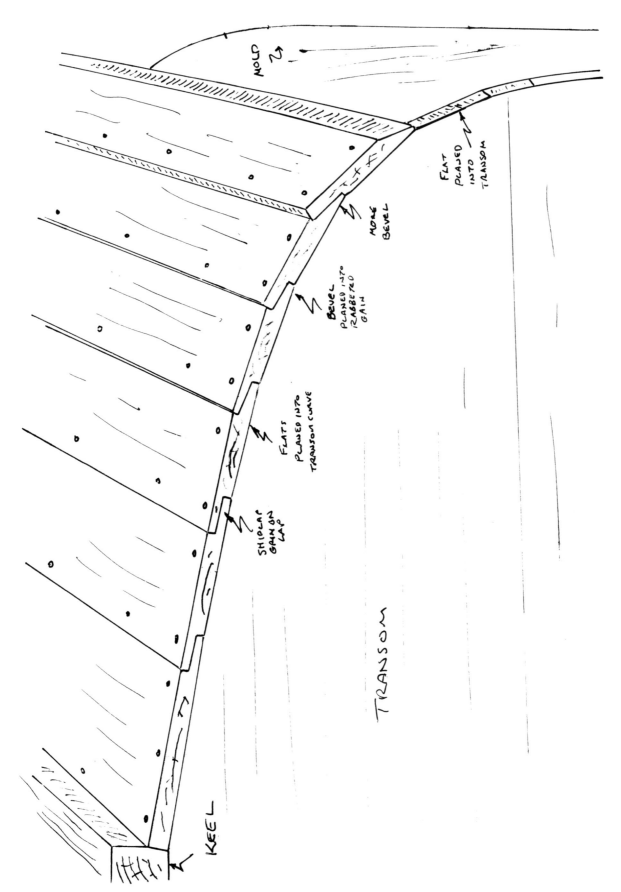

MOLD 2

FLAT PLANED INTO TRANSOM

MORE BEVEL

BEVEL PLANED INTO RABBETED GAIN

FLATS PLANED INTO TRANSOM CURVE

SHIPLAP GAIN ON LAP

TRANSOM

KEEL

Lapstrake planks on a round transom.

of the forward dory-lap mark, and goes to a feather-edge at the hood end.

So much for the forward end, but what to do about the transom? The new plank at the transom may be dead on top of the previous one (like at the stem). You can simply plane in a complementary bevel like at the stem. More likely, however, the new plank will lie over the preceding one's lap at an angle as it comes around the curve. If so, the next job is to determine what angle is necessary on the overlapping plank to match the featheredge of the dory lap on the preceding strake.

Take a bevel gauge and place it on the edge of the transom adjacent to the previous plank. Then swing the blade out to capture the angle of the lap. Take that angle to the transom end of the new plank and record it with a pencil or by cutting in a notch with a chisel. From the aft 20″ dory-lap mark, plane in your rolling bevel to the transom mark.

All that remains to be done is to bring the plank to the boat to check the fit, make any last adjustments, and fasten it.

When checking the fit of the laps, it's best to clamp along the entire length rather than just holding it in place by hand, as this shows more accurately how tight the joint will be after fastening. To avoid surprises, remember to inspect the lap on both the inside *and* the outside faces of the plank—especially when working upside-down.

▪ 4 ▪

Dory-Lap Planking

Dory lap is a modification of the familiar lapstrake style, the basic difference being that instead of having one edge of the plank planed square and the other beveled, dory lapstrakes have bevels on both the top and bottom edges—but on different sides. All the planks (with the exception of the sheer) have a constant bevel on the outside face of the sheer (upper) edge. The mating bevel, on the lower edge of the inside face of the plank, is compound, changing in response to the shape of the boat. Although at first blush this might seem a horrible concept, the technique is actually no more difficult than standard clinker construction and the result of the matching plank bevels is less exposed plank width—in other words, a rounder hull.

CHECK THE LINES

For the most part, the hull was already lined off on the lofting board, since the planks follow the angles or "knuckles" formed by the flats on the molds and transom, and the planks' forward end points were established on the stem when it was laid out. Nonetheless, the line of the planks does define the looks of the boat, so it's worth taking a few moments to check these lines with a batten. Tack a batten to the lines and sight down it for fairness (especially at the stem). Modify it if necessary by pulling a tack and letting the batten correct itself. Also, check that the plank lines' endings are equal on either side of the stem. This homage paid to the gods of symmetry will pay dividends as it allows you to cut out two planks at the same time from a single spiling. The only difference between them will be that the bevels will be (near) mirror images of one another.

Spiling

In Chapter 24, we show how to loft a Chaisson semi-dory from plans, and we'll use the same boat here for our example. (A photo of a sailing version of the same design appears in Chapter 35.)

A Dion dory in autumn.

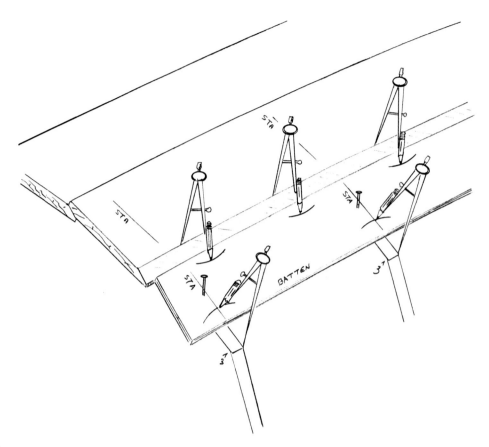

Spiling a plank.

The spiling batten is a flexible pattern that wraps around the hull between the plank line marks and is tacked down to the molds, transom, and stem. All the data necessary to fashion the plank are recorded onto this pattern. A good choice of stock for the spiling batten is ¼" plywood, as it is stiff enough to easily span the distance between the molds without sagging and to resist edge-set, a pernicious side twisting phenomenon that often bedevils the builder. An edge-set batten will straighten out when removed from the boat, and a plank made from it can be a cranky affair to fit, as all of its recorded dimensions will be correct but the shape will be all wrong.

To accommodate the sweep of the strakes, it's generally much easier to build up the spiling batten from several pieces of plywood that are first wrapped around the boat, then joined with gussets and glued. The batten should be fairly wide, landing on the bevel of the previous plank and stretching to just shy of the knuckle on the molds.

While there are myriad spiling techniques that work, for dory-lap planking it's hard to beat the compass method. The theory is this: if you strike an arc with a compass, and then swing two more arcs—using any two locations on the first arc as a starting point—the intersection of the two arcs will be at the point that you started the first arc from in the first place. To replicate a curve of a plank, just move along the length of it swinging a series of arcs onto an anchored spiling batten. The batten can then be removed and tacked in place on top of the construction stock. Then, from the series of arcs on the batten, swing your intersecting arcs onto the planking stock. Spring a flexible batten through the series of X's and there you'll have the curve.

Spiling the Garboard

To spile the garboard, work from the shoulder of the bevel on the bottom board and run a series of arcs along the length of the spiling batten. On the sheer side of the garboard, swing an arc from the first knuckle on each of

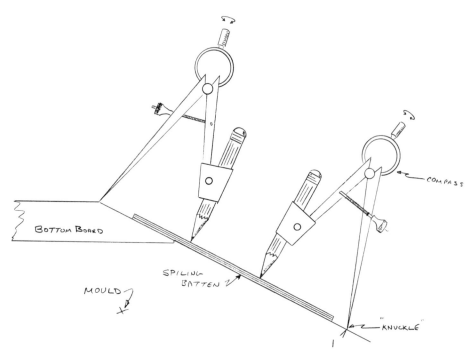

Spiling the garboard.

the molds and the transom and the plank line on the stem. Then mark the curve of the forward face of the stem and the aft edge of the transom onto the spiling batten. Also mark and number the stations.

Making the Bevel

Dory garboard planks tend to be quite wide and may require scarfing. They also have a considerable amount of twist and are miserable to replace if they go bad, so it pays to be finicky in your stock selection. When laying out your plank from the spiling batten, be sure to avoid sapwood, rot pockets, deep checks, and large knots (especially those on the edge of the plank). When cutting out the garboard, leave the plank long at both ends and the bottom edge a bit oversize. This will accommodate any problems in fitting. The sheer side can be planed right to the line. Then the constant bevel can be scribed on the outer sheer (i.e., top) edge of the plank. This bevel will be the same for each plank (except the sheer plank, which has none). Set your combination square to the width of the lap (on this boat, it is 7⁄8″) and use it as a gauge to run a pencil along the sheer edge of the plank, scribing the lap line on the outside face. Next, draw a line on the edge of the plank that is 1⁄16″ out from the inside edge. Plane down to these two lines and—Eureka!—there is your bevel

with just a little step at the edge. One last thing: from a point 2′ from the ends, roll the bevel gradually to a featheredge at the stem and transom. This eliminates the step and will allow the next plank to sit flush.

Fastening the Garboard

The garboard can now be bent to the hull. Screwing wooden cleats to the sides of the molds will give the planking clamps additional purchase points. The hood end of the garboard has quite a bit of twist and will need to be heat-softened into submission. Although steaming is an option, a better choice is the boil-in-place technique. Just clamp the aft part of the plank in place and wrap the hood end in rags. Slide a piece of plastic sheet between the boat and the plank. Boil some water and pour some onto the rags. Wrap the plastic around them to keep the heat in. Every 5 minutes or so, unwrap and repeat the drill. After 30 minutes, remove the sodden steaming swaddling, bend the plank easily into place, and clamp. It's a crude technique but effective. Just remember to use caution and your hot mitts!

After cooling, the plank can be fastened. Due to the rolling shape of the plank, this job will take a symphony of hardware: shorter screws for the stem and transom, longer screws for fastening horizontally

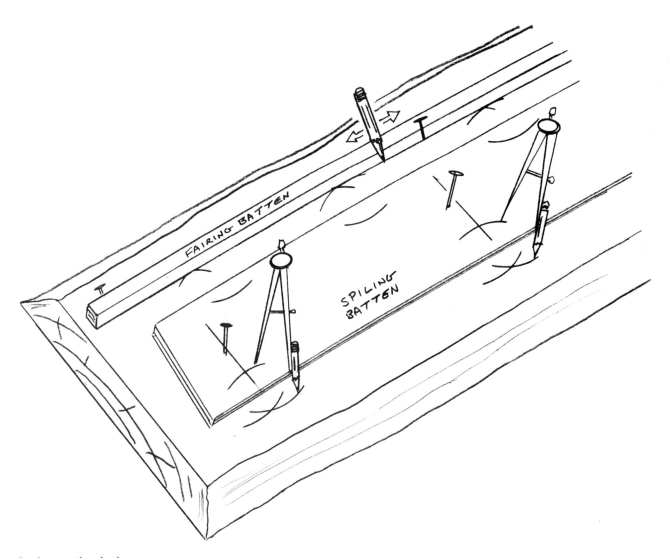

Laying out the plank.

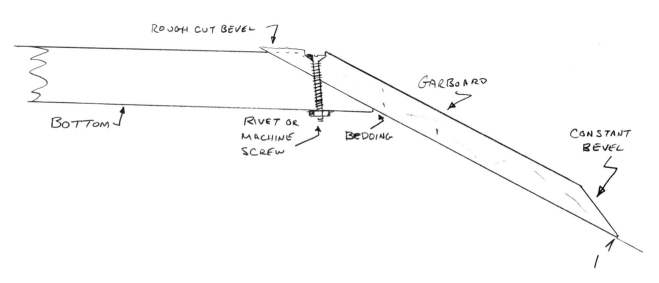

Fitting the garboard to the bottom.

into the edge of the bottom forward of Station 2, and machine screws or rivets to through-fasten the garboard to the long bevel of the bottom aft. The garboard plank benefits from the use of a flexible adhesive 3M 5200 or Sikaflex in the joint with the bottom. Dry-run the job to be sure you have enough clamps (and places to clamp them to). Deep-throated "clothes pin" clamps are a real plus. Then, working fore to aft, fasten the plank. Afterward, the ends of the plank can be trimmed flush with the transom and curve of the stem face and square to the centerline of the boat. (This boat has a two-piece stem. The planks are fastened to the inner stem, which has a bevel but no rabbet. The outer part—a "false" stem—will be affixed to the forward edge of the inner stem and squared plank edges later.) Next, plane the edge flush with the bottom of the boat. (Watch out for those vertical fastenings.)

Repeat the operation for the other garboard.

Finishing the Planking

The rest of the planks are spiled in a similar fashion to the garboard. The only real difference is that subsequent planks are spiled to the shoulder of the constant bevel (or lap line) of the previous planks. The plank is again laid out on the stock and cut and trimmed square to the top and bottom scribed batten lines. Establish and plane in the constant bevel on the "sheer" edge of the plank just as you did with the garboard.

The next job is to generate the compound bevel. Begin by drawing another 7⁄8" lap line with the combination square on the inside face of the lower edge of the plank.

To pick up the rest of the bevels at the stations and transom, place the bevel gauge so that the pivot lands on the lower edge of the constant bevel of the previous plank. One leg of the gauge will follow the bevel; the other will stretch out until it contacts the knuckle for the next plank. Transfer the measured angle directly to the edge of the new plank at each station. One method to record the bevel onto the plank is to cut "spots" with a chisel to match the angle of the bevel gauge, working from the lap line to the edge. Another technique is to scribe the angle from the gauge onto the edge starting from a point 7⁄8" from the station line drawn on the edge. Either method will give you the low point of the bevel. The plank bevel at the stem will

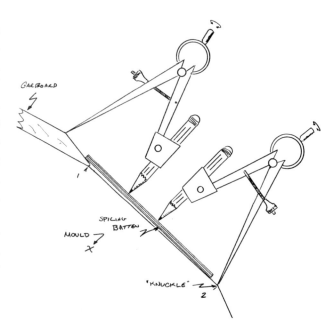

Spiling a broad strake. Note how the spiling batten sits on the "shoulder" of the previous plank, and not on the mold.

always be planed to a featheredge (both top and bottom) to allow all the planks to lie flush with one another. Fair the spots (low points) together with a batten and trim the entire edge with a plane. Check that your bevel is dead flat, as any crown on it will prevent a good fit between the joints. In a straight-or slab-sided dory, the plank lap bevels are all the same, while on a Swampscott-style dory, these bevels are compound or constantly changing.

Now it's time to fasten the planks to one another by either rivets or clench nails. Generally, no compound is used in the joints. When laying out the fastening locations, many builders like to pre-mark the points equally by "walking" them out with dividers. It pays to move your clamps along as you fasten to ensure a tight joint. Vibration from hammering fastenings can loosen the clamped strake and cause it to droop from its intended position. To defy gravity, check the fit and reclamp several times as you work.

The sheer (i.e., shop floor) edge of the sheer plank will not have the bevel and instead is left square. Rather than planing to the sheer line as spiled, leave this edge a little full. The final sheer line can be planed in after the boat is off the jig, and the extra width is a bit of insurance just in case the plank slips out of place while fastening.

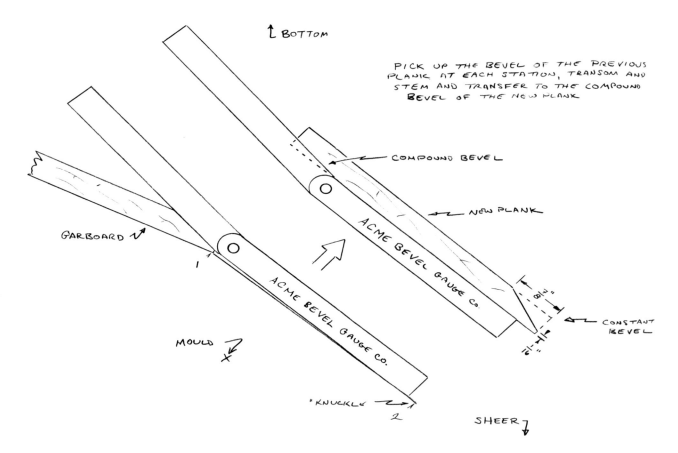

↑ BOTTOM

PICK UP THE BEVEL OF THE PREVIOUS
PLANK AT EACH STATION, TRANSOM AND
STEM AND TRANSFER TO THE COMPOUND
BEVEL OF THE NEW PLANK

COMPOUND BEVEL

NEW PLANK

ACME BEVEL GAUGE CO.

GARBOARD

1

ACME BEVEL GAUGE CO.

MOULD

8½"

CONSTANT BEVEL

6½"

"KNUCKLE"
2

SHEER

Picking up the bevels.

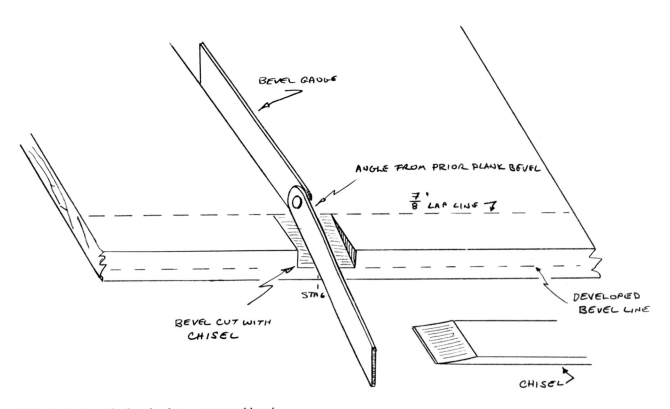

BEVEL GAUGE

ANGLE FROM PRIOR PLANK BEVEL

7/8" LAP LINE

DEVELOPED BEVEL LINE

BEVEL CUT WITH CHISEL

STA 6

CHISEL

"Mechanical" method to develop a compound bevel.

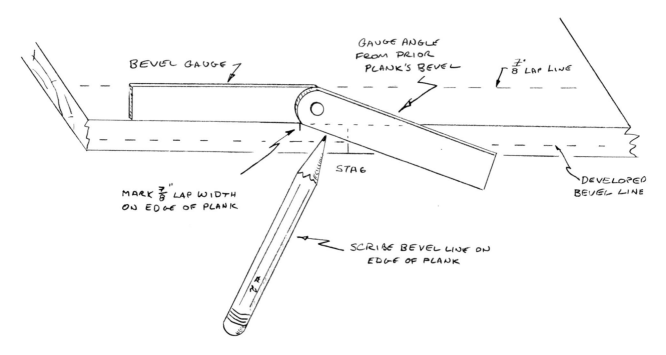

BEVEL GAUGE

GAUGE ANGLE FROM PRIOR PLANK'S BEVEL

$\frac{7}{8}"$ LAP LINE

STAG

MARK $\frac{7}{8}"$ LAP WIDTH ON EDGE OF PLANK

DEVELOPED BEVEL LINE

SCRIBE BEVEL LINE ON EDGE OF PLANK

"Geometric" method to develop a compound bevel.

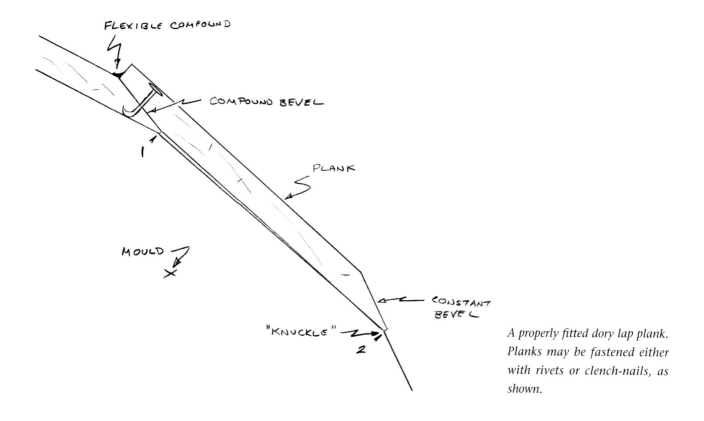

FLEXIBLE COMPOUND

COMPOUND BEVEL

PLANK

MOULD

CONSTANT BEVEL

"KNUCKLE"

A properly fitted dory lap plank. Planks may be fastened either with rivets or clench-nails, as shown.

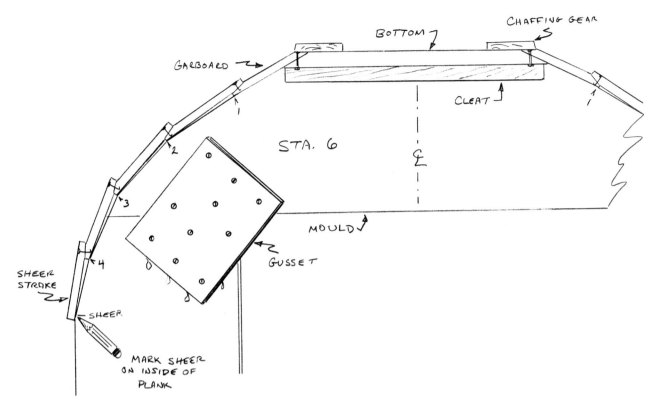

CHAFFING GEAR
BOTTOM
GARBOARD
1
STA. 6
CLEAT
¢
2
3
MOULD
GUSSET
4
SHEER STROKE
SHEER
1
MARK SHEER ON INSIDE OF PLANK

A dory-lap hull all planked up over the midship mold.

· 5 ·

Planking a Traditional Flat-Bottomed Boat

Mention the term "cross-planked hull" and the mind immediately conjures up the vision of practical blue-collar boats—sensible working craft such as clamming skiffs, flatiron skiffs, garveys, sharpies, sailing scows, and sloop-rigged flatties. And indeed they are practical and sensible. Using very few and generally unsophisticated tools and locally available woods, they are among the simplest and most economic craft to build. They excel in shallow-water operations, are handy on the beach, and can be moved easily with rollers. In addition, they are safe and stable platforms for either heavy-duty work situations or

A Will Angel–designed sharpie skiff.

explorations by adventurous youngsters. It's no wonder so many of them show up in city park ponds.

But the flat-bottomed boat need not be simply a clunky reliable workhorse. Add a little design and flair and you have an elegant thoroughbred. The long and lean "sharpie" is a good example of the marriage of practicality and performance. Extensively used on the East Coast of the United States in the second half of the 19th century, these high-capacity working vessels were ideal for working shallow inshore fisheries and then returning home quickly and safely in a variety of sea conditions. Yachtsmen soon took notice. Influential yacht designer Commodore Ralph Munroe popularized the type in the 1880s when he put his 28' *Egret* into commercial service carrying passengers and mail in south Florida. It was faster than the competition and could run the shoal inlets near his Coconut Grove home in almost any weather. According to Howard Chapelle, the sharpie's popularity was due to its low cost, light draft, speed under sail, graceful appearance, and seaworthiness.

As with any hull type, however simple, the quality of craftsmanship will make all the difference—especially with planking. Slap-dash construction and shoddy materials can make a vexatious leaker out of the finest design. Conversely, attention to detail will allow the humblest skiff to rival any of its more pretentious cousins in longevity and durability.

An Egret sharpie at Commodore
Munroe's homestead in Coconut
Grove.

*A bit of fancy detail is a good thing, even on a utilitarian work-
ing boat.*

A LITTLE HISTORY

The earliest cross-planked prototypes were built by eye.
Hulls were commonly planked with one or two enormous, straight-grained pine boards per side. (One 1917
boatbuilding manual called for using stock 13 feet
long, 17 inches wide, and ⅞ inch thick.) If two boards
were used, they would simply be cleated together edge
to edge and then treated as a single plank for the purpose of shaping and planing. The planks were then
spiked to a triangle-section stem. A trapezoidal transom was fashioned and roughly beveled, and a center
"shadow" mould (again trapezoidal in shape) was
made and inserted between the two planks. A rope
tourniquet known as a Spanish windlass was slipped
around the aft ends of the planks and used to pull the
sides together around the mould to the transom. The
planks were nailed to the transom, the bottom boards
were nailed on crosswise, and the projecting ends
sawed off. The centre mould was then popped and
replaced with a thwart or two, the bottom was caulked,
a keel-board and skeg added, and you were pretty
much in business.

While this "eyeball" method works, how *well* it
works depends on the eye and experience of the

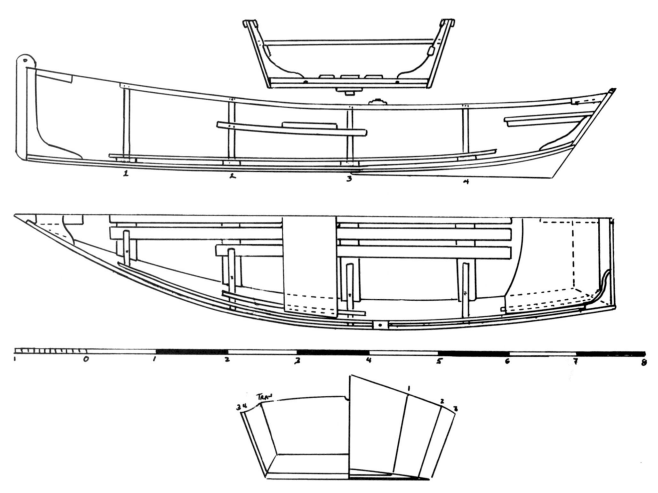

A flat-bottomed skiff intended for the circa-1890s home boatbuilder—from the old Forest and Stream *magazine (redrawn by the author).*

builder. A more reliable method is to loft out the lines. The loft is simple (only a few lines) and well worthwhile, as it will give not only the shape and location of the moulds, but also the shapes and bevels of the stem and transom.

SETTING UP THE HULL

These days, most small flat-bottomed hulls are built upside down over conventional molds set up on a strongback. Better hulls have chine logs and an interior keelson. The chine logs are hardwood (usually oak) longitudinal pieces that are bent around the interior of the hull where the bottom joins the side planking. They run from stem to stern and not only stiffen the hull but also give the lowest side planks something solid to fasten to. Chines often need to limbered up by steaming to get them to fit. The keelson is a hardwood board that runs down the centerline on the inside of the hull. It too stiffens the hull, backs up the bottom planking, and provides a good base for a centerboard trunk. Occasionally sheer clamps are fitted. These are hardwood strips running along the inside top edge of the sheer strakes to stiffen them and provide a wider landing upon which to fasten oarlock pads. The molds have to be notched to accommodate the chine logs, keelson, and sheer clamp.

These boats commonly have a beveled dory-type stem with no rabbet. The planking runs entirely on the outside of the stem and, at the apex where opposite-side planks meet, they are cut off and trimmed square to the boat's centerline, presenting a flat face upon which to fasten a false stem, as shown in the accompanying drawing. On some old-time sharpies, the side planks ran past the forward edge of the stem

Building on a jig.

and were mitered to form a sharp cutwater that was then covered with a brass band. Yet another option is the rabbeted stem that the planks fit into. Whichever type of stem is used, the chines and keelson will be bent to it and fastened.

Along with installation of the stem, a beveled transom is added and connected to the rest of the boat by the chines and keelson. The bottom edges of the chines are beveled to assure a good landing for the bottom planking. A hand plane and good straight-edge, such as a four-foot carpenter's level, works well for this. A batten is sprung around the entire assembly to check the fairness of the molds and the bevels on the transom and stem. Then all surfaces that will land against planks are painted with red lead or another good primer. The boat is now ready to plank.

An unrabbeted sharpie stem.

A sharpie transom. Note the joinery of the chine, keelson, and transom framing.

PLANKING THE SIDES

Flat-bottomed boats can be planked either edge-to-edge, carvel style, or lapped using a standard clinker lap or the dory lap. The argument for clinker is that it produces a stronger and somewhat lighter hull. Spiling is done in the usual fashion. For length, the planks can be scarfed or (in the case of carvel) butt blocks can be used.

For either carvel or clinker, the garboard plank goes on first. It will be bedded and fastened to the stem, chine, and transom.

With carvel planking, sawn frames are added at regular intervals. They should be notched to fit around the chine and long enough to run past the sheer. (The length can be trimmed after all the planking is on.) Clamp the frames in place and fasten them to the chine and garboard. The arrangement looks a little odd, but the frames need to be there to hold the rest of the planks in place. Spile and fit the next plank and fasten it into place by screwing it into the stem, frames, and transom. (Don't forget the caulking bevel.)

With clinker, mark the location of the frames on the garboard but don't install them until all the planking is done. The plank-to-plank fastenings will hold everything in place. Prior to putting on the bottom, fit the frames to the chine and flush to the planking, allowing for the step of the laps.

It is not unusual for the optimistic nineteenth-century sheer plank to be too wide for the reality of twenty-first-century planking stock. The builder has the choice of either relining the plank locations and adding an additional plank or simply adding a wedge-shaped "stealer" fore and aft. In the past a stealer would be fit and mechanically fastened. Nowadays, the easiest way to add a stealer is to simply lay the spiling batten onto the planking stock to determine how much extra stock is needed. Then cut out, join, and edge-glue (with epoxy or resorcinol) a piece that adds the necessary

NAILS VS. SCREWS

For the parsimonious builder of the past, the galvanized square-sectioned boat nail was the fastening of choice for planking. The modern equivalent is the bronze ring nail. Nails should be prebored for using slightly undersized bits. They should be installed at an angle that draws the planking together, but care must be taken to avoid breaking out of either the chine or the transom.

While nails are cheap and fast to use, they also make damaged planks almost impossible to repair. For small boats intended for long-term use, bronze screws are the way to go. Installation is nearly as quick as the nails, and if you ever need to get that plank off you'll be able to do so without using a chainsaw.

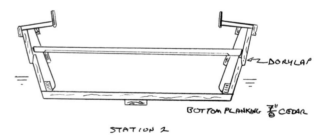

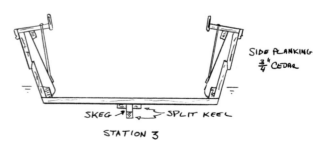

Section construction details on a dory lap sharpie.

width to the plank stock. The plank can then be spiled onto the widened stock and cut out.

PLANKING THE BOTTOM

For the builder with a traditional bent, the tried-and-true method of cross planking is a good way to go. The planking that connects the sides eliminates the need for the heavy framing required in fore-and-aft-planked flat bottoms, such as banks dories. Efficient and expeditious, this technique has changed little over the years.

On launching, boats with traditional cross-planked bottoms and caulked garboards often leak a little bit before the caulking swells up to tighten the seam and keep the water out. These days, however, cross planking is often eschewed in flavor of plywood. "Why mess with caulking and swelling when I can just slap on a plywood bottom and be done with it?" asks the progressive builder. A point well taken. It is true that compared to a plywood bottom, the planked version does require a modicum of care in painting and caulking. But a job is only as good as the materials that are put into it, and many do not have ready access to good quality marine plywood, while sawn lumber may be readily available. For others, the rugged reliability, easy repair, and classic appearance make old-time cross-planking their first choice. Besides, some will argue that the new flexible, adhesive seam compounds alleviate much of the angst over leaky bottoms.

Bottom Wood

One of the advantages of the flat bottom is that it allows the builder to use stock that otherwise would have been neglected. Often an inspection of the wood pile will reveal numerous planks that have a short run of wonderfully clear wood from the "butt of the log," while the other end of the stick is a study of narrow heartwood, enormous knots, and rot. These orphan "leftovers" can make great candidates for cross planking. In addition, random widths are permissible (within reason). Indeed they can be used to advantage: wider planks in the flat runs and narrower ones in areas where the bottom has a lot of curve.

Does this mean anything can be used for bottom planking? Not quite. The stock for working craft tends to be hefty: say ¾" to 1" in thickness. Also, wood can change dimension as it gains or loses moisture. This can cause distortion, checking, warp, or cupping. Quarter-sawn or vertical grain lumber is therefore a top choice for the job, as it is more resistant to cupping than plain-sawn or live-edge (flitch-cut) boards (see Chapter 12). Unfortunately, this commodity is easier to specify than to find at the local lumber emporium. It is far more likely that the builder will be using the less stable but more readily available plain-sawn lumber.

Which brings us back to the question of plank widths. Using overly wide plain-sawn planks can be problematic as they cup more easily and shrink more when they dry out, compared to narrow planks, leading to open seams. The Forest Products Laboratory's *Wood Handbook* suggests that for best cup-resistance, the width of a board should not exceed eight times its thickness. (The Forest Products Laboratory is part of the U.S. Department of Agriculture. Go to www.fpl.fs.fed.us.) On the other hand, very narrow planks, while more

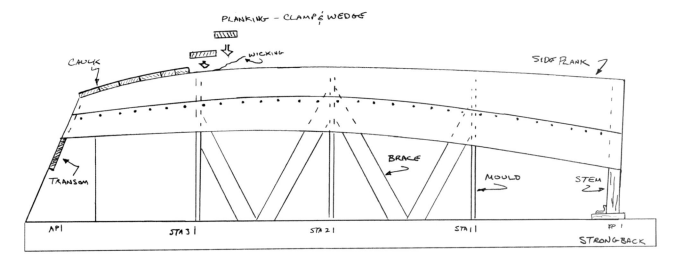

Crossplanking a flat-bottomed skiff on a jig.

stable, can be overly limber and may flex too much when installed on the bottom. Yet another consideration is that some species exhibit greater resistance to cupping than others. The cedars do better than the pines or larch, while hardwoods tend to be the worst offenders. So, what to do? Try to use planks 5" to 6" wide, and avoid excessively wide stock. If using narrower board, check beforehand for excessive flex.

Tight Bottom Planking

Before planking gets underway, check once again that the lower or mating edges of the chines and side planks (and keelson, if there is one) are planed fair and true relative to one another.

That being done, a caulking seam bevel can be planed onto the lower outside edge of the lowest side plank. This will allow for a strand of cotton to be driven in after the bottom has been installed. An alternate method is to bevel the bottom edges of the lowest side planks flush to the bottom and run a strand of twisted cotton wicking along the edges for the bottom planking to land on as it is installed. In addition, some builders like to run a thin coating of bedding compound on the bottom edge of the chine before planking.

The edges of the bottom planks need to be planed dead true. This is a good job for an electric jointer or a well-set-up table saw followed by a #7 handheld jointer plane. Then add a caulking bevel to the outside edge of each plank.

Cross planking usually begins at the transom and works its way toward the bow. In the case of double-enders, planking can start at the center and work toward

the ends, but make sure that the first plank is dead square across the hull.

The planking can be roughly cut to size and laid out beforehand. This will ensure that you have all the stock needed to complete the job without interruption and that all the boards have been planed to the same thickness. It's okay to leave the ends square and over-long, as they can easily be trimmed off as you go along (rather than waiting to cut them off after all the planking is on). If the previous plank is temporarily left long, it will give you a place to clamp to when drawing the next plank in tight. Clamping wedging blocks to the chines and keelson (if it has one) will also help draw the new plank tight to its neighbor. The plank should also be clamped downward onto the chines if the design calls for them (not all do). Be sure to use wooden pads between the clamp and the plank. After the plank has been clamped tight, fasten it to the chine logs and inner keel (if there is one) with nails or screws.

John Gardner wrote of another way to draw planks up tight. He planked in sections no wider than could be pulled together with a bar clamp, and he would leave slightly wedge-shaped openings the width of a plank between the sections. He would then install a tapered shutter plank that could be driven in tight with a mallet.

As the planking crosses the station molds, transfer the centerline mark from the mold onto the plank. These marks will make it a lot easier to establish an accurate centerline for the outer keel. After the planking has been all installed, fair the bottom with a long plane and sanding board and give it a good vacuuming.

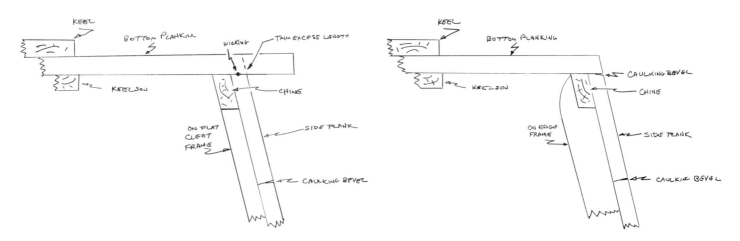

Two traditional ways to keep the water out. Left: The lowest side plank is flush to the bottom planking, with a strand of wicking between. Right: A conventional caulking bevel is planed into the bottom edge of the first side plank, and caulking is driven or rolled in place.

Caulking

Like all carvel-type planking, caulking the bottom with cotton not only makes it watertight but also hardens and strengthens it in a way that elastic caulk by itself cannot. The cross planking should fit tight on the inside of the boat and have a caulking bevel on the outside. While the seams can be caulked with an iron, the job is probably most easily done with a caulking wheel. After the cotton has been tamped in, the seams should be primed with red lead or another good oil-based undercoat paint.

After the paint dries, top the seam off with an elastic seam compound. This is a good place for one of those industrial-strength adhesive sealants that come in a tube. These products cling tenaciously to the sides of the seam, stretching or compressing as the planking shrinks and swells. The goops are notoriously messy, however, so masking the seams beforehand is recommended. Then pump the seam full by pushing the caulking gun ahead along the seam. Finally, tool the filled seams with the bottom side of a teaspoon and pull the tape.

A Laminated Bottom

Another bottom-planking technique that combines a traditional look with modern technology is the double laminated bottom. Planking is put on in two layers of half-thickness stock that are laminated in place with epoxy at right angles to each other. This is best done with stable woods that glue well, like cedar, in boats with keelsons to support the relatively limber first layer.

If the plans called for ¾″ planking, run your first layer of ⅜″ stock athwartships. Run a bead of adhesive flexible caulk between each plank to prevent epoxy leaking through. After the caulk has cured, fair the bottom, apply epoxy, and lay down and fasten a layer of ⅜″ planking in the fore-and-aft direction. For extra durability, a layer of fiberglass cloth can be set into the epoxy between layers. Wait for the epoxy to cure, then recoat over the glass with fresh epoxy and install the second layer of planks. After curing again, trim the bottom to size. What you essentially end up with is a cedar plywood bottom that will never leak or need swelling.

Plywood

Of course, manufactured plywood can also be used on the bottom if the amount of fore-and-aft rocker (curve of the bottom) allows for it. Applying the plywood in two lighter layers with epoxy between makes it easier to get the curve. Use quality marine plywood, and be sure to seal the edges with epoxy.

Keel Board and Skeg

Next add the outside hardwood keel board and skeg (if the boat has one). Begin by marking a centerline on the bottom. Then measure out from the centerline the dimensions of the keel board at each station.

Chances are, the keel is tapered, so spring a batten through the points and scribe a line. Give the planking between the lines a coat of primer. Prefit the keel to make sure that everything joins well. Apply a thin coating of bedding compound, and then bend the keel board into place.

If the boat has a keelson, the keel board can be fastened directly through the planking into it. If there is no keelson, use only enough fastenings to hold the keel board in place on the planks and run the rest of the fastenings from the inside of the boat through the planking and into the keel.

There are a number of different ways to add a skeg. Some plans simply call for a wedge to be fastened to the bottom with a cleat on either side. Others call for a notch or fork to be cut into the keel that is as wide and long as the skeg. The narrow end of the wedge-shaped skeg is nibbed to the thickness of the keel board. The skeg is then attached to the bottom, and the keel is bent around the bottom with the two tines of the fork running snugly on either side of the skeg.

A third way is the split-sprung keel method. This works well on bottoms that have a gentle curve and then suddenly kick up toward the transom. A wedge-shaped skeg is fit to the bottom of the hull along the strong curve up to the transom, and the top edge carries on the gentle curve of the bottom a bit farther forward. The skeg is fastened into place. The outside shape of the keel is cut. As in the forked-keel method, two kerfs are cut into the keel to accommodate the skeg. This time, however, the center "tine" is left in place rather than removed to make a notch. The keel is bent and fastened into place. When the keel board reaches the keel, the two outside tines fit tightly to the bottom and sides of the skeg, while the center tine runs on top of the skeg wedge and is fastened with screws. The skeg ends up elegantly ensconced by the three tines of the keel.

With that done, the bottom is complete. Lift the whole rig off the jig, flip it over, and finish it out!

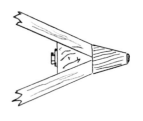

STEM DETAIL

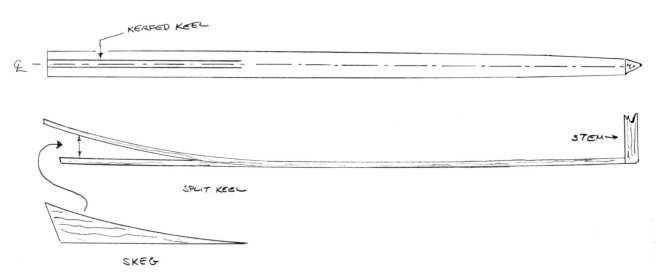

KERFED KEEL

C_L

SPLIT KEEL

STEM →

SKEG

A split-sprung keel. Two kerfs are sawn into the aft end. The side pieces are fastened to the bottom, while the center section becomes the bottom of the skeg.

Just off the jig, ready for fitting out the interior.

∎ 6 ∎

Batten Seam Construction

Occasionally there are construction techniques that, despite their utility and past popularity, have fallen from favor. Let's take up the case of batten seam construction.

Reminiscent of old-time wooden airplane fuselage construction with formers and stringers defining the shape of the hull, batten seam is a modification of standard sawn-frame carvel construction. The battens are screwed (and many times glued) into prenotched sawn frames. The planking is then fastened to the battens with each batten centerline falling under a planking seam. The method has worked for a plethora of light, strong, high-speed hulls and was often used in production mahogany speedboats.

In many ways, batten seam construction takes the best attributes from both carvel and lapstrake. Like the rigidity offered by the lapped edges of the lapstrake planked hull, the battens add stiffness at the seam line. This not only reduces the number of frames used, compared to conventional carvel construction, but also permits reduced plank thickness and greater plank width. (If desired, additional light frames can be added later in the process.) And the battens keep the seams leak-proof (mostly).

PREPARING PLANKS AND FRAMES

V-shaped batten seamed boats tend to be relatively slab- or flat-sided. With little if any hollow or curve to be sculpted into the planking, as in regular carvel, the planking stock can be milled out to the final thickness right from the get-go. Indeed, if you've got thick enough stock, you can get the plank's shape out of the heavy stock and then resaw it into matching port and starboard planks and plane it to the final thickness. Even if the stock is too thin to be resawn in half, you can still work up two planks together. When sawing, simply use the first plank as a guide or pattern for the second. Then tack them together, put them in a vice, and plane their edges down as one.

The setup of batten seam frames is about the same as in standard sawn-frame construction—including roughing out the chine notches before setup, but saving the final beveling and tuning until later. As in regular hard-chined construction, the transom will have an internal frame or cheeks on which the chines and battens will land. Some builders treat the transom frame like the rest of the frames, setting it up and bracing it at the proper angle and adding the transom planking only after the chines and battens have been attched. This scheme allows the notches for the chines and battens to be easily cut in and faired without interference; then the chines and battens can be installed over-length and fastened, and their ends can be trimmed off flush to the after face of the frame. Then (finally) the transom can be planked up. It's all in the timing.

Next you can bevel the frames for the planking. While the compound frame bevels could have been derived from the lofting, for small craft, it is often easier to do it when the frames are standing vertical and

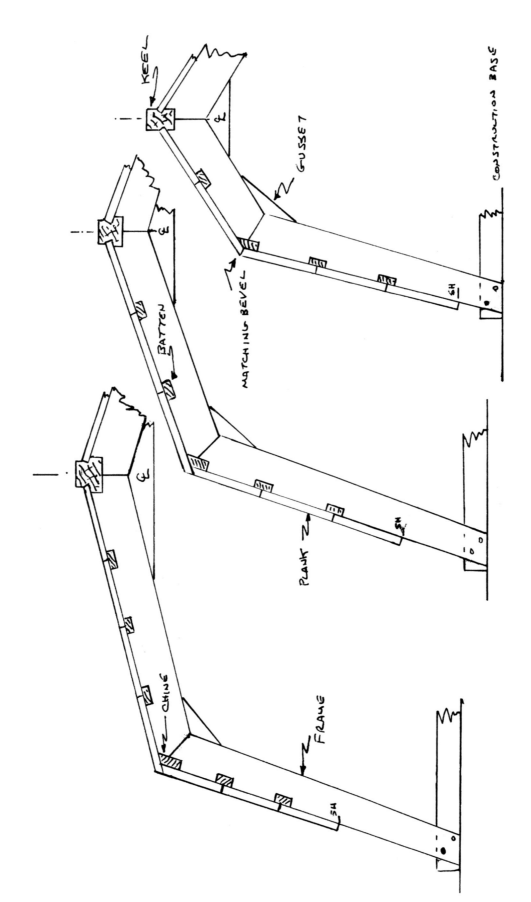

SECTIONS - NOT TO SCALE

KEEL

GUSSET

CONSTRUCTION BASE

MATCHING BEVEL

BATTEN

PLANK

FRAME

CHINE

In batten seam construction, sawn frames serve as the building molds. Longitudinal battens are let into notches cut into the frames, and every plank seam falls over a batten, for a tight, rigid structure.

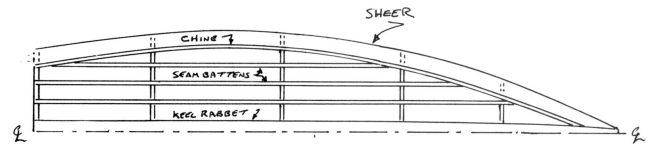

Layout of parallel seam battens on the bottom of a V-shaped hull.

are well supported and you can have your way with them. Simply wrap a fairing batten around them and hone down the "high" sides of the frames to the correct bevel with a spokeshave, chisel, or rasp. After the frames have been faired, it's time to mark out the batten notches.

Some builders lay out, notch, and bevel for the battens before cutting the bevels into the frame edges. Then they install the battens. The notch naturally ends up deeper on one side of the frame than the other. Then the frames are beveled flush with the seam battens.

The chine is installed next at the corners of the frames and transom. The forward end is fit into a notch directly behind the rabbet on the stem.

TOPSIDES

The planking locations may be given numerically on the construction plan. Then again, maybe not. If not, you can divine pretty close locations by measuring the plan with a scale rule. If your planking stock is a bit on the width-challenged side, it's not a big deal to install an additional batten to accommodate more but narrower

Fairing the frames with a batten prior to cutting in the notches for the seam battens. (Photo: Ford Reid)

planks. On the topsides, above the chine, the planks will run in the conventional fore-and-aft fashion and are mathematically diminished so that they are all of equal width on each frame—with the possible exception of the sheerstrake, where it might be a bit wider to accommodate the rub rail. The plank lines need to be faired by eye with a good batten.

You can then mark and cut in the notch locations and fit the bevels so that the battens will be flush with the inside face of the planks when installed. Either bevel the forward end of the battens or notch the stem to allow the outer face of the battens to come in immediately behind the bearding line of the stem rabbet.

ON THE BOTTOM

Below the chine, you have a choice. You can continue to line out the planks in the same fashion as the topsides, with planks and battens running from the transom to the stem. The planks will be slightly curved, and shaped wider in the center than at the ends. Option two is the straight-plank approach, in which all plank seams and battens run parallel to the centerline, and each plank retains the same width

The parallel arrangement of seam battens allows for efficient use of planking stock, and requires careful cutting of compound bevels where the battens meet the chine logs.

throughout its length. This makes for very efficient use of stock. The look is a bit unconventional, however, since instead of ending at the stem rabbet, the planks soon start to run out over the chine and have to be trimmed off following the curve of the chine. The last plank out may not touch the transom either and will have one edge following the chine, giving it a bit of a half-moon shape. Either style works fine. For the parallel plank style, up toward the bow, the seam battens in the boat's bottom will have to join or land against the chine. This joint forms a compound bevel.

SPILING AND PLANKING

Since batten seam construction is a form of carvel planking, the planks for it can be spiled onto a flat spiling batten in the conventional manner. As the shapes are relatively simple, some builders use a scribing block and pencil like a compass to scribe the gentle curve onto the spiling batten. There is no bevel between the planks for caulk as the batten does the job for keeping the water out. The garboard is caulked in the conventional manner, however.

The planks are screw-fastened to both the battens and the frames. As usual, pilot holes need to be bored to prevent splitting the planking or chines. There is generally bedding of some sort between the inside of the plank and the batten. This slippery stuff can gum up the process of getting a joint tight enough for screwing the plank down properly. To guarantee a good fit, some builders choose to clamp the plank in place, prebore for the screws, remove the plank, anoint the batten with bedding, reclamp, and install the fastenings.

To glue or not to glue: that is the question. For a truly bullet- and waterproof seam, an adhesive caulk such as Sikaflex or 3m 5200 can be used in place of traditional bedding compound. It works great. The drawback is that it makes repairs to the planking fairly horrible to do as the planks will be essentially welded to the battens.

Due to the twist coming into the stem and chine, the forward ends of the lower planks will likely need to be steamed or at least given the boiling hot compress treatment (see Chapter 27).

Planking progresses in two directions. On the bottom, it is done from the keel toward the chine. On the sides, it is done from the sheer to the chine. The transition between the lowest topside plank and the outermost bottom plank along the chine is a bit tricky (but it sounds worse than it is). Here's the deal: for most of the length of the boat, the bottom planking is run or lapped over the side planking at the chine. The edge of the bottom plank is simply planed to match the angle of the side planking. As you approach the vertical stem, however, the increasing angle between the topsides and bottom makes this impossible. So in the bow region there is a compound mitered angle that will eventually transition to the overlap back aft. This can be a gradual transition or you can choose to stop the miter at a natural break point such as a joint or a butt block in the bottom. Before fastening down the planks, be sure to put bedding in the joints.

With that done, it's time to putty those screw holes and fair the hull.

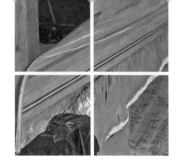

∎ 7 ∎

Strip Planking

Long a favorite technique of the home boatbuilder, the practice of planking hulls with narrow strips of wood has a somewhat murky origin. Some Maine chauvinists claim strip planking was invented by parsimonious Downeast fishermen who would plank their hulls with the free edge-trimmings otherwise discarded by sawmills after squaring up pine planks. Others argue the method can be traced further back into antiquity. But no matter: whether used in the construction of ultralight kayaks and canoes, as a substrate for cold molding in elegant yachts, or simply as a straightforward method for planking a workboat, the humble art of strip planking is now experiencing a bit of a renaissance.

And why not? The technique is versatile: nearly anything that can be built in conventional carvel can be built with strips. First-time builders appreciate not having to spile each plank. It is extraordinarily rugged, as the interconnected strips form a truly monocoque hull. Indeed, it is possible to use fewer frames in a stripper than in a standard carvel-planked hull (although, for appearance's sake, you may not want to).

A strip-planked Cosine Wherry, built by the (much younger) author.

There is little waste of wood in milling, and the strips can be gotten out of stock that is too narrow for conventional planking. And there is no need for caulking.

Of course, there is always a downside. Old-style beveled-strip-and-nail planking can be time-consuming and labor intensive. Unless the builder depends totally on mechanical fastenings (and few do these days), there will be plenty of glue to contend with. And down the road, the boat will be more difficult to repair than a conventionally planked hull.

All that being said, a well-built and faired strip hull is not only an elegant and long-lasting alternative, but in areas that have poor access to high-grade planking stock it may be the only way to go.

THE CHANGING GIRTH

Part of the appeal of strip planking is its apparent straightforward manner of construction. It involves none of that troublesome spiling found in carvel and lapstrake. Just take a pile of strips, start at the keel, stack and nail 'em all together, and there you go. Unfortunately, the builder using that technique soon discovers that instead of the planking finishing up nicely at the marked sheer, the strips hit the top of the stem rabbet and transom considerably before arriving at the sheer amidships. That modest daysailer now looks more like a Viking ship. What tripped up our hapless mechanic was his failure to account for the changing girth of the vessel.

To better understand this phenomenon, take a measuring tape to the setup molds of a pulling boat. Up forward at station 1, where the boat exhibits that splendid fine entrance, the distance measured will be short—maybe 24″. Amidships, where the tape travels across a relatively wide, flat bottom, then goes around a quick turn of the bilge before striking upward, the girth is at its greatest, say 35″. Then back at that wineglass transom, the girth again decreases to 20″ or so.

Standard carvel excels in its ability to cover the ever-changing girth of a hull. When planking in carvel, it is a simple matter to vary the width of the plank to reflect the facts on the ground, er, boat. A carvel plank can start off at 2″, go to 4″, then retreat to 2½″. For strip planking, we use a more subtle technique.

There are probably as many approaches in lining out strip planking as there are designs and builders' proclivities. On larger craft, tapered planks are quite effective in making up the difference in girth. They can be used continually throughout the construction, punctuating occasionally with straight strips as the need arises, or even just clustered in the underwater section of the hull. The strips should be wide enough at the stem and transom (say 1″ minimum) to accept a fastening. In areas of greatest girth and little twist, tapered wedge-shaped "stealer" strips can be incorporated to help even things out.

There is much to recommend starting off using a conventional garboard plank, then switching to strips. Not only does the garboard allow you to build in a good deal of the middle girth, but that extra plank width at the hood end makes it a lot easier to make that fiendish twist into the stem rabbet. (Indeed, some strip-plank boats have been built with a broad garboard and a second broad strake as well.) The first strip can simply be edge-fastened to the garboard. If a garboard is used, conventional floor timbers should be installed to fasten the plank to.

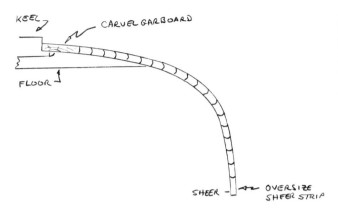

KEEL

CARVEL GARBOARD

FLOOR

SHEER

OVERSIZE SHEER STRIP

Using a conventional garboard in wood-strip construction can make it much easier to plank into the stem rabbet.

Canoe and kayak builders have a number of options as well. On vessels that are fairly narrow and have little curve to the sheer, the boat can be planked from the sheer to the keel. The bottom planks then get trimmed to fit the curve of the stem and the bottom. On a canoe, with its upturned ends, often a "master sheer plank" is installed at the lowest part of the sheer at the center mold. This strip follows the sheer in an arc until the curve becomes too great near the ends of the canoe. At that point, it continues in a fair shallow arc to the stems. The space above it is planked in later with shorter pieces. Below the master plank, planks are edge-fastened to each other down toward the keel, and their ends are trimmed to fit the stem and keel as before. If the boat has a lot of girth amidships (as in a Whitehall type or a wherry), you could use the "double run" method. Here, the location for the master plank is installed at the turn of the bilge, roughly equidistant from the sheer and the bottom. The boat then can be planked up to the sheer. A second "master plank" is installed down the centerline of the bottom, where a keel would normally appear. From there, planks are installed upward toward the first master plank at the turn of the bilge. This is the most time-consuming and tricky method of the three, because the fore and aft ends of every strip have to be trimmed to a wedge shape to fit to the first master plank. Care must be taken not to develop a "hard" or unfair shape where the two planking schemes meet.

Keep in mind that if you choose to bevel the strips as they go around the turn of the bilge, the bevel will "shrink" the width of the inside of the plank and can throw off your layout. To keep on track, some builders use a batten to mark an occasional plank line (sort of

PLANKING STOCK

Strip-plank stock is fairly basic stuff and is rectangular in section. (For example ½" thick stock might be 1¼" wide.) As with any planking material, selection and quality are important. When shopping for strip-plank stock, look for clear, defect-free, straight grain. Getting out strip plank is much akin to making battens or stock for steam-bent frames. Knots and defects that would be acceptable for standard planking can be the cause of vexatious breakage with strips. Sapwood must be avoided and, as green lumber is sure to be problematic, the stock needs to be acquired early enough to be thoroughly air-dried.

The decision of what wood to use often hinges on prosaic considerations such as what is available locally. The choice of wood also depends on the method of construction. If the strips will be edge-nailed and painted, select a good quality, rot-resistant species. If the hull will be built monocoque style (glued and glassed), the density, weight, availability, and color of the strips will be of greater importance. Some rugged hulls are built with relatively cheap, lumberyard pine or spruce. More durable candidates include cedar, yellow pine, Philippine mahogany, and sassafras. Steer clear of oily woods if the strips are to be glued.

To get the proper length of a plank, it is often easiest to scarf the wide stock on the workbench prior to ripping out the pieces.

a "false sheer") at several locations on the hull. If, as you reach each line, you find the planking is deviating significantly, it is a fairly easy matter to set things right by adding more tapered planks or a stealer.

At any rate it is a good idea to have an oversized strip to use at the sheer to accommodate any slight deviation from your original lining.

Fitting the Joints

Before selecting and cutting out your stock, you must decide on the nature of the strip-to-strip joints. If the strips are simply wrapped around the hull, they will contact on the inside but, alas, will be gapped on the

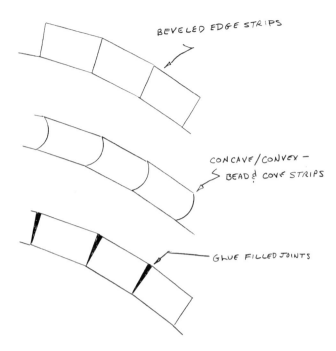

Three methods of edge-joining the strips.

outside. There are three popular solutions: beveling, inter-connecting bead-and-cove (and occasionally, tongue-and-groove, or ship-lap), and square-edged planks with the outside gaps filled with goop.

Beveling is the oldest, most traditional method and not a bad choice for those who do not have access to a shaper and are finishing the hull bright. The strips are treated in the same way as standard carvel, with one edge square and the other edge beveled with a hand plane to meet the adjoining plank. If you think this is tedious, you are correct. But after a few planks, the process becomes "second nature" and proceeds relatively quickly.

For heavy planking, the bead-and-cove method requires a shaper. For thin stock, the router is the tool of choice, and bits are cheap compared to shaper cutters. The shaper knives or router bits cut matching surfaces on the upper and lower edges of the strips: concave on one edge, convex on the other. When the planks are joined, they fit together nearly at any angle—hence no need for beveling. The joint also provides more glue surface than the plain bevel, and tends to hold the edges of the glue-slippery strips in alignment.

The square-edged method is perhaps the easiest, and certainly the messiest, and a joy for the adhesophile. The gaps between the strips are filled with epoxy resin thickened with filler.

A FEW TOOLS

Strip planks are like lofting battens that you twist into shapes they really don't want to be. Because they are so narrow, it's often difficult to apply enough torque to make them take a severe twist. The secret to controlling strip planks is to maintain control in two directions. Holding them to the form usually doesn't take much, but holding the planks against each other is something else. So before going into the planking business, it is worthwhile to take a few moments to whip up a couple of persuasion tools:

- *The Horseshoe Strip Alignment Clamp is sort of a cross between an old-fashioned wooden clothespin and a tuning fork. The gap between the two prongs is the width of the strips, while the depth of the cutout between the prongs is at least two strips wide. When hanging the new plank,*

this little wonder can be slipped over the new strip and the previously fastened one to help hold the planks in alignment until they are nailed.

- *Strip Twisting Spanners—When building with heavy strips, these are just the ticket to get the proper leverage to twist the strips into place. The "one-handed" model is used amidships to cajole recalcitrant strips into alignment. It is similar to the horseshoe tool, with the exception that the prongs are only one strip long and it has a long handle. Just slip it over the strip and tweak it up or down as necessary. The "two-handed" version is akin to a pipe-threading tool. In the center is a cutout that matches the cross-section of the strip plank. The tool is slid over the strip as it runs past the transom. The strip can then be easily contorted to land properly on the transom.*

A FEW TOOLS (CONT.)

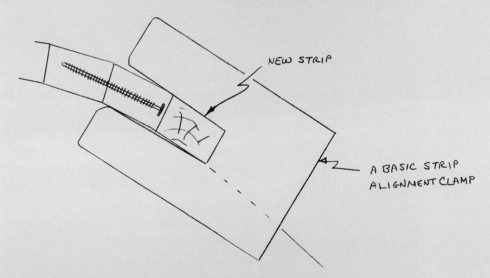

NEW STRIP

A BASIC STRIP ALIGNMENT CLAMP

A simple horseshoe-shaped tool to align strips before fastening.

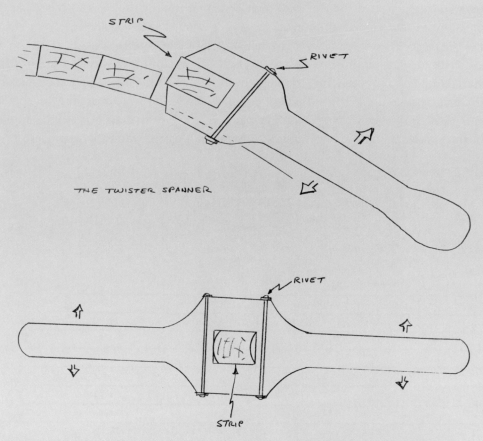

STRIP

RIVET

THE TWISTER SPANNER

RIVET

STRIP

THE TWO HANDED TWISTER

Two tools to twist planks into alignment. The two-handed version is useful for applying maximum torque where the ends run out over the transom. The one-handed version can be used anywhere along the strip to force it to lie fair against its neighbor.

Fastening the Planking

Traditionally, builders of boats using heavy strips would place only white lead luting (if anything) between the strips. Of course there was not much else to use anyway. Today, you are more likely to see the strips glued. Resorcinol and epoxy both afford a truly tough and waterproof bond. If the wood is of an oily variety (such as teak), resorcinol is the way to go. Some builders prefer epoxy due to its gap-filling qualities, variable pot life, and lack of the classic resorcinol "purple."

For a light, thin-strip hull that will be covered with fiberglass on both sides, the glue's only purpose may be to hold the pieces in alignment long enough to fair them, while it's the fiberglass cloth that holds things together in the final analysis. When that's the case, yellow carpenters glue is easier to use than epoxy, and much less unpleasant to work with, since there is no mixing and it's nontoxic.

There are several philosophies on glue application. For traditional heavy strips, some prefer a small paintbrush or roller, while others opt for the palette and spatula approach. Some use the pastry decorator's approach: load a plastic bag with the glue, tie off the top, cut a small hole in a bottom corner, and squeeze the stuff onto the strips. Whatever glue is used, apply enough to fill the joint plus a little more for soaking into the wood, and take the time to clean off the excess squeezings before it sets up, both inside and out. You'll be glad you did.

Traditional construction calls for the planks to be fastened to one another by edge nailing, and this can serve either as a primary fastening, or simply to hold the strips in place until the glue cures. (Strip garboards can also be nailed to the keel.) The nails act like bantamweight drift pins, and are installed with staggered spacing. For example, if the nails are installed every 4" on the first strip, the next strip's nails would be set over by 2". The actual nail schedule is based on the shape of the hull. Predrilling for the nails with an undersized bit will prevent splitting. To get more locking action, some builders prefer to install the fastenings at a slight angle. The old-time favorite was galvanized iron nails (probably because they were cheap). Today a better bet would be bronze ring nails. The heads should be slightly set into the wood. Be sure to install the nails at enough of an angle so your smoothing plane won't find them when fairing the hull. If a strip garboard is used, it gets edge nailed to the keel.

Where the strips don't want to lie against the molds, use a drywall screw equipped with a washer right through the planking into the mold. A plywood pad and a light box nail will do the same trick for canoe planking. If a plank is reluctant to draw close to the adjoining one, anchor a block of wood to the nearest mold

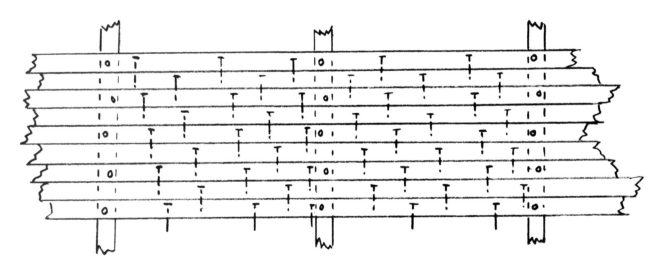

When edge-nailing the strips, stagger the nails to avoid running into the previous row. Set the heads slightly below the surface, and watch your angles so you don't run into the points when fairing the planking.

and drive a wedge between it and the strip. This should cajole the wayward plank into place.

With very light strips that will be covered with epoxy-saturated glass cloth (such as the ¼" thick stock used in canoes) there is neither room nor need for strong edge fasteners. Apply yellow carpenters glue with a glue syringe and drive removable staples through the planks into the molds to keep the planks in place until the glue dries. Some builders have used hot-melt glue, which sets almost instantly so few if any staples are needed. I don't recommend it, however. It's difficult to get the planks to close tightly, and the stuff sands like bubblegum.

Fairing the Hull

After the planking is completed and the anchor screws, nails, or staples are removed, the next job is fairing. This is where the time previously spent cleaning off excess glue will pay off. The task of smoothing and sculpting a standard strip hull is roughly the same as for a carvel one. The weapons of choice are sharp

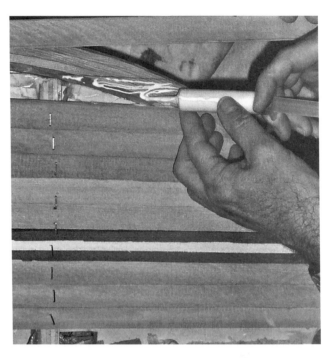

A glue syringe is especially useful when working with thin bead-and-cove strips. Temporary staples are driven through the strips into the molds, to hold the strips in place until the glue sets.

After the hull is faired and sanded, a layer of fiberglass and epoxy is applied. When finishing a strip-planked boat "bright," strips of contrasting wood make a nice accent.

block and smoothing planes, a disc sander, and a fairing board. The trick here is to remember that rather than smoothing individual planks, you are smoothing the hull in its entirety, shaping a series of flat planks into fluid curves. When using a plane, working at a diagonal to the run of the planks will reduce tearing out the grain and result in a better, smoother job. Keep the plane's blade sharp and set for a shallow cut. (Some builders refer to the planes that they use for fairing as "fastening detection devices with cheese grater blades." This can be avoided by careful placement of your ring nails.)

A disc sander with a foam pad is a most effective way to smooth up a heavily built hull. Like the hand plane, it works best when running on a diagonal. Work expeditiously and avoid staying in any place too long or you'll produce an interesting but unwanted crater. Finish up the job with a long sanding board. Use your hands as well as you eyes to detect unfairness. Good ventilation, eye protection, and a high-quality dust mask are essential; fairing with a sander will convert your shop into a collapsed mineshaft in short order.

Some builders use a disc sander first to get rid of glue and some of the high spots, and then switch to the plane once the blade-dulling blobs of glue are gone. The plane gets it close, and then the long board does what it does best, cleaning up the little high spots.

Smoothing light canoe planking requires considerably more finesse. This is not the job for the industrial belt sander with the 40-grit paper. A sharpened paint scraper, block plane, spokeshave, random orbit sander, and long board are the tools de jour. Again, work at a diagonal and let the sander, not your muscles, do the work.

With a little care, you'll have such a smooth hull that even if it's a chunky, utilitarian fishing boat, it will earn the ultimate accolade: "Is that boat wood or fiberglass?" Ouch.

· 8 ·

Traditional Hard-Chined V-Bottomed Construction

Let's begin with some definitions. The *chine* is the angle, or line of intersection, where the bottom strakes meet the sides of a flat- or V-bottomed boat. In a hard-chined boat, this angle is pronounced. In a soft-chined vessel, it is rounded. A *chine log* (chine piece, chine) is a piece running fore and aft, where the side and bottom edges of the frames meet. It runs from stem to stern and is notched into and fastened to the frames.

V-shaped hull construction has long been a favorite for home boatbuilders. Countless plans and "how-to's" have been printed in boating and do-it-yourself magazines over the years. Whether for power (think of a Chris Craft-style mahogany runabout or a Simmons Sea Skiff), sail (how about the popular 25½' Sea Bird yawl or a 15' plywood catboat by Wittholtz), or just a humble dinghy, V-shaped construction is an alternative that is easy to comprehend and easy to plank.

CONSTRUCTION STYLES

There are a number of different construction styles, including: sawn frames with notches cut in for batten-seam planking (a method often used in mahogany speedboats); sawn frames spaced relatively far apart

A Sea Bird yawl.

with lighter, often bent, frames in between; or unnotched sawn frames all by themselves.

For sailboats, the hard-chined V-shaped hull has greater initial stability than the round-bottomed style. On the other hand, round-bilged hulls ride softer and have less wetted surface, for potentially greater speed in displacement hulls.

Howard Chapelle wrote that compared to flat-bottoms, the V-bottom has several advantages: greater displacement without an increase of driving power, less pounding when upright, better performance under power at medium and high speeds, and better sailing qualities in light airs.

The V-bottomed powerboat can be fuel efficient and an all-round good performer if designed properly. William Hand was a pioneer in the genre. Working in the early part of the twentieth-century, he struck a balance with his designs that achieves good handling both at displacement speeds and when planing. His work has inspired many other builders and designers, including Weston Farmer and Harry Bryan. Many modern high-speed V-bottomed boats, however, operate efficiently and handle well at planing speed, but wallow and are hard to steer and fuel inefficient at low speeds. While this design tradeoff may be acceptable if your trade involves eluding law enforcement authorities in the waters off Miami in the dead of night, it may not be the best choice for those who prefer casual and economical recreational cruising.

Lofting

Lofting is generally straightforward. If there is no curve to the sawn frames (which is not uncommon), the builder only has three fore and aft lines to deal with: the rabbet (or apex), the chine, and the sheer. If there is some shape, waterlines will fair up the topsides and a couple of buttocks will take care of the bottom (see Chapter 24). That said, care needs to be taken to get your lofting right. On some hulls, the stations are not mere frames—they may be bulkheads—and taking the time to lay them out properly on the lofting board will pay big dividends later.

Setup

One of the most appreciated qualities of the V-hull is the simplicity of setup. Some find the complexity of round-bottomed construction with steam-bent frames daunting and wasteful. You have to build and erect molds and get out and install ribbands, and none of these remain in the finished boat. Yes, they can be used to build another boat, but is that your intention? Then there are all those persnickety bevels and the complex shaping of round-bottomed carvel planking.

The setup and construction of a hard-chined boat is relatively simple. In most cases, your molds are also your frames, and they remain part of the boat. (Some lapstrake versions add sawn frames after planking.) If the boat will be planked batten-seam, the battens (the moral equivalent of ribbands) remain a part of the boat.

Sawn frames serve as construction molds in hard-chine construction. (Photo: Ford Reid)

Battens can be used to fair the frames to accept planking, or the bevels can be taken from the lofting.

Most small V-bottomed hulls can be built upside down. If your shop floor is straight and true, you can simply screw the cleats to the floor at the station lines and fasten the frames to them and brace the frames plumb.

While the setup of a hard-chined boat is easier than the setup for round-bottomed construction, the same amount of care and attention to detail should be exercised. The frames still have to be beveled for the planks to land on. The angles can be taken from the lofting or the bevels can be done on the setup, using a batten tightly wrapped around the hull and a plane or spokeshave. For strength and rot prevention, the notches for the chine logs in the hull frames and inner transom frame must be well fitted. On very shapely hulls,

installing chine logs made of straight stock can be akin to wrestling a giant squid into submission. Often it is best to spile and steam them into place, or laminate them from a number of thin pieces. For a good-looking and easy to plank hull, the planking locations should still be lined out. It's important to promote ventilation and avoid standing water, using ample limbers and beveling surfaces that might otherwise entrap water.

Using Sheet Plywood

Occasionally a builder will select an older V-bottomed hull that was designed for standard planking and attempt to use sheet plywood on the hull. This can be

WHAT'S THIS "DEADRISE" BUSINESS, ANYWAY?

Much marine terminology ranges from the nonintuitive to the utterly counterintuitive. Such it is with the mystical word "deadrise." Despite the evocative name, there is no direct connection to Transylvania or boxes of native earth. Instead it is just a measurement of the steepness of the angle (or amount of rise) of the underwater part of the hull below the turn of the bilge, relative to a horizontal line drawn out from the rabbet. "Deadrise" is also often used as a generic, catch-all term for a V-shaped bottom.

From whence the name? Catboat designer Fenwick Williams conjectured that the term came from the terminology of larger craft:

> *The bottom members of heavy, sawn frames were called floors, and a flat, horizontal surface was often called rise of floor above the dead flat. We know it was called rise of floor, and then dead-rise.*

So now you know.

(continued on next page)

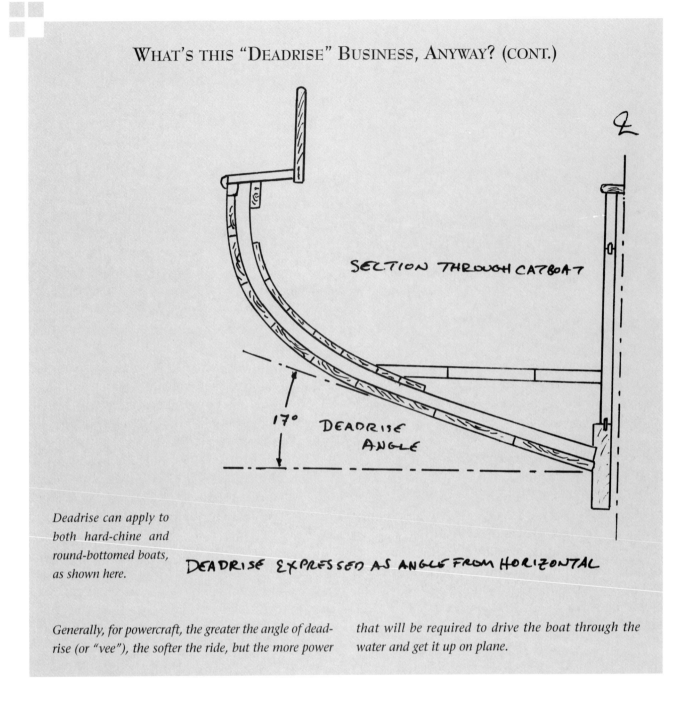

SECTION THROUGH CATBOAT

17° DEADRISE ANGLE

Deadrise can apply to both hard-chine and round-bottomed boats, as shown here.

DEADRISE EXPRESSED AS ANGLE FROM HORIZONTAL

Generally, for powercraft, the greater the angle of deadrise (or "vee"), the softer the ride, but the more power that will be required to drive the boat through the water and get it up on plane.

problematic. According to Ted Brewer in *Understanding Boat Design,* "The only boats that can be sheet plywood planked are those having all the sections relatively parallel or those designed by the conical method of projection." Individual wood planks are more flexible and can assume greater shape than sheet plywood. Before attempting plywood conversion, it is best to consult the designer.

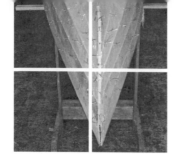

·9·

Stitch-and-Glue Construction

Stitch-and-glue is the new kid on the construction method block. It had to be, as the technique simply wasn't possible without reliable marine plywood to use as hull panels and truly waterproof glue to "weld" the panels together.

In many ways, the method is a stage of evolution from the earliest hard-chined and multi-chined hulls. Think of a traditionally built dory or a sharpie. You have a series of curved planes or panels anchored at the ends to a stem or transom. Longitudinally, there is a series of stiffeners: a keel, chines, sheer clamps, or simply plank laps. Vertically, you have stiffeners in the form of frames, bulkheads, floors, and hanging knees. These not only dictate the shape of the hull, but also serve to hold the individual components of the panel—i.e., the planks—together.

After plywood was introduced, the panels could be one piece. The cross-laminated nature of the curved material had great strength. You still had your stems, transoms, and chines, but in many cases the number of frames could be reduced.

Stitch-and-glue took the process a couple of steps further. The plywood skin became sort of an exoskeleton, and the shapes of the curved panels dictated the hull's shape. There is little in the way of frames or molds, especially for very small craft. Glued fiberglass tape over epoxy fillets—thickened epoxy radiuses on the interior angled joints—is used in place of the venerable chine log. To hold the bent panels together so that the epoxy and tape can be applied, the plywood panels are drilled and temporarily wired together at the chines, sort of like when a tailor pins fabric together before sewing. That's the stitch part. The result is a very rugged hull that is built from the skin inward, eliminating much of the heavy internal structure that is necessary in more traditional construction. As an elaboration on the basic method, the plywood can be treated as the core

Stitch-and-glue is one of the most popular methods for building kayaks and, indeed, of amateur boatbuilding in general. Although a bit less common for canoes, it can produce very fine results nonetheless.

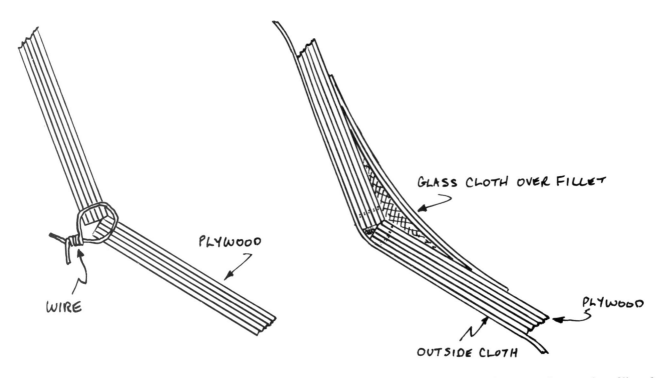

WIRE

PLYWOOD

GLASS CLOTH OVER FILLET

PLYWOOD

OUTSIDE CLOTH

The anatomy of a stitch-and-glue joint. Twisted wire holds the plywood panels in place just long enough to apply a fillet of thickened epoxy, cover it with glass cloth and more epoxy, and give it time to cure. Then the wires are cut off or pulled out and another layer of glass cloth is applied to the outside of the joint.

material in a laminate, and the entire structure encapsulated between layers of glass and epoxy. This further increases the strength and results in a monocoque structure.

A LITTLE HISTORY

As with many innovations, various approaches to stitchandglue were developed by a number of innovative individuals working somewhat simultaneously and independently all over the planet. That said, many credit Ken Littledyke of England as the first to develop a pioneering procedure for his KL canoe design in which, instead of using a conventional chine log to hold the plywood side panels in place, he simply wired them together and joined them with polyester resin and fiberglass tape.

Others note the early-1960s experiments of British television DIY handyman Barry Bucknell to use sewn-seam construction methods to build a boat for his son. The *London Daily Mirror* took note and soon recruited Jack Holt to refine Bucknell's boat, and design a sailing pram suitable for amateurs to build with simple tools and little experience. The resulting product was the popular 10' one-design called the "Mirror" dinghy.

The Mirror dinghy enabled thousands of people to become boat owners for the first time.

A decade later in the Pacific Northwest, builder Sam Devlin and his father were rediscovering stitch-and-glue. For the Devlins, using plywood sheet goods for boatbuilding was a natural as the material was so popular in the region. Sam had already experimented with balsa sheet models and saw how the shape of a hull could be varied by simply changing the shape of the planking (panels). They scaled up the models and cut the sides out of plywood and brought them together. Unlike earlier plywood designs, these would have little internal framing and would employ panels that were first sewn, then glued together with polyester (soon to be epoxy) and cloth. Over time it was found that the technique worked just as well for larger designs as it did for dinghies and canoes. And these boats could be built quickly with a minimum of fuss.

In the early 1980s, sea kayaker and software engineer John Lockwood began experimenting with computerdrawn designs for stitch-and-glue kayak building. When you think of it, plywood is a natural for kayak construction. Look at a traditional Inuit skin-on-frame design, with its skin stretched flat and tight over the stringers, creating a series of chines, and it's not difficult to picture replacing that skin with panels or planks of light plywood. A plywood skin will remain tight, reinforcing and stiffening the hull structure. The plywood sections are joined with butt blocks or scarf joints to get any desired length of plank. Cover it with glass cloth and you get a strong, lightweight, engineered composite that has a great resistance to puncture. The trick was how to tailor those plywood panels so they would fit together.

Consider that these panels are not unlike the iron or steel plates on an old-time battleship that had to be wrapped around a complex, curved surface without buckling. Certainly the desired shapes can be developed by the old method of lofting. Nowadays, however, the computer can design and generate compound plates in a jiffy.

Research led Lockwood to a mathematical approach to plating development introduced by Tim Nolan in a 1971 issue of *Marine Technology*. At the time, the only existing software that could do the job was prohibitively expensive and designed to run only on mainframe computers. In 1985, Lockwood quit his job to create what would become the first commercially available hullplate expansion computer program that would run on personal computers. Lockwood (and his new company, Pygmy Boats) introduced his first computer-designed production kayak kit.

Other design programs, some of them optimized for use with plywood, soon followed. These programs promote efficient use of materials, optimize hull performance, and allow for the development of very complex hull shapes for both hard- and multi-chined designs. Computer design led naturally to computer machining and fueled a growing industry producing kit boats. CNC (computer numerical control) machines using a high-speed routerhead allow quick and cost-efficient cutting of highly accurate kayak pieces that fit easily and accurately together.

A FEW CAUTIONS

As with any kind of boat construction, attention to detail is important with stitch-and-glue and tasks need to be done in the right order. In standard carvel and lapstrake construction, the system sort of arm-twists you into righteousness. Stitch-and-glue is a wonderfully straightforward technique, but that simplicity is a sultry siren that lures some onto the shoals of complacency,

assuming they can simply stick tab "A" into slot "B" and offer up three "Hail Marys," and everything will come out great with the finished boat popping off the assembly line in maybe two hours.

There's more to it than that. The designers have done a great deal of work to produce the panel shapes that will dictate the shape of the hull. When building from scratch, the mechanic should give as much (or maybe more) attention to laying out and drawing the lines as he or she would in old-time lofting. If working from a kit, the builder shouldn't assume that the planks can just be slapped together. It is important to check and double-check by eye. Small misalignments can have a multiplier effect that causes big problems later. The builder should label the components that go together.

The standard operating procedure of doing dry runs applies here as well. For example, if you are gluing, make sure that the pieces to be glued are properly aligned and indexed, that you have enough clamps, that there is a release plastic between your work and your gluing table, and that the hardener you are using will allow you enough time to do the job. Glue (usually epoxy) is what makes this process work. Be sure to use the appropriate safety precautions (see Chapter 15). Plan to work neatly. Using just enough epoxy will save you time and materials and result in a better-looking boat. Read the kit manual several times and follow the instructions. For example, if the book says to join the sheer clamp to the sheer panel while it's still on the bench and before the boat is assembled, it is probably better and easier to do it that way.

BUILDING PROCEDURES

For most of us, the natural place to start is to begin knocking out planks from the builder's patterns or from the precut kit pieces. But before we start pulling our socks over our boots, it's worth considering how much control is needed during the building process. True stitch-and-glue designs (at least for small boats) need little in the way of a traditional construction jig. In theory, the precut pieces will dictate the final shape—mostly. (Though some designs do use temporary forms to bend the planks around and guarantee the final hull shape.) But that doesn't mean you may not want some sort of a cradle to put some stability in your life. A simple cradle (an outside female mold) can help keep everything level and square, prevent possible twists or

These kayak side panels have already been scarfed to length. Per the designer's advice, the sheer clamps are being glued in prior to assembly of the panels. Make sure you have enough clamps in hand before spreading the glue!

hogs, and more or less anchor the pieces in place, saving you time in the long run. In boatbuilding, whenever something is moved inadvertently, there is wasted time, energy, and sometimes materials. If the designer has not included plans for a cradle, the desired shapes can usually be derived from temporary interior forms or bulkheads. Just add the thickness of the planking (and maybe a bit more) and you have the outside-of-plank cradle shape for that location. Care needs to be taken to make sure that cradle shapes are level relative to one another and aligned to a proper centerline.

Assembling the Panels

The stock size for most plywood panels is 4' by 8'. Unless you are planning to build a really short boat, you are going to be in the plywood joining business. While some kits require fiberglass-and-epoxy-reinforced butt joints or plywood butt blocks for strength, glued scarf joints are the most elegant solution (see Chapter 28). With their long, tapered glued surfaces, scarf joints are strong, and because the joint is the same thickness as elsewhere on the panel, they generally allow the plywood panel to bend in a natural curve without "hard" spots. If plank sections are cut to shape before being scarfed together, care must be taken to get the pieces properly aligned so that the finished shape is correct.

(Remember that it's the shape of the planks or panels that will drive the final shape of the boat.) It helps to glue the planks in pairs (with plastic in between, of course) so at least they will be symmetrical.

Begin by pulling together the pieces of a stitch-and-glue sewing kit: precut wire "sutures," a tray or can to hold them in, linesman's pliers, a small hammer, a drill motor, and a small bit. On larger boats, some builders prefer to use self-grabbing plastic cable ties instead of twisted wire.

Lay out the bottom panels, and tape or clamp one atop the other, interior face to interior face. Draw a stitch line along the "keel" side. Lay out the bored hole locations (a divider works well for this) and drill the holes right through the panels. After boring, separate the pieces and bevel the inside edge of the keel side of the plank to roughly 45°. Bevel only to half the thickness. The bevel will help the two panels align together after they have been pulled together with the wire. Place the panels back on top of each other, inner faces together, pass the wire ties through the holes, and use the pliers to loosely twist the ends together. Leave enough slack for the bottom panels to be opened booklike into their locations, yet still fit snugly. At this point, many builders insert a spreader stick or a temporary mold to spread the bottom panels to their

With the stitches in place, it's time to begin folding the panels up.

A multi-chine canoe hull, all stitched up.

proper angle before planking the sides. Support the ends and sides as necessary, and then get ready to bore and wire together the next panels.

On many shallow V-bottom, multi-chined, and flat-bottomed boats, the planks are assembled "edge-butted" when drawn together at an angle. This system produces a series of flats or facets on the hull. Care needs to be taken when tightening the wires so that the planking does not get misaligned, especially when working with lightweight panels as on kayaks.

On hulls where the V-shape is pronounced, the side planking ends up overlapping, lapstrake fashion, the upper edge of the bottom panels. For most of the way around the hull this works out fine, only requiring that a bevel be planed into the overlapped panel. Like all lapstrake techniques, however, there is always the question of how to go from overlapped plank to planking lying flush at the stem.

One method that allows the overlapping panels to blend together at the bow is the *transition joint*. Basically, the joint is a notch or step as deep as the amount of overlap that is cut into the lower edge of the overlapping plank. The notch starts off as a line drawn parallel to the bottom edge of the upper plank. The distance that

the notch carries aft varies with the length of the boat. For boats up to 10' long, a notch 12" to 18" works well; 24" for craft from 11' to 17'; 36" for boats to 36', and so on. The notch on the upper plank (or panel) stops square at the end of the prescribed distance.

Meanwhile, the lower (or bottom) panel needs to be dealt with. Scribe a line on the outside face that indicates the amount the upper panel overlaps. Then measure back the same distance that you measured for the notched panel. Forward of that mark, the top edge is left square just the way you cut it. At the mark, use a hand saw to cut a small kerf into the outside face of the upper edge of the plank that runs from the inside upper edge to the lap line on the outside of the panel. Now go to the stern (top) edge of the bottom panel and plane a bevel that runs to the depth of the lap into the outer face. Stop the bevel dead at the saw kerf on the forward end of the panel. The panels can then be bored and stitched. The forward ends of the panels will roll in, one above the other.

Bulkheads and Bracing

Virtually all boats need internal structures that add stiffness. Conventional small boats have thwarts, knees, risers, inwales, outwales, stanchions, and more that all work to cross-brace and strengthen the hull. Another way to add strength is to incorporate bulkheads. Bulkheads are transverse panels that are fitted to the shape of the hull. In a stitch-and-glue boat, the panels are made of plywood and bonded in place with the same epoxy fillet and fiberglass tape joint used on the rest of the hull. Like the hull panels, the bulkheads can be temporarily tied into place prior to applying the thickened epoxy.

Welding the Plank Seams

The epoxy fillet covered by fiberglass not only acts like a chine log and welds your hull together, but also helps to transfer structural loads from one surface to another. Needless to say, once the epoxy has cured, whatever you've glued, you've got. So before gluing, make sure the hull is straight and true.

While the stitches can be left in place, you'll end up with a much cleaner job if they are removed before the fillets are installed. To remove the stitches without having the boat fall apart, simply apply small tabs of thickened epoxy to the joints between the stitches to effectively "spot weld" the hull together. After the glue has cured, the stitches can be pulled.

A Well-Done Fillet

With the stitches gone, the fillets of thickened epoxy can be applied to intersecting surfaces. There are a number of epoxy additives out there, including:

- Microfibers: Fine cotton fibers used to thicken and reinforce epoxy to create a multipurpose adhesive.
- Wood flour: Finely ground wood fiber. Also known as sanding dust. Look in the bag of your sander.
- Colloidal Silica: Used to control the viscosity of the epoxy.
- Microlite or microballoons: Soft (sometimes hollow) spheres used to make a low density, easy-to-sand fairing filler.

One recipe, which calls for a mixture of epoxy, colloidal silica, and microfibers, is rugged but somewhat hard to sand. A blend of epoxy, wood flour, and Microlite sands easier and is probably sufficient for more small human-powered craft. As every epoxy manufacturer offers slightly different products, it's best to consult them. In any case, the fillers must be blended into premixed epoxy. A popular description for the proper consistency of this sticky amalgam is the technical term "peanut butter."

If you are looking for a nice clean job with as little mess as possible, it's worth the time to mask off the edges of the fillet. To avoid any possibility of glue starvation, some builders will first saturate the wood under the fillet with a coating of unthickened, mixed epoxy. Next, the thickened epoxy is applied and "squeegeed" into the joint and sculpted with a custom trimmed plastic spatula.

Reinforcing fiberglass tape that has been precut to length can be laid into the epoxy fillet while it is still soft. The tape is wet out with straight mixed epoxy (no thickeners needed). Use just enough to saturate the fabric and stick it down. Excess tape on the fillet is most easily trimmed when the epoxy is in its "green" or partially cured state.

Adding fiberglass to the outside of a hull built with heavy dimensional plywood adds both strength and abrasion resistance and is a very desirable option. For kayaks and canoes built with okume or gaboon plywood, glassing both the exterior and interior is the best way to go. Okoume is generally considered nondurable, but when it is used as a core material sandwiched between glass and epoxy, it is quite rugged.

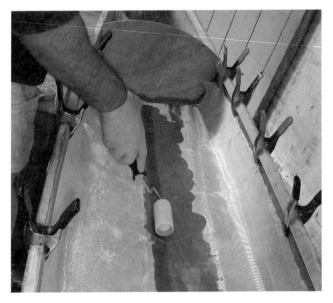

Glassing the interior of a hard-chine kayak hull. Note the bulkhead already filleted in place. Epoxy turns the glass cloth transparent, which leads to a large percentage of stitch-and-glue boats being finished "bright."

A brace of stitch-and-glue kayaks nearing completion. The hull and decks have already been glassed; the cockpit rim and hatch covers come next.

LapStitch Construction

LapStitch is an innovative planking technique that was developed by designer Chris Kulczycki, founder of Chesapeake Light Craft. The method could be thought of as a hybrid of glued lapstrake and stitch-and-glue that allows a lightweight, traditional-looking round-hulled boat to be built quickly without molds. A CNC machine not only cuts the planks to shape, but also cuts a constant 90° rabbet into the inside lower edge of each plank. During assembly, the square outside upper edge of the adjoining lower plank fits into the rabbet. The planks are drawn in and held together temporarily by wire ties in stitch-and-glue fashion. The planks do not have the rolling compound bevel that is found on traditional lapstrake construction, so the voids in the rabbet are filled in (injected actually) and the planking fastened together with a thickened epoxy slurry. Less glue is used in this method of construction, since the laps do not require the large fillets and fiberglass reinforcement of "conventional" stitch-and-glue (except along the keel). Lightweight, with classic looks. Not a bad combination.

· 10 ·

Glued Lapstrake Planking

In glued lapstrake construction, epoxy replaces the rivets or clinch nails used in standard lapstrake or dory-lap construction to edge the planks lengthwise. While there are some similarities to stitch-and-glue in that epoxy is holding the planks in place, glued lapstrake will not develop the hull's shape, so it requires a standard kind of setup involving offsets and lofting, and building molds and setting them on a strongback. The boat will also have the usual components, such as a stem, transom, and board keel, or at least some sort of keelson on which to land the garboard plank. On boats with extremely light planks that might easily distort during construction, it may be worthwhile to install ribbands that are let (notched) into the molds behind the laps. The flatter the section shape (i.e., the shallower the angle between the planks) the more support the planking needs.

Glued lapstrake construction produces a strong, good-looking hull with little (or vastly reduced) need for the frames found in conventional lapstrake construction. Due to the crosswise lamination of veneers, the lapped plywood is extraordinarily strong for its thickness. The glued plywood lap seam is leak proof, and it neither shrinks nor requires swelling, which makes it a great style for boats that spend most of their lives out of the water, in desert climes or on a trailer. If the boat is built with high quality plywood, maintenance will be reduced, as plywood makes a very stable substrate for either paint or varnish. And when you are painting or varnishing, there are far

Lapstrake canoe. (Photo by Koji Matano)

fewer interior components to cut in around with your paintbrush.

The thickened epoxy in the laps can fill minor *faux pas* in the beveled plank landings, so the beginning builder will still end up with a tight hull. In comparison to some other glued-construction methods, it is not necessary to sheath the hull with fiberglass and, if one is careful when applying the glue, much less work is

Filling the laps with thickened epoxy.

required fairing with a plane or toiling behind an electric sander or manual long sanding board.

There are, of course, a few caveats:

- Glued lapstrake only works well with plywood, and the higher the quality of the plywood, the better. Very thin cheap plywood is no bargain as there may be flaws within, and without proper sealing, it is subject to rot.

- Regular wood planking is not a good candidate for gluing. Real wood needs to be able to move at the joints or there is risk of breakage.

- Having your planks permanently cemented together can make repairs extremely difficult. Having a plank fail just once can make one consider long and hard before welding up a pile of planks a second time.

- Unlike naturally grown wood, which can be purchased in a variety of lengths (and shapes), plywood is generally only available in 8' lengths. Every plank will need to be scarfed (spliced). Entire sheets of plywood can, however, be scarfed and the planks can be cut out later.

- On the matter of aesthetics: A traditionally designed hull that has been built in glued lapstrake can have a very nontraditional look on the inside. All those frames that you no longer need once served as design features as well as structural members, and your eye may wonder where they went.

The new, clean and modern interior may take some getting used to.

SPILING AND BEVELING

Spiling of glued lap planking is done exactly as in standard lapstrake, but even more care is required when developing the spiling batten, since the plywood planks cannot be edge-set nearly as effectively as natural wood planks.

Cutting the bevels into the planking also duplicates the standard lapstrake method. When planing bevels into very light planking that is not backed up with a ribband, take care to avoid distorting the plank edges.

At the stem, where the planking comes in flush against the bevel or rabbet, gains need to be worked into the hood ends. Of the three methods described in the lapstrake section, the matching rabbets (or ship lap) version works the best for glued lapstrake.

At the transom, there are a number of options depending on hull shape, plank thickness, and the builder's proclivity. For example, on boats where the transom is as rounded in shape as the stations, flats or facets are planed into the transom to allow the planking to lie flush. In regions where there is plenty of shape or curve in the transom—in other words, where each plank lies at a fairly large angle to the previous one— all that needs to be done is to work a bevel into the previous plank that continues the bevel on the transom for the next one. Then the next plank will land nicely on both the transom and the beveled plank.

It's where the angles are shallow between the planks at the transom that the process gets interesting. When the two planks meet at a shallow angle, the previous plank is too thick to work a proper tight bevel into it: too much would have to be planed off. What to do? Thin the plank metaphorically, so that you can bevel it.

One way to do this is to cut a tapered rabbet into the lap part of the previous plank with a rabbet plane, as described in Chapter 3. After this has been done, the effect is that the plank (in the lap area) has been "thinned." The bevel can now be worked into the plank as usual with the bevel continuing right along the tapered rabbet. The new plank will fit flush against the planed bevel, from stem to stern with the edge of the lower edge of the new plank fitting snug against the edge of the cut rabbet of the previous plank.

Another way to reduce this metaphorical thickness is to notch the transom to let the previous plank set

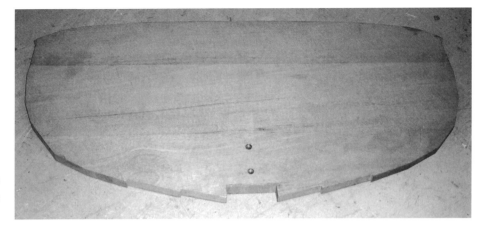

Flats are planed on the transom to accept the planks (John Brooks method).

in further to allow the lap area to be simply beveled for the landing of the next plank. Your plans may indicate where this notch lands and how deep to cut it.

CLAMPING THE LAPS

Before we start planking, let us consider the disappointing notion of gluing the boat to the jig. To preclude doing this, be sure to either wax or use a nonstick tape on the outer edge of the molds.

As in standard lapstrake construction, the planks must be pulled together with clamps before they can be fastened to each other—with rivets in the case of conventional planks and with glue in our present case. Conventional clamps become ineffective as the glue (at least until it hardens) acts like a lubricant and allows the planks to slide past each other when pressure is applied. Fortunately, epoxy only requires that the planks be brought together into alignment and held there so as not to move around.

Some builders simply use a line of Sheetrock screws as their clamps. After the epoxy has been spread on the lap, the plank is brought into position and screws are slowly installed in the laps, tightening just enough to pull the laps together but not enough to strip the holes in the inner plank and cause the screws to spin. Screws should be used sparingly and, to avoid low spots, the planking should be supported from the interior.

To get more uniform pressure, glued lap builder John Brooks uses a waxed clamping batten or stringer that he positions over the lap on the outside of the hull. He drives screws through the batten and the laps and into the station molds. Between the stations, he screws into blocks of wood held in place inside of the hull. To minimize wrestling with the batten, first attach it to a mold amidships and then work out toward the bow and

stern. You can do a cleaner job, with less chance of plank breakout, if you predrill the batten and the lapped planks with clearance holes that are just large enough for the shank of the screw to pass through easily. Again, start at a midship mold, predrilling and screwing into the molds as you work toward the ends of the boat. Then lay out holes between the molds (a compass or divider works well), predrill, and install the screws through the batten and laps and into the blocks. The holes in the planks will be plugged later with epoxy.

If you have installed temporary ribbands at the lap line, both the ribband and the batten must be thoroughly waxed to avoid adhesion. Working as described previously, the lap will be sandwiched between the fore and aft strips. If the planking is narrow, C-clamps may be used instead of screws.

Whatever method you use, be sure to clean up the squeezed out glue before it sets—you'll be glad you did.

Fastening a clamping batten.

· 11 ·

Cold Molding

Laminated cold molding produces a light, strong, and elegant hull. In my opinion, however, it's not the best choice for a first-time builder. Cold molding is a form of composites engineering, and the techniques, safety concerns, materials, and required skills are different from all of the construction methods previously described. It involves large quantities of epoxy, and there are plenty of places to go wrong. It usually requires building a jig that is so elaborate that it justifies series production of multiple hulls rather than the construction of a one-off boat.

That said, after you've built a few boats by more conventional methods and developed several of the basic skills, you might have a hankering to give cold molding a try. So let's dip our toes into the wonderful world of epoxy.

A BIT OF HISTORY
The technique of molding, or laminating, wooden craft has been around for many years—and it hasn't always been confined to boats. Perhaps the most famous such craft was the DeHavilland Mosquito, a twin-engined fighter/bomber/reconnaissance plane from World War II. The fuselage of this excellent plane was made by hot molding, a process in which thin layers of wood were bonded together with adhesives that were cured at high heat (usually in excess of 200° F) and under high pressure (in excess of 75 pound-force per square inch, or psi). This system required a lot of tooling with expensive equipment, but resulted in a plane that was strong, lightweight, and well shaped, and that required a minimum of strategic materials.

After the war, surplus technology was used to produce a number of different kinds of hot-molded production boat hulls such as the Luders 16 and the Wolverine outboard runabouts. The introduction of low-cost and easy maintenance fiberglass (GRP) hulls, however, soon took the starch out of the hot-molded boat business.

Cold molding, made possible by the later development of epoxy glues, is really room-temperature molding, and it refers to a type of laminated construction that requires neither great heat to cure nor extreme pressure. Epoxy requires only light contact pressure to hold everything together until the resin self-cures at room temperature. Epoxy is further well-suited to the task because it is waterproof, has gap-filling qualities, and has a controllable "pot life." The laminates can be laid up with epoxy over a form or jig and held in place with staples. Alternately, pressure can by applied by vacuum bagging, in which the panel is enclosed in plastic sheeting and the air is evacuated with a vacuum pump, thus enabling ambient air pressure to do the job of pressing the laminates together.

These laminated structures are really shaped plywood, incorporating multiple layers of wood veneers (or *plies*) with the grains running in opposing directions. The result is a very strong monocoque shell or hull skin that bears most or all the anticipated stresses with little internal bracing required. Because the plywood is built *in situ,* it has none of the built-in stresses associated with stitch-and-glue construction.

BASIC METHODS

There are several ways to build cold-molded hulls. For very small hulls, the most efficient, albeit initially the most expensive, way is to build over a mold. Building the mold can be nearly as time-consuming as building the hull itself. You have to construct a jig with mold frames similar to those used in conventional construction, and then strip plank it, or at least let in enough ribbands to support the lightweight plies of wood without drooping. An inner keel and stem are usually placed in the jig. Then you can plank and fair the boat and add an outer keel and "false stem." To prevent the heartbreak of bonding the new hull to the jig, you need to cover the whole business with polyethylene sheeting. After all this has been done, you can (finally) build one or a succession of hulls by laying up multiple layers of the diagonal laminates over the jig. As in other sorts of planking, the complex shape of the hull still requires the planking to be spiled (actually scribed) to shape. Each of the veneers must be bonded and fixed with staples into place until the epoxy cures. Final epoxy and fiberglass work on the exterior can be done before the hull is lifted off the jig.

Another way is to laminate the veneers right onto a strip-planked hull. You can build the jig in a more conventional fashion with the mold frames waxed to prevent glue adhesion. As in standard strip construction, the keel, stem, and transom are set in place before planking. Strips can be square-edged, bead and cove, tongue and groove, or ship lap. The strip planks are glued to one another. A sheer clamp can be included in the setup to attach the planks near the sheer to add stiffness.

This strip-planked structure is then faired in preparation for the application of the laminations, either veneers or light plywood, usually applied in a double diagonal pattern. On V-shaped hulls, some builders use the combination strip/veneer system on the bottom and laminated plies on the topsides.

A third version of cold molding is the stringer frame method. This is quite similar to wooden aircraft (and balsa- and tissue-paper model aircraft) construction, except that the skin consists of load-bearing panels rather than dope-stiffened fabric. This method eliminates the need to build an elaborate mold, as the hull is laminated over the stringers and frames. It's light and strong, but as the Gougeon brothers note, the main drawback is that you must begin laminating over a marginally adequate mold and take great care as you install the first two layers of veener. As with conventional carvel batten seam construction, the fore and aft stringers (or battens) are visible in the interior.

All these methods are heavy in the production of dust and use of epoxy resins, hardeners, and solvents. Cold molding is probably the most demanding method of boatbuilding in terms of shop conditions. Building under the spreading chestnut (or palm) tree is unlikely to produce good results. The shop must be well ventilated, and climate control is extremely important when working with large quantities of epoxy. If it's too hot, your pots of glue can begin fuming insidiously and hardening prematurely. If it's too cold, the epoxy may not cure at all. How many heat lamps can you plug in before the electric meter self-destructs?

Always follow safety precautions when using epoxy resins. Avoid contact with your skin; wear protective clothing; keep solvents off your skin; avoid breathing vapors; wear safety glasses; and work clean. A couple of good books to consult before going into the cold-molding business are *The Gougeon Brothers on Boat Construction* and Reuel Parker's *The New Cold-Molded Boatbuilding.*

Part Two

SETTING UP SHOP

Building a boat involves a symphony of products that need to work well together: wood, fastenings, glues, beddings, paints, and more.

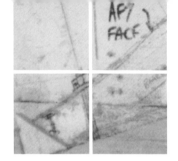

· 12 ·

Traditional Hull Materials

The selection of lumber for boatbuilding involves different considerations than when shopping for cabinet-making or even house-framing stock. The mechanic has to consider the strength, rot resistance, fastening holding capabilities, gluing performance (and with what kind of glue), steam-bending potential, moisture content, and lots more. And after one decides what kind of stock to build with, it may not be available or practical for a number of reasons: cost, embargos, or perhaps the predilections of a merchant who reserves his better stock for high volume customers. Expect a good degree of perusal and peregrination when stalking boat lumber. It's best to start accumulating it ahead of time so you'll have it when you need it.

BUYING WOOD

While boat lumber can occasionally be purchased from local building centers, most likely you will end up dealing with merchants or local sawyers who specialize in this sort of stock. This is not a bad thing, as they are probably acquainted with your needs. Some outfits ship wood or may even have delivery trucks in your region. It's worth enquiring about.

Since boat lumber is a specialty item, it costs more than the construction-grade stuff that you might pick out of the bin at the Mega-Mart home improvement center. But you get what you pay for.

Here are some woods commonly used for boatbuilding:

Cedar. Generally sold in flitches, cedar is highly prized for planking small boat hulls. Relatively soft and rot resistant, the wood is easy to shape; it doesn't shrink and swell excessively; and it is very forgiving of amateur caulking jobs. There are differences between the cedars, however.

- Northern white cedar is a slow growing tree found mostly in the northeastern part of the United States and Canada. It tends to be a small tree with a lot of branches, which means clear stuff is hard to find, and you can forget about quarter-sawn lumber. It is still an excellent planking wood. It is very decay resistant; stands up to abrasion very well; has low shrinkage; resists puncture; and is sinuous, pliable, and tougher than a boiled owl. It can be scarfed to get desired lengths.

- Atlantic white cedar (aka juniper) is relatively light in weight, has low shrinkage, has high decay resistance, and is available in good lengths and widths. It is weaker than northern white cedar, however. It's brittle and splits easily.

- Alaska cedar has a distinctive yellow heartwood. It has low shrinkage and high resistance to rot. It is moderately light (but heavier than northern white or Atlantic cedar) and moderately low in strength. It has excellent working and finishing qualities.

- Port Orford cedar is grown in southern Oregon and northern California and reputed to be one of the heaviest and strongest of the cedars. It has moderate strength and hardness and high resistance to decay. It can be obtained in substantial widths. Its color runs from light yellow to pale brown and it has a distinctive spicy smell.

- Western red cedar is light, has slow shrinkage, and is quite rot resistant. It is also very weak, soft, and brittle. One can easily drive a fastening right through the wood and it can break like a pencil. It is often used for planking—with caution. It works very well in laminations such as cold molding, or as strip planking for kayaks and canoes.

- Spanish cedar (cedro, cigar box cedar) in many ways resembles "Honduras" mahogany, which is not surprising, since it is not really a cedar at all, but a member of the mahogany family. It is lighter and softer than Honduras mahogany, however, and worth considering as an alternative for planking. It is easy to work with; shrinkage is low; and it has good decay resistance. It doesn't easily split or warp, and its gluing performance is acceptable.

Spruce, sitka. This wood's moderate strength, light weight, and straight-running tight grain make it a top choice for spars, oars, and lofting battens. It has moderate shrinkage and hardness and low rot resistance.

Spruce, northern white. If selected carefully, northern white spruce can yield many of Sitka's qualities at a fraction of the cost. It makes a good laminated spar. It is sometimes used in deck framing when weight is a consideration.

Pine, white and sugar. These pines are still occasionally used for planking for dories and strip-built hulls. They are weak and prone to rot, can have knots as big as a coffee cup, and crack easily. But many boats have been built with them, partly because very broad planks can be obtained. The wood should be dosed with preservatives, and kept well drained, ventilated, and painted. Not bad for thwarts.

Pine, longleaf yellow. This a board of a different color. An East Coast wood whose range is from New Jersey to the Gulf of Mexico, this pine is heavy and straight-grained, quite durable, and strong. It's too stiff for most small-craft planking, but it can be used for clamps, stringers, and backbone structural members such as keels and deadwoods.

Cypress. This species grows in southern U.S. swamplands and has very rot-resistant heartwood. It works well and can be used for planking, but it does make for a heavy boat due to its ability to soak up water.

Douglas fir (western fir). This West Coast wood is strong, is straight-grained, and has low to moderate decay resistance. It has many uses: structural, planking, battens, and spars. A fir spar, however, is a good deal heavier than a spruce one—something worth considering when using it in a small boat.

Larch (hackmatack, tamarack). While it has been said you can build an entire boat with larch, what sets it apart are the strong, rot-resistant crooks formed by the tree's roots. It is great for knees, breasthooks, and such.

Oak, white (and a little bit of red). White oak has a lot going for it. Whether it is used for frames, coamings, sheer strakes, toe rails, or tillers, the stuff will stand up to just about anything the weather throws at it.

The wood isn't really white, but rather a subtle cream that, with a clear finish, develops a warm amber tone. Oak is relatively heavy: the charts place it at 47 pounds (dry) per cubic foot. Green, it tips the scale at 62 pounds. That makes it heavier than ash, mahogany, and teak. It is strong and tough, and holds fastenings well. Screw holes should be prebored and the fastenings well lubricated to prevent them from seizing and twisting off. Carefully selected stock is excellent for steam bending.

The single greatest edge that white oak has over its red-tinged brethren is that the pores of the heartwood of the white oak are usually plugged with a growth called tyloses, which prevents movement of liquid into the wood. Red oak, on the other hand, is like a bundle of pipettes. Capillary action can draw fresh water right up into the stick. Indeed, you can dip an end of a short piece into water and blow bubbles, or even blow smoke through it. (A real crowd pleaser at parties.) As you'd expect, untreated red oak is far more prone to rot, while white oak is fairly rot resistant.

Wood for steaming is best used freshly cut or "green." For all other purposes, white oak should be well seasoned as it shrinks a good deal in the drying process. It should be protected from the weather, as oak left in a stack unprotected will warp and twist. The end grain should be painted to avoid checking at the ends. Plain-sawn oak tends to be less dimensionally stable than quarter-sawn, but finding quarter-sawn stock of a usable width can be a challenge. Gluing can be problematic with some adhesives. Consult the glue's manufacturer before attempting to laminate white oak.

Ash, white. This wood is strong and straight grained and steams well. It does have very poor rot resistance but, in a pinch, it can be used as a substitute for oak in dry, well-ventilated areas. It can be used for rails, oars, tillers, and joinery.

Mahogany (sometime referred to as Honduras mahogany). Mahogany is decay resistant and relatively strong, exhibits low shrinkage, and seasons well. It also finishes very well and is often chosen for transoms and joinery of all sorts. It works well for small-craft accent sheerstrakes and occasionally for backbone members.

Mahogany, African (Khaya, Utile). This wood is very similar to mahogany of the Americas. It is hard, strong, and decay resistant. It is also handsome under varnish but difficult to work with.

"Lyptus." This is a new Brazilian hardwood on the market. A natural hybrid of *Eucalyptus grandis* and *E. urophylla*, lyptus promises to be an alternative with good workability, machining properties, density, finish tolerance, and overall strength. The wood is grown on plantations, where stands of indigenous trees are interspersed to preserve natural habitat. Wood can be harvested in just 14 to 16 years. All the returns aren't in, but it's something worth experimenting with.

Tangile (lauan, "Philippine mahogany"). This tropical cedar common to the Philippines is moderately heavy and decay resistant and available in good widths. The color ranges from light (almost pink) to a burgundy. It holds fastenings well and is often used for trim and planking. It is considered "hard" and caution should be used to not over-caulk.

Teak. This wood is very durable and contains natural oil that excludes moisture. It's commonly used on decks. It shrinks and swells little and is quite expensive. It is tough on edge tools and challenging to glue.

Iroko. This wood hails from tropical Africa. It has similarities to teak but is not as strong. The heartwood is decay resistant and moderately easy to work.

Locust, black. This is a heavy and hard wood with high shock resistance and strength. It has low shrinkage and high rot resistance, and is good for small boat stems, knees, floors, and hardware such as cleats, bitts, and tillers. It finishes well. Some wags refer to it as "American teak."

Elm, rock. This wood is difficult to obtain these days but may occasionally be found from a local sawyer. It is very pliable and a top bending wood—better than oak. It's great for frames in small craft. It's strong, tough, and sinuous. As anyone who has tried to split elm for firewood will tell you, it has interlocked grain. It tends to warp.

WEIGHTS OF BOATBUILDING WOODS

Wood	per cubic foot @ 15% moisture*
White ash	42 lbs
Elm	44
Greenheart	61
Iroko	40
Ironbark (Eucalyptus)	62**
Mahogany ("Khaya")	32
Mahogany ("Honduras")	34
Lauan ("Philippine mahogany")	31
Locust (black)	50
Oak (white)	47
Oak (red)	43
Okoume (Gaboon)	27
Teak	43
Iroko	40
Cedar (Alaska yellow)	32
Cedar (Atlantic, juniper)	23
Cedar (northern white, Maine)	21
Cedar (Port Orford)	30
Cedar (Spanish)	35
Cypress	32
Douglas fir (Oregon pine)	34
Larch, eastern (hackmatack, tamarack)	30
Lyptus	40***
Pine (white, eastern)	25
Pine (sugar)	27
Pine (longleaf yellow, southern)	41
Spruce (eastern)	28
Spruce (sitka)	28
Apple	47

For weight per board foot (12" × 12" × 1"), divide by 12

** *Oven dry*

*** *Source: West Wind Hardwood*

Source: Wood: A Manual for its Use as a Shipbuilding Material.

This list is but a sampler. Many builders have had good luck using so-called nontraditional local woods such as black cherry (handsome, good rot resistance, glues well), apple (low rot resistance but makes elegant exposed knees for small craft), black walnut (good rot resistance, handsome in interiors), and sassafras (highly durable). The trick is to do your homework and check with your local university, department of agriculture, marine museum, and local builders to see what works in your area.

A LOT TO CONSIDER

Back in the discussion of carvel construction (Chapter 2), I mentioned that boatbuilding is probably more like dressmaking than cabinet making (at least pattern wise). Joinery-wise, it's also more like bridge building than cabinetry.

Furniture making is characterized by tight joinery, matching woods, uniformly dry stock, and a static, controlled environment for the finished product. In contrast, traditional boat construction is all about movement, flexibility, and weight considerations. The wood must have the strength to hold fastenings, sufficient stability to keep shrinking and swelling to a minimum, and durability to stand up to collision, grounding, wave-bashing, and hobnail-booted passengers, plus exposure to the worst elements that nature can dish out: wind, sun, water, and pernicious wood-eating molds. All of this is a lot like the demands placed upon highway bridges, except that boats, like furniture, are also expected to finish well.

Species

The wood species you select, by necessity, will be a compromise, so it pays to do some research. Take spruce, for example. It is straight grained, has a high strength-to-weight ratio, and carves and glues well, all of which make it an excellent choice for spar making, even though its resistance to rot is poor. Just make sure you keep varnish on the spar and keep it out of the bilge water, and you'll be in good shape. In contrast, consider ash. It bends well (think snowshoes), has good shock resistance, and holds fastenings well. But even with its fabled penchant for bending, it's a bad choice for steam-bent frames since it, too, has very low decay resistance. In bilges it tends to turn into black mush in short order.

Sawn Lumber

Quarter-sawn (or radial-sawn) lumber shrinks and swells less in width, and it cups, twists, and checks less than plain-sawn lumber. Quarter-sawing, however, is a labor-intensive process that only uses a portion of the log, and in order to get boards of decent width, the tree must be very wide. All of this makes quarter-sawn lumber expensive. Fear not, for in most cases, plain-sawn will work fine.

Some lumber—especially cedar and sometimes oak—is sold as live edge or flitch sawn. This means the log has been sawn straight through without trimming the edges and leaving the bark on. This is a good thing. The curved edges of the stock may be just what you need to fashion that curvaceous plank, frame, or deadwood. A lot of usable wood is left on the sawmill floor when a board is "four-sided"—in other words, cut square on all four sides.

Sawn boards generally exhibit two kinds of woods: more durable inner heartwood and more rot-prone outer sapwood. There is usually a difference in color between the two. You are interested in the heartwood. With plain-sawn lumber, the side of the board closest to bark will have more sapwood. Keep that in mind when laying out your work. If your patterns are all traced onto heartwood on the outside (or "bark" face) of the board, you can be sure that you will still be in the heartwood on the other side.

Defects

Other defects (or at least shortcomings) include knots, through-cracks, rot, and stray fastenings.

Not all knots are bad. A small, solid knot from a live branch can actually make the wood tougher due to whorled grain structure. A "black knot," formed where the tree grew over the base of a dead branch, or a rotten knot should be avoided or repaired. Very large knots of any sort should be avoided altogether.

Rot can be detected by looking for punky, soft, or discolored spots. Some minor rot can be repaired, but keep in mind that the condition of the wood you buy is the best it will ever be. It's all downhill from there. The better the quality of the wood you install, the longer the boat will last.

Cracks are problematic. If they are at the end of the board in between the grain (probably due to improper drying) they will likely limit the length of the board

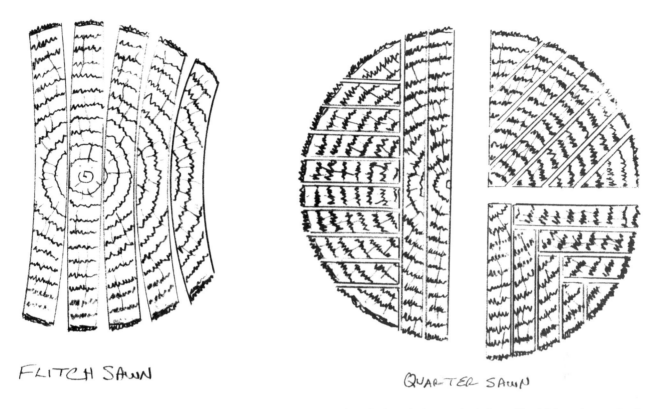

FLITCH SAWN   QUARTER SAWN

Flitch-sawn, or plain-sawn, lumber is quicker and cheaper to mill, but the boards from a single log will exhibit grain running in different directions—some of it nearly perpendicular to the surface (which is good), and some of it more nearly parallel, which can lead to cupping. Quarter-sawn lumber all has nearly vertical grain and is more stable.

you can use. Cracks across the grain can seriously weaken the stock. Some light surface checks that run with the grain are just cosmetic and can often be planed out.

Wood can warp in different ways, including twisting, bowing, crooking, and cupping. Warping severely reduces the usability of a piece of wood. To check for warp, sight the wood down its length, preferably before buying it, and certainly before running it through a saw.

Moisture

The moisture content of boat wood is another consideration. "Green" or unseasoned wood has been very recently cut, and it needs to be dried to reduce its moisture content before it is used. (Green wood does work well for steaming, however.) Air drying outside or in sheds is the oldest and simplest way to season lumber. It can reduce moisture to between 12% and 15% during the dry season of the year. Generally, this wood is fine for construction. Kiln drying is done at temperatures that are high enough to kill any fungus that may be

present. Some builders dislike kiln-dried wood because they feel it is too stiff, or too dry to use in underwater applications because it will swell excessively.

POLITICS AND WOOD

Oh no. . . . There's politics with wood too? I'm afraid so.

Although it is sometimes hard to picture, wood is an internationally traded mass commodity right up there with coffee, cocoa, and petroleum—with all the intrigue and consequences that status bestows. Wood has long been shipped overseas, but the equation has changed because technology allows us to cut more wood faster and more efficiently than ever before, and the demand for exotic species has encouraged industry to exploit undeveloped lands at any price. Another difference is that we're more aware of it due to modern media that often allow us to see what is actually going on.

Not that long ago, however, boatyards constructed their vessels with woods that were available locally from nearby sawyers and merchants. In New England, the planking was of white cedar or pine; in Mexico, perhaps Spanish cedar; in Indochina boats were built of teak. If the vessels that reside in marine museums are any indicator, the local woods worked out just fine. Somewhere along the line, however, local woods were deemed unworthy, or at least too plebian. What now was needed was wood with bulletproof panache that finished like a Steinway piano.

So what's the problem with a wood that varnishes up well and is rot resistant? Well, nothing—as long as the social or environmental prices are not too dear. For example, consider the highly desirable clear spruces and cedars that come from a very narrow band of specialized forest in the Pacific Northwest. Much of that wood is sawn from very large ancient growth trees that, when gone, will be gone forever. From the south comes handsome mahogany lumber. Alas, in recent years a great deal of the mahogany sold has been sawn illegally in protected rain forests—some of it slave labor. In the same fashion, money accrued from some teak sales in Asia has been used to prop up despotic military juntas. These are all very bad juju and yet the topic is not much discussed around the boat-shop coffeepots— even ones filled with "fair trade" coffee.

As an alternative to building with materials with dodgy credentials, consider how you are using the wood, and employ good old-fashioned consumer demand to affect the marketplace. For planking, there is little need to use ultra-clear stock: second-growth stock is fine, and so what if there are a few knots? High quality glues have made scarfing shorter lengths of wood practical for planking, spars, and rails. Investigate which local woods work as alternatives, and consider species such as eastern spruce, sassafras, and rot-resistant and elegant black locust. Demand wood that has been certified (by an independent organization) to be grown in a sustainable fashion. This technique has already influenced the way large home improvement centers purchase their lumber and will still allow you to get the wood you need. Investigate plantation-grown tropical species such as lyptus, which is marketed as an alternative to mahogany.

Finally, look into other methods of construction. For example: instead of a teak deck—pricy in terms of cost, politics, and environmental impact—why not consider epoxy-filled Dynel cloth over plywood. When painted, the Dynel is a near dead ringer for canvas and is very traditional looking. It is skid proof, leak-proof, very rugged, and nearly maintenance free.

With just a bit of creative investigative enterprise you'll have a boat that you can be proud of not only for the craftsmanship but also for what it is made of.

·13·

Plywood

There is considerable debate over the notion of what is, and what is not, "traditional boatbuilding." The discussion can become quite heated when "traditional" becomes synonymous with the concept of historically correct restoration. Often "traditional boatbuilding" boils down to perspective, e.g., if it was being done when I learned the trade, it's traditional. Probably, somewhere down the line, Nat Herreshoff was darkly considered an apostate for using screws in his boats.

Yet boatbuilding has always been about innovation and the introduction of technologies that allowed for faster and more efficient construction. Replacing rivets and trunnels with screws and bolts is a good example of this. Glues made from horse hooves being replaced by epoxy and resorcinol is another. Then there was the introduction of an engineered construction material known as plywood.

PLYWOOD TODAY

Despite its cachet of modernity, plywood has been with us in one form or another since the days of the early Egyptians and Romans. It wasn't until the introduction of truly waterproof glues in the pre–World War II era, that plywood could be used as a reliable boatbuilding wood.

Indeed some say that plywood was on track to be the construction material of choice for production pleasure boats until the introduction of "fiberglass." Fiberglass, or the more technically correct term "glass reinforced plastic" (or GRP), opened the door to mass production of inexpensive, reliable hulls.

What fiberglass couldn't offer was much of an opportunity for the home boatbuilder who was looking for a traditional hull. By its nature, fiberglass construction

TYPICAL WOODS IN MARINE PLYWOOD

Douglas fir. Strong and moderately durable. Generally used in American marine plywood.

Lauan (shorea). Sometimes called Philippine mahogany (although it is not a true mahogany) or Meranti. Most comes from Southeast Asia. It is rated moderately durable.

Okoume (gaboon). A lightweight hardwood from Africa with low durability. It is usually sealed with epoxy for protection. It bends well and has a high strength to weight ratio.

Sapele. A moderately durable hardwood from Africa. Stronger than lauan, Honduras mahogany or khaya (African mahogany).

Utile and sipo. Both moderately durable African hardwoods. Harder than okoume or lauan.

African mahogany (khaya). An African hardwood with moderate decay resistance. Moderately strong, it finishes well.

requires a sophisticated mold that is simply impractical for "one-off" construction. Small boatbuilding shops had the choice of continuing to work with old-time plank-on-frame methods, or adopting plywood by switching to rather slab-sided hull designs with minimal compound curvature.

Today, the picture is very different. The availability of easy-to-use, bulletproof glues and reliably high quality plywood has inspired a school of "modern traditional" boat shops that design and custom build graceful and efficient small craft using the material. Modern technology is now being used to create and interpret elegant traditional designs. Sophisticated computer hull design programs assure that the hulls are efficient. The panels and planks are precision cut by CNC machines, saving time and materials and reducing costs. Innovative techniques such as stitch-and-glue, glued lapstrake, and "LapStitch" were developed so that boats could be built faster, lighter, and with less interior framing. According to one builder, whose shop is noted for its highly efficient pulling boats, plywood is the best material for

the job since it is light, tough, resilient and elastic. It also creates a watertight, light hull that finishes beautifully.

WHAT IS PLYWOOD ANYWAY?

Plywood is a manufactured panel or sheet composed of many layers called veneers or "plies." The plies are created either by rotary cutting or flat slicing. In both processes, a log is soaked to soften the wood prior to cutting. In the rotary method, the log is spun on a lathe and the surface is peeled off by a big knife as a continuous sheet. Flat slicing is just like it sounds: the log is sliced fore and aft into long thin slices. The veneers are then sandwiched at right angles to one another and glued together under great pressure. This produces a panel with high dimensional stability by restraining movement across the grain. The number of laminates can vary in a given thickness. Generally, more and thinner laminates will impart greater stiffness and strength in both directions of the panel.

Sheet stock may be stamped with a number of labels. The term "marine plywood" indicates that the sheet

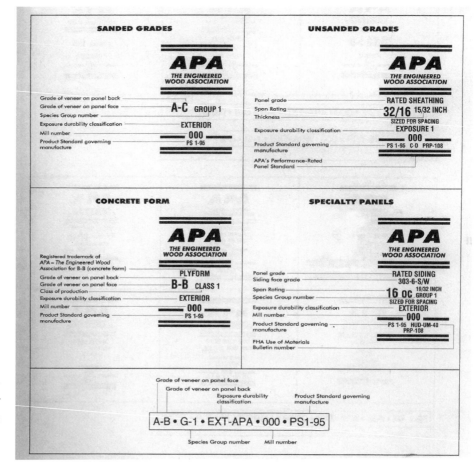

APA—The Engineered Wood Association ("APA" once stood for American Plywood Association but is no longer used) sets U.S. standards for plywood.

BS 1088 is the British Standard Specification for marine plywood.

has been certified by an accreditation agency and is a guarantee that the stock is made with WBP (weather and boil proof) glue such as phenolic formaldehyde (or in some American plywoods, resorcinol). U.S. marine-grade plywood standards are from the Engineered Wood Association (APA), while the British standards follow BS 1088–British Standard Specification for Marine Plywood. In addition, there are U.S. military standards. And there are nonmarine types of plywood that have applications in certain conditions. If you choose to use an alternative, you need to do your homework. Otherwise, specify a true marine-certificated sheet and buy from a reputable dealer.

There are considerable differences between the APA and the BS 1088 standards. For example:

- APA standards call for Douglas fir or Western larch, while the British standard applies to plywood made with untreated tropical hardwood veneers having "a suitable prescribed level of resistance to fungal attack."
- In any edge of a BS 1088 board, not more than one gap is allowed, which shall be not wider than 0.5 millimeters. The maximum APA core-gap is ⅛" (more than 3 millimeters).
- The British standard for veneers requires that they shall be free from knots, other than sound pin

knots. Open splits are not allowed. The APA requires that the grade of all plies be "B" or better. (B-grade veneers may have knots but no knotholes. Grade A allows no knots or knotholes.)

Making the Choice

The question, of course, is: what kind should you use on your boat? On a small boat, cost should not be the primary motivator. The cost of the wood is a relatively small part of the entire cost, especially if you consider labor. For the all-round working craft where durability and cost are concerns and an "okay" paint job is the finish of choice, APA rated A/B fir plywood (Grade A on one side; Grade B on the other) is a good option. Where lightness is a concern and the entire hull structure will be sealed, Okoume BS 1088 plywood does well. Where the hull is not to be embalmed in epoxy, a little extra weight is not a problem, and the job calls for defect-free stock and good durability, Sapele or Meranti BS 1088 certified plywoods are good bets.

Whatever the panel has been made from, it should be stored in a protected location. Sun and rain can weather and degrade a panel. After the plywood has been cut to shape, the edges should be sealed with a coating that is compatible with the material that will eventually cover or coat the panel.

· 14 ·

Hull Knees

The quest for good curved stock for knees, stems, and breasthooks, while not quite in the same league as the Holy Grail, is a continuing challenge for the builder. Naturally curved members are head and shoulders above straight-grained stock for bracing, gusseting, and otherwise reinforcing the hull. Steam bending stock to shape, and lamination, are also options.

The natural knee has a lot going for it. Using the sinuous grown curved grain found in branches and roots, these gnarled units not only exhibit prodigious strength but also look great when varnished. Indeed, when one considers the work the near-right-angle larch (aka hackmatack) root does in buttressing the whole of the tree against the winter's wind, or the weight of the fruit borne by the apple branch, it is easy to get an appreciation for the elegant brawn of these structures.

NATURAL KNEES

Which wood to use? This calls for a visit to your local agricultural extension agent and/or marine museum to inquire about the durable woods growing in your area and what the old-timers used. Fruitwoods such as apple

The grain is running all the right way in this well-selected and gotten-out breasthook.

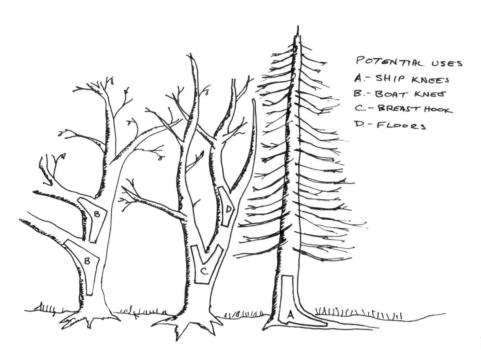

POTENTIAL USES
A.- SHIP KNEES
B.- BOAT KNEE
C.- BREAST HOOK
D.- FLOORS

Where knees come from.

and wild cherry offer up grand stock for thwart knees or breasthooks for small boats, while locust or white oak may yield a stem, stern knee, or dory frames. The knee you need may be right in your own back yard or at least nearby. But chances are that you will need to venture further afield for your quarry.

Try visiting an orchard. In an effort to encourage more production, many farmers are replacing venerable standard varieties with semi-dwarfs. Often the old trees will be piled at the edge of the field and readily available, with prices ranging from cordwood value to free. Pick your stock cautiously, however: discard any dead branches, as apple gets punky quickly, inviting boring insects that you don't need.

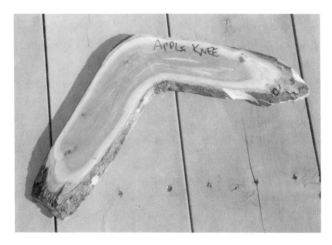

This apple knee will look just fine supporting a thwart or deck.

Another resource is street trees that are trimmed for any number of reasons: overhead utility work, highway visibility problems, or storm damage to name a few. Let your local officials and arborists know that you are interested in the waste products of such operations.

Lastly, in these days of wanton proliferation of highways, malls, and housing developments, there is an opportunity to salvage useable stock before the bulldozers plow it under.

If your knee needs are small, the local lumberyard may be the answer. Many times these emporiums will have planks of oak or mahogany on hand that have been graded out due to the presence of large knots. The whorled grain surrounding the knot can be just the ticket for laying out thwart knees or even small gaff jaws. Just be sure the stock is well dried to avoid excessive shrinkage. In fact, whatever your source, it's a good idea to cut the stock overlong to accommodate checking, shrinking, and pattern fitting. (More on this shortly.)

Going Underground

Roots are yet another source. Although some black spruce knees are harvested for Adirondack guide boats, in the United States the root of choice when it comes to ship knees comes from the Eastern larch (*larix laricina*, also known as hackmatack or tamarack). Most abundantly found in the cool swamps and sphagnum bogs of northeastern North America, the larch forms a right angle or lateral root that with a section of the lower trunk, forms the knee.

Compared to live oak, larch knees were historically considered "small" ship knees. That being said, specimens are still being harvested that are 10" thick and stand as tall as a man. The wood is durable, coarse-grained, hard, and heavy, and holds fastenings well. These jumbo knees are prized by ship and boat carpenters alike. For the small-boat builder, the near right-angled shape makes it a good choice for single-piece stems for traditional rowing and sailing craft, and for transom knees. Waste from a larger knee will often yield a few extra thwart or transom knees as a bonus.

Harvesting larch knees requires some different techniques than those used to gather aboveground stock. Longtime knee harvester Newman Gee recommended that you begin by looking for a stand of larch in the uplands or a a bog. After finding a likely spot and getting the owner's permission, cruise the lot looking for a basin: a flat depression or hollow, often with a steep berm at the edge that flattens off, and is

Newman Gee and his big knee.

full of peat. Peat makes the easiest digging, although the "dirty soil" at the edge of the peat bog may produce the best knees. As the roots hit the clay bottom, they are forced to turn to form a sort of right-angled pedestal.

When prospecting, Newman carried a shaft to plunge into the peat like a dipstick. After finding a promising location, the next chore is to round up some likely suspects. He recommended looking for a tree that looks healthy, with one-third of the tree being the crown.

Having found the tree, the next job is to inspect the base, as not every tree has roots that qualify as knees. Look for an "instep" or swelling on the side of the tree that indicates a heavy root. If there is only one big knee it is called a bull root—used for one ship knee. The soil can then be softened up with the chainsaw (the peat is about the consistency of parcel packing filler), the main knee exposed, and side roots sliced off. The tree can then be pulled over, the upper trunk cut off, and the knee yarded out to where it can be carefully roughed out with a chainsaw with a special saw chain with chipper teeth designed for rip cuts.

Said Newman, "Digging hackmatack knees is like treasure hunting—not every tree has a knee on it. When you find one, dig it and if it is healthy, it's been a good day."

Roughing Out the Stock

It pays to rough out knee stock as soon as possible after harvesting it, since knees take a considerable amount of time to season, and leaving the bark in place is an invitation to wood boring insects that can spoil your hard-won prize. Knees can be debarked with a spud or drawknife. The next task is rough milling. Although some builders slab off the sides of small knees by free-handing them through the band saw, this is a *very* dangerous procedure. The round-sided stock has only tenuous contact with the saw table, and one miscue can cause the blade to catch and pitch the knee sideways, ruining the blade and possibly the operator's hand. It is far safer to flatten the stock using hand tools, either by saw kerfing and breaking the pieces out with edge tools, or with a handheld power planer. Large knees can be slabbed with a chainsaw but the stock must be well supported, the saw well sharpened, and the operator well skilled (and wearing proper safety equipment). Some traditionalists have been known to use an old-time handheld ripsaw.

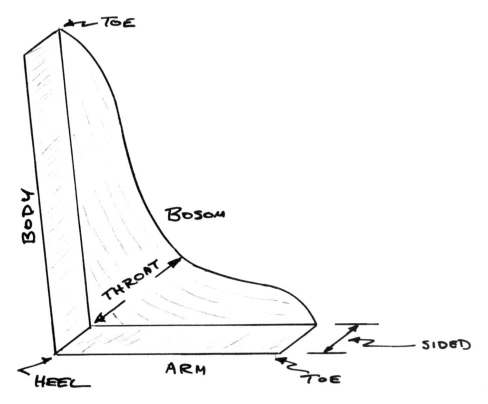

No patella, but no shortage of other anatomical references. The parts of a knee.

Finish surfacing of small knees can be done with either a stationary power planer or a handheld planer. Care should be taken when surfacing knees, as they have constantly changing grain that can easily pull out. For large knees that have been slabbed nearly to size, a belt sander with a rough grit belt may be all you need.

Curing

To avoid excessive shrinkage, twisting and checking, knees should be cured or dried slowly in a dark, ventilated environment such as a woodshed or barn with a dirt or gravel floor. One technique is to rack them up on sleepers or stickers a bit off the ground and out of the wind.

There is a good deal of folklore on the best way to retard the drying process. Some believe painting knees with used motor oil or hot wax will do the trick. Others think sealing the ends and bosom with red lead or some other sealer is sufficient. Pete Culler once wrote that he found soaking them in oil and kerosene and placing them in a steam box for a bit would quickly season the stock. Anyway, it's a pretty good bet that knees that have not been sealed with something will check.

Laminated Knees and Frames

Building an unnatural knee by lamination is an excellent alternative to the homegrown sort. If well fashioned, it will be quite strong and capable. This sort of structure can often be seen in the laminated arches of high school gyms and civic centers. They do look like what they are and may have too much of a high-tech appearance for some boats. That said, with a coat of paint, both kinds of knees look the same.

The technology is the same as when building a laminated stem except that instead of laminating the stock to near-exact size, here we will produce the raw material from which the knee will be made—much like the raw stock provided by the natural crook. Begin by making your knee or sawn frame patterns. Then build a lamination jig that is a compromise shape that will work for all your patterns. Mill out and steam or boil the laminations and bend them to the jig. Before gluing, place your pattern on top of the clamped stack to ascertain that the laminated stock will be large enough to work for all of the various knees.

STEAM-BENT KNEES

The steam-bent knee is an elegant solution, either as a single bent piece of heavy stock or with a fitted filler block behind. Like many elegant and simple-looking solutions, however, there is more to it than it seems.

Here's the problem. When wood bends around a curve, the outside of the curve is stretched while the interior is forced into compression. You can get an idea of this if you take a stack of thin strips of wood, clamp one end, and bend the stack. You'll see that the outer layers will offset or come up short relative to the inside ones. On the laminated knee described previously, that's no problem as the thin laminates bend easily and everything is glued up oversized anyway. For a single-piece bent knee, the plot as well as the wood thickens.

If we try to bend that heavy stick of wood around a tight curve, chances are good that the outside of the stock will fail. This will be true even if the bending stock is of the highest quality. We need to somehow limit the stretching of the outside fibers while encouraging the inside fibers to compress. To do this, we'll use a bending strap, which is just a flexible piece of metal with stops on either end that fit the length of the wood exactly. When we bend the wood around a form, the length of the wood will be contained so that the only recourse for the wood is to compress the inner fibers.

Boatbuilder Harry Bryan of New Brunswick, Canada, has devised an effective jig for bending knees and stems that harkens back to versions used at the old Herreshoff yard. Harry's jig accepts an extra-wide piece of wood so two knees can be cut out of a single bent unit. One part is a rugged bending form that can be bolted to a workbench. The other part is a bending strap with stops and a lever at the far end for mechanical advantage. The steamed wood is inserted into the bending strap between the keepers and one end of the strap is clamped to the form. As the strap is bent around, the wood is pressed tightly to the form, and then clamped tightly for a couple of days. The wood can then be released and the knee's shape traced on and sawn out.

WATCH YOUR PATTERNS

No matter whether your knee is steamed, laminated, or natural, patterns are essential in selecting which piece of stock to use. Patterns help the builder visualize the final product and maximize its strength by judiciously aligning the curves of the part with the grain of the wood or laminations. They can also lure the builder into overconfidently tracing their shape and cutting to the line, only to find that the piece is too small.

What happened? The pattern is two dimensional, and it represents only one face of the knee. It does not

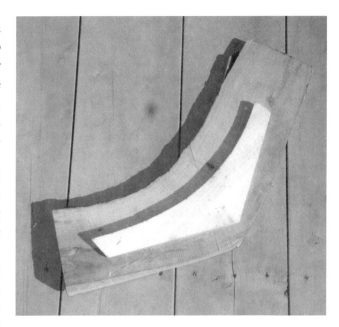

When fitting a pattern to the knee stock, try to obtain the maximum values of the grain's strength and beauty.

Consider the bevels carefully before you begin cutting.

take into account any bevel cut into the two side faces, nor does it allow for mistakes or necessary trimming the mechanic might make in fitting the piece. That romantic inside curve that is so inviting to cut on the band saw could leave you short of the last knee needed for the job. So leave the bosom full, fit those plebeian side faces, break out the pattern one last time, trace, and then cut that last gracious bow. 'Tis a thing of beauty!

· 15 ·

Selecting a Glue

Marine adhesives have come a long way. It wasn't that long ago that the top-of-the line glues were only water resistant at best. If you really wanted something to stay in place, you had better have had some pretty fancy locking joinery, or at least a fastening through it.

Many modern glues are truly waterproof. But as with most technology, the more sophisticated the product, the more demanding (or cranky) the parameters in which it is used. Reliability and success are highly dependent on mixing ratios and thoroughness, temperature, clamping pressure, time clamped, the amount of glue in the joint, and contamination. We are no longer cooking up horse hooves: this is chemistry. The good news is that successful gluing is nearly guaranteed—if the manufacturer's instructions are followed to the letter.

The two most popular types of glues, resorcinol and epoxy, each have their devotees who have fervently sworn eternal faith to one or the other. There are the conservative resorcinol Pharisees who disdain all things epoxy and grimly predict imminent failure of any epoxy-laminated hull setting out to sea on a hot summer day. Then there are the epoxy zealots who would never consider using resorcinol—or anything else, for that matter. Within the epoxy camp there have been theological schisms producing factions that have pledged their allegiance to particular manufacturers' formulations. As always with questions of faith, the best course is one of moderation. In fact, both resorcinol and epoxy have their specific strengths, uses, and shortcomings, and there is room for both in the boat-shop locker.

GLUE CHARACTERISTICS

One thing both products have in common is that they are composed of chemicals that must be blended into one another to activate the ingredients. Protective gear should be worn to keep the stuff off your body and face. Wearing disposable gloves and an apron is good practice, and long sleeves or gauntlets to protect your forearms are also worthwhile. Be sure to also have plenty of ventilation, just as you would when working with any chemicals.

Another trait the two glues hold in common is limited "pot life." Once a batch is mixed up, the clock starts running and it's a matter of limited time before the concoction starts to harden. So before opening a can, unscrewing a jug, or pumping a squirt, complete all joinery, make the gluing jigs, have all the clamps ready, and work out the clamping techniques.

So much for the similarities—on to the differences.

RESORCINOL

Resorcinol (i.e., resorcinol resin paraformaldehyde-based adhesive) is one of the original truly waterproof glues and it is rugged stuff. Favored by wooden aircraft builders, the purple, two-part adhesive produces highly durable bonds able to withstand continuous salt- or freshwater immersion, outdoor exposure, tropical or sub-zero temperatures, cold or boiling water, and molds.

In addition, the stuff is impervious to solvents, oils, grease, mild acids, and bases, and it works well with relatively oily woods.

Unlike epoxy, which can also be used as a coating or as a reinforcement in conjunction with a fabric such as fiberglass, resorcinol is only intended for use as an adhesive for gluing one piece to another or in multi-layered laminated structures.

Resorcinol is a two-part glue consisting of a syrupy purple liquid resin and tan powder catalyst. It can be mixed either by weight (recommended) or by volume into a noncopper container. After measuring, slowly add the powered catalyst into the resin and stir for five to ten minutes, until the mixture is uniform.

The workable liquid "pot life" of resorcinol is dependant on temperature. The glue cures at room temperatures—from 70°F to 95°F. The cooler it is (down to about 70°F), the more time you have before it gets too thick to use. DAP, the manufacturer of Weldwood brand resorcinal glue, says that temperatures below 70° can cause poor bonds. This can be a consideration for those working in unheated shops in cold climates.

Using Resorcinol

As with many other adhesives, the mixture must be spread on both mating surfaces to assure proper adhesion. There should be enough spread so that, when the pieces are clamped together, there will be squeeze-out. This is a good thing (aside from the mess) as you are assured that there is enough of the stuff in the joint. Before clamping, allow time for the adhesive to absorb into the wood.

Joinery demands when using resorcinol are pretty high. DAP suggests that glue-line thickness should be about 0.005″ and clamping pressures should be between 25 and 75 psi. The bottom line is that you need tight-fitting joints and should honk down on the clamps pretty tight.

Moisture is another concern in curing resorcinol. For a reliable bond, the moisture content of the wood should be between 8% and 12%. (The same for goes for epoxy, by the way.) You may find yourself pining for that pricy, up-town digital moisture meter promoted in *Neurotic Woodworker Magazine*. Bonds on wood with moisture content below 5% or above 15% are usually inadequate.

A nice feature of resorcinol is that you can clean your spreaders, brushes, and containers with water, as long as you do it immediately after use and before the glue sets.

On the other hand is resorcinol's seriously purple color, which will show at the glue line. This is not a problem for painted woods, but it is not a particularly desirable quality for brightwork.

EPOXY

Compared to the one-stop shopping approach of resorcinol, epoxy offers a cornucopia of choices that can make a first-time user's head spin. Even the ingredients sound industrial strength: the resin is the diglycidyl ether of bisphenol A. Most of the hardeners are amine-based. These *are* hardeners, and not catalysts. A catalyst promotes reactions but doesn't become part of the product. Epoxy hardeners do become part of the cured epoxy and affect its final properties.

What sort of properties? Resins can be formulated to be thick, to resist running, or of water-thin viscosity to penetrate wood. The flexibility of the cured epoxy can be modified. Hardeners can be of the "fast" variety that will let you work down to temperatures as cool as 40°F (4°C) or produce a swift cure at room temperature, slow, that lets you work at a warmer temperature for longer times, or *really* slow for hot weather or for really long (for epoxy) working time. There are special clear coating hardeners that are preferred by kayak and strip boatbuilders. There are rot stabilizing epoxies, versions formulated to wet out fiberglass cloth better, and varieties formulated to glue oily woods (which epoxy generally doesn't do all that well), and more.

Choosing the Brand

Which manufacturer to go with? It is a difficult choice, as the companies' advertising literature tends to indicate that they all produce the best product on the market. And in fact, all the major manufacturers do a good job. Many builders base their decisions on one or two properties of the product line, such as the visual appearance of the epoxy when used for clear coating, or the pot life, or the curing temperature range. Other considerations include: Does the manufacturer make its product easy to use with easy measuring ratios, or different self-metering pumps and such? Does it offer products to augment its epoxy, such as fillers and thickeners? Does it have good reference material and someone to staff a technical help line to answer questions? Is the product available locally? (This can mean a lot if you are halfway through a job on a Friday afternoon and your discount supplier is located above a sandwich stand in Timbuktu.) Usually, when a satisfactory manufacturer is found, builders stick with it (so to speak). This avoids duplication of products that may not necessarily work together, and having to deal with different curing times, mixing ratios, and performance.

Using Epoxy

When using epoxy, it is necessary to rethink the paradigms learned with the older glues. Epoxy thrives on less-than-perfect joints, needs only enough clamping pressure to pull the pieces together, and (when the proper mix is used) can work in a wide temperature range, from 40° to 95°F (4° to 35°C).

When a coat of epoxy is applied, it seeps into the wood pores, helping to create a strong bond. But this quality can also lead to glue-starved joints, if so much is absorbed that not enough is left in the interface between the pieces. But epoxy can be modified with myriad additives to change its consistency, both wet and cured. There are microfibers to thicken the epoxy, preventing excessive running and absorption and allowing it to fill large gaps and generally hang out in a joint until it cures. There are high-density fillers to build strength where high loads are anticipated (like when mounting hardware). There are fillers that are intended to make strong fillets (see below), fillers that can turn epoxy into an easily sanded putty, fillers to create fairing compounds, and more.

Epoxy fillets are used to "weld" or reinforce parts where they join at a difficult angle, such as when joining a watertight bulkhead to the inside of a hull. This is done with epoxy thickened with a filler the consistency of peanut butter. It can then be installed in a thick bead between two parts that need to be joined, then smoothed into a nice arc. Fillets can replace cleats or chines in construction, although this works best when bonding lighter materials.

Epoxy is also used as a laminating agent to stick down fabrics to sheath and reinforce hulls and decks. Years ago, polyester was used for this purpose because that's all there was, but it never worked very well because it doesn't bond well with wood. Epoxy does, however, and it is the combination of epoxy and fiberglass that makes lightweight strip plank and stitch-and-glue hulls possible. Dynel and epoxy over a plywood deck is a great long-lasting alternative to canvas.

Are there any drawbacks to this miracle elixir? Of course. The stuff is forgiving but not totally. Many of the difficulties experienced with epoxy are due to operator error. As mentioned, joints can be clamped too tightly or there can be too little glue in the joint, both of which can cause failure. Improper mixing ratios of epoxy and hardener, or too little mixing, can cause the stuff to gel rather than cure. Working in conditions that are too hot, mixing too much, or mixing it in a container that is too small can produce disconcerting (though interesting) results as you get a runaway exothermic reaction. The material starts fuming and frothing and solidifying immediately in the mixing container. Joints can fail because they were contaminated by the residue from a salami sandwich you had for lunch, or simply because of the natural oils in the woods.

Coating a hull with epoxy has its pros and cons. Glass and epoxy encapsulation can toughen and reinforce a plywood or thin strip hull. Simply coating the outside of a conventional hull with the impermeable stuff can entrap moisture, causing blistering or even rot. Epoxy is not resistant to ultraviolet light, and it must be protected from sunlight with either paint or a UV-resistant varnish.

Perhaps the greatest concern about epoxy is its effect on human health. All materials used in boatbuilding have a certain level of toxicity. With the potential to cause respiratory ailments and skin and eye allergies, even wood dust has its problems. But at least the dust is visible and most builders wear dust masks. The health threats of epoxy are more insidious in that they're not so obvious. The most common problem with epoxy is dermatitis or skin inflammation. This comes from an allergic reaction to the stuff, not unlike poison ivy. Different people have different levels of sensitivity. The problem is that it's really easy to get too comfortable around epoxy, adopting the old "I'm just doing a little bit of this" approach. Nearly clear, epoxy lacks resorcinol's high-visibility purple that makes it obvious when you have a lot spread around and encourages neat work habits, such as wearing gloves and protective clothing, and careful application of appropriate and not excessive amounts. Once you get sensitized to epoxy, reactions can recur with tiny levels of exposure, so that you may never be able to work with the stuff again. Sanding uncured epoxy is bad news as well, causing respiratory irritation. Epoxy chemicals remain active until fully cured. As with many other boatbuilding processes and materials, the answer is to wear that safety stuff, work cleanly, maintain good ventilation, and not use any more of the product than you have to.

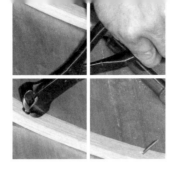

·16·

Fastenings

Even a small boat can have thousands of fastenings in the planking alone, so you want to put in the right kind. Likewise with stem-to-knee joints, built-up rudders or centerboards, and the dozens or hundreds of other places where components are held together by something other than glue: each type of joint or connection has different requirements, so fastenings must be selected carefully, considering type, size, and material. Often, newer plans will specify what kind of fastening is called for. For old plans, you need to make your own informed decisions.

For example, rivets, screws, clench nails, and ring nails are the usual options for planking. Which to use can depend on how heavy the planking is, how much

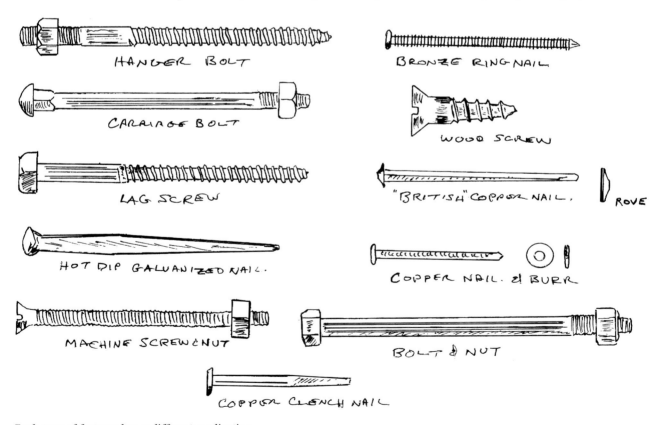

Each type of fastener has a different application.

strength the boat requires, and how strong the frames are. Are you working by yourself or do you have a helper? Are you working upside down or right-side up? Do you anticipate having to do repairs in the future?

While you're pondering these questions, and especially when you're installing the fastenings, keep in mind that they aren't intended to draw components together upon installation. You do that with clamps, and the fastenings just keep the components in place.

SCREWS AND RIVETS

Let's begin with the debate on the relative merits of screws vs. rivets, particularly as they relate to planking. For most builders, the screw is the hands-down first choice. It's fast and easy to install, you can use the cordless screw gun (carefully), and you can work single-handedly. Screws can be used in places where it would be difficult or impossible to get a rivet in. By the way—when we talk about screws, we generally mean the shanked drill-the-hole-and-install wood-screw variety, not the ubiquitous, all-thread, point-and-shoot drywall screw.

The holding power of the screw is dependent on it being inserted into a properly drilled hole. In many cases, drilling that hole can be thought of as a four-step process, although some of the steps may occur simultaneously. Picture joining two pieces of wood together. In the lower piece of wood, the hole must be big enough for the root of the screw to pass, but narrow enough so that the threads can tap into the wood. The holding strength of the screw depends on those threads. In the upper piece of wood, the hole diameter must be large enough to allow the shank of the screw to spin without binding. The shank should be long enough to reach the bottom of the top piece of wood, since screw threads in

the upper piece can keep the joint between the two pieces from closing. Then, the hole must be counter-bored so that the head of the screw will snug down below the upper surface of the wood—the space above it to be filled with a bung or putty. And at the bottom of the counterbore, the hole must be countersunk, to provide a solid seat for the screw head. Fortunately, there are factory-made boring bits that do the entire job in one pass. The most popular sort that does a reasonably good job is the Fuller brand adjustable tapered drill and countersink/counterbore. The company also manufactures bung cutters that produce plugs to match the diameters of the counterbores exactly.

Even with a properly bored hole, caution needs to be exercised when installing the screw. If the screw is pushed too far into the wood beyond the bored hole, the screw changes from a fastener into a splitting wedge. Hence, the power driver must be used carefully. Some power drivers have a torque adjustment. It is possible to power the screw in part way and finish up by hand. Other options are the old-fashioned "Yankee" screwdriver or a brace and bit.

Wood screws, especially those made of silicon bronze, can be quite brittle, and you can too easily wring the head right off if the threads are not lubricated. Oil, soap, wet paint, paraffin, bedding compound, and boot dressing can and have been used. My favorite is a wax toilet bowl seal. This ring of softened wax will hold a bunch of screws stuck into it and the wax will cling to the screw threads when the screw is inserted into the hole.

Screws come with flat, oval, and round heads. Flathead screws are used for flush or countersunk assembly while the oval and round heads are generally used for

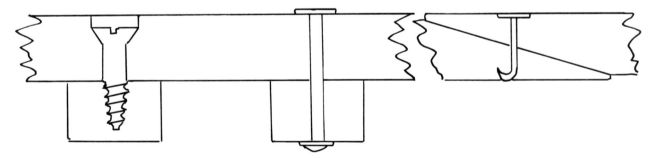

The effectiveness of a screw (left) is dependent upon a properly drilled hole: narrow enough for the threads to bite into, snug in the shank, and countersunk for the head to seat properly. Rivets (middle) are held in place by the nail head on one side and a rove or washer on the other. The rove itself is held in place by peening down the end of the nail after nipping off the excess. The wood should be predrilled for a snug fit. For clench nails (right), predrill for a snug fit and drive the nail through until it hits and turns upon the holding iron, forming a one-legged staple.

trim or for attaching hardware. Screw heads are milled to accept either the familiar slotted, Phillips/Frearson or square drive. Square drives—also known as Robertson drives—are gaining in popularity quite rapidly for power installation.

Rivets

There have a number of advantages over rivets. They cost less. They hold the pieces of wood together like a C-clamp does—from the outside—provided that you have access to both sides. They make fastening repair or replacement easier, as the new rivet can go into the old hole without concern about cross threading the threads in the wood. The narrow shank of the rivet can be used in very light frames that would be easily broken by the wedge-like screw. On the downside, the rivet is labor-intensive. It often requires two people to

do the job: one to drive the rove on, nip off and peen the end; the other to back up the fastening with an iron. Some locations are difficult to get a rivet into.

Rivets come in two different styles. Traditional U.S. construction typically uses rivets with round shanks and flat heads. These are actually common nails made of copper that are similar to steel construction nails. The popular rivets in Europe consist of a copper nail that is square in cross section (similar to old-fashioned cut flooring nails) with either a flat or proud rosette head and a dished or conical copper ring or rove.

Common riveting nails can be sold by the "penny" (D) size or by wire gauge. The nails are turned into rivets when combined with a washer-like rove or burr that is driven over the nail. The nail is cut outside of the burr and the end is peened (mushroomed) with a ball-peen

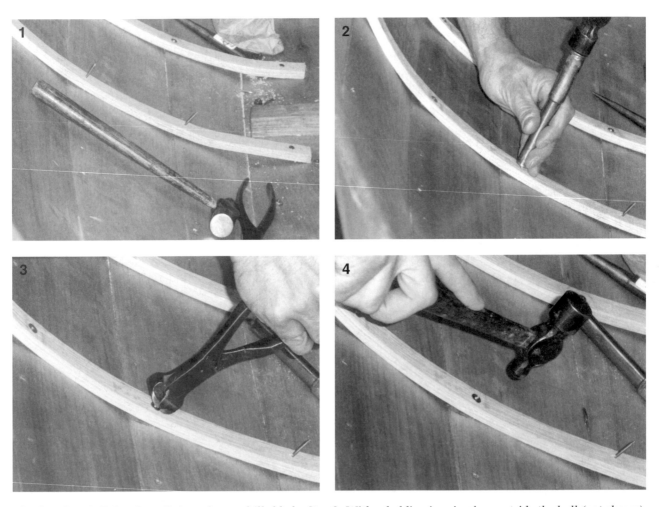

Riveting. Step 1: Drive the nail through a predrilled hole. Step 2: With a holding iron in place outside the hull (not shown), drive the rove over the nail with a rivet set and hammer. Step 3: Nip off the excess nail shaft. Step 4: With the holding iron still in place, peen over the cut nail.

Backing up a rivet with a holding iron. Riveting is truly a two-person job, and gaining access to the opposite side can often be awkward.

hammer. See the accompanying tables for specifications of American-style rivets.

Clench Nailing

Copper clench nails are cut nails with the sharp beveled point of a tack. Generally they are used in light planking-to-frame situations or when fastening the laps of lapstrake planks between frames. When installed, they can best be described as one-legged staples. Instead of peening the end of the nail over a rove, the nail is turned back on itself as soon as it emerges from the wood. Clench nails can be used just about anywhere a rivet can, and although they are probably not quite as good a fastening as the rivet, they certainly are adequate for light construction; they are also faster to install and they can usually be done single-handedly. They have particular value in fastening the laps between the frames in lapstrake and dory-lap construction.

The tools required for the job are few: a light hammer, an electric drill with a slightly undersized bit, and a curved clenching (or clinching) iron for turning the nails. This last item can be a large hammerhead or even an automotive bodywork iron. As for the nails, their overall length should be roughly ⅛" longer than the clamped-up width of the laps.

U.S.-STYLE COPPER RIVETS

NAIL SPECIFICATIONS

Penny	Gauge	Length	Shank Diam.	Head Diam.	Count per/Pound
2D	15	1"	0.072"	³⁄₁₆"	685
3D	14	1¼"	0.083"	³⁄₁₆"	424
4D	12	1½"	0.109"	¼"	205
5D	12	1¾"	0.109"	¼"	165
6D	11	2	0.120"	⁹⁄₃₂"	133
8D	10	2½"	0.134"	⁵⁄₁₆"	86
10D	9	3	0.148"	⁵⁄₁₆"	55
16D	8	3½"	0.165"	⅜"	40
20D	6	4	0.203"	⁷⁄₁₆"	23
40D	4	5	0.2381"	¹⁷⁄₃₂"	14

(continued on next page)

(continued from page 119)

BURR-TO-RIVET FIT

Size Nail	Loose	Drive
15	15	N/A
14	14	N/A
12	12	13
11	12	13
10	9	10
9	8	9
8	7	8
6	5	6

Source: Jamestown Distributors

COPPER BURRS

Size	Hole I.D.	Approximate Count/Pound
14	0.093	2050
13	0.106	1350
12	0.124	1240
10	0.138	750
9	0.146	580
8	0.166	465
7	0.176	380
6	0.206	184

Source: Jamestown Distributors

EUROPEAN STYLE RIVETS

European style copper nails are mated with slightly cupped or conical washers. The burr or rove is driven over the nail with the cupped side toward the wood.

COPPER ROSE HEAD NAIL

Size	Length
#14	¾"
#14	1"
#13	1¼"
#13	1½"
#12	2"

CONICAL COPPER ROVES

Size	O.D.
#14	⁵⁄₁₆"
#13	⅜"
#12	½"

Source: Jamestown Distributors

Copper clench nails and the tools to use them: a ball peen hammer and a clenching iron.

As with riveting, it takes a bit of practice to become proficient in clenching, but the rewards are well worth the time. Begin by clamping your stock tightly together. Next, drill a sightly undersized pilot hole. There are occasions when you can get away with driving the nail directly, but you stand a much greater chance of splitting out the wood.

Next, while holding the clenching iron to the inside of the pilot hole, drive the nail in. When the beveled point contacts the face of the iron (you'll feel it), roll the iron ever so slightly to turn the point back on itself. The nail should be rolled from the beveled side of the point and turned inward, across the grain of the wood and away from the edge of the plank. When the head of the nail is flush with the plank, you're done.

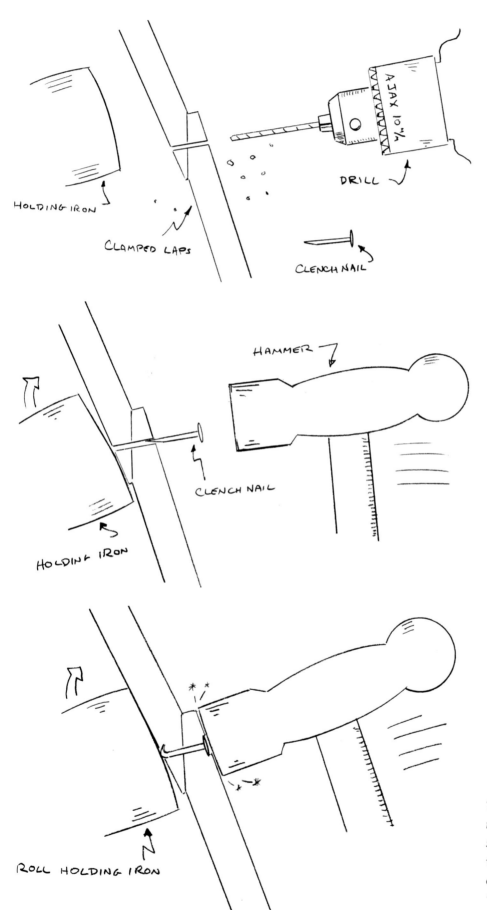

HOLDING IRON

CLAMPED LAPS

DRILL

CLENCH NAIL

HAMMER

CLENCH NAIL

HOLDING IRON

ROLL HOLDING IRON

To fasten plank laps with clench nails, (left) drill a slightly under-size hole; (middle) drive the nail while holding the clenching iron on the opposite side; and (right) "roll" the iron to turn the point of the nail back into the wood.

OTHER USEFUL FASTENERS
Drift Pins

Drift pins are used to hold together an assembly such as a keel, centerboard, or rudder. Similar to homemade nails, they are made from metal rod that has been roughly pointed or beveled at one end and peened or mushroomed, with perhaps a washer added, at the other end. They are driven into very slightly under-size holes that have been predrilled slightly longer than the pin. When several are used to hold an assembly together, the piece is tightly clamped and the holes are generally drilled at different angles. If the piece tries to come apart, the angled pins will lock and prevent the joints from opening up.

Ring Nails

Threaded or "ring" nails are close cousins to the ringed drywall nail. When they are driven into a prebored hole of the proper size, the ringed or burred shaft grips the wood and resists loosening. They are fast and easy to install, but if your hole is a bit too large, they don't hold very well. If your hole is too small and you are driving into oak, the nail will likely buckle, and you will discover how difficult it is to pull these nails. They can be most unpleasant to run into if you are doing a repair job and want to be able to remove a piece, say a plank, without destroying it. They do have their place, such as when you are fastening plywood planking to a chine that is going to be embalmed with epoxy.

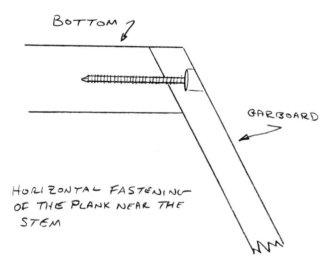

When ring-nailing a plank into the bottom of a hard-chine boat, drill and drive horizontally, rather than perpendicular to the plank.

Galvanized Boat Nails

Hot-dipped galvanized steel boat nails are generally used for heavier commercial craft. They are forged and have a rectangular shaft, a blunt or chisel point, and a blob-like head. Expect them to have a shorter life than more durable metals.

Carriage Bolts

Available in bronze, stainless steel, and galvanized iron, the carriage bolt has a round head and a shaft that is usually only threaded partway. Under the head, where it meets the shaft, the bolt has a short square section that sinks into the wood and keeps the bolt from rotating when it is being tightened. These bolts are quite useful for the assembly of keel and stem structures. To be effective, the holes in the structure should be bored the same diameter as the shaft of the bolt.

Machine Screws

Machine screws with matching nuts (and usually, washers) are used to fasten a multitude of hardware aboard boats. These straight-sided screws may be fully or partially threaded, and can also be used for hard-wood-to-hardwood applications. For example: if you want to install an inwale to the top end of a line of frames, but are concerned that the wedge-like action of a standard wood screw might split the frame heads, select a machine screw with a coarse thread instead. Clamping the inwale tightly in place, bore holes of the diameter of the root of the screw, and tap threads into the holes in the same way you would tap metal. Then rebore the inwale slightly larger, to allow the screw to pass through freely as it threads into the frame beneath. Tighten and you are in business.

POPULAR FASTENER METALS
Silicon Bronze

This is the most versatile metal for small craft fasteners. The metal is hard and quite corrosion resistant. Screws are available in round, oval, and flat-head versions. Carriage bolts and machine screws are available in many different lengths and diameters. Solid rod (useful for shop-made bolts, drift pins, and bracing) and threaded rod are available, as are annular ring nails.

(continued on page 124)

JUST CHARGE IT

When I was a teenager and owned my first boat, I remember the old-timers at the boatyard giving me dark warnings about the dread "electrolysis" that could eat boat fastenings. They had seen firsthand how the affliction could turn bright brass fastenings into pink mush in a few short years, and every spring would see the boys clamping ever-larger talismanic sacrificial zincs to their shafts and rudders to fend off the affliction.

While there are a number of causes of "electrolysis" in hulls including bum electrical systems, what they were referring to is basic galvanic action between dissimilar metals. If you think back to your high school chemistry class, you'll remember that different metals have different electrical potentials. If you suspend two different metals (say a galvanized steel bolt and a bronze one) in a tub with an electrolyte (saltwater, for instance) and hook a voltmeter to the bolts, you'll see you have a battery. An electric current is flowing from the anode (the galvanized bolt) to the cathode (the bronze one). The more "noble" metal (in this case, the bronze) attacks the less noble one (first the zinc, then the steel itself), causing it to corrode or waste away. The farther the metals are from one another in the galvanic series, the greater the intensity of the attack. If mixing metals, it is better to select two that are as close together as possible on the galvanic series. Copper rivets are better paired with silicon bronze screws than with galvanized steel ones.

Galvanic Series in Seawater

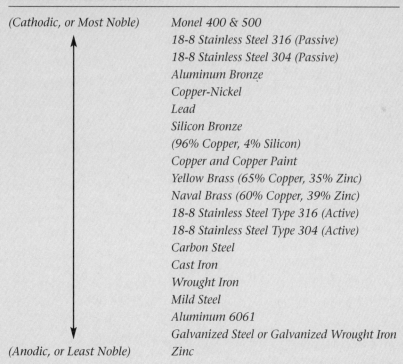

(Cathodic, or Most Noble)	Monel 400 & 500
	18-8 Stainless Steel 316 (Passive)
	18-8 Stainless Steel 304 (Passive)
	Aluminum Bronze
	Copper-Nickel
	Lead
	Silicon Bronze
	(96% Copper, 4% Silicon)
	Copper and Copper Paint
	Yellow Brass (65% Copper, 35% Zinc)
	Naval Brass (60% Copper, 39% Zinc)
	18-8 Stainless Steel Type 316 (Active)
	18-8 Stainless Steel Type 304 (Active)
	Carbon Steel
	Cast Iron
	Wrought Iron
	Mild Steel
	Aluminum 6061
	Galvanized Steel or Galvanized Wrought Iron
(Anodic, or Least Noble)	Zinc

(continued from page 122)

Copper

Perhaps the most ancient of fastening metals, copper is soft and malleable and resistant to decay. Nowadays it's used primarily for rivets and clench nails.

True Hot Dip Galvanized Carbon Steel

This steel is useful for larger commercial work. Square-cut boat nails, common nails, screws, bolts, and rod are generally available. Beware of discount electroplated hardware store varieties. These are merely zinc flavored and will rust quickly.

Yellow Brass

This material is still used for escutcheon pins and half-oval and half-round strap (for things such as trim and bang strip on the stem). Silicon bronze, being stronger, harder, and less susceptible to decay, has generally replaced brass for fastenings.

Stainless Steel

This is a catch-all term for many different alloys offered under that name. They are generally strong and have utility for fastening small hulls that are not kept in the water all the time, or for above-water applications. Galvanic action problems can arise if stainless is used along with nonferrous metals in hull fastening, and fasteners can break down if they are installed in low oxygen conditions. Unlike bronze or copper, stainless is at its best when it is exposed (uncovered by plugs, paint, or putty), as it requires oxygen to maintain its passivity and self-repairing oxide protective coating.

Monel

If your lifestyle tends toward BMWs and Rolex watches, you might want to consider Monel. It's very pricey, extremely durable, and harder and stronger than silicon bronze. It is excellent for keel bolts that you don't ever want to replace.

· 17 ·

Bedding Compounds

Wooden boat construction often offers bountiful opportunities for options and opinions on the matter of materials and techniques. One such example is humble bedding compound. Bedding compound can be described as a nonhardening putty that is used as a flexible gasket between two pieces of mechanically fastened material—generally wood to wood or hardware to wood. The primary purpose of the mixture is to exclude water from the joint.

Certainly it is an advantage for a port light to be well bedded, to prevent water from dripping onto to your head while you're in your bunk. A more important purpose of bedding is to prevent decay-promoting freshwater from sneaking into a joint and turning it into a nautical petri dish.

While most agree that having some sort of stuff in the joint is a good idea, opinions vary as to what stuff is best. Although it is somewhat counterintuitive, a prime consideration in deciding which product to use when assembling something is whether you will want to take it apart again. Most of the synthetic "in-the-tube" compounds produce a flexible yet very tenacious bond, curing to the consistency of a rubber tire or a motor mount. This stands up to vibration so that as the wood moves, the compound can stretch and compress and still maintain its bond. The stuff is strong: indeed, after it cures, you could pull out your fastenings and everything would hold together nicely. So what's not to like? Consider that to do any sort of repair, you'll likely need either a saw or blasting powder.

Wooden boats have a lot in common with the old Volkswagen Beetle. You can easily take them apart to do repairs. Worn out or damaged parts can be relatively easily replaced. Anything that gets used a lot will wear out eventually. That's why automobile wheels are rarely welded to the axle and lightbulbs aren't cemented to their sockets. With a bit of care, traditionally built wooden boats can last indefinitely, as their parts are replaceable.

Types of Bedding

There are two basic kinds of bedding: the nonadhesive oil-based putties that come in cans, and the flexible/adhesive synthetics that come in the tubes.

Good candidates for nonadhesive bedding are grab and toe rails, hardware, transoms, deck hardware, butt blocks, breasthooks, frame sockets in keels (if you believe in them), and knees. Using an adhesive polyurethane bedding between the laps of conventional wood lapstrake planking is a really bad idea. To repair it you might find yourself heating a putty knife with a torch to melt the bond apart. Quite unpleasant. Trust me, I've done it.

But then there are situations where those high-tech beddings are just what the doctor ordered, such as backbone assemblies. Consider the stem for a small pulling boat. Traditionally, that boat would have had a one-piece grown crook for a stem. As crooks became unavailable, an alternate stem was developed that was assembled from fitted and bolted pieces. These pieces shrink and swell at different rates, which precludes effective rigid gluing. Stopwaters can be installed between the pieces to prevent water from working its way through the joint, but they can lose efficacy, and eventually water might get in. To take that stem out to repair the leaks would require intensive surgery, probably involving replacing the entire stem assembly. In this case, one of the flexible/adhesive concoctions is a fine alternative. The pliable compound will follow any contortions of the stem components and still keep things leak-free (usually).

There are the situations that can go either way. Centerboard trunks come to mind. A good argument can be made that they should be bedded to the keel with a nonadhesive product, so that when they start to leak, the bolts can be removed and the trunk easily taken out, rebedded, and reinstalled. Of course, a counter argument could be made that, if the trunk bed logs were bedded in that flexible adhesive, it wouldn't leak in the first place. Your call on this one.

APPLICATION

Whatever the compound you use, there are a few general rules:

- Bedding compound is not intended to make up for defective joinery. Fits should be as good as if you were joining them dry.

- When rebedding, have both surfaces clean and dry. Scrape away every bit of old caulking and contaminants and, if in doubt, use a solvent/degreaser on the surfaces to be bonded.

- The consistency of bedding compound is relatively thick and will resist squeezing out and allowing the joint to close up. Oil-based bedding can be thinned sparingly. To avoid overapplication, spread with a putty knife, then use a notched trowel-like device such as a hacksaw blade (as though you were laying bathroom tile) to ensure a uniform thin spread.

- To avoid misalignment of holes in an assembly that will be bedded and bolted, clamp up the assembly dry first and bore for the bolt holes. Then remove the clamps, butter on the bedding, reclamp, and insert and tighten the bolts.

- After the fasteners are tightened, bedding compound may continue to ooze out of the joint for a time. Many builders will then retighten the fasteners. That's a mistake, because it breaks the waterproof seal that has formed around the screws. To get a good joint and avoid excessive "squeeze-out," use only a thin coating of compound, then tighten the fasteners down snug and leave them alone.

- When installing butt blocks, use oil-based bedding so that repairs can be made. Paint the adjoining wood so that it does not absorb the oils from the bedding.

- To avoid unwelcome surprises, experiment to ensure that paints and varnishes will cure over the compound, and that it will not attack plastics.

- When applying synthetic compound, wear gloves; to minimize cleanup, mask the edges of your work. Pull the tape before the stuff starts to skin. Work clean: these goops can mysteriously migrate to your varnish, decks, rails, chair, coffee cup, car . . .

WHAT TO USE?

When choosing what kind of product to use you will always find a dynamic tension between repairability, durability, and some other considerations. Let's take a closer look at the candidates. (See Appendix B for sources of supply.)

Historic and Traditional Elixirs

Back in antediluvian days, the mechanic had the choice of a number of classic compounds: white lead paste, red lead paint, soft copper paint, pine tar, and reinforced black roof-patching tar to name just a few. While these concoctions were efficacious (and still are), they have their drawbacks. The lead-based products are now difficult to come by in some localities, and maintaining a good finish over tar can be problematic at best.

Next came the "boatyard bedding" compounds. These oil-based, flexible, semipaste potions offered consistency and ease of use. Early versions were enhanced with the pernicious preservative named pentachlorophenol, whose effects are deleterious to both fungus and humans.

Today's oil-based bedding compounds are thankfully free of the noxious chemical. They are also particularly user-friendly. They are not overly messy, and whatever mess does occur can be scraped up with a putty knife and thinner on a rag. They don't even smell bad.

With the consistency of peanut butter, and natural or greenish-tan in color, these modern boatyard bedding compounds are flexible and nonadhesive, making for easy disassembly. They should be used as a gasket compound between two pieces that are held together with mechanical fastenings. They can also be used between layers of double planking. The stuff dries fairly hard and it can be painted over after it has skinned over. Joined wood surfaces need to be sealed with paint to prevent them from sucking the compound's juices out and causing it to dry out prematurely.

All the brand-name products are pretty much the same in application. One may be a little thicker in the can than another, but they can be thinned slightly to the desired "spreadability."

THE STUFF IN THE TUBES

As opposed to the simple oil-based compounds, these polymers never dry out and they stay flexible for a very long time. There are a plethora of potions available: polysulfides, polyurethane, polyethers, silicones, and more. There is quite a bit of difference between the chemical formulations and even within brands. Curing time, strength, adhesion, and even cleanup solvents can all vary. What they all have in common is that they are "one part" and come in a tube. Looking at the panoply of goops and deciding which one is best for you can be daunting. Perhaps it is best to use the same approach as when hunting for wild mushrooms—i.e., you don't have to know everything about all of them; you just have to know everything about the one you are going to eat (or in this case, use). And if you're not sure, ask someone who does, such as the manufacturer.

Polysulfide

Polysulfide compounds have been around for many years. Polysulfide is basically a synthetic rubber with decent adhesive characteristics. It bonds well to most surfaces (even teak) and is nonshrinking and flexible. Polysulfide compounds make a much better bond with wood than silicone, but not as strong as the industrial strength polyurethane. That makes them a good candidate for repairable bedding situations. They can be painted over.

Some one-part polysulfide compounds, such as 3M Marine Sealant 101, cure by exposure to oxygen, while others, such as BoatLIFE Life Caulk, cure by exposure to water. For water-curing compounds, a base material is mixed with a dry catalyst and a desiccant. When the

stuff is pushed from the tube, the desiccant picks up moisture from the air, which causes the catalyst to dissolve and initiates the chemical action between the catalyst and the base material. Cure time is dependent on temperature and humidity. Polysulfide compounds can have a rather distinctive sulfurous aroma until they cure.

Generally speaking, polysulfides should not be used to bed plastics, so check with the manufacturer before any such attempts. Cleanup can be done with mineral spirits or lacquer thinner.

Polyurethane

Polyurethane compounds are best known in the boat shop by either their product name or number—Sikaflex (291) or 3M 5200. Generally speaking, the polyurethanes should be considered an adhesive first and a sealant/bedding second. Tougher than a boiled owl, they are flexible and make a robust and tenacious bond between materials. Although the bond can be cut with a knife, razor blade, or piano wire, it's generally best to use it only for assemblies you wish to consider essentially permanent. About the only things these compounds will not adhere to are nylon, teflon, most rubber, and polypropylene.

To address differing construction demands, manufacturers offer modifications of their basic polyurethane compounds. For example, 3M has introduced its 4200 compound that is certainly rugged, but less strong than its 5200, so that parts have a better chance of being taken apart for repair. Then there is the matter of cure time. Many polyurethanes are fairly slow curing, which can be an advantage when working on time-consuming assemblies. Basically, cure time depends on air temperature and humidity: the more moisture, and the warmer it is, the faster the material will cure. Some manufacturers have adjusted their products to either speed up or slow down the cure. 3M has its 5200 Fast Cure that is said to be tack-free in two hours and cured in 24. Going the other way, Sikaflex's 291 LOT promises a longer open working time: three to four hours, as opposed to an hour or so with 291.

Some polyurethanes may have compatibility problems with plastics, so it is best to check the manufacturer's specifications before using. Sikaflex 295 is designed as an adhesive for Lexan windows and as a UV-resistant sealant.

To get a good bond, these compounds do need a sound base. Make sure all surfaces are clean and dry and free of contaminants before application. In certain instances, a cleaner and/or primer is recommended. Check with the manufacturer.

Polyurethane compound can be cleaned up from your work area with mineral spirits, and from your hands with citrus hand cleaner.

Some paints (especially alkyd-based paints) have difficulty curing when applied to polyurethane. The only way to be absolutely sure of compatibility is to make a test panel on which you can try your coating over some cured compound.

Polyether

3M manufactures a polyether-based product called 4000 UV. The compound cures to a firm, rubbery, waterproof seal. It is similar to their 4200 in strength (meaning that it can be taken apart), but it is more UV resistant (so that its white color remains more white) and it will bond to metal better than many polyurethanes.

Cleanup can be done with alcohol, acetone, or citrus cleaner.

Silicones

Silicones are most often associated with bathtub and fish tank installations, but there are some limited marine bedding applications. While some silicones are suitable for underwater use, generally, they are best used in above-the-waterline applications. They have difficulty accepting paint or varnish: indeed they can contaminate the surfaces that they touch.

Silicones have little adhesive quality and can best be thought of as a gasket compound like the oil-based beddings. On the upside, they are flexible, they won't attack plastics, and they work well for bedding hardware on already finished surfaces.

BoatLIFE makes a product called Life Seal, which is a blend of silicone and polyurethane. It has better adhesion than straight silicone, yet it can be removed without blasting. It can be used on plastics such as ABS and Lexan. It is not paintable.

· 18 ·

Boat Finishes

The look of the final paint or varnish on a boat is dependent on a number of factors, such as the smoothness and quality of the hull surface beneath, the conditions under which the finish is applied, and the quality of the products used. Let's take a look at some of these.

Too much of a good thing?

FILLING, SURFACING, AND FAIRING

Counterbored fastening holes, shallow gouges, and imperfections and low areas can be filled with a number of products before paint is applied. These are the moral equivalent of auto body putty and are not intended for structural repairs. They range from "surfacing putty"—a fast-drying compound used right out of the can—to the two-part epoxy putties (both store-bought and shop blended varieties) and the fast-curing vinyl ester compound with glass bubbles—a fast-sanding first cousin to the auto body shop "Bondo." These are for use over unpainted wood. To fill spots where there are things such as shallow dings and pulled grain, there is trowel cement. This is the boatbuilder's feathering compound. The stuff sands well and is for use only over painted wood.

If you are using varnish on a surface, all imperfections will show, so quality workmanship is paramount. You should sand in line with the wood grain and fill fastening holes with bungs (plugs). Be sure to line up the grain of the bung with the surrounding wood.

In preparation for either paint or varnish, sand the wood to perfection with 80-grit sandpaper and remove all the dust with a tack rag.

PAINTING CONDITIONS

While the ideal painting and varnishing conditions are like those in an auto body shop, few boatshops have them. If you are working indoors, clean the area up as much as possible and avoid running shop tools for as long as possible before finishing. Some builders will wet down the floor to discourage dust. Try to restrict breezes in the shop but not to the detriment of good ventilation. Good light is essential to see what you are doing. Overhead light is great, if combined with side lighting (such as reflector lamps) so it is easy to see where the wet and dry areas are, and any runs. Beware of overhead hanging fluorescent shop lamps–they can harbor a Sahara's worth of dust on top. Vacuum them down or suspend plastic to protect the boat. When painting (or varnishing), get into the habit of looking back at the area just coated to check where you have left off and for imperfections such as runs, pinholes, and uncoated areas.

If working outside, look for "shirt sleeve" temperatures and settled weather without the threat of rain. Avoid fog, wind (which kicks up dust and dries the paint prematurely), and direct sun (which can cause poor brushing conditions, prevent the paint from "leveling" or flowing properly, and even cause the finish to blister). Also, plan to stop outdoor painting by midafternoon to allow for any evening fog.

With the hull and a place to work prepared, you are ready to start, almost. Before you pop the lid off that can, there is a bit more to do to ensure a good-looking job. The following is a look into the paint locker at some of the products you will need.

MODIFIERS

Most oil-based paints and varnishes are not designed to be used straight out of the can, but must be amended with other liquids to allow them to flow better and to control the speed of drying. Which to use depends a great deal on the weather. Here are your primary options:

- Thinner is a fast evaporating solvent that improves drying in cold conditions.
- Brushing liquid or retarder is a special slow evaporating thinner useful in warm weather and windy conditions. It extends drying time to allow for proper flow of the finish and permits brush marks to settle and cover evenly. Not all thinners use the same chemical formulation. Some have aggressive solvents and can attack alien (i.e., not the same brand) paints. To be on the safe side, use the type and brand of thinner recommended by the manufacturer.
- Japan Drier is another, somewhat mysterious, amendment. It is designed to speed the drying of oil-based paint and varnish. It is generally used when the weather is damp or cool.

SEALERS AND STAINS/FILLERS

Some woods need to be treated with a sealer prior to painting. Open-grained woods such as mahogany need to be prefilled to provide a consistent, smooth surface for a good finish. Bare fir plywood has a special need for presealing as it often incorporates both hard-grained, winter-harvested wood and softer-grained, summer-harvested wood in a single panel face. These woods absorb paint at different rates, causing dried paint to have high and low spots. To that end, one can apply a clear sealer that will allow uniform coating after a light sanding off of wood "fuzz."

Even after being sealed, open-grained woods can take forever to fill to a uniformly smooth surface with straight varnish. That's where the paste stain and wood fillers come in. These are formulated to do exactly as the name suggests. The product is worked into mahogany to fill its open grain, while at the same time, staining all the wood to a uniform color.

Undercoaters are heavy bodied paints designed to provide an even base color, fill porous grain, and create a smooth but durable surface for good adhesion of the finish coats. Sanding surfacers are heavily pigmented paints that fill grain and small surface imperfections. Undercoaters can attract unwanted moisture that can cause problems for subsequent paint coats, so it is important to almost totally sand them off until the coat is almost translucent.

PAINTS AND VARNISHES

Despite the allure of Mercedes-quality sheen and durability, there is little need for high-tech, high-price, bulletproof, two-part finishes on traditional boats. Not only are they finicky to apply, but the paints simply don't look right. Standard, low-gloss, one-part marine enamels work fine. The paints are flexible, are abrasion resistant, cover well, and are easy to apply. Some builders have had good luck using porch and deck enamel as an alternative to marine paint.

The materials used for brightwork on a boat are more persnickety than paint. They require more preparation and more coats. There are, however, some situations where the extra work is worth it: varnished wood is elegant when used as an interior for a canoe, on a bright finished strip canoe, or as accent trim in an otherwise painted hull. The key here is to use a top-quality product with a high solids content with strong ultraviolet resistance.

Mixing

There is little joy in mixing paints and other finishes. Scientific tests (perhaps performed by Einstein) have indicated that when one is stirring either paint or epoxy, time actually slows down to the point where a minute can approach an hour in length. Despite that anomaly, good stirring is essential to getting a good finish. Poor mixing of paint can lead to variable consistency—thin at first, and thick later—and can cause runs and sags and even lead to the paint drying in different shades.

One thing you can do to get a good mix is to pour the top third of the liquid into a separate container. With a wide stirrer, mix both containers using a lifting motion to capture and blend the heavier solids from the bottom. After thoroughly mixing, blend the two containers back together and continue mixing. Remember to stir the can every now and then while applying the paint, and to provide lip drain holes around the lip of the can by poking holes in the bottom of the lip with an ice pick or nail.

To avoid bubbles in varnish, do not shake it, and keep stirring to a minimum. That said, consult the manufacturer's specific recommendations on the can. Some products, such as satin finish varnish, require regular stirring.

Avoiding Contamination

It is a good idea to strain varnish before using it. Standard cone-shaped paper-and-mesh filters work well. Paint and varnish brushes can pick up a lot of dust and detritus while the finish is being applied. If you tip off or wipe your brush into the original container, eventually you will end up applying a nonskid surface. To reduce this interesting phenomenon, after thoroughly stirring, pour a portion of your finish into a separate painting container and seal the original can. Then tip the brush into a third can. By using a separate can to paint from you can vary the amount of thinner in that can without changing the mix in the original can.

A FEW APPLICATION SCHEDULES

Once you have gotten all your materials together you are ready to start work. There are many different schools of finishing. The following are just a couple of approaches to applying paint and varnish.

Painting a Bare-Wood Hull

To paint a bare-wood hull, begin by sanding with 80-grit production paper to bring everything up to a uniform surface. You can pick up any dust with a tack cloth. Next apply one coat of undercoat (or sanding filler) and then sand lightly. Fill any minor imperfections with an easy sanding trowel cement, and then sand and tack. Once that is done, apply a second coat of undercoat, and sand and tack any dust. Finally, apply two coats of enamel.

Applying Varnish over New Wood

To apply varnish over new wood, begin by sanding with 80-grit production paper, and then tack the surface. Next apply sealer. Then apply filler stain and work it in well and let it dry. Once this step is complete, coat with thinned varnish (10%) or sealer, let it dry, and then very lightly sand with 220-grit paper. Apply a second coat, full strength, let it dry overnight, and then sand and tack it. Finally, repeat the operation—apply, dry, and sand—for at least three more coats.

As an alternative, natural wood can be left unfilled and unstained. That will probably require two more coats. In recent years, other products have been developed to speed the varnishing process. Billed as "wood finishes," they are designed to build coats quickly and easily, one a day without sanding in between. After the desired thickness has been built, it can be overcoated with standard varnish.

ALTERNATIVES

Looking for an alternative to varnish? Manufacturers have come up with a number of different potions that produce finishes that are similar to varnish, with good ultraviolet protection, but are much easier to apply. Some products to consider are Epifanes Rapid Clear (a modified alkyd/resin with strong ultraviolet protection), Armada Wood Preservative (a microporous, translucent oil alkyd resin finish), and Sikkens Cetol Marine (semitransparent and imparts a color similar to antique spar varnish).

Then there is the old-time oil finish. This is usually mixed up at home according to the following recipe: one quart of turpentine, one quart boiled linseed oil, half pint of pine tar, half pint of Japan drier. This is a very traditional, easy to apply finish. It also smells great. Just make sure your tradition calls for a dark gray or black interior as that is the color that this finish eventually imparts.

Speaking of linseed oil (but this goes for other oils as well), a pile of oily rags can self-ignite and burn your shop (and everything connected to it) down. Hang the rags on the line or burn them, but never keep them in the shop.

PAINT AND VARNISH OVER EPOXY

If you have an epoxy-covered hull, most of your preparation work has been done. Before getting ready to coat the hull, check to see that there is no amine blush. This residue is a waxy byproduct of the epoxy hardener that will feel greasy to the finger. It is water-soluble and must be removed before you coat the hull with varnish or paint. Some builders recommend removing the blush with clean, warm water and a "Scotchbrite" type scrubbing pad. The hull should be rinsed well, toweled dry, and rechecked for greasy areas.

Next, prepare the surface for coating by giving it a quick sanding with 220-grit sandpaper. Vacuum the dust and tack the hull with a water-dampened rag. Seal any nonepoxy-covered wood trim so that the finish will build at the same rate as the epoxy-covered wood.

If you have any concerns about whether your paint will cure on the hull, coat a test panel with the same brand of epoxy and run some experiments.

FINISHING AS YOU GO

While the matter of finishing can be put off until the boat is completed, many people prefer starting when the hull has been planked and framed. Why? Painting (like filing income tax forms) is a tedious business and can be overwhelming if left to the last minute. Doing it in bits and pieces seems to make things easier. Also, the paint (or varnish) hardens and protects the surface from damage and shrinkage while allowing you to seal areas such as under a deck or in lockers that would be difficult (if not impossible) to reach if the job were done later.

RUMINATIONS ON VARNISH

There is something about brightwork that stirs emotions in a boat owner. For some, it is the signature of elegance on a classic hull. It provides a crystal clear finish that is like tranquil spring water over blemish-free tropical hardwoods. For some people, the application can be a near spiritual ritual. Exotic boar hair brushes are carefully combed and coiffed. An alchemist's cupboard filled with amendments, thinners, reducers, driers, fillers, and tack rags is assembled. Ultraviolet filter charts and weather oracles and prognosticators are eagerly consulted; the paint room is carefully purged of dust and insects, and offset lighting is arranged. Then, with measured strokes, the resinous amalgam is flowed, maintaining the sacred wet edge, over the meticulously prepared woodwork.

For others, varnish is the great Satan of finishes. It is a task filled with tedium and frustration. Horror stories of implanted brush hairs, small embedded boulders, anomalous flat regions, holidays and oozing runs abound. Horizontal surfaces are barely tolerable; vertical ones are beyond the pale. For these apostates of the bright finish faith, the notion of switching to gray deck paint has great appeal.

Is there no hope for the committed varnish phobic?

Perhaps. Many of the woes in applying the clear stuff can be tracked to the brush. Good quality brushes are expensive, take maintenance, and require skill to avoid applying either too much or too little coating. Replacing the brush with a more efficient application device would go a long way toward making the job more tolerable.

An example of such an implement is the yellow high-density polyurethane roller cover that is commonly used for epoxy application. (The gray foam rollers sold down at the hardware store are less suitable, as the foam is prone to becoming unstuck from its cardboard tube and affixing itself to the newly varnished surface like a large garden slug.) The quality of the polyurethane foam seems to meter out just the right amount of finish that is neither too heavy nor too light. The roller also allows for much faster application of the varnish.

To begin, cut in the edges of a manageable portion of the job with a conventional or foam brush. Then you can fill the acreage in between with the roller—just like painting a wall at home. (To avoid entrapping air bubbles, be sure to thoroughly saturate the roller with varnish.)

Lap marks and residual bubbles can be quickly removed with a homemade foam brush. This can be easily constructed by slicing up another yellow epoxy roller cover on the band saw into roughly 2″ sections. Then resaw those sections along their length so that you have a selection of foam half moons. These segments can be either attached to a homemade handle or just grabbed by an edge. Like the full roller, the new brush should be well saturated with varnish. Then you can quickly draw or strike the brush over the newly rolled varnish, pulling any offending bubbles or excessive amounts of liquid finish from the surface. Then roll out another section and repeat with the brush. And that's all there is to it.

To get the hang of the technique, practice on a sample plywood panel set vertically.

Does this mean that you now can get away without sanding, tacking, staining, or adding thinners, and arrogantly apply the stuff on a sunny day in a dust storm? Will it make having a varnished deck practical? Nope. But it may just be the thing that saves that elegant stripper canoe or treasured Chris-Craft from being painted out in good navy fashion.

Paint Coverage

The approximate square-foot coverage of paint or varnish will appear on the label of the can. To compute coverage of the surface of the boat:

Topsides = (length overall + beam) × average freeboard × 2

Bottom, heavy displacement hull = (waterline length × beam × draft) × .75

Bottom, light-displacement hull = (waterline length × beam × beam) × .50

Deck = (length of deck × beam) – (area of deck structures) × .75

Source: 2005 The Mariner's Book of Days

BORATES

Protecting your vessel against rot used to mean applying coal-tar, creosote, pentachloraphenol, or copper naphenate. All these potions smelled bad, stained the wood, and were unpleasant to use—but they worked. You could also use timber that had been pressure-treated with copper arsenates. But after laboratory and medical research demonstrated the toxicity to mammals of these products, governments began regulating or banning their use. In search of a new, effective wood preservative that wasn't hard to obtain, bad for their health, and bad for the environment, some boatbuilders turned to an old idea: borate wood preservatives.

Borates are a salt or an ester of boric acid, which is derived from naturally occurring borax, a white, crystalline mineral salt. Their use as a wood preservative goes back at least to 1875, when their value in British ship construction was noted in "A Treatise on the Origin, Progress, Prevention and Cure of Dry Rot in Timber," by Thomas Allen Britton. They became popular in Australia and New Zealand during the last century, but it is only recently that they have begun to catch on in the United States.

Borates offer highly effective protection against wood-eating fungi (and insects), but not against mildew fungi. They penetrate and diffuse readily through wood, have low volatility and low toxicity to humans, and are colorless and odorless. Writing in *WoodenBoat* magazine, Professor Richard Jaegels said that the greatest potential for the use of borates was in areas above the waterline, especially in cabins. High humidity in enclosed spaces often leads to wood decay from the inside out, he said, and borate-treated wood that is well painted should resist this kind of threat from decay fungi.

The most basic borate preservative is simple boric acid, but other formulations, such as disodium octaborate tetrahydrate, have been developed to address particular needs such as chemical stability and improved penetration of wood.

Applying Borates

One of the most positive aspects of any borate preservative is its ease and safety of application. It is usually added to water and stirred, and can be brushed, sprayed, dipped, or even rolled on. The typical schedule calls for two applications.

If the wood is already wet through, the borates will be drawn deep into the wood. For dry wood, heating the mix will aid in penetration, but it does not appear to be necessary. Wood may be wrapped in plastic to decrease evaporation and increase penetration time. Another way to lengthen the drying time of the solution is to thicken the liquid borate with polyethylene glycol.

Borates are also available in solid rod form for commercial pest control applications. The end grain of large timbers can be bored to accept these rods, which will dissolve when and if they get wet. It is important to note, however, that what water will give, it will also take away. Leeching of the borate from the wood is a concern, and treated wood subject to flowing water should be protected with a good coating of paint or varnish.

· 19 ·
Tools

Can one have too many tools? Theoretically there is a limit, but modern science hasn't yet been able to determine it. For boatbuilders, however, the number of tools required is few. Consider that in remote regions, mechanics have been building vessels for millennia without the latest in high-tech, laser driven, whiz-bang technology. What they do have is a limited number of quality tools that are kept in good repair and, most importantly, are sharp.

As far as availability of tools, it's the best of times, it is the worst of times. Not so long ago, one could go to a corner hardware store with oiled floors run by a knowledgeable proprietor and buy reliable hand tools right off the shelf. They had to be of good quality since customers made their living with them. There were brand names you could trust, and shop classes were still taught in school.

Nowadays, everyone uses the power tools hawked on home-improvement TV shows, shop classes are on the endangered species list, and corporate decision makers have found it easier to buy venerated manufacturers' names and apply the trusted brand to sub-quality tools and pop them into bins. On the other hand, the poor availability of high-quality hand tools in most hardware stores and building centers has inspired a number of entrepreneurs to open specialty tool stores and catalog operations that cater to the discerning craftsperson. There are new manufacturers that are building high-quality replicas of hand tools that were dropped from the big manufacturers' lines years ago. Other outfits are even developing and inventing new hand tools.

Some tool prices are very high, but the old adage "you get what you pay for" applies in spades with woodworking tools. One very good plane will shave circles around a pile of discount paperweight versions. Some imported implements are diamonds in the rough, with coarse castings and funky paint jobs, but good basic design and tool steel underneath. With a bit of tuning and honing, these can develop into very high quality instruments. And then there are flea markets and tag sales. These places can be a treasure trove of wonderful old tools just waiting to come out of premature retirement. Antique stores are also a possibility. Avoid ones that display their spokeshaves and block planes in locked glass cases and sell books titled *Iron Hand Tools–A Golden Investment Opportunity*.

Only a few handheld power tools are necessary. They should be good quality and are probably best purchased new. Heavy, sparking, and sputtering flea market specials are rarely a bargain. New tools are lighter and better designed and insulated against shock.

Below is a list of useful tools. Some items, such as the caulking gun and stapler, are already in the average household waiting to be given new tasks. The ones with asterisks are must-haves, even for building kit boats. The rest come in very handy and are worth acquiring over time.

Large rabbet planes like the one shown are available with an array of accessories, such as fences to make sure the tool rides straight and parallel to the edge of the workpiece, and shaped irons to plane various profiles. The small, bullnosed rabbet plane can be used to plane an L-shaped channel in the edge of a board, or a U-shaped channel away from an edge.

The convex irons on these backing planes are used to hollow out the interior face of carvel planking. You'll find some planes with a simple hardwood wedge to hold the iron in place, but the mechanical components on these planes make them much easier to adjust.

HAND TOOLS

- *Chisels. A set with long blades ¼″, ½″, ¾″, and 1″ wide. Medium quality is fine. These do get beat up running into fasteners and such.

- *Wooden mallet. To drive the chisels (never use a metal hammer) and encourage recalcitrant fits. May also be used with a caulking iron.

- Caulking iron. #0 is a good size for most small carvel seams and lapstrake rabbet seams. Found at good marine suppliers.

- Caulking wheel. Occasionally found in antique stores. Easily made up in the shop.

- Hand planes. Standard length jack and long jointer.

- Rabbet plane. For cutting and finishing off rabbets in stem, keel, and lapstrake planking.

- *Block plane. Low angle is best, 12–13°. For all-around trimming and plank fashioning.

- Backing out plane. A round-bottomed wooden plane with a curved iron that is used for hollowing the interior of carvel planking. This is occasionally found at antique stores or can be made by modifying a wooden hand plane.

- Spokeshave. For general shaping.

- *Sharpening stone. There are many types—natural and manufactured stone, water stones, and diamond stones. All work and should be used often.

- *Hammer. For general nail driving and lots more.

- Small ball peen hammer. For peening rivets, and drift pins.

- End cutting nippers. A long-handled pliers with cutters aligned like giant toenail clippers.

- Bucking iron and rivet setting tool. Used for fashioning rivets. The iron is used to support or back up the nail head. The set drives the rove or burr over the shank of the nail. The nippers cut off the nail beyond the rove. These can be bought or homemade. The iron can be an auto body iron. The set can be a piece of iron rod with a long hole drilled in the center of its core for a few inches of the length.

A spokeshave is invaluable for shaving surfaces where a plane won't fit.

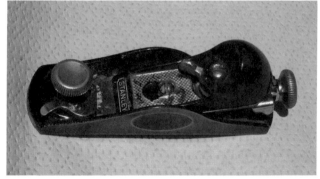

A low-angle block-plane (the iron is set at about 12° or 13° from the horizontal) is needed for trimming end-grain.

Use a wooden mallet, not a metal hammer, to drive your nice, wood-handled woodworking chisels.

There are all kinds of sharpening mechanisms on the market. One of the most effective and inexpensive is a simple jig that maintains the blade at the correct angle as you roll it back and forth across the stone.

- Bevel gauge. Use a large one for lapstrake, and a small one for carvel plank. Used everywhere, including fitting bulkheads, floors, knees, breasthooks, and thwarts.
- *Hand saw. Either a western style, that cuts on the forward stroke, or a Japanese-style that cuts on the back stroke.
- Hack saw. For trimming off bolts and cutting metal stock to size.
- *"4-in-1" rasp. Just like it sounds. One side is round and the other is flat; one end of each side is fine toothed and the other is coarse.
- Putty knife. For application of putties and gunk, and removing squeezed out putties and gunk.
- Heavy duty stapler. For pattern making, strip planking, and tacking the plans to the wall.
- *Heavy duty scissors. For cutting fiberglass fabric.
- *Linesman pliers. For twisting those stitch-and-glue wire sutures.
- *Lots of C-clamps and spring clamps. For countless clamping situations.
- Pipe clamps. For wide gluing jobs such as fabricating transom panels.
- *Canvas tool apron. Help keep those tools handy where you can find them.
- Hand screwdriver. Oval-handled versions will give you the best leverage.
- Brace and bit. For slowly but surely putting large screws in and taking them out. Much better than a screw gun for this purpose.
- "Yankee" screwdriver. Yes, they still make them. A spiral, automatic screwdriver. Archaic? Perhaps,

but also very handy. The original cordless screwdriver.

- *Sharp paint scraper. Mostly for scraping glue instead of sanding.
- Plastic squeegee. For shaping and forming epoxy.
- Ice picks or awls. For starting screws in wood, aligning holes, testing for rot, and holding lofting battens in place.
- Chalk line. For establishing a long straight line.
- Adjustable wrench (i.e., a crescent wrench). For general quick-and-dirty nut tightening.
- Socket set and ratchet. For precision tightening where you don't want to round the nuts.
- Cold chisel. Various and sundry metalworking tasks.
- Tap and dies. A few sizes for either cleaning up beat-up threads on bolts or for making your own bolts out of bronze rod.

Unlike Western-style saws that cut when you push them into the wood, Japanese-style saws like these cut on the pull stroke. Many boat carpenters find them easier to control for fine work.

A big mallet like this is appropriate for driving caulking on between the heavy planks of cruising-size boats and ships. To caulk the lighter planks on small craft, you'll want a smaller mallet that lends itself to a bit more finesse. You'll also need a variety of caulking irons, including different widths and straight and curved blades.

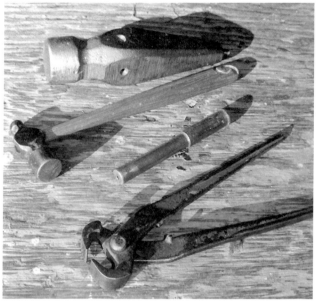

Riveting gear: a nipper, ball peen hammer, and bucking iron.

Handheld propane torch. To heat and temporarily anneal metal to make it less brittle so that it can be bent (like brass stem bands) or peened (as when making drift pins).

MEASURING TOOLS

- *25′ measuring tape (¾″ wide or wider). Used all the time for everything from lofting to launching. Get a good one.
- *Combination square. Used for drawing lines square and as a marking gauge.
- Framing square. Used for lofting, jig setup, taking lines, and all-around boat construction.
- *Spirit level (bubble level). Used all the time to keep things on the level.
- Plumb bob. Like the level, it is used a lot: setting up molds, plumbing stem and transom, determining frame locations, taking lines, and more.
- Good quality dividers and pencil compass. For lofting, spiling planks, and fitting bulkheads.

ELECTRICAL HAND TOOLS

- *Cordless hand drill/driver. Used all the time. It's worth buying a good one.
- Drill bits: A set of twist bits, screw driving bits, and countersink/counterbore bits.

- Saber or jigsaw. An underappreciated tool. A good quality saber saw will do much of the work of a band saw at a fraction of the cost. Use it to cut out planks, bulkheads, circular holes, and more.
- Circular saw. Like the jig saw, the circular saw can stand in for a standing power tool: the table saw. In some cases, it is the tool of choice as it can make controllable long cuts that would be dangerous when done single-handedly with a table saw. Again, quality matters.
- *Block or palm sander. For light and controllable sanding.
- Router and bits. A plethora of uses, such as inlays for plank repairs, mortising for keys or tenon joints, shaping, rounding, and making strip planking. Get at least 1½ horsepower.
- Handheld power planer. For topical application of planing—spars, sides of keels.
- Extension cord(s). Good quality, 14-gauge wire minimum.
- Angle grinder. 4½″. For shaping metal and cut off use. Always use eye protection.
- *Wet/dry shop vacuum. A boon for general shop cleaning. Much better (albeit louder) than a home vacuum for removing wood debris and dust.
- *Boom box—preferably one with a bent antenna, knobs with hardened glue, and the ability to play tapes.

These handy but hard-to-find clamps (available from Conant Engineering; see Appendix B) are useful to edge-set planks tight against their previously installed neighbors. The wooden-handled screw clamps the tool against a frame, while the T-handled screw does the edge-setting.

STATIONARY EQUIPMENT

Small boats can be built with hand tools alone. But if you are getting into larger craft or building more than one, standing power tools are worth considering. They don't have to be expensive, have digital readouts, or have satellite guidance systems.

Power tools are not your friends. Allies of convenience, yes, but buddies, no. They are just waiting for you to let your guard down once to pounce. Hence it is extremely important to learn how to use standing machines properly. Take your time when working and plan out every operation. Avoid distractions: turn off that cell phone—they'll call back if it's important. Stand out of the "firing line" of the machine. Keep only the minimum of blade exposed needed to do the job. Don't feed the machine any more than it can handle. Use lumber roller supports (dead man) when working by yourself. Wear face, dust, and ear protection. Don't let clutter build up around the machines. And don't work while tired, sick, or angry or after a beer (or two). And quit work when tired. Pushing late in the night will only cause mistakes that take half the next day to correct.

- 14" band saw. This is the boat-shop standard. Small enough to not take up much room, heavy and powerful enough to cut just about anything you want. If you only have money for one shop tool, this is the one.
- Thickness planer. If you are building a traditional hull, you will need stock in various thicknesses.

While this work can be outsourced, it is better if it can be done on site. A small standing planer (13"–15") is great. The smaller (12") "portables" also do a surprisingly good job.

- Table saw. Great for milling up long stock such as keels, frames, centerboards, and transom boards. It needn't be fancy but should have enough power to run a 10" blade.
- Drill press. Not absolutely necessary but handy for boring repeated holes in wood or metal and for cutting bungs (plugs).
- Grinding wheel. A bench-mounted grinding wheel is quite handy when working up metal parts, fashioning drift pins, and (if equipped with a "cool" grinding wheel) repairing and hollow grinding cutting irons. Always wear eye protection.
- Dust collection system. By its nature, boatbuilding is a dusty business. Especially when you are milling and cutting planking, the shop can quickly come to resemble a collapsed mine shaft. The dust and shavings not only prevent efficient work, but are also unhealthy. Get rid of them with a dust collection system.
- Finally (although nonelectrical and nonpowered): a long workbench complete with a couple of woodworking vises and a metalworking vise goes a long way toward civilizing a boat shop.

SAFETY GEAR

- *Top quality dust and mist masks. Keep nuisance dust out of the lungs.
- *Multipurpose cartridge respirator. Keeps more noxious dust and fumes out of the lungs.
- *Ear protection. Hearing loss is cumulative and can sneak up on you. Wear ear protection when working around power equipment.
- *Disposable gloves. Either latex or blue nitrile.
- *Chemical resistant gloves. *De riguer* when working with aggressive solvents such as acetone or lacquer thinner.
- *Safety glasses and/or face shield. Absolutely necessary, especially when grinding.
- *First-aid kit. Accidents do happen. Keep the kit well charged with adhesive bandages for the occasional cut and tweezers for splinters.

· 20 ·

Setting Up Shop

After deciding on a design, buying the wood, and rounding up the tools, it's now time to find a place to build the boat. This can be a tall order—especially in colder climates. Alfresco construction is an option—indeed, it may be the only option if the project is large—but it does have its drawbacks. The vicissitudes of sun, rain, and wind can raise the devil with wood, causing it to shrink, warp, and weather. And the onset of winter with hip-high snows and freezing temperatures tends to slow progress considerably.

THE GARAGE SHOP

For many builders, a permanent shop is the best way to go, and the standard two-car garage works well for most small boats: one "bay" for the boat itself, the other for a bench, standing power tools, room for saw horses, lofting boards, lumber racks, and so on. A wooden floor is best—even if the shop is built on a slab. Wood is a lot easier to set up jigs on and, more importantly, much easier on the legs than concrete. A trussed roof will allow for a shop floor that is unencumbered by posts as well as second-story storage of stock. The workbench should run the entirety of the wall. This luxury will permit you to easily scarf and glue up planks, assemble spars, work up oars, and the like. And speaking of indulgence, if building new, install as many windows as possible. It's hard to beat natural light to work by, especially in the dead of winter. As far as electricity goes, figure out how many outlets you

need and double it. The cost is relatively small and convenience and the safety of not having extension cords writhing serpent-like underfoot is worth it.

Consider how you are going to get the boat in and out of the shop. On skids? Maybe you need a loading dock. By trailer? Maybe you need a ramp or at least a ground-level entrance. And while we're getting things in and out, let's consider stock. What happens if you are running an 18' plank through the planer and your building is only 24' long? Incorporating small "doggie doors" on opposing walls will allow you to feed wood in from outside, through the machine and back out through the other door. Again, if building new, now is the time to think insulation and heating plant. It's a lot easier to do it now than to wait until the walls are covered by wood racks, tools, radios, charts, blueprints etc. And one more thing: you might want to consider a dust evacuation system. The price on the equipment has dropped significantly and its use will generate dividends for your health and working efficiency.

PLASTIC SHELTERS

A plastic-covered shelter is another good, low-cost way to go, especially if you or your spouse prefers to continue using the garage, or if you need more room for a bigger project. It will offer protection from the wind and (if properly built) the rain. It will certainly provide enough light, and can be set up with a workbench and adequate (well-grounded) electricity. As these

A plastic-covered shed can be an acceptable workshop, even in winter. Heavy-duty shrink-wrap plastic—the same stuff used for boat covers—is durable and cuts down on constant, annoying flapping.

"greenhouses" tend to be lightly built, care does need to be taken to preclude snow buildup from collapsing the structure. Dead-of-winter working conditions can be rather nippy—especially on overcast days. But if you can time your work for only sunny, wind-free days, temperatures can get quite balmy inside, even without auxiliary heat. Plastic sheds have other limitations as well. They are susceptible to condensation problems.

Well-built (i.e., more than one season) plastic buildings can tie up considerable time and material in their construction. They do not age gracefully. The best they will ever look is when they are first built. And unless you use "greenhouse" quality plastic that has ultraviolet protection, the plastic itself will start to weather and break down in fairly short order. Your exfoliating polyethylene atelier may offer you an opportunity to become acquainted with folks you had not had a chance to meet previously—such as the neighbor whose fancy home overlooks your shop, or perhaps the local code enforcement officer. A possible alternative is one of the prefabricated steel-framed plastic covered garages. These come with ground anchors to keep them from blowing away at inconvenient times and often fly under local building permit radar.

A LOBSTER POT BOAT SHOP

How about a modular, double-sawn-frame lobster pot boathouse? This is an inexpensive, temporary (and hopefully nontaxable) shelter that is light enough for easy assembly, rugged enough to stand up to the elements, and easy to disassemble when the job is done.

This method was developed in a moment of exigency one January for the accommodation of a large mahogany speedboat that had been delivered for repairs just after a major storm. A spot could be cleared beside

The "double-sawn lobster pot boathouse" is strong, is easy to set up and break down, and offers a lot of flexibility.

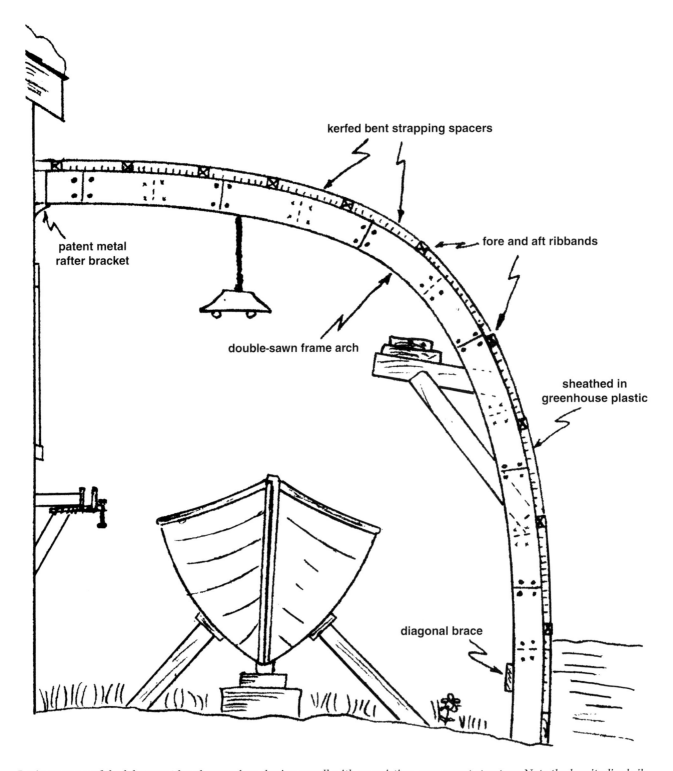

kerfed bent strapping spacers

patent metal
rafter bracket

fore and aft ribbands

double-sawn frame arch

sheathed in
greenhouse plastic

diagonal brace

Basic structure of the lobster pot boathouse when sharing a wall with an existing, permanent structure. Note the longitudinal ribbands (see from the ends) that tie two individual frames together, and the curved, saw-kerfed spacers that keep the ribbands parallel to one another.

the shop and the boat moved into place, but then what? Casting about for an idea, my eyes lit upon a sepia photo on the wall of an early twentieth-century shipyard. Set up on the ways was a series of tugboats under construction, with battens already wrapped around their stout, double-sawn frames, serenely awaiting planking. Of course! Half double-sawn frames could be built production-fashion on the shop floor, using scrap cedar ends left over from planking construction stock, and fastening them together with drywall screws and glue. They could then be erected like flying buttresses over the boat.

With this approach, you have a system of standardized, interchangeable, reusable arches. The units are relatively light, easily assembled and disassembled, and versatile. After the arches are set into place, they need only be connected with wooden strapping, sheathed in plastic, and—*voila!*—an instant boat shop (or nearly so). And when the project is finished, the strapping can be removed and the arches stacked knocked down to await the next project. How many of these modules will you require? Think of them as roof rafters and work accordingly. The greater the span and/or the greater the expected snow load, the more you will need.

Building the Frames

Begin by calculating the height and width of the structure, based on the size of the project. Remember to add plenty of space for a workbench, stationary power tools, and room to move around. Next, clear a space on the shop floor to draw the curve. Start by drawing a base and erecting a perpendicular centerline, much as you would if you were setting up to draw a body plan on the lofting floor. After driving nails at the ends to work against, spring a flexible batten into a curving arch similar to a midships section of a boat. Then stand back and admire your artwork. How does it look? Is there enough slope on the upper side to shed snow and rain, yet still allow headroom to work on deck? Make it a little bigger, because this is the outside dimension. Tweak it until it looks right (sketch in your boat if you have to), and then commit it to the floor with your pencil. Next, draw the inside face of your arched frame, parallel to the first curve. A depth of 6″ to 8″ seems to work well.

Each frame or arch is composed of two layers of curved pieces of 1″ thick wood that is 6″ to 8″ wide. The joints between the individual pieces of the frames should fit tightly, at near right angles to the curve, and be staggered from one side to the other. Since we'll be building these flat on the floor, the joints of the "top" layer should fall roughly halfway between those of the "bottom" layer. When laying out your joints, check that the full depth of the frame can be gotten out of your lumber. The joints may need to be closer in the "turn of the bilge" region.

Okeydoke? Then it's time to start transferring the drawn shapes to the wood by using the old nails-in-repose trick.

We'll start with the piece of frame at the top of the arch. Place 3d box or pot nails every few inches along both of your layout curves so that the heads on the drawn lines and the shafts of the nails are perpendicular to the curve. Next, lay your first piece of stock carefully atop the bed of nails. After checking that all the nail heads are covered by your stock, gingerly climb aboard and squash the board down onto the nails. Removing the board, you'll see a whole lot of nail heads stuck into the bottom of the board in a shape that corresponds to the curve. Remove the nails and using a straightedge and flexible curve, connect the dents and draw in the shape with a pencil. Cut it out on the band saw, label it "A," and there you have the first piece (and pattern) for the frame. Continue this process until you have made and labeled all the pieces for the bottom side of the frame. Huzzah! You're halfway there.

Okay, let's repeat the steps for the pieces of the top side of the frame. Remember, this time, the joints will fall roughly half way between the joints of the bottom half. After making the pieces for the top half, we'll be ready for mass production.

Setting Up the Factory

Using the original master pieces as templates, trace and cut duplicate futtocks for as many frames as needed. For seven frames, cut six more frame section A's, six more section B's, and so on until you've got a whole stack of parts prepared for assembly.

Using any scrap wood you have kicking around the shop, cut up a batch of keeper blocks. These will be screwed down around the perimeter of the frame that is drawn on the floor, turning the drawing into a construction form and keeping the pieces in their rightful place.

Now comes the part we've been waiting for: the high-speed assembly. Plug all the pieces for the bottom side of frame one into place. They should fit just as snug as a bug in between the keeper blocks. For extra security, spread a layer of that yellow carpenters glue on top—like peanut butter in a sandwich. Then plug in the pieces for the top layer.

Then, you can fire up the screw gun and drive plenty of drywall screws through the top layer into the bottom. That's all there is to it! The completed frame

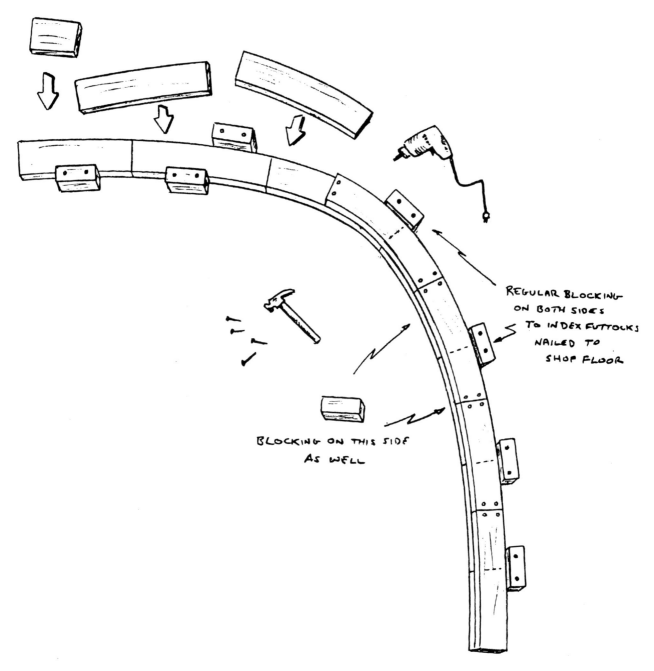

REGULAR BLOCKING
ON BOTH SIDES
TO INDEX FUTTOCKS
NAILED TO
SHOP FLOOR

BLOCKING ON THIS SIDE
AS WELL

Building the boathouse frames. Because the joints of the top and bottom layers are staggered, you can get away with using fairly short pieces of scrapwood for this.

can be lifted out of the form and set aside and a new one can be started.

Ribbands

Now is the best time to determine the location of the fore and aft strapping or ribbands that will tie the whole business together. Lay the frames flat, one on top of the other, so they are dead square. Cut a small piece of strapping stock to use as a marking gauge. Where do the ribbands go? This is basically eyeball stuff, but the idea is to have them fall at regular intervals over the curve of the frame. The more there are, the stronger it will be. You should have more on the top where the greater snow load will be, and less on the sides. Take the ribband gauge and mark the locations along the edge of the top arch. Take a framing

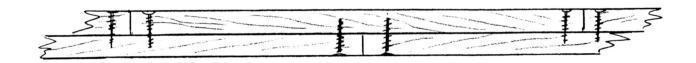

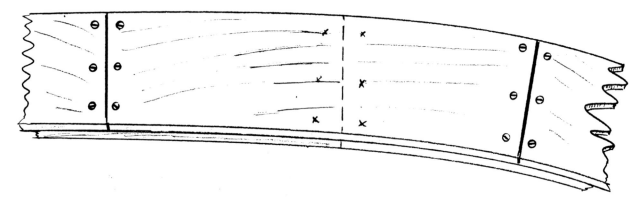

A closer look at the staggered joints.

Installing the spacers is the easiest way to keep the ribbands parallel. The saw kerfs make them easy to bend over the frames. Line up the spacer stock edge to edge, with the ends even, and make the cuts all at once with a circular saw or radial arm saw.

square and bring those marks down square onto the rest of the frames. The ribbands want to be flush with the outside face of the curve, and the easiest way to do this is to make saw kerfed spacers to fit snugly between the ribbands. The kerfs will allow them to be bent and screwed down around the curve.

Assembly

Now it's time to assemble the enclosure. When using the frames against an existing structure, the first job is to install a series of sockets along the wall at predetermined intervals and level heights for the frames to drop into. These can be made of plywood or you can use steel rafter brackets from the lumberyard. These can remain a permanent feature on the building, ready

anytime you need to set the frames up again. Next, drive stakes into the ground and set up a sill board that is as long as the building, level and parallel to the permanent structure. The distance from the building comes from your construction jig.

Begin construction with the center frame. Hoist it up, and plug and fasten it into the socket on the building. Swing the frame out until it is perpendicular with the building, screw fasten it to the bottom of the sill board, and temporarily brace it plumb with diagonals. This arch will be the keystone of the operation as everything will work off of it. Mark the frame locations onto the sill board, measuring out in either direction from the erect frame, and drive stakes and anchor them with screws at each location. Install a few ribbands

It looks a little odd as a free-standing shed, but it works just fine with some minor modifications.

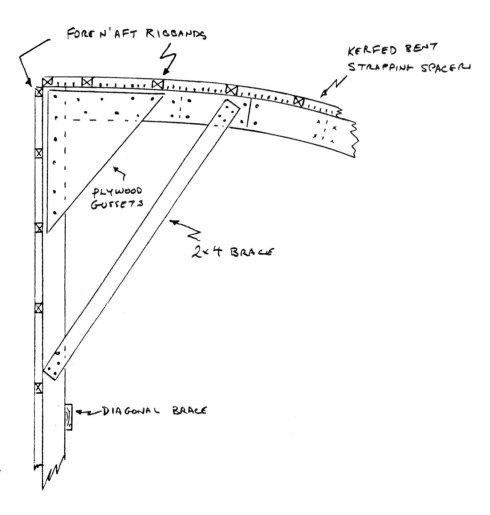

FORE N' AFT RIBBANDS

KERFED BENT STRAPPING SPACERS

PLYWOOD GUSSETS

2×4 BRACE

DIAGONAL BRACE

Bracing for the free-standing version.

into their slots, leaving them to stick out on either side equally.

Then pop another couple of frames into place, one on either side of the first. The sockets will hold the top, the sill will align the bottom, and the ribbands will drop into their notches, indexing the frames. When they are plumb and perpendicular, fasten with screws. Add a few more ribbands and set up a couple more frames. Plumb and fasten as before. Set in a few diagonal braces internally to stiffen the structure and prevent wracking. Then install more ribbands, add more frames, and set more diagonals. The more you add, the stronger the building becomes. After you reach the end of the building, you can frame in the ends, customizing by adding doors, access ports for lumber, or whatever. Don't forget the ribbands. Attach the plastic to the frames with staples, or by nailing strips of wood over the ribbands through the plastic.

What about using the trusses in a free-standing structure? This can be done. Vertical legs need to be added to replace the strength afforded by the adjoining building. Hefty gussets and diagonal bracing are important to resist the pressure of a snow load, and plenty of cross-bracing is needed on the back wall. As with any freestanding plastic building, thought should be given to placement. They should only be set in sheltered locations with an abundance of anchors to the earth.

The Greenhouse Effect

While there are several products that work well for sheathing the building—shrink wrap and reinforced polyethylene to name a couple—it is hard to beat the plastic specifically designed for greenhouses. It is rugged, difficult to tear, and quite resistant to ultraviolet breakdown from the sun—which probably has something to do with its eerie greenish tinge. It also is extremely flexible at low temperatures (I have successfully worked with it at minus 15°C, rolling it out flat without any signs of cracks or other problems) and it's plenty slippery to let snow slide off. As with any roof, a snow load can be a problem, especially a heavy wet snow that is reluctant to slide on its own. Not to worry; pushing against the plastic from the inside will get the snow to move. Just don't forget to do it!

And how does it work for a shop? Just as advertised! You'll find plenty of room for the workbench and storage racks on the vertical wall; lots of space to work on deck; and enough solar heating and sun in February to make you feel like you're in the Bahamas.

· 21 ·

Wood Dust

It is easy to forget how toxic wood dust can be. After all, wood is natural, versatile, and pleasant to work with, it finishes beautifully, and it smells ever so much nicer than polyester. To top it off, if you select the right wood, it is naturally rot resistant. That natural rot resistance is likely due to the natural poisons in the wood.

Wood dust has long been known to be dangerous to your health. Indeed, years ago, workers in western red cedar shake and shingle mills exhibited a disease euphemistically called "cedar lung."

Nonetheless, in the past woodworkers generally maintained a cavalier attitude toward what was considered "nuisance dust." Times have changed, however, and what used to be termed a mere nuisance has turned out to be downright hazardous. The federal government recently updated its list of compounds either "known" or "reasonably anticipated" to cause cancer in humans, and it now includes wood dust as a known human carcinogen. According to the Occupational Safety and Health Administration website, "As a general rule, hardwoods are more hazardous to human health than softwoods. There are exceptions—in particular western red cedar, a softwood, is usually identified as one of the most hazardous to human health. The health effects appear to be related to the concentration of tannin and similar compounds in the wood." Other studies note that the same chemicals that encourage rot resistance can also damage the respiratory tract, causing chronic respiratory disease and asthma.

As if all that natural organic toxicity were not enough, the boatbuilder and repairer also has to contend with organisms such as fungi and mold that grow on the wood and can be released during sawing and sanding. Grinding dust from repairs can also contain particles of polyester and epoxy, as well as detritus from past applications of preservatives such as copper napthanate, creosote, formaldehyde, red lead, and the ever-popular pentachlorophenol. And there is the potential to release arsenic and chromium dust when sawing and milling CCA (Chromated Copper Arsenate) pressure-treated lumber. However skeptical one may be toward governmental studies, the overwhelming weight of evidence and common sense indicate that it is a good idea to limit exposure to airborne particulates in the workplace.

CLEANING IT UP

Vacuum cleaners have come a long way, and the home boatbuilder is no longer sentenced to having to use traditional eardrum splitting Banshee Brand shop vacuums when trying to capture dust. Manufacturers now offer quiet units that feature washable automotive-type filters that promise 99.85% filtration efficiency and even automatically start and stop when the tools are activated. These units can be paired with handheld tools such as orbital sanders so that the vacuum will only run when the sander is turned on.

A tool that will enhance the efficiency of the common shop vacuum is the so-called "trash can cyclone lid," available from several manufacturers. The lid has inlet and outlet openings and is set atop a standard garbage can between the shop vacuum and the dust-collection nozzle, essentially creating a two-stage dust-collection unit. The lid, which has no moving parts, allows the larger and heavier shavings and dust to precipitate out into the garbage can before they reach and foul the impeller and dust collection bags of the shop vacuum.

To further clean the air in the working space, there are now compact portable air cleaners that scavenge from the air fine (as small as 5 microns) dust particles produced from sanding, routing, and sawing.

PROTECTIVE WEAR

After getting the work environment as clean as possible, it is time to properly suit up for the job. For heavy-duty work such as sanding epoxy, you should consider wearing protective Tyvek overalls with the sleeves and pant legs taped closed. Proper ear protection will allow you to work longer and help keep your mind on the work. And eye protection should be worn, in addition to a suitable facemask or respirator.

There is (or should be) quite a bit to consider when selecting the right respirator for the job. Generally speaking, the paper version that can be purchased at the local discount store is not adequate. Before selecting your respirator, you need to know what sort of contaminants you'll be working with. Will you just be sanding new wood or will it be contaminated with fiberglass, epoxy, or lead paints? How heavy will the concentration of dust be? Try the respirator on and find out if it can be properly fitted to your face, and if it is comfortable enough so that you will actually use it. Quality respirators come with a proper instruction sheets, warnings, and use and time limitations, as well as telephone numbers to call with technical questions.

With all that low-cost groundwork done, you are ready go. Not only will you be working in an environment that is healthier, but you will also save hours in tedious cleanup time. Indeed, setting up a dust-safe worksite is a small investment that will pay guaranteed long-term benefits.

FAD (FEDERAL ACRONYM DECODER)

When looking into health and safety issues, you're sure to encounter an alphabet soup of government agencies. Here are a few acronyms to look out for:

- *NIOSH/MSHA stands for the National Institute for Occupational Safety and the Health/Mine Safety and Health Administration. NIOSH is the federal agency responsible for conducting research and making recommendations for preventing work-related illness and injuries.*

- *RELs are the recommended exposure limits for a given material during a workday of up to 10 hours during a 40-hour workweek.*

- *PELs are the permissible exposure limits under the same standards.*

- *OSHA is the Occupational Safety and Health Administration, whose duties include proposing statutes and enforcing laws.*

Part Three

BUILDING TECHNIQUES

*B*oatbuilding is a compendium of operations. Generally speaking, none of them are difficult or high tech—but they must be done right and in the right order. The following chapters offer a sampler of common construction tasks.

▪ 22 ▪

Construction Planning

Boatbuilding, like life, is full of those little moments of regret—if only I had done "X" or "Y," things would have gone a lot easier. The construction of a boat is a continuum, a matrix of interdependent pieces that should be installed at the proper time. That doesn't mean those pieces can't be incorporated out of order (this is called repair), but planning ahead to get it right the first time is certainly more efficacious.

Here is a partial compendium of common miscues, tribulations, and solutions.

THE STEM

With its (usually) complex joinery, rabbets, bevels, and other components, the stem offers ample opportunity for avoidable mistakes.

Many potential difficulties can be dealt with right on the lofting board. Take the time to draw in the complete stem construction: the rabbet, joints, bolts, and stopwaters. This not only assures that you know what you need for stock, and offers an accurate source for patterns, but it also makes it more likely that you'll discover conflicts before they become real problems—like planning to put a bolt right where the stopwater wants to be. The lofting board also makes a dandy construction jig. Small wooden blocks screwed down to the board will immobilize finished pieces while you fit the rest of the assembly to them. No more wrestling loose pieces into submission and wondering if you are getting the fit right.

Of course, patterns represent only two dimensions of a three-dimensional finished product. Patterns are great for tracing shapes onto the stock, aligning the grain of the wood as you would like it, and laying out complex joints. But, alas, if the stock is cut exactly to the drawn pattern line, the very first shaving made with a hand plane to clean up the stock will make the piece too small. Also, the joinery in a stem can be a complex business, and the wood can be hard to work. When fitting the pieces, it is common to get a small gap (say 1/16") on one end of one part of a joint. With little wood to work with, it is easy to say "Oh, the bolts will close it up." And the bolts will, but due to the multiplying effect over the length of the assembly, the top of the stem can end up being kicked forward or aft with no way to correct for it.

What to do? Simply make the cutting of stock a two-stage process. First, cut the joints of your stem right on the money, but leave the rest of the stock slightly oversized. Concentrate on getting the joints perfect. You can work faster, because there will be less angst wondering whether you will have enough stock. If you do a good job joining the wood, you know you will have enough. Use blocks to hold the joined pieces together on the lofting board. Place the patterns on top of the blocked-up stock, and retrace the lines onto the wood. Cut out the pieces (leaving the line), plane the pieces to size, and you're in business (mostly).

It's a good idea to leave extra wood at the top of the stem as well. If you wish to raise the sheer, you will have the wood to do it, plus you'll have surplus stock to screw stabilizing braces to, without having to worry about unsightly screw holes. The stem head can be trimmed off to size at the very end. It's also a good idea to put off fairing the forward end of the stem. Those parallel sides of the stem can come in handy when you're clamping in planking.

Anticipating having to bore for bolts for a false stem or a towing eye? Instead of "eyeballing" it after the boat is planked, why not bore for them ahead of time, right after assembling the stem?

Lofting is also tremendously helpful with floors. It can help you place them where keel bolts and station molds aren't. Floors (like transom quarter knees) can be tedious to fit, and a pattern will only give you one face (you hope the larger one). As with the stem components, to give yourself a bit of insurance and to avoid waste, cut the stock out oversize and do the difficult fits first. Wait until after the sides and keel have been fit to trim the top edge level. Don't forget to put the limbers in before installation—while you can still get at them.

STEAM BENDING

Probably 90% of what goes into a successful steam-bending job is proper preparation. Take the time to do proper stock selection: green wood, straight grain, and no sapwood or other defects. Relieve the edges—this will help prevent breakage.

Wait until there is abundant steam. Have clamps, tools, and assistance all at the ready. Premark the location of frames. In fact, make two lines, marking the fore and aft edges of the frames to avoid confusion.

FINISHING

"Finishing" may be a misnomer here, because I'm advocating doing some of it before you're finished assembling the boat. Much rot can often be avoided by priming the end grain of stock, painting the tops of deck beams, and sealing the inside faces of butt blocks. A preemptive paint strike can be a great time-saver. Prime the interior of a hull before bending in frames, and fully paint out the forward end of the boat *before* the deck goes on.

Considering bright topsides? Varnish finishing a hull is a bit like planting a very large lawn. It requires more maintenance, but gets less use. Paint is cheaper, easier, and in many ways, more elegant.

THE KARMA OF FASTENINGS

One reason wooden boats can last so long is that they are generally repairable. When making an assembly, give consideration to whether it will ever have to be fixed. Will that quick, cheap and ever so inextricable ring nail be such a great way to go if the plank you just fastened with it cracks overnight and needs replacement? The same goes for adhesives such as Sikaflex and 5200. They do exactly what they are advertised to do: provide a flexible bond that holds like grim death. Maybe that's not the best choice for toerails, portlights, cleats, or lapstrake plank seams. A more benign gasket material such as old-fashioned oil-based bedding compound is often a better choice.

LINING OUT PLANK LOCATIONS

Some builders feel they are far too busy to line out the hull. "I can line that plank when I get to it" says our irascible friend. True enough, but predetermination of the plank lines will ensure well-proportioned topsides, avoid giant banana-shaped planks, help you to locate butt blocks and stealers in reasonable locations, and ensure that lapstrake planking will go on with a minimum of fuss. And besides, you are going to have to line out those planks sometime.

TRANSOM

Chances are that you'll be using patterns for the transom, and that the transom has camber on its top edge. Some builders will cut the transom out to shape, including the camber, right from the get-go. While expeditious, one miss-step in the fashioning process can make the transom too small.

Consider leaving the top of the transom square to the centerline and about an inch above the top of the crown. This will allow a little wiggle room in case of a faux pas in shaping. If that occurs, you only need to move the patterns upward and you will still be able to use the transom stock. There are other benefits to the square top. The flat surface allows for easy leveling, whether the boat is upright or upside down. The crisp edge permits easy horning to assure the transom is at right angles to the centerline. The waste stock at the upper edge is a great place for screwing bracing to. After you do cut in the camber, don't lose track of the waste stock: it's just the stuff for cutting matching bungs for your fastenings.

DON'T FORGET TO . . .

- Plumb the depth of drift pin holes before you start to hammer in the pin.
- Install a push-down hole in the centerboard trunk cap.
- Check that you've cut enough threads into that bolt to allow you to actually tighten up the nut.
- Leave those pencil construction lines on the waterlines, centerlines, stations, and elsewhere. They can be an invaluable reference when building and can easily be removed later with thinner and a rag.
- Put that garboard drain plug fitting in before the boat is on the travel lift heading to the water.

· 23 ·

Lofting Basics

Boat plans document the shape of a 3-D hull, similar to the way a topographic map documents the shape of a mountain. But where a topographic map shows only one view (looking down), boat plans portray three interdependent views: looking down (the half-breadths), from the side (the profile), and fore and aft (the body plan).

Lofting is the process of expanding the lines from the plans to full size, in order to develop forms and patterns for the real boat. In order to transfer the shapes in the drawing onto a full-size lofting board, coordinates are plotted on a grid (sort of like latitude and longitude), and long flexible strips of wood, called *battens*, are sprung through them in smooth curves. The battens quickly show up any bad or unfair coordinates, allowing you to correct them.

When the three views are used together on the lofting, you can fair the stations in much the same way as you would springing a fairing batten around molds on a construction jig. But doing it on the lofting board is a lot faster, since you're working with a pencil and eraser rather than a spokeshave, a tub of glue and shims.

As a bonus, lofting also allows you to develop the bevels and patterns for the stem and transom; lay out the details of your construction jig, including any necessary brackets for the stem and transom; and determine the length and quantity of the backbone fastenings. It even acts as a construction jig for your molds. What a deal!

Double-checking offsets.

THE TOOLS

You'll need a 25' steel measuring tape, a framing square, trammel points, 1 pound of 3d nails, a hammer, a chalk line, knee pads, pencils, and (most certainly) erasers. A good, long straightedge is a necessity. An easy way to obtain one is to slice a 4" piece off the mill cut edge of a sheet of plywood. (Remember to mark which edge is the mill end.) A roll of adding machine paper will come in handy as a tick strip to transfer offset distance information from one view to the other. For this job, common cash register tape would work. An alternative is to have a bevy of long, thin strips of wood to record data onto.

A note on steel measuring tapes: the hooks on the end of the tapes tend to be funky and mendacity prone. It is much safer to use either the 10" or 1' mark instead; 50" just becomes 60", and 1'6" becomes 2'6" and so on.

Battens

Battens are long, straight-grained strips of wood that are used to fair (smooth) the drawn lines. They are held in place on the lofting by driving small nails alongside, not into, them. They should be rectangular in section and available in an assortment of sizes to accommodate different kinds of curves. For example, a batten ⅜" × ¾" might be used for a fairly tight curve, while one ¾" × 1" might be employed on a much slacker one. The best woods to use are those that are stiff with a limited "memory" of shape—i.e., they will spring back to straightness when released. Spruce and Philippine mahogany are good, and pine will work. Hardwoods, such as oak, will take a set easily and tend to give false readings.

Smaller caliber battens called drafting splines are mighty handy for tight turns such as may be found at the stem. Store-bought versions made of plastic are the best, although shop-made wooden ones will do the trick as well. Splines are generally held in place with lead spline weights (called ducks) that have hold-down hooks at one end.

The Floor

Think of the lofting floor as a giant drafting table. What you need is a smooth, stable surface that can stand up to a lot of service. We will be getting a lot of mileage out of our lofting, not only drawing the shape of the hull onto it, but also pulling all of our patterns off of it and assembling our construction molds atop of it. Two sheets of A-faced (sanded smooth) plywood should do the trick. An extra quarter sheet may come in handy if the views are spread out a bit more. Screw the boards down to the floor and paint them with a good coat of flat white paint. For the deluxe version, some builders will build a frame under the lofting boards and set it on sawhorses. This saves considerable wear and tear on the knees.

As with any sort of drawing, good light is essential, but avoid direct sunlight, as the crisp shadows will create irksome and distracting phantom lines.

THE TABLE OF OFFSETS

The Table of Offsets is the Rosetta Stone for interpreting any set of plans. The table contains most (but not all) the control points for plotting on the reference stations and drawing the lines of the hull as well as other useful information.

Despite a global reverence for metrics, most reference coordinates on plans in the United States and the United Kingdom are in English (Imperial) measurement and given in feet, inches and eighths. That means a notation 1-2-7 is read 1'2" and ⅞. Awkward, you say? Actually, this shorthand makes things a lot easier, as it eliminates the need to convert everything to inches and fractions thereof, and also makes it difficult to transpose the numbers (at least, once you get used to it). The vertical measurements are given as heights (above base), and the horizontal measurements, the half-breadths, are measured out from the centerline. The table usually indicates whether the lines are measured to the inside or outside of planking.

Why inside versus outside of the plank? It just depends on what the designer or architect felt was more accurate or convenient. Either method works equally well. Round-bottomed boats, especially historical ones that were measured in the field, or that have rabbeted stems, are often (but not always) drawn to the outside of the plank. These lines are drawn to the *rabbet line*, where the outside of the planking intersects the keel or stem. It's accurate and easy to understand. To build the boat, however, it is necessary to deduct the plank thickness from the finished drawn lines on the lofting board to get you to the "inside of plank" so that you can make an accurate rendition of the stations (or frames), transom, and stem and keel rabbets.

Hard-chined boats and dory-style hulls are commonly drawn to the inside of the plank. These lines will either end at the *apex* (or *middle line*) of the rabbet, or the *bearding line*. The apex is the deepest point in a rabbet, where the inside face of the plank would end. In a profile or side view of a cut rabbet, it lies between the rabbet and the bearding line. The bearding line is where the inside of the plank touches the outside face of the stem or keel. This line is often used on boats with beveled stems (such as dories). The advantage to lines drawn to the inside of the plank is that what you see is what you get. There will be no deduction to give you the edges of the transom or molds (or frames). It can, however, be a little trickier to get the rabbet just right.

Caveat Emptor!

Designers generally spend a lot of time to accurately record the reference numbers onto the table of offsets. This care, however, does not guarantee that all the numbers are accurate (although most of them will be). What's the deal? Weren't the lines on the plans drawn from these numbers? The answer is, maybe yes, but probably no.

Let's consider the case of a historical nineteenth-century boat measured in 1932. The historian, using levels, squares, and plumb bobs, surveyed the boat as best he could in a dimly lit, cobweb-bedecked, leaking shed with a large barking dog on a too long chain outside. He then took the numbers, sketches, and maybe photos and beat feet back to the drawing board. On the drawing board, he dutifully recorded the numbers and other data. Being that the drawing had to fit on the table, the plan had to be drawn in scale, maybe 1" equal to 1'. Although most of the recorded numbers worked, some of the numbers (due to the recording conditions) may have been funky. By springing a flexible batten through the points, the bum or outlier numbers or offsets were revealed by the fair sprung line. By the time the drawing was done, it was covered with accurate lines that had been distilled and faired until they worked. The historian then took his scale rule, measured the line intersections, and created a table of offsets. This new table was probably quite accurate, but since he was working in scale, measuring to a curved pencil line, the potential for human error was high. These are the numbers you will be working with. It is only when the lines have been lofted full size that the accurate numbers are generated and a true shape is rendered. Just think of it as quality control.

A NOTE ON SCALE RULES

Those of us who have taken shop or mechanical drawing classes have received the sermon from the imperious instructor in lab coat: "Thou shalt not measure from the plans with ye olde scale rule!" And yes, he did have a point. Paper blueprints can shrink and swell with changes in the weather. That said, you will find yourself measuring the blueprints with a scale rule. There is so much information on a set of plans that some measurements will invariably be left off accidentally. Judicious use of the scale rule can help when figuring out the depth of the stem knee, the spacing of the frames, or the width of a thwart. The scale rule is also useful in debunking the aforementioned bum offsets.

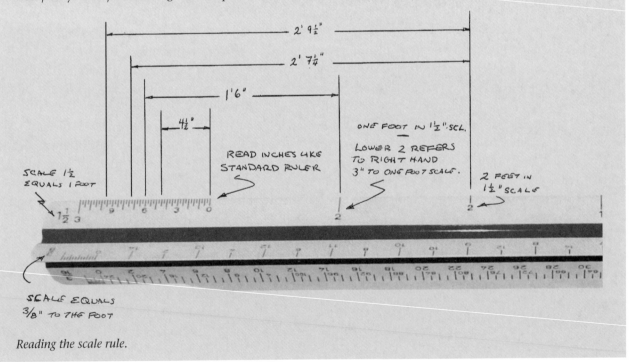

Reading the scale rule.

LOOKING AT THE PLANS

If there is one constant in marine plans, it is that they are all different—and we're not just talking about the boats. There are distinct differences in what information is given, how much information is given, whether the lines are drawn to the inside or outside of plank, where the lines end up, what scale they are drawn in, and much more. Different designers and builders have different styles and vastly different notions of how much information is enough to build the boat. That being said, there are commonalities to which everyone (well, almost everyone) subscribes.

Generally, every plan will contain at least three views: the body plan, the profile, and the half-breadth.

The Body Plan

This view shows the form of the hull at regular transverse vertical planes, called *sections* or *stations*. If the boat was a loaf of bread, and you pulled out a slice and traced it with a pencil, there you'd have your station. As the vessel is symmetrical, only one half of the station needs to be shown. For convenience and clarity, the aft stations are usually displayed on the left of the centerline, and the forward ones to the right. Unless, of course, they're reversed.

On complex round-bottomed hulls, you will need more information. On a round-bottomed body plan, you will find horizontal lines called *waterlines*, vertical lines called *buttocks*, and diagonal lines called, well, *diagonals*. More on these little wonders soon. Additionally, there will be a *base* (or *baseline*)—actually a flat plane that serves as the starting point for all vertical measurements on both the profile and body plans.

The Profile

The profile is a longitudinal view. It shows the shape of the boat at the centerline as viewed from the side. The more complex the hull, the more information will be contained in this view. Usually, the profile view will show you the curve of the sheer, the shape of the stem and bottom, the rabbet line, and the rake of the stern. In this view, the curved stations in the body plan appear as vertical lines at regular intervals from fore to aft and perpendicular to the base. Many plans have a vertical *forward perpendicular* (or FP), a line parallel to the stations that touches the very forward end of the stem. On the other end of the drawing, there will be an *aft perpendicular* (AP) touching the aftermost point of the transom.

In some plans, curved *plank lines* are shown. Other plans show horizontal slices through the hull called *waterlines*. In the profile view, these are just straight parallel lines, almost always drawn parallel to the base; you'll see their curves when viewed from above as half-breadths. Additionally, there will be buttock lines that represent vertical slices lengthwise through the hull. In this view, they will be curved in a manner similar to the rabbet line. We'll look at these in more detail later.

Half-Breadths

This is a plan view, showing half of the hull, split at the centerline, with the bottom up and you looking down at it like a seagull (sort of). (You can also imagine the boat right-side up but transparent, like a wire-frame rendering.) A line indicates the edge of the keel or bottom, and a curve shows the shape of the sheer from above. Also illustrated are the shapes of the outside faces of the transom and stem.

There are other curved lines as well. On a flat-bottomed boat, the curve of the chine is shown. On a multi-chined hull, the inside-of-plank lines are depicted. For a round-bottomed hull, the waterlines that appeared as straight lines in the profile are shown as curved lines in the half-breadth view.

Still in the half-breadth view, a *centerline* (actually a vertical center plane) runs down the middle of the hull, dividing it into two equal, mirror-image halves (only one of which is shown). The centerline is also visible in the body plan view. The station lines appear as straight lines perpendicular to the centerline.

Diagonals

Round-bottomed hulls often have long curved lines that overlap other views. These are the diagonals and their job is to provide a final check on the fairness of the hull. We'll discuss these further when we address the lofting of round-bottomed hulls in the next chapter.

Separate from the three views in the lines plan, there is usually a *construction plan* (which may be drawn on several sheets). On this plan are shown the shapes and dimensions of the various parts and pieces, how they go together, and their placement in the hull.

SETTING UP THE GRID

The grid that the lofting is drawn onto is like a jumbo piece of graph paper. The lines should be drawn with

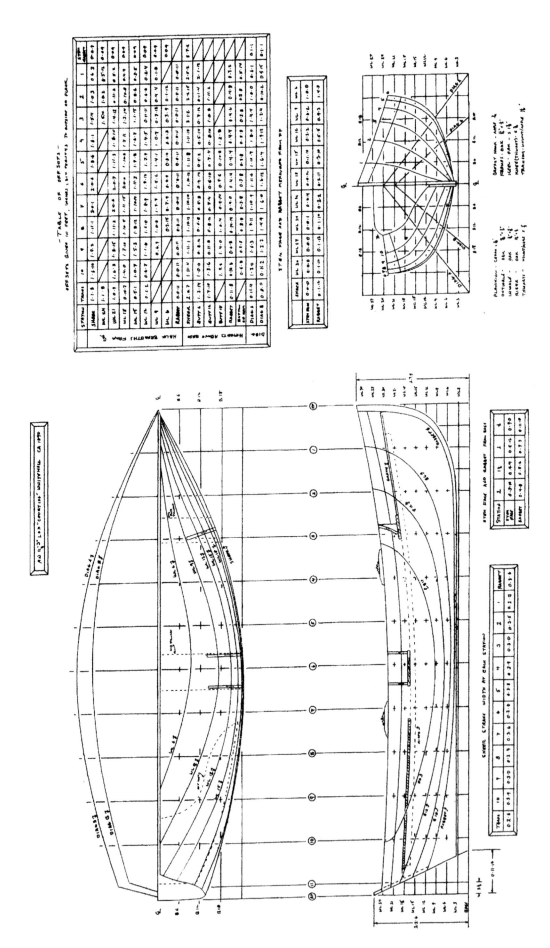

Upper left: diagonals (above the centerline) and half-breadths with waterlines (below the centerline). Lower left: Profile view with waterlines (below the centerline). Lower right: Body plan, with aft stations to the left of centerline, and forward stations to the right. Upper right: tables of offsets.

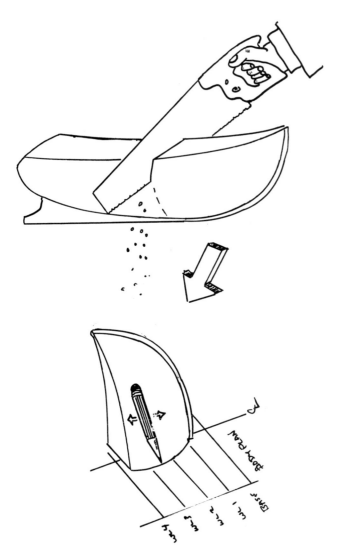

Where body plan lines come from. All the stations share the same centerline and baseline.

high accuracy at their proper locations. For clarity, consideration should be given to keep the overlapping of the drawn views to a minimum. A good way to do this is to establish the long baseline (aka base) on one side of the lofting board and the separate but parallel centerline (CL) on the other side of the board. The base and the centerline will share the same drawn perpendicular station lines. Drawing the profile from one side of the board and the half-breadths from the other means that the sheers in each view will tend to nest together, keeping confusion as to which line is which to a minimum. If possible, it also is good to either place the body plan off to one side of the grids for base and centerline or have it drawn on a totally separate board. Not only does this cut down on further clutter on drawing of the profile and half-breadths, but it also will

allow you to build your molds or frames right on top of the drawn body plan without trashing, smudging, or otherwise disfiguring the other drawn views.

If possible, try not to run the aft perpendicular and forward perpendicular right to the edges of the plywood. As we'll soon see, the extra room will come in handy when we will need to expand the transom and run sections through the stem.

The place to start is with the straight baseline for the profile that will run the length of the plywood, an inch or two in from the edge. This seems a simple enough task but it often goes awry. Just snapping a chalk line isn't good enough, as it often hangs up or bounces, giving you several lines to choose from. One good way to get a true line is to stretch a chalk line between two nails so that it is humming tight, and then place a thin wooden spacer at either end under the line to elevate it. Then, with the assistance of a square, make marks directly under the string. Remove the string and connect the points with a straightedge and scribe the line and label it "base, profile."

Check the plans to see where the baseline actually runs. The keel may rest on the baseline, or it may be above it; in either case all profile offsets are measured vertically up. The baseline can also be the designed flotation waterline, in which case offsets are given to measure both up and down from the base. If this is the case, be sure to allow enough room on the lofting board to measure in both directions.

Next, lay out the vertical line intersections on the baseline. The locations of the stations and forward and aft perpendiculars will be given on the blueprint. Be sure to record the proper spacing onto the lofting board. Some plans have some pretty oddball measurements for the stations. They may seem weird but must be replicated all the same.

To avoid unsightly cumulative error, stretch out the measuring tape and mark the distances as a continuum: forward perpendicular, to Station 1, to Station 2, to Station 3, and so on, until you reach the aft perpendicular. Label all these points, then erect perpendicular lines that run to the other side of the board. Check the lines for squareness with a 3-4-5 (i.e., 30°-60°-90°) triangle or with trammel points.

Draw a line an inch or two in from the opposite edge of the board and parallel to the baseline. Label this line "centerline, half-breadth." Then move to the body plan grid, draw the base and, finally, erect the centerline.

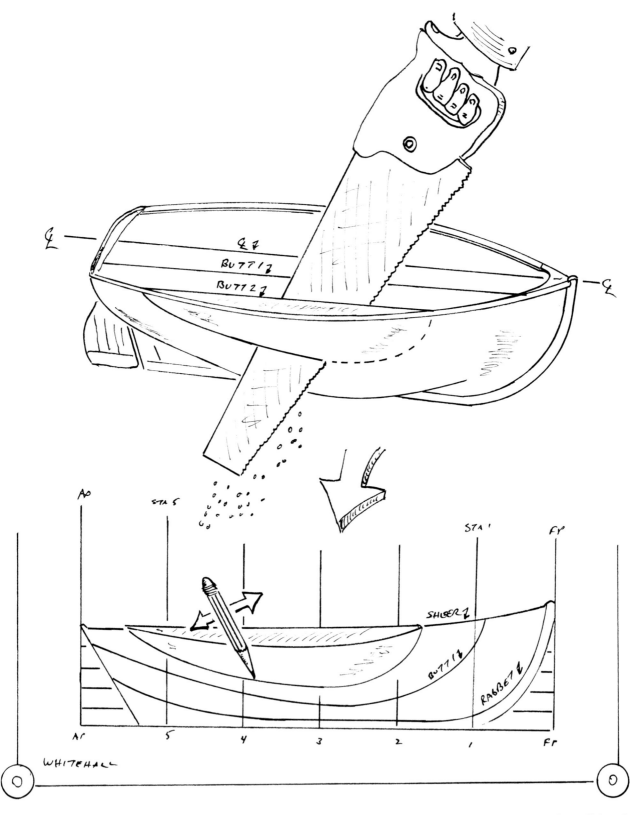

The buttocks, shown as curved lines in the profile drawing (bottom), represent lengthwise slices through the hull parallel to the centerline. The rabbet can be considered a special-case buttock, right up against the side of the keel and stem. Like the stations in the body plan, the buttocks all share a common baseline and centerline.

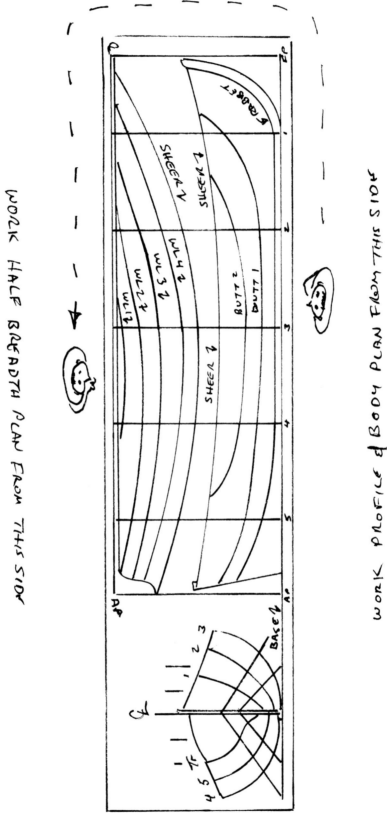

All the views in the full-size lofting relate directly to each other. To save space, it's handy to "nest" the convex curve of the waterlines in the half-breadth view into the concave curve of the sheer in the profile view, but you'll want access to both sides of the lofting board.

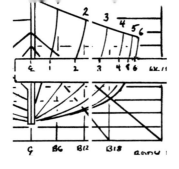

· 24 ·

Let's Loft Some Boats

Here are just a few more comments on basic lofting procedures before we actually begin to loft some boats.

It is tempting to drive nails into the flexible batten. Don't do it. The whole idea of the batten is to use the nature of bendable wood to create a fair line and not to slavishly follow each and every offset point. Instead, place nails (or ice picks) alongside the batten to anchor the ends and push the curve out in the middle to meet the drawn offsets. (Besides, good, straight-grained softwood battens are hard to come by, and driving nails into them will shorten their lives.) Also, never drive a nail into your drawn point—it will disappear and you'll never again be sure where that point actually was. Whenever possible try to work from the outside or the tension side of the batten. It is easier to sight and it will give you a better-drawn line than the inner or compression side of the batten. Try not to leave a batten bent on the board any longer than necessary—over lunch or, worse, overnight, as it can cause the batten to take a permanent set. Try not to overstress the batten. If it starts to get cranky and feeling like it's getting ready to break, it probably is going to break. Downsize to a lighter batten.

The builder ends up moving a lot of information around when lofting. Remember that we have at least three different views going on at all times. Most times there is going to be repetition of distances. For example, if you measure out distance "X" for the sheer at Station 2 in the half-breadth view, the distance to the sheer at Station 2 in the body plan is also distance "X." Same sheer, same distance, only a different view. So, after establishing the distance in one view using a tape measure, there is no reason to use a tape measure again. The distance on the first view can be recorded as a couple of marks on a stick or, better yet, a strip of paper cash register tape. Bring the tape over to the other view and just transfer the measurement at the right location.

THE FLAT-BOTTOMED BOAT

The simplest type of boat to loft is the hard-chined, flat-bottomed hull. For this example, we'll be lofting a sharpie-style skiff designed by Will Ansel. The lines were developed using both a half model and the original boat. This boat exhibits a number of classic details. The two-piece stem is dead straight and raked slightly back. The bottom exhibits considerable rocker and it kicks quickly up back aft, keeping the transom well clear of the water. The bottom is cross-planked, with a skeg and steam-bent keel added after the boat is planked.

The lines for this sharpie are drawn to the inside of plank. The simple plan does not contain a classic table of offsets. Instead, the dimensions of the components are noted directly on the plan.

Setting Up the Grid

The boat is just a bit over 10' long. This will allow us to draw the profile/half-breadth grid and the body

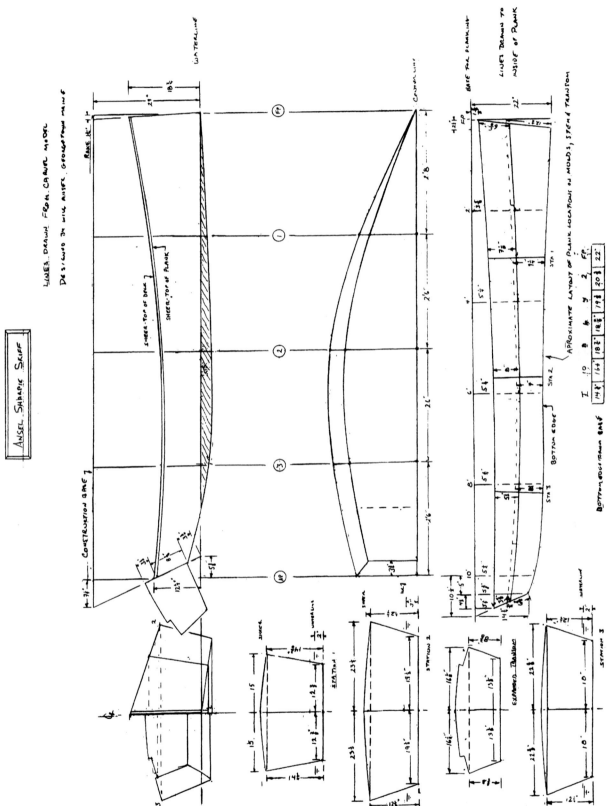

Because of its simple lines, all the critical measurements could be drawn legibly directly on the lines plans for this little sharpie skiff, rather than recorded in a table of offsets. The expansion of the transom (i.e., its flat view when layed out on wood) has been done for you—twice!—once in the profile view, and again on the left, second from bottom. Another bonus is the expanded plank shapes (bottom right).

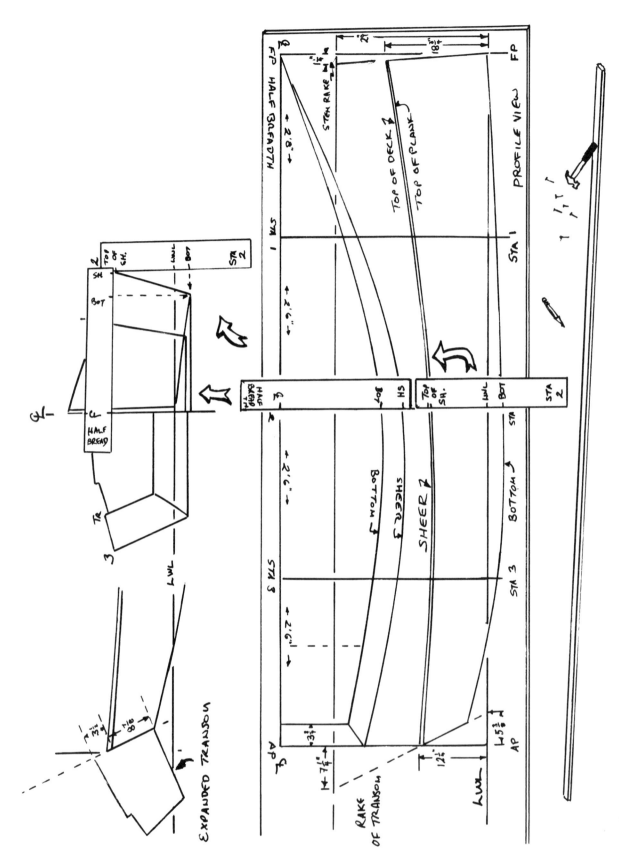

To loft the sharpie, lines are faired and drawn from the data on the "offsets" drawing. Heights and widths are recorded on a wood or paper "tick strip," then the body plan is drawn using the tick strip data. The expanded transom combines measurements of the profile and half-breadth views.

plan onto two 8' sheets of plywood. The profile base-line is the waterline of the original boat. The greatest depth of the bottom is 3". To be on the safe side, we'll draw the baseline 6" from the edge of the plywood. The centerline (CL) of the boat can be drawn in 2" from the other edge of the plywood. To get the real shape of the transom, we will have to "expand" it. This involves drawing the transom out full size using the after face of the line of the raked transom as the centerline of the expanded transom in the profile view. The transom width is 16⅛" so let's move the aft perpendicular over to 1½" from the edge of the plywood. Station spacing is all 2'6" except the space between Station 1 and the forward perpendicular, which is 2'8". To clarify details and give us a line to eventually build to, let's also draw a *"construction base"* reference line that runs 29" from, and parallel to, the already drawn (waterline) baseline. This construction base will be the two-dimensional equivalent of the top of a strongback or a dead-level floor on which we'll build the boat.

Drawing the Profile

We'll start the process by drawing the rake of the transom onto the profile view. To get the sheer at the transom, measure up 12¼" from the base on the aft perpendicular (AP) and make a mark. Then, measure 5⅜" forward of the aft perpendicular on the baseline and make a mark. Take a straightedge and connect the two points and draw in the line, running it past the sheer height to the construction base. This line should intersect the construction base 7¼" aft of the aft perpendicular.

Next, we'll get the rake of the straight stem. On this boat, the bottom of the true stem is at the intersection of the forward perpendicular (FP) and the base. To get the rake of the stem, go to the construction baseline and make a mark 1¼" aft of the forward perpendicular. Take a straightedge and connect the two marks. This is the rake of the stem. To get the sheer of the stem, measure up the forward perpendicular 18¾" and square back until you hit the stem rake line. Mark and label it.

Now we can establish the curves of the sheer and the bottom. The information for this is given on the individual station sections on the left side of the drawing. On Station 1, the bottom of the boat is 2" below the waterline/baseline. Take that distance and mark it onto the station grid line on the profile. From that bottom point, then measure up the given 14¾". This

is the sheer line for Station 1. Repeat this operation for stations 2 and 3.

We have nearly enough information to draw the profile. The last thing we need to do is to go to the transom rake line, and measure up the rake (from the baseline) 3¾". Make a mark and we are ready to run the sheer and bottom lines. Connect the sheer points on the stem, transom, and stations with a batten. Hold the shape with nails driven alongside. Sight along the batten to eliminate any humps and get it as fair as possible; then scribe a line with a pencil. Repeat the operation and connect the points to give you the curve of the bottom. Scribe the line and it's on to the half-breadth view.

Drawing the Half-Breadth View

Move to the drawn centerline. Using the body plan numbers on the blueprint, record the offset distance for the sheer and chine at each station. At the transom, the sheer falls on the aft perpendicular, so measure out that distance from the centerline to the top-of-transom.

Next, the bottom-of-transom distance needs to be established. The plan gives us the numerical distance (13⅜") for the width. This plan also gives us the distance forward of the aft perpendicular (3¾") from where the width is measured. If that distance forward of the aft perpendicular had not been given, we could have simply squared down the bottom-to-transom location from the profile view onto the centerline in the half-breadth view.

Last we need to get the ending at the stem. On this boat, both the sheer and the bottom end ¼" out from the centerline. The bottom ends right at the intersection of the forward perpendicular and the centerline. The stem is raked aft, so the sheer at the stem is actually aft of the forward perpendicular. Take a divider or a piece of paper tape and pick up that distance aft of the forward perpendicular at the sheer from the profile view and bring it down to the centerline in the half-breadth view.

With those points established, measure out ¼" and connect the sheer and bottom points with a batten. With a straightedge, connect the transom points. Label those and then it's . . .

The Body Plan

Moving to the body plan grid, we'll draw the forward section (looking aft) of the boat on the right-hand side

ANSEL SHARPIE SKIFF

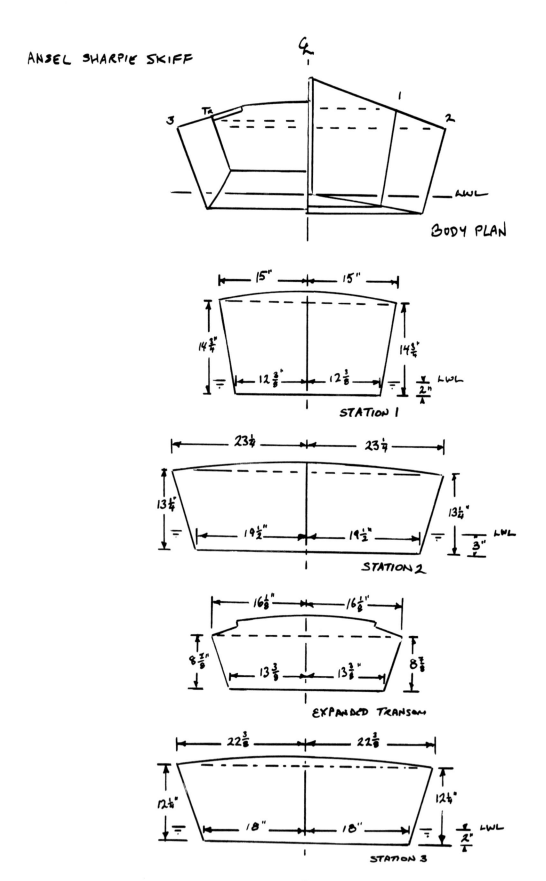

A FLAT BOTTOM "TABLE OF OFFSETS" - INSIDE OF PLANK - SHEER = TOP OF DECK

A closer view of the simple body plan "offset" drawing in lieu of a table of offsets.

of the centerline and the aft side (looking forward) on the left. Instead of using the offsets given on the plan, we'll simply combine the distances already established on the half-breadth and profile drawings. Just measure up the height and out the width.

First, go to the profile view. Mark the waterline base on a piece of paper tick strip tape, then slide it back and forth to record the heights of the sheer and bottom, both above and below the base, for all the stations, the stem, and the transom. Be sure the tape is indexed on the baseline. Bring the tape to the body plan and, after indexing the tape to the base, record the heights onto the centerline.

Next, draw a line ¼" out from the right-side centerline. This is the same stem ending line we established on the half-breadth plan. Then, take a second piece of tape and, after establishing an index centerline, slide the tape along the half-breadth plan, picking up the width of the sheer and bottom at each station and the transom.

Bring the tape to the body plan. Place the tape horizontally (i.e., parallel to the base) and index the centerline of the tape to the centerline of the body plan. Slide the tape up and down to match each of the recorded heights on the centerline. For example, to get the shape of Station 2, slide the tape up to the height of the sheer and, squaring the tape out, mark the width of the sheer. Then, slide the tape down to the bottom height and measure out the width. Connect the dots and then go on to stations 1, 3, and the transom.

Expanding the Transom

Looking at the drawing, we see that the transom is shown three times. Each is accurate (for what it is), and each is unusable by itself. In the half-breadth view and the body plan, the widths of the sheer and bottom are correct, but the length from top to bottom is foreshortened since it is angled from the viewer's perspective. The profile has the proper length of the transom (from top to bottom) but no widths. So what we need to do is to combine the width and length (much like we did in drawing the stations) to come up with the real shape of the transom.

The easiest location to generate the expanded transom is right at the transom in the profile view. We will use the rake of the profile as the centerline of our drawing. That automatically gives us the proper length. Take a framing square and draw out lines square from the top and bottom of the raked transom. Then take a tick strip and pick up the width of the transom at the sheer and at the bottom from either the half-breadth or body plan. Record those distances onto your new grid. Connect the lines, and you have the accurate shape of the after face of the transom.

This is the small, forward face of the transom, so we only have half the information we need. If we make this into a pattern and use it to cut out the transom, it will be too small. Now we will get the inner, larger face of the transom. The plans say that the transom is 1" thick. So draw a line parallel to and 1" forward of the raked profile transom. This will be the centerline of the inner face of the transom. Once again, draw lines square out from the sheer and bottom intersections. Now all we need to do is record the widths onto the new grid. But where do we get that information? We can't use the body plan as that only has the small transom face on it. We can, however, get it from the half-breadth view.

Go to the profile and find the point where the inside of the transom line hits the sheer. (It will be a little bit ahead of the aft perpendicular.) Square that distance down to the sheer in the half-breadth plan. Mark that point. The distance from there to the half-breadth centerline is the distance we need to plot on our new grid. Pick that distance up with a tick strip and transfer it to the inner face grid.

Go back to the profile and find the point where the bottom hits the new inner transom line. Once again, square it down to the half-breadth view and mark the intersection on the curved bottom line. Pick up the width to the centerline and plot it on the expanded inner transom grid. Connect the lines like we did for the outer face and we are in business.

Make patterns (actually half patterns) for both the inner and outer transom faces. Fashion the transom panel so that it is exactly 1" thick. Make sure it is longer and wider than the finished transom. Draw a squared centerline on both sides of the panel.

Place the large pattern on the panel. Align the bottom edge of the pattern with the bottom edge of the panel. Align centerline to centerline. Scribe in the bottom-to-sheer angle. Then flip the pattern and repeat the operation on the other side, making sure the centerlines on both sides line up.

Next (and very important!), pick up the bevel of the transom bottom on the profile view with a bevel

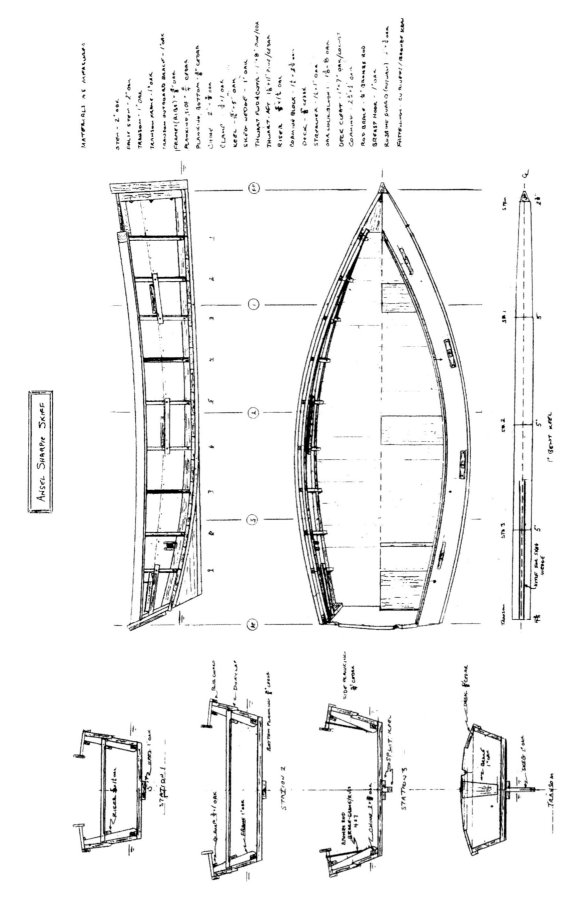

ANSEL SHARPIE SKIFF

MATERIALS AS MEASURED:

STEM - 2" OAK
FALSE STEM - 2" OAK
TRANSOM - 1" OAK
TRANSOM FRAME - 1" OAK
TRANSOM OUTBOARD BRACE - 1" OAK
FRAMES (BILGE) - 7/8" OAK
PLANKING, SIDE - 5/8" CEDAR
PLANKING, BOTTOM - 3/4" CEDAR
CHINE - 2" × 7/8" OAK
CLAMP - 3/4" OAK
KEEL - 5/8"-5" OAK
SKEG WEDGE - 1" OAK
THWART FLOOR/CONTA - 1/8" OAK/CEDAR
THWART AFT 1/8" × 11" OAK/CEDAR
RISER 5/8" × 4" OAK
CORMING BLOCK - 11/2 × 2 1/2 mm
DECK - 5/8" OAK
STRAKTER - 3/4 × 1" OAK
OAR LOCK BLOCK - 11/2"-8 OAK
DECK CLEAT - 1"× 7" OAK/CONST
CORMING - 21/2" OAK
ROD BRACE - 1" BRONZE ROD
BREAST HOOK - OAK
RUBBING GUARD (OUTWAL) - 1" OAK
FATTENINGS CU RIVETS/BRONZE SCREW

The construction drawings and list of materials show how it goes together. In addition to the scantlings (thickness dimensions of the structural members), note the dory lapped planks, notched frames, seat risers, side-deck supports, and unusual split/sprung keel.

gauge. Transfer that bevel to the side of the panel with pencil—starting at the bottom edge of the inner surface. Remember that the transom is raked or tipped back. Thus, the bottom edge will have a bevel cut into it and the bottom of the outer face will be "higher" than the inner face. Square the result of the bevel drawn on the side across the aft face of the panel.

Like we did with the large, inner face pattern, we'll trace the smaller pattern onto the outer face of the panel. Align the bottom of the pattern with the newly traced "bevel" line and the centerline of the pattern with the centerline of the panel. Flip the pattern and trace again on the other side of the centerline.

Then all that needs to be done is to take the panel to the saw and cut to the larger, inner-face lines. (Leave the top long for trimming later.) Then simply hand plane down from the sawn inner face line to the drawn, outer face line. The proper bevels for the bottom and side planking will automatically develop.

The Stem Bevel

To have planks land properly on the stem, a correct bevel needs to be planed into it. This angle too can be gotten from the lofting. Checking out the materials list on the sheet of construction drawings, we see that the stem is 2″ thick. Up at the stem region, draw a line on the half-breadth view that is 1″ out from the centerline. (That's half the stem thickness. On old plans this is known as the *half siding*.) Mark where the bottom and sheer cross that 1″ stem thickness line. Use a piece of tick strip tape to record those two intersection distances aft of the forward perpendicular. Bring (square) these distances up to the profile view and record them at their respective locations. Connect the two points with a straightedge. This is the bearding line. Using the scale rule, we can determine that the stem is 3″ wide, so this line too can be drawn (aft of the face of the raked stem) onto the profile. To cut the bevel, transfer the drawn bearding line onto the two sides of the 2″ × 3″ stem. Put a centerline onto the forward face of the stem. Draw a ¼″ line on both sides of the centerline. Then just plane a bevel in from the ¼″ line to the bearding line.

Final Steps

While we have the lines drawn on the lofting, we might as well get our money's worth.

Let's start off with designing our construction jig. Transfer the construction base from the profile view to the body plan. From the sheer at each station, draw a line square to the construction base. When each station mold is built, it will extend to the construction base. Built this way, all the stations will self-align at the right height (relative to one another) when they are set up.

On the profile view, draw the stem so that it continues all the way to the construction base. The pattern and the finished stem will have this extra length. A bracket can be installed on the floor or strongback to hold the stem at the proper angle and location. On the other end of the profile view, design a bracket to hold the transom at the proper height, angle, and location. Then, using the tick strip tape, bring the station spacing and location of the transom and stem holding jigs from the lofting board to the strongback or floor.

Is there more? You bet. If you wish, the bottom can be "planked" on the lofting in ⅞″ stock, which will allow you to design the keel and skeg and make patterns. The false stem can be drawn on and the bolts "installed" to see what is needed for length. The chine notches can be drawn into the station molds. Even the frames and seat locations can be drawn in so you'll know where they go. How far to go is up to you. It is a neat process, though, as it allows you to predesign most of the tricky parts to save wood and time later on. And it's almost fun.

THE ALMOST-ROUND-BOTTOMED HULL

For this example let's select a Swamptscott-dory-type boat—the Chaisson Semi Dory from John Gardner's excellent *The Dory Book*. This little 10-footer exhibits all the techniques needed to loft a much larger boat of this sort. The Chaisson profile includes the sheer curve, the inside-of-plank lines, the curved bearding line, the shape of the inside of the bottom, and the outside face of the transom. Stations appear as vertical lines. The profile also includes coordinates to help get spacing of the stations, the rake of the transom, and the bearding line.

The table also informs you that the lines are measured to the inside of the planking, the inside of the bottom, the outside face of the transom, and the bearding line.

Logistics

Before starting your lofting, it is best to plan ahead as to layout. Your lofting board is only 16′ (two plywood

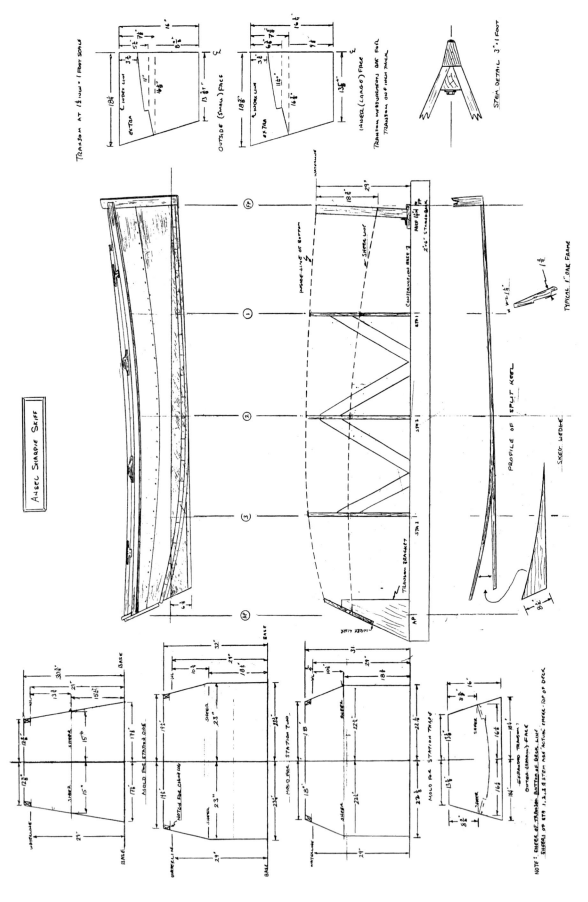

Use the lofting to design the construction jig, including the station molds, transom bracket, and stem support.

STATION SPACING IS 24"
LINES DRAWN TO INSIDE OF PLANK
OFFSETS GIVEN IN FEET, INCHES, EIGHTHS

STATIONS		STEM	2	4	6	8	TRANS
HEIGHTS ABOVE BASE	Sheer	2.4.0	1.11.6	1.9.0	1.6.4	1.6.7	1.8.4
	Plank 2	2.2.1	1.9.2	1.4.7	1.2.7	1.5.3	1.6.1
	Plank 3	1.11.1	1.5.5	1.0.7	0.10.3	0.10.5	1.3.0
	Plank 4	1.7.4	1.1.7	0.10	0.4.7	0.8.1	0.11.2
	Plank 5	1.6.2	0.10.0	0.5.6	0.3.3	0.6.3	0.8.3
	Bottom	0.4.5	0.4.4	0.8.1	0.1.5	0.3.5	0.4.6
HALF BREADTHS	Sheer	0.0.6	1.0.2	1.8.6	1.11.6	1.9.6	1.4.2
	Plank 2	0.0.6	0.11.7	1.8.4	1.11.2	1.9.4	1.4.6
	Plank 3	0.0.6	0.10.5	1.6.3	1.1.1	1.8.0	1.4.1
	Plank 4	0.0.6	0.6.6	1.1.6	1.5.3	1.4.4	1.2.2
	Plank 5	0.0.6	0.6.7	0.11.1	1.0.9	1.0.1	0.10.5
	Bottom	0.0.6	0.11.3	0.7.6	0.7.2	0.8.1	0.1.0

10' CHAISSON SEMI-DORY

Lines for a 10' Chaisson semi-dory, a nice little semi-round-bottom hull that works well for both oar and sail.

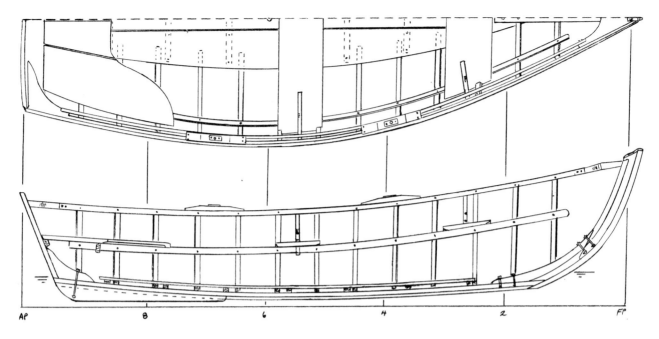

Construction details for a rowing version of the Chaisson semi-dory.

sheets) long. On it, you need to get the profile, half-breadths and body plan—with, for clarity, the minimum of overlap of the views. You also will need to do a transom expansion working off of the aft of the transom in profile. That calls for pretty good figuring—although the worst that can happen if you miscue is that you will need to add part of another sheet of plywood. The easiest way to reduce overlap of views is to draw the profile from one side of the board and the half-breadths from the other. In this way, the two sheers will "nest" in one another. The body plan can be forward of the stem of the profile and use the same baseline. (By-the-by, don't forget to label everything. The biggest bugbear in the lofting biz is the question "What is that point anyway?") With that done, set up the grid as usual.

The Profile

Now we can start to loft the boat. Begin with the transom. Referring to the table of offsets, plot the transom top 1-8-4 (20½") up the aft perpendicular. Then plot the bottom at a point 0-5-6 up from the base and aft 1' 6¾" from Station 8. Connect the dots and there's the transom.

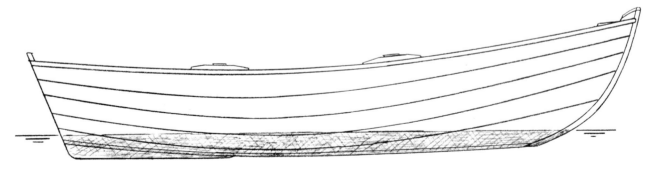

Nicely lined planks will make this workmanlike little dory-planked boat as elegant as many a longer, leaner, lapstrake craft.

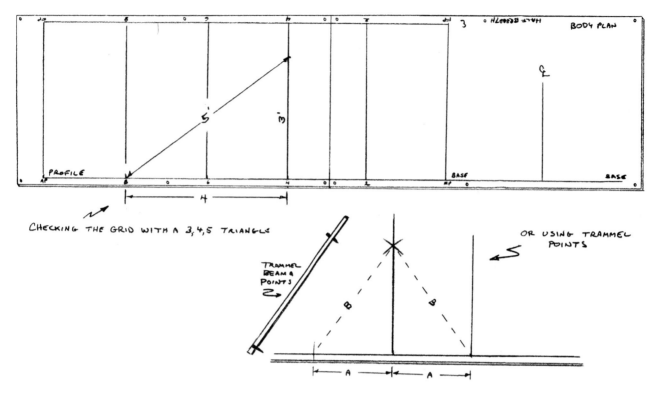

Careful planning will pay off when trying to loft a boat full-size onto a couple of pieces of plywood. So will scrupulous attention to getting things straight and square.

For the sheer, plot the sheer heights from the table on their respective stations and forward perpendicular. Spring a batten through the points and hold it in place with nails driven alongside. Sight along the curve and pull any nails at the stations causing unfairness. (The whole idea of lofting is to get those smooth lines.)

Now move to the stem. Remember we are drawing to the bearding line and not to the forward edge of the stem. The plans give several points to establish the curve of the stem that are measured up and aft. The uppermost ones also give you the end points for planks #2–5. (Label these.) The lowest gives you the end point for the bottom and the others are just for reference. Plot these points and spring a batten through them and scribe the line.

For the bottom, just plot the heights on the stations and spring the batten from stem to transom and draw.

The planks can now be drawn in. To get the plank endings on the transom, just measure the transom heights given on the offset table up the aft perpendicular and square across until you hit the transom. Plot each plank height on the stations, then spring your batten through the points and check it for fairness as

you did at the sheer. Label everything and then it's off to the half-breadths.

The Half-Breadths
First, draw the half thickness or half siding of the stem on the lofting as shown. This is just a line ¾" out from the centerline. Next, from the offsets, plot all the half-breadths for the planks, sheer, and bottom onto stations 2 through 8.

Now the distance out for each plank at the transom can be plotted. The half-breadths are taken from the offset table. How far forward of the aft perpendicular each plank ends is taken from the profile. Take the distance from where each plank, sheer, and bottom hits the raked transom and bring that vertically to the centerline on the half-breadth plan and mark and label it. Then, using a framing square as a guide, measure out the given offset distance and mark it. After establishing the marks, you can connect the dots and there you have the transom (at least in half-breadth).

In a similar fashion, to get the endings at the stem, square up the intersections of the bottom, planks, and

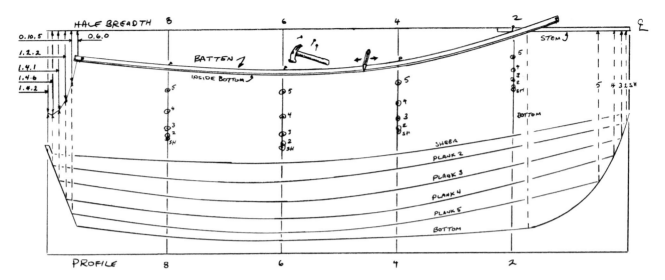

Transferring the plank line endings from the profile to the stem and transom on the half breadths and marking the half-breadth offsets.

sheer with the bearding line in the profile to the half siding of the stem on the half-breadth plan.

All we need to do now is to run our batten from stem to stern to get our lines. Let the batten run by the bearding line on the half siding of the stem until it contacts the centerline. As the stem is beveled to the centerline, this will generate the forward face of the upper stem for each plank line, the sheerline, and at the bottom.

Now we can get the forward face of the stem on the profile. Take a short batten (or even a ruler), place it onto the drawn plank, sheer and bottom lines in the profile view, and extend these lines forward of the drawn bearding line. Then square the forward face distances for each line on the half-breadth view down to the extended lines on the profile view and plot them. Connect these points with a light batten.

Again, sight the lines for fairness and adjust if necessary. If the lines aren't fair here, they won't get any better on the boat.

The Body Plan

To get the body plan, all we need to do is to combine the information generated in the other two views. For example, to get the sheer at Station 4, use a tick strip and pick up the height above the base from the profile (mark both the height and the base on the strip) and the width from the half-breadth plan (mark the width and the centerline). Take this information to

the body plan. Measure up the vertical centerline and mark the height, then square out the width. Label this point. Repeat this exercise for each plank and the bottom. Connect the dots and there you have the shape of Station 4.

Perform this operation for each of the stations and the transom. And there you have it: the finished lofting. Well, almost.

Stem Sections

We need a bit more information to generate the forward face of the stem. Why is this important? The distance between the forward face and the bearding line is what will generate the bevel on the stem that will allow the planks to land properly.

Some of the information we have already. As you recall, when we ran the plank lines in the half-breadth view, the lines were allowed to extend to the centerline. Where the lines contact the centerline is the forward face of the stem at that plank. All we need to do is to square that distance down to the profile and plot it on the plank line in that view. But first, we have to extend the line of the planks out forward of the bearding line by placing a short batten on the plank lines in the profile and marking it. Now the distances can be squared down for the planks' sheers and bottoms.

But we still don't have enough information for the lower part of the stem. To get it, we'll need to run a section at a right angle to get an X-ray view of the lower

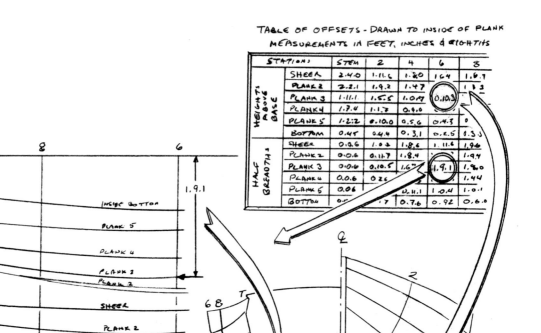

TABLE OF OFFSETS - DRAWN TO INSIDE OF PLANK
MEASUREMENTS IN FEET, INCHES & EIGHTHS

	STATIONS	STEM	2	4	6	8
HEIGHTS ABOVE BASE	SHEER	2.4.0	1.11.6	1.8.0	1.6.4	1.6.7
	PLANK 2	2.2.1	1.9.2	1.4.7		1.3.3
	PLANK 3	1.11.1	1.5.5	1.0.4	0.10.3	
	PLANK 4	1.7.4	1.1.3	0.9.0		
	PLANK 5	1.2.2	0.10.0	0.5.6	0.4.3	0
	BOTTOM	0.4.5	0.4.4	0.3.1	0.2.5	0.3.3
HALF BREADTHS	SHEER	0.0.6	1.0.3	1.8.6	1.11.6	1.9.4
	PLANK 2	0.0.6	0.11.7	1.8.4		1.9.4
	PLANK 3	0.0.6	0.10.5	1.6.7	1.9.1	1.9.0
	PLANK 4	0.0.6	0.2.6			1.4.4
	PLANK 5	0.06		0.11.1	1.0.4	1.0.1
	BOTTOM	0.-	.7	0.7.6	0.92	0.6.0

To generate the body plan, first plot the heights above base on the profile and fair them. Next, plot and fair the half breadths. Then use tick strips to transfer heights and half breadths to the body plan.

stem. A stem section is nothing more sophisticated than a station that is cut in at an angle. Picture slicing through the stem with a chainsaw. Although this would be deleterious to flotation, you would see exactly how the planks land on the stem. We'll do the deed with a pencil.

Begin by drawing a line that is roughly at right angles to the stem. This will be our centerline. Since our stem is 1½" thick, we'll draw another short line, ¾" to the right of the section centerline and parallel to it to represent the side of the stem in the section.

Next, at the point that each plank crosses the section's centerline, draw a grid line out square. Also square a short line out from where the bearding crosses the centerline to the side-of-stem line.

Okay, now, back to the section centerline. At the point where plank 2 crosses it, draw a line vertically to the centerline of the half-breadth plan. Lay a tick strip along that line and record the distance from the centerline to where it contacts plank 2 (distance A). Take that distance and plot it on the section grid line that radiates out from plank 2 in the profile. Repeat the operation for planks 3 and 4.

Then take a flexible batten and spring it through plotted points for planks 2, 3, 4, and the bearding on the "stem face." Let the batten run past the bearding until it contacts the centerline. That point is the forward face of the stem.

Run another section in an area where you don't have enough information. Then, using the data developed by squaring down from the half-breadth plan and the stem sections, you can spring a batten and get the forward face of the stem.

Expanding the Transom

Once again, this business is about getting the right shape and bevels of the transom. Although we have the transom portrayed in each of the three views,

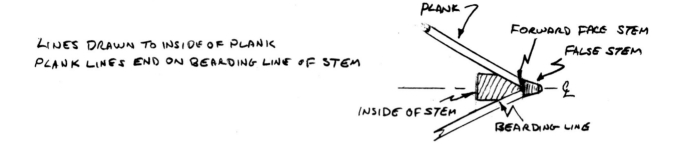

LINES DRAWN TO INSIDE OF PLANK
PLANK LINES END ON BEARDING LINE OF STEM

PLANK
FORWARD FACE STEM
FALSE STEM
INSIDE OF STEM
BEARDING LINE

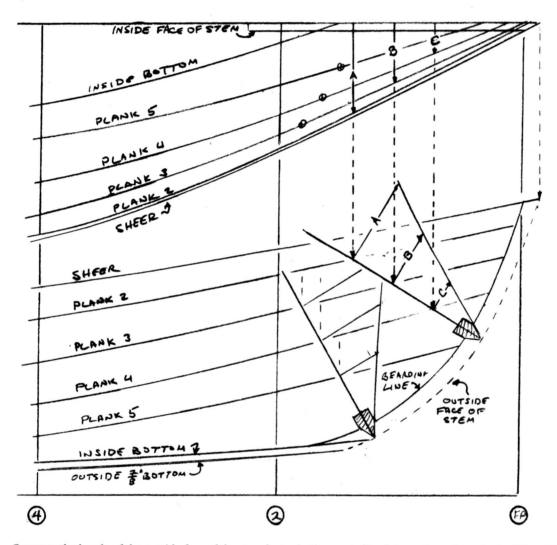

INSIDE FACE OF STEM
INSIDE BOTTOM
PLANK 5
PLANK 4
PLANK 3
PLANK 2
SHEER
SHEER
PLANK 2
PLANK 3
PLANK 4
PLANK 5
INSIDE BOTTOM
OUTSIDE ⅜" BOTTOM

BEARDING LINE
OUTSIDE FACE OF STEM

④ ② FP

Generate the bevels of the outside face of the stem by projecting centerline intersections from the half breadth to stem sections on the profile drawing.

none of them is accurate enough to allow us to make a pattern. In the half-breadth and body plan, the widths are correct, but the length is compressed (too short). On the profile the length is correct but there is no width all! What to do? Employ the same technique used on the stem. We are going to swing the

transom out flat by plotting it on a grid, so we can make a pattern.

We will be using the aft face of the transom as the centerline of the grid. Square lines out from the points where the sheer, planks 2–5, and the bottom strike the transom. Then, as with the stem sections, draw a vertical

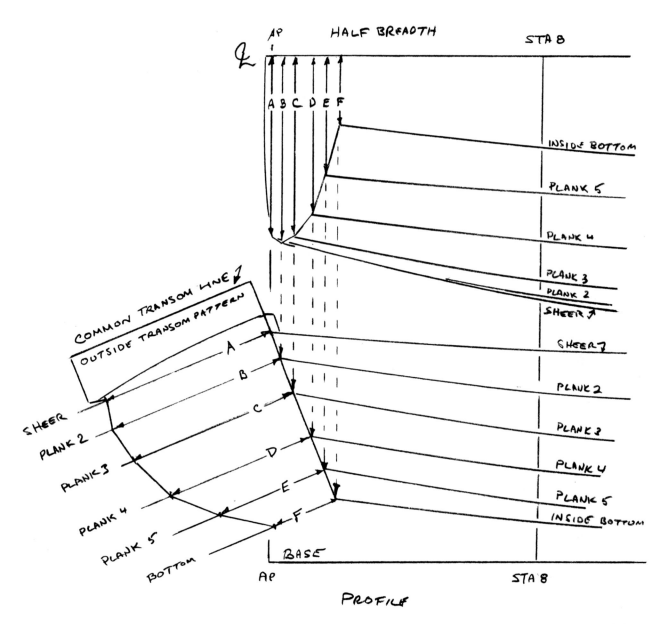

A B C D E F

INSIDE BOTTOM

PLANK 5

PLANK 4

PLANK 3

PLANK 2

SHEER

SHEER

PLANK 2

PLANK 3

PLANK 4

PLANK 5

INSIDE BOTTOM

COMMON TRANSOM LINE

OUTSIDE TRANSOM PATTERN

A

B

C

D

E

F

SHEER

PLANK 2

PLANK 3

PLANK 4

PLANK 5

BOTTOM

BASE

AP   STA 8

PROFILE

To expand the outer (smaller) face of the transom: 1) Square out the gridlines from each plank/transom intersection. 2) Square up to the plank lines on the half-breadth view and mark. 3) Record the distance from the centerline to the intersection marked in Step 2. 4) Plot the recorded distance on the transom grid. 5) Connect the points with a straightedge. 6) Complete by drawing in the common transom line.

line from each intersection to the centerline of the half-breadth. Pick up the width for each plank/transom intersection on the half-breadth with a tick strip, plan, and plot in on the corresponding grid line on the expansion. When all points have been plotted, you can connect the dots and you will have the outside face of the transom—correct in both length and width.

Just one more task. From a convenient point above the crown of the transom, square out one more line.

Label this "common transom line." This line will not only help keep the transom square; it will also index it to maintain the proper bevel. Label this pattern aft or outer. With this action, we are halfway there.

The outside face of the transom is, of course, the smaller face of the transom. If one used only the outer face pattern (even if it were accurate) and cut the transom out square edged, the results would be fairly horrible. There are several ways of dealing with

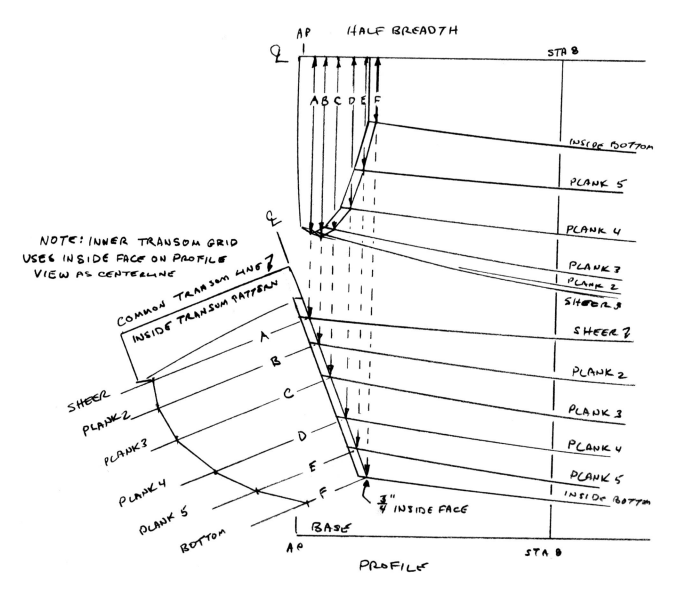

AP HALF BREADTH

STA 8

A B C D E F

INSIDE BOTTOM

PLANK 5

PLANK 4

PLANK 3
PLANK 2
SHEER 3

SHEER 7

PLANK 2

PLANK 3

PLANK 4

PLANK 5
INSIDE BOTTOM

STA 8

NOTE: INNER TRANSOM GRID
USES INSIDE FACE ON PROFILE
VIEW AS CENTERLINE

COMMON TRANSOM LINE 7
INSIDE TRANSOM PATTERN

A

B

C

D

E

F

SHEER

PLANK 2

PLANK 3

PLANK 4

PLANK 5

BOTTOM

$\frac{3}{4}"$ INSIDE FACE

BASE

AP

PROFILE

To expand the inner (larger) face of the transom: 1) Trace the ⅞" thickness line on the profile. 2) Square out the gridlines from each plank/transom intersection. 3) Square up to the plank lines on the half-breadth view and mark. 4) Record the distance from the centerline to the intersection marked in Step 3. 5) Plot the recorded distance on the transom grid. 6) Connect the points with a straightedge. 7) Complete by drawing in the common transom line.

this conundrum. One sure-fire way that works, but is quite time-consuming, is to trace the outside face pattern onto one side of a transom panel, cut it out considerably oversized, install it on the boat, and using a batten and a spokeshave, keep cutting and fitting until you get the transom down to the size traced.

Another method is to expand the inner (larger) face and make a pattern. You can then trace the small face pattern on one side of the panel, the larger on the other, cut the panel out to the large pattern, and spokeshave to

the small. You end up with a transom that is the correct size fore and aft and the compound plank landing bevels develop automatically. This is the method we'll talk about here.

The method of expanding the forward face is the same as used in expanding the after face. The only difference is that you will be using the forward face of the transom for the centerline of the new grid. Begin by drawing the line of the inside face of the transom on the profile, which in our case is ⅞".

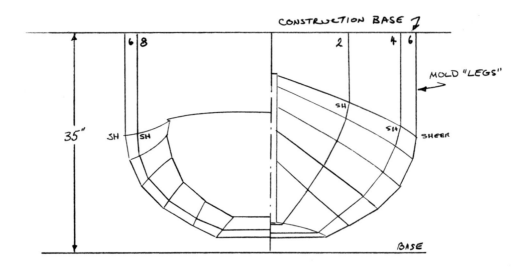

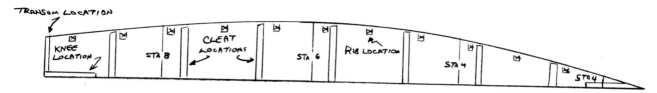

Establishing a common base for the molds (top). *Laying out the expanded bottom pattern.*

Establish the grid in the same fashion, squaring-out from the plank-line intersections. This operation has been known to become confusing due to the number of lines, and for clarity, some builders use different colored pencils or even tape down a piece of cardboard on which to draw their expansion.

As before, draw a vertical line from each intersection of the plank lines with the *inside* of the transom line, to the centerline of the half-breadth. With a tick strip pick up the width for each plank/transom intersection in the half-breadth plan and plot it on the corresponding line on the new grid for the expansion. Again, connect the points and you will have generated the inside face. Lastly, carry over the same common transom line used for indexing the small face onto the drawing of the large face. Label it forward or inner face and you have it.

Note: This system works only if the thickness of your transom panel is the same as the one lofted on the profile. Change the thickness on the stock, and the angle of the bevel will change; then all bets are off!

Remaining Pieces
Now we are entering the home stretch. There is enough information on the drawing to allow us to draw in the various parts of the assembly that either need to have patterns made or will at least affect the placement or shape of the parts that need patterns. Some of the items have their dimensions given on the plans (such as the thickness of the bottom and transom). Others, such as the stem, transom knee, and skeg, do not. This is not uncommon. Rarely will a set of plans have all the dimensions of all the vessel's components expressed numerically. But, *no problema* if one uses the magic of the grid! For example, you can draw a grid with 2″ blocks (in scale) over the stern knee on the plans, using the straight inside face of the transom as your base. Then place the same grid, only full size, on the lofting. Pick up the intersections of the curve of the knee on the scale grid on the plans and transfer them to the full-size grid on the lofting. Connect those points with a drafting spline and trace the curve. *Voila!* This is also the time to make any design modifications. Case in point: dories traditionally had naturally grown curved stems cut from knees. If you do not have any such in your back yard, or your lumber merchant doesn't carry them, you may need to go to straight stock, which means, for strength, a two-piece stem would be in order. This design change can easily be

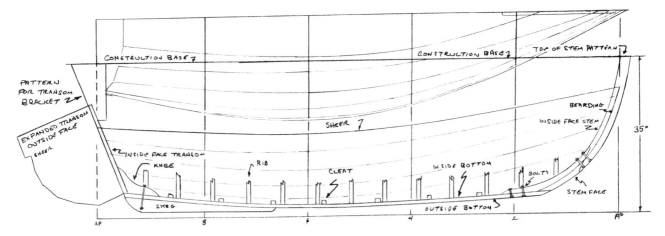

Using the lofting to generate construction patterns.

made on the lofting, as shown. Another design change from the original to consider is increasing the depth of the skeg by ½". This will improve the tracking of the vessel and can be done by just drawing a line parallel to the one shown on the plans ½" down and extending the skeg a bit forward. When you have all the parts drawn in, you can lay out your bolt locations, and note the placement of the bottom cleats (to be sure they are not where the molds are) and even the rib locations (this information will come in handy much further down the line).

Expanding the Bottom

When making a pattern for the bottom, it too will need to be expanded from the lofting, although in a slightly different fashion. The reason is the same, however—the correct measurements are there, but just not in the right places. The bottom has curvature that must be taken into account and if a pattern (and bottom) were simply made from the dimensions shown on the half-breadth, when it was finally bent into place, it would end up being too short. Fortunately, this expansion is an easy task.

Begin by springing a batten over the inside face of the bottom in the profile view—from the aft face of the transom to the forward face of the stem. Mark the location of the fore and aft faces of the stem and transom, the station lines, and the cleat and rib locations onto the batten. Release the batten and place it against the straight edge of your pattern stock (¼" plywood works well for this). Transfer your points to the edge of the plywood. This is the expanded fore and aft distance of

the bottom. Square out all the points. Using tick strip tape, capture the half-breadth distances of the four stations and the transom from the half-breadth plan. Plot these distances onto the plywood. Spring a batten through these points to the forward face of the stem and scribe the line. Cut to the line and there you have your pattern.

Preparing to Build

Our last job is to use the lofting to help us design our construction jig. This can be a real boon as it eliminates a lot of tedious on-the-site measuring, squaring, and angle divination. We will be building upside down, so the first task is to establish a "construction base" on the lofting floor that is parallel to the profile base and will correspond to the top of the strongback or shop floor. This height can be at the builder's discretion—the only consideration being that it should be of a height as to make planking convenient—not so low that you'll have to saw a hole in the floor, nor so high that you'll need a scaffold; 35" above the profile base works well for the Chaisson. Scribe the line and label it.

Next, on the body plan, square lines up from the marked sheer on each station to the 35" line. These represent the extensions or legs of each station mold. The common 35" line will square each mold, and will properly index them so they will all be at the right height relative to one another.

Moving to the bow on the profile, extend the top of the stem up to the 35" line. Note its location on the line relative to the forward perpendicular. The stem pattern will be made to this new length. When setting

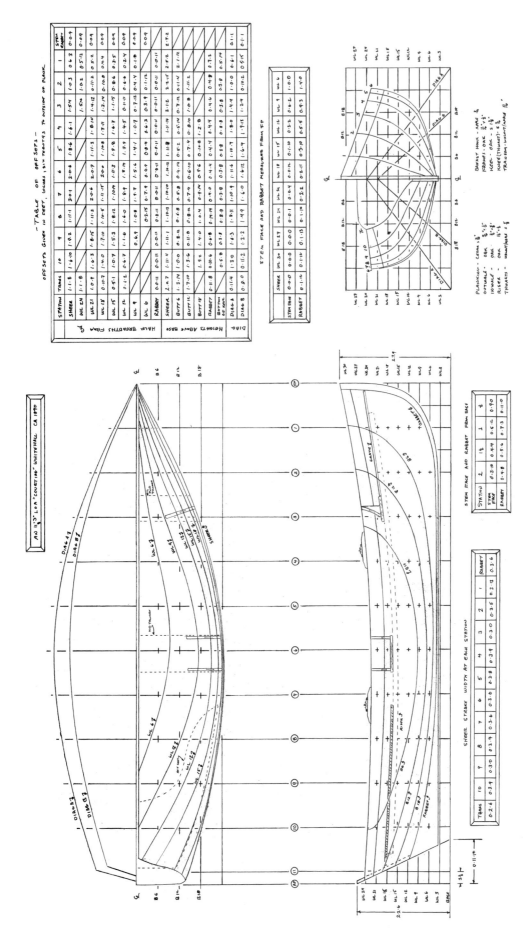

At less than 12' LOA, this miniature Whitehall is nearly as beamy as a full-size one. Careful lofting is required to make such a "curvy" boat fair in all respects. The diagonals in the body plan (also shown above the centerline in the half-breadth view) will help with that.

up the boat, the 35″ line will index the stem at the proper height, and the distance from the forward perpendicular will provide the proper location.

Going aft—working off the construction base, you can design the bracket to fit the common transom top line you drew in the expansion. When the bracket is made, the aft perpendicular will be marked on it to allow it to be indexed on the jig. When the bracket is installed on the jig, it will automatically square the transom, and hold it at the correct angle and in the right location. Engineering. Ain't it grand!

THE ROUND-BOTTOMED HULL

The round-bottomed hull represents the most sophisticated and difficult form of lofting. It involves lots of information, lots of intersections, and lots of views. It also can generate the most elegant hulls. If you enjoy jigsaw and crossword puzzles, this round-bottomed version is for you. The distilling and refining that takes place can also save a barrel of time later on when building. A great subject for this version of lofting is the Whitehall. These boats are noted for their streamlined shape, "hollow" efficient entry of the underwater planks, and wineglass transom.

The original designer/builder of our little subject Whitehall is unknown. It was likely a one-off, built by eye, using a movable single central mold and wrapping battens around the hull at many locations from stem to transom to determine the boat's final shape. Although considerably smaller than the classic Whitehall, this boat is no toy. It rows well and contains all the construction details found on its larger cousins. The lines were taken from, and drawn to the outside of, the plank.

At first blush, the drawing of our round-bottomed boat appears to have a lot in common with the sharpie skiff and the semi-dory. And so it does. There are the three views—half-breadth, profile, and body plan. Again, all three views are inextricably linked together. Also present are the familiar base, centerline, stations, fore and aft perpendiculars, and sheer lines. There are some important differences as well. As mentioned, the lines are drawn to the outside of plank, and the stem is rabbeted instead of being simply beveled. Also, there are a lot more reference lines in the three views, and there is a whole new view called diagonals. What's up? The round hull is simply more complex to get right, so more enhanced information is necessary. Let's take a look at some of these differences.

Curved Lines

In the half-breadth plans for the semi-dory, the curved fore and aft running long lines corresponded to the run of the planks. In the round-bottomed blueprint, the long, curved lines portray parallel lines of elevation—similar to contour lines on a topographic map.

In the Whitehall plans, the baseline is used as a starting point and the "contour interval" is 3″. These contour lines are called waterlines ("WL" on the plan). To further muddy the waters, these lines rarely have anything to do with the actual flotational waterline of the hull. When viewed on the profile and body plan, waterlines appear as straight lines that run parallel to the base.

In the profile of the Whitehall, the drawn curved lines are called *buttocks*. These are the vertical, fore and aft slices or planes that run through the hull at regular intervals parallel to the centerline. These really are contour lines too—they just happen to be vertical ones. When viewed on the half-breadth plan and body plan, the buttocks appear as straight lines that run parallel to the centerline.

Diagonals

Diagonals are the bugbear of the first-time loftsman. So, what's the deal with them? The diagonals are used in the same way the waterlines and buttocks are—to check the fairness of the hull. Indeed, all these lines are used just like when the old-time builder wrapped the fairing batten around the setup frames (or molds) at different locations to check for lumps, bumps, or hollows.

Intersecting lines are most accurate when they meet at near right angles. (Think of the accuracy of latitude and longitude intersections.) Lines that intersect one another at low angles have more ambiguity and uncertainty. So the waterlines are most accurate in the upper part of the hull where they cross the stations in the body plan. The buttocks are most accurate down near the keel, where they intersect the stations at near right angles in the body plan. The area not well served by either the waterlines or buttocks is the turn of the bilge.

This is where the diagonals come in. If we look at the body plan, we see a diagonal line that comes from a point on the centerline. The angle of the line was set to intersect the turn of the bilge at as close to a right angle as possible.

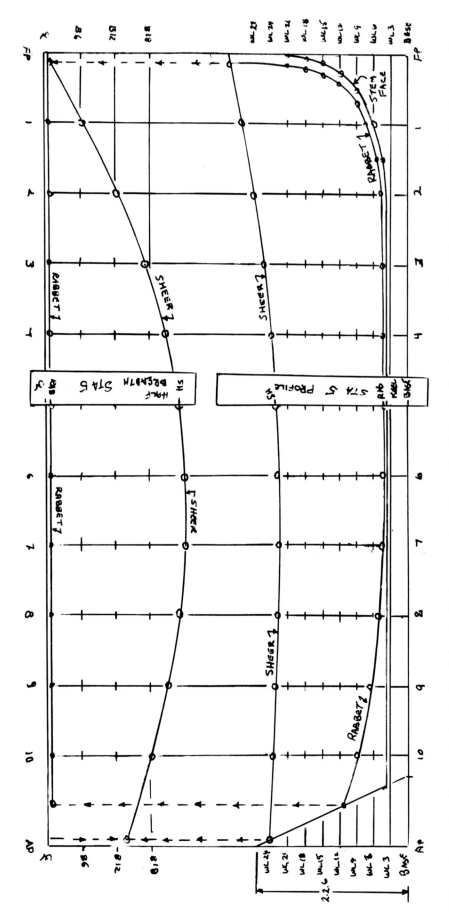

After setting up the grid, start the drawing by: 1) drawing the sheer on the profile; 2) drawing the transom rake on the profile; 3) drawing the rabbet, keel, and stem on the profile; 4) squaring the transom and rabbet endings to the half breadths; 5) drawing the half breadths of the keel and sheer; 6) picking up the height of the sheer, rabbet, and keel on the profile with a tick strip; 7) picking up the half breadth of the sheer and keel on the half breadth; and 8) bringing the distances to the body plan.

Think of it like the face of a (analog) clock. Waterlines radiate from the centerline like the hour hand at 3:00. The diagonal is like the hour hand at 4:30 or 4:45. Both are uniform planes sliced through the hull, fore to aft, that have station lines marked on them. Like the waterline, diagonal offsets are measured out from the centerline onto the stations, and a batten is sprung through those offsets to check for fairness.

Setting Up the Grid

Our little Whitehall is approximately the same size as the sharpie and the Chaisson, so we'll be able to fit all the drawings on two pieces of plywood. There are more lines to contend with, however:

- There are 11 stations to be drawn on the profile and half-breadth plans (of which 10 will be used).
- There will be waterlines (running parallel to the base) every 3", running from 3" to 30", drawn on the body plan and profile plan.
- Then, there are three buttocks that will be drawn every 6", parallel to the centerline, on the half-breadth plan and the body plan. In the half-breadth plan the buttocks will be horizontal, and in the body plan, they will be vertical.
- Finally, there are the two diagonal reference lines in the body plan. Commonly, these lines run out in two directions (sort of teepee like) from a given height on the centerline and through a given intersection on the grid. On our blueprints, Diagonal A (Diag. A) runs from waterline (WL) 24 on the centerline (CL) to 30" out on the baseline. Diag B runs from WL 21 on the CL to Buttock 18 (B 18) on the baseline.

With that completed, let's begin.

The Profile

Once again, the transom is drawn first. To get the rake of the transom, go up 2-2-6 (26⅜") on the aft perpendicular and 11⅞" forward of the aft perpendicular on the base. Connect the dots with a straightedge. Note that it's the top of the transom that touches the aft perpendicular—not the sheer.

Next, we'll tackle the sheer. Go to the table of offsets and record all the sheer "heights above base" onto the drawing. To get the sheer at the transom, measure up the aft perpendicular the given transom height (2-0-7)

and square over until you hit the rake of the transom. Connect the points with a stiff wooden batten and draw in the line.

To draw in the stem and rabbet, we'll be using two smaller tables of offsets. The first (just below the main table) is titled "Stem Face and Rabbet measured from FP." These offsets are (as advertised) to be measured back from the forward perpendicular. The second table is located right under the stem and is called "Stem Face and Rabbet from Base." These are measured up vertically. Connect these points with a light plastic batten and drafting ducks.

Next, it's back to the main table of offsets to plot the heights of the bottom of the keel and rabbet from the stem to the transom. Then it's on to the half-breadth view.

The Half-Breadth View

We can now run the keel rabbet and sheer in the half-breadth view. The plans indicate that the keel and stem are 1⅜" s (for *sided* or width) and 1⅛" m (for *molded* or height). When we draw the keel, it is half the thickness (⁹⁄₁₆") out from the centerline. As the lines are drawn to the outside of the plank, the width of the rabbet line is the same thing as the width of the keel. This keel rabbet line runs from the forward perpendicular aft to where the transom hits the keel. Where is that on the half-breadth plan? Just go to the profile view and look where the rabbet in that view hits the rake of the transom. Square that distance down to the half-breadth plan. That's the distance forward of the aft perpendicular that the rabbet/keel ends on that view as well.

Now we can plot the sheer. Using the table of offsets, measure out the location of the sheer at each station. Then plot the sheer at the transom. To get where this point actually lies, go back to the profile view and find where the sheer hits the rake of the transom. Square that distance down to the centerline in the half-breadth view. Then, using a framing square, measure out the given offset distance.

Finally, let's plot the location of where the sheer hits the rabbet. Again, go to the profile view and locate the point where the sheer meets the rabbet. Square that distance (aft of the forward perpendicular) down to the rabbet/keel line in the half-breadth view. Spring a batten through all the points from the rabbet to the transom. Sight the line and when its looks fair, scribe it in.

TABLE OF OFFSETS
OFFSETS GIVEN IN FEET, INCHES, SIXTEENTHS TO OUTSIDE OF PLANK

	STATION	TRANS	10	9	8	7	6	5	4	3	2	1	STEM RABBET
HALF BREADTHS FROM ℄	SHEER	1·1·8	1·6·10	1·9·2	1·11·1	2·0·1	2·0·6	1·8·6	1·6·1	1·5·4	1·0·3	0·6·3	0·0·9
	WL 24	1·1·8								1·5·4	1·0·2	0·5·12	0·0·9
	WL 21	1·0·9	1·6·3	1·8·15	1·11·2	2·0·6	2·0·7	1·11·3	1·8·10	1·4·12	0·11·2	0·5·2	0·0·9
	WL 18	0·10·7	1·4·0	1·7·10	1·10·5	1·11·15	2·0·0	1·10·8	1·7·11	1·3·14	0·10·8	0·4·4	0·0·9
	WL 15	0·5·1	1·0·7	1·5·3	1·8·12	1·10·14	1·11·3	1·9·8	1·6·7	1·1·15	0·8·6	0·3·5	0·0·9
	WL 12	0·1·2	0·6·7	1·1·6	1·6·0	1·8·9	1·8·14	1·7·9	1·4·5	0·11·11	0·6·6	0·2·4	0·0·9
	WL 9			0·6·9	1·0·8	1·9·7	1·5·6	1·4·1	1·0·7	0·7·12	0·4·4	0·1·8	0·0·9
	WL 6			0·3·15	0·7·9	0·9·9	0·8·4	0·6·3	0·3·9	0·1·12			0·0·9
	RABBET	0·0·11	0·0·11	0·0·11	0·0·11	0·0·11	0·0·11	0·0·11	0·0·11	0·0·11	0·0·11	0·0·11	
HEIGHTS ABOVE BASE	SHEER	2·0·7	1·11·11	1·11·1	1·10·13	1·10·10	1·10·12	1·11·8	1·11·14	2·1·2	2·2·15	2·5·2	2·7·2
	BUTT 6	1·3·14	1·0·0	0·8·12	0·6·8	0·5·8	0·4·14	0·5·2	0·5·14	0·7·12	0·11·4	2·1·12	
	BUTT 12	1·7·10	1·3·6	0·11·8	0·8·12	0·7·4	0·6·10	0·7·4	0·8·10	1·0·8	1·11·2		
	BUTT 18		1·9·2	1·4·0	1·0·4	0·9·14	0·9·6	0·10·8	1·2·8				
	RABBET	0·11·8	0·10·6	0·6·8	0·14·14	0·4·0	0·4·4	0·4·4	0·4·4	0·4·6	0·4·8	0·7·2	
	BOTTOM OF KEEL		0·5·8	0·3·8	0·8·8	0·3·8	0·3·8	0·3·8	0·3·8	0·3·8	0·5·14		
DIAG	DIAG A	0·11·4	1·3·0	1·6·3	1·8·11	1·10·9	1·11·6	1·10·7	1·8·0	1·4·4	1·0·0	0·6·1	0·1·1
	DIAG B	0·8·0	0·11·2	1·2·2	1·4·9	1·6·0	1·6·12	1·6·4	1·9·13	1·2·4	0·10·2	0·5·15	0·1·1

STEM FACE AND RABBET MEASURED FROM FP

	SHEER	WL 30	WL 27	WL 24	WL 21	WL 18	WL 15	WL 12	WL 9	WL 6
STEM FACE	0·0·0	0·0·0	0·0·0	0·0·1	0·0·4	0·0·12	0·1·10	0·3·2	0·6·2	1·0·0
RABBET	0·1·12	0·1·12	0·1·13	0·1·14	0·2·2	0·2·11	0·3·10	0·5·5	0·9·3	1·4·0

Table of offsets.

The Body Plan

In the sharpie and the semi-dory, the body plans were done late in the game, combining the faired heights and widths from both the profile and half-breadth views. We could do the same with the Whitehall. But there's a lot to be said for developing the body plan at an earlier stage. Here's the deal: compared with our first two boats, the Whitehall has a ton of information in the offset table coming in from three other views. Some of those offsets are going to be mildly funky—incorrect but not standing out like sore thumbs. Because the station spacing is relatively far apart, we might not pick up the bum offsets when running the waterlines, buttocks, and diagonals. But when we transfer the developed distances to the cramped body plan and try to create a fair station, all of a sudden those bad points that came from the lines drawn previously through the bad points will jump out and will have to be corrected in the previous view. And that might force us to change yet another view. Ugh, who needs it?

So here's what we'll do. For the sheer and the rabbet at the keel, we'll combine the information from the sheers and keel rabbet already drawn on the profile and half-breadth views. Those lines have already been faired and they look good. So unless something extraordinary happens, those faired offsets are written in stone. Bring those distances over with the tick strips and plot them on the body plan grid as we did previously. Then, for each station (one at a time to avoid confusion) dump in all the offsets from the table. So when running Station 8, there will be the sheer, the rabbet, six waterline offsets coming in from the centerline, three buttock offsets coming up from the base, and two diagonal offsets coming down at an angle. Spring a batten through all these points and look for a fair line. If we hit twelve out of thirteen points with a nice smooth line, that's a pretty good indicator that the thirteenth offset is a bummer or at least an outlier. Just to be on the safe side, we can check the distance by

measuring the blueprint with a scale rule. Often the offset was incorrectly recorded on the table by the draftsman. Note that the offset is bad, draw the line, and move on to the next station. And the next, until the full set of stations has been completed. This is now our new, corrected set of offsets for the rest of the plan. The rest of the waterlines, buttocks, and diagonals will come from distances brought over by tick strip from the body plan.

Running the Waterlines

With the body plan out of the way, much of our work is done. It's a lot like when the old-timer made and set up his construction molds or frames. The next step was to wrap battens around them to check them for fairness.

The waterlines are run in the same manner that we ran the sheer in the profile. Only it's easier as we

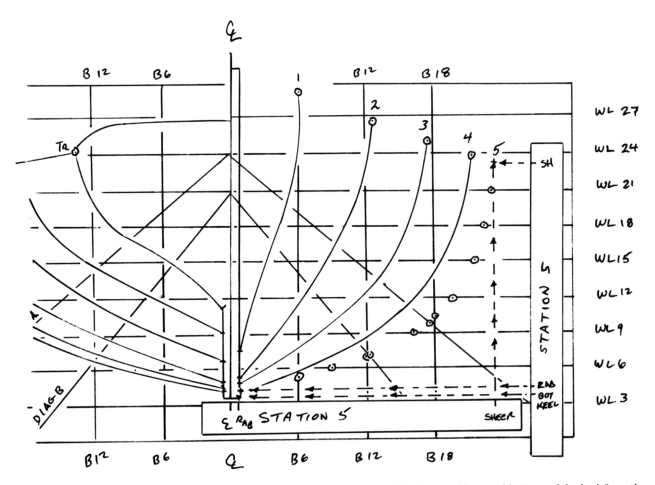

Draw the body plan as follows: 1) Use tick strips to bring the intersections of the sheer, rabbet, and bottom of the keel from the half-breadth and profile views. 2) Plot the intersections on the body plan. 3) Plot offsets for waterlines, buttocks, and diagonals onto the body plan. 4) Fair with a batten.

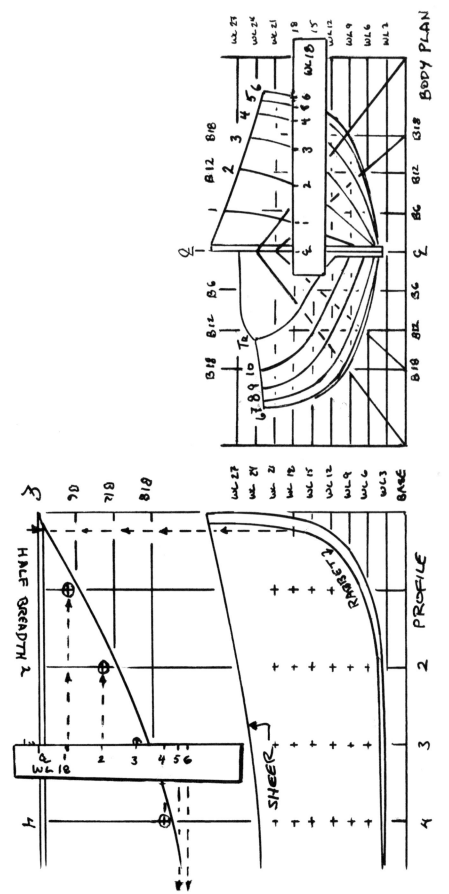

To run the waterlines: 1) Pick up the waterline widths at each station on the body plan on a tick strip; 2) Bring the widths to the half breadth plan for each station; 3) Square the waterline endings up from the profile waterline intersection to the rabbet line in the half-breadth view.

don't need to use the table of offsets (or at least, not very much). Instead, we'll use tick strip tape and the body plan.

Let's run waterline 18. Stretch a paper tape along waterline 18 across one side of the body plan to the other. Mark and label the tape at each station, the transom, and the centerline. That's it: the table of offsets for waterline 18.

Go to the half-breadth plan. Place the centerline mark on the centerline and stretch the tape out on Station 1 and record the Station 1 distance for waterlineL 18 on the board. Move the tape to Station 2, align the CL, and record that WL 18 distance. Then on to Station 3 and so on for all the other stations. At the transom, it's just like when we ran the sheer: go back to the profile view and find where the waterline hits the rake of the transom. Square that distance down to the centerline in the half-breadth view. Then, using a framing square, measure out the "tape-recorded" distance of the transom.

Where waterline 18 meets the stem, go back to the profile view and locate the point where the waterline crosses the rabbet. Square that distance (aft of the forward perpendicular) down to the rabbet/keel line in the half-breadth view.

Spring a batten through all the points from the rabbet to the transom. Sight the line and when it looks fair, scribe it in. If there is a bump in the batten, the body plan needs to be corrected. Let the batten fair through and take the distance generated back to the body plan and correct it.

All the rest of the waterlines are run in the same fashion. In the lower waterlines, we get out of the transom and the aft end is treated like a double-ender. Waterlines 12 and 9 come into the keel just as they do at the stem.

With the waterlines done, we've tuned up the topsides. Now let's check below with the buttocks.

Running the Buttocks

Now the plot thickens. To run the buttocks, we'll take intersection information from both the body plan and the half-breadth plan. To start, place a tape on buttock 12 on the right-hand side of the body plan. Record the baseline and the station line intersections onto the tape. Then, slide the tape to the left side of the body plan. Align the baseline of the tape with the drawing and capture the rest of the stations.

Bring the tape to the profile. Align the baseline of the tape with the base of each station line and transfer the height from the tape to the profile. Then do the Station 2 height from the body plan to the Station 2 line on the profile, and so on. Mark the height on the transom as well. Label them all. That takes care of the bottom and middle of the boat. Now we need to deal with the ends.

To do that, we are going to square the waterline/ buttock intersections from the half-breadth view to the profile view. (Same old intersections on the hull, just a different view.) These can simply be squared down with a framing square, but the easiest way is to use a tick strip tape.

Stretch out a piece of tape on buttock 12 on the forward end of the half-breadth view. Mark a couple of stations onto the tape as index marks (maybe Stations 1 and 2). Record the sheer and all the waterline intersections onto the tape and label them. Mark the tape buttock 12.

Then slide the tape horizontally down to the profile view. Index it to stations 1 and 2 and mark the sheer point on the profile sheer. Label it B12. Then, slide the tape down to waterline 24 in the profile. Again, index the stations and transfer the waterline 24 point to the line and label it B12. Slide the tape to waterline 21 and repeat the operation. Continue for each waterline.

Capture the half-breath intersections back aft in the same way we did the forward intersections, and bring them down to the profile. After checking that everything is labeled, it's time to (finally) run the batten through the points.

Actually, this is usually a two- to three-batten operation. Use a heavier batten through the run of the bottom and, at the ends where the batten starts to feel cranky and unbendable, use lighter, more flexible battens to finish up the line. What we are especially looking for is the heavy batten to land easily on each station. If it does, so will your bottom planking on the boat.

Repeat the operations for the other buttocks.

For many boats we could stop here and be fairly certain that our lines would work. But to make absolutely sure, we can run the diagonals.

The Diagonals

The diagonal has gotten a lot of bad press over the years. The terms "difficult," "odious," and "fiendish"

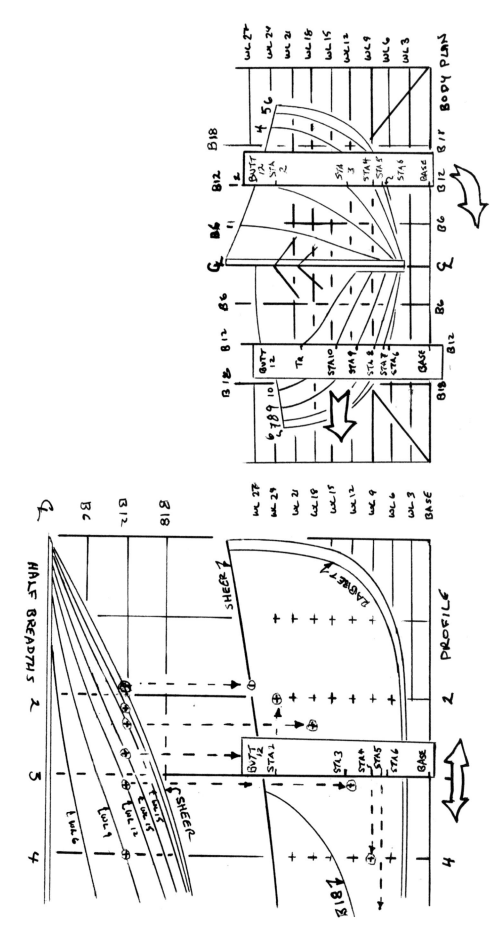

Running the buttocks: 1) On the body plan, use a tick strip to record the heights of the intersections of the buttocks at each station. 2) Bring the heights over to the profile and record them on each station. 3) Square down the waterline/buttock intersections from the half-breadths to the profile (or use a tick strip).

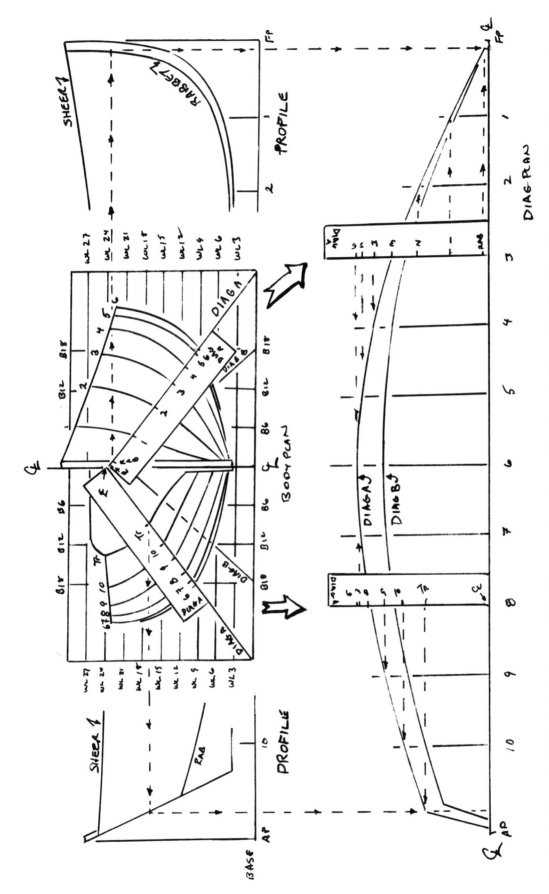

Running the diagonals: 1) On the body plan, record the distance out from the centerline along the diagonal for all stations, the transom, and the rabbet onto a tick strip. 2) Plot the distances on each station line on the diagonal plan. 3) Record the height above base of the diagonal/rabbet intersection and the transom/diagonal intersection on the body plan. 4) Square the transom and rabbet heights to the profile. 5) Square the intersections to the centerline of the diagonal plan. Plot the rabbet and transom widths on the diagonal plan.

come to mind. Baloney. The diagonal is run very much like the humble waterline: just pick up the width of the intersections of the stations measured out from the centerline and plot them on the board. Then figure out the endings, plot them, and spring the batten through the points. No big deal.

Strangely enough, the biggest problem with running the diagonals is finding a place to run them that doesn't cause confusion. If one had the space, another lofting board could be set up that just had a centerline, stations, and a forward perpendicular and aft perpendicular. Then the diagonals could be drawn just as they are on the blueprints. But chances are, room for lofting will be limited, at best. So the next best thing is to run the curved diagonal lines onto a lofting board in a direction that is obviously contrary to the lines already drawn below. Often, the profile baseline will serve as a centerline for the diagonals.

Start by stretching a tape down along the diagonal (diag A) line on the right side of the body plan. Record the centerline, the rabbet line, and each of the stations. Then, swing the tape to the diag A line on the left side of the body plan. Index the centerline and record the rest of the stations and the transom onto the tape. As with the waterlines, plot the captured station distances onto the grid.

Next we need the endings. Like the waterline endings, we'll need to go back to another view to show us where on the centerline we have to measure out the recorded distance on the body plan tape.

First go back to the body plan and (measuring vertically) record the height above the base where diag A crosses the transom and record on a tape where it crosses the rabbet line.

Take the second tape to the profile and slide it across the drawing until the "height of diag. A at rabbet" contacts the rabbet in the profile. Square that distance aft of the forward perpendicular down to the centerline on the grid for the diagonal. From that point, square out the rabbet distance from tape one. This is the forward endpoint. For the transom, it is the same operation: slide the second tape over until the transom height contacts the rake of the transom. Square that distance forward of the aft perpendicular to the centerline on the grid for the diagonal. From that point, square out the rabbet distance from tape one. This is the aft endpoint. Now we have all the points for the diagonal line. Strike the line in.

Expanding the Round Transom

As with the sharpie and the semi-dory, the round-bottomed boat needs to have its transom expanded. The transom has more shape, but we also have more information.

First, create the grid off the aft face of the raked transom. The transom line in the profile will be the centerline for the grid. Square out lines at the sheer and the rabbet, and from where each waterline intersects the rake of the transom. On that new grid, also draw in the gridlines for buttocks 6 and 12. Take a tape and from either the body plan or half-breadth plan, pick up the transom widths for the sheer, rabbet, and waterlines, and plot them on the new grid. Then, square over the points where buttocks A and B hit the transom to their respective lines on the new grid. Connect the points with a flexible batten and draw it in.

As before, we'll need the forward, larger face of the transom. Our transom is ¾" thick. Draw that line parallel to the aft raked transom line. Again draw the grid including all waterlines and buttocks.

To get the sheer, rabbet, and waterline widths, square down from those intersections on the inside face transom line in profile to their respective lines in the half-breadth view. Pick up each of those distances to the centerline with a tick strip tape. Plot them on the new grid. Square the buttock intersections with the inside-of-profile transom to their grid lines on the expanded transom grid. Connect the points and we have the inside face of the transom. Now the transom patterns can be made.

Remember, like the two previous transoms, this one is raked. This means the reference lines will be higher on one side (the smaller after face) of the transom panel than the other. So while the centerline of the transom can be squared around, the reference waterlines cannot. Pick up the angle that the waterlines cross the transom in profile with your bevel gauge. Plot the grid on the aft face of the transom panel. At the edge of the panel, record the angle of offset for each waterline and draw those offset waterlines onto the forward side of the panel.

Plotting the Rabbet and Stem Sections

To cut the rabbet into the stem, we will have to develop the locations of the apex and bearding line and plot them onto the profile view. From there, the rabbet, apex, and bearding line can be transferred

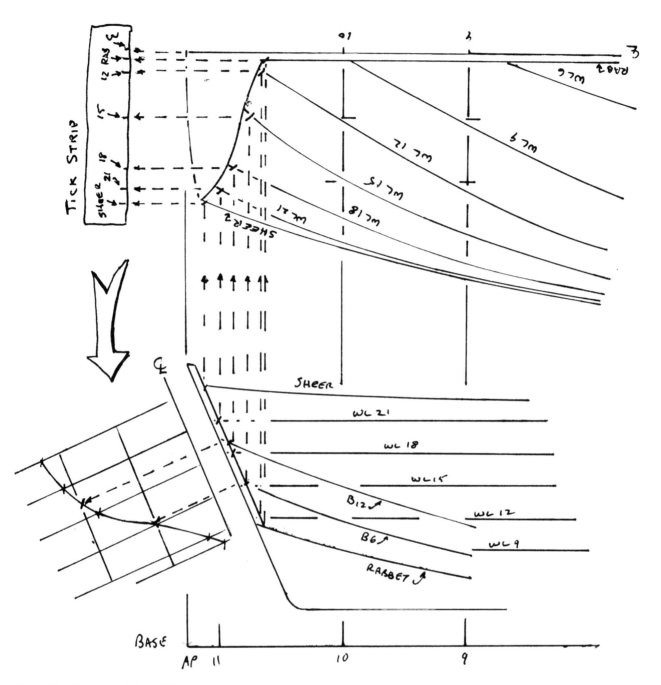

Expanding the forward face of the transom.

to the keel and stem of the real boat. These lines are quite easy to develop and the only specialty tool you'll need is a slip of wood that is the thickness of your planking. This can be called a plank sample or "fid." We'll combine information from a few different locations.

Let's start with the stations. Our planking is drawn to the outside of plank. Place the fid on the inner side of each of the drawn station lines with the outside edge touching the rabbet line. Draw around the fid with a pencil. The inner corner of the fid makes the apex. Where the "inside of plank" face of the fid hits the outer face of the keel is the bearding line. Mark and label both. Pick up the heights above base for the apex and bearding lines with a tick strip tape and transfer them to the stations and transom on the profile plan.

Expanding the aft face of the transom.

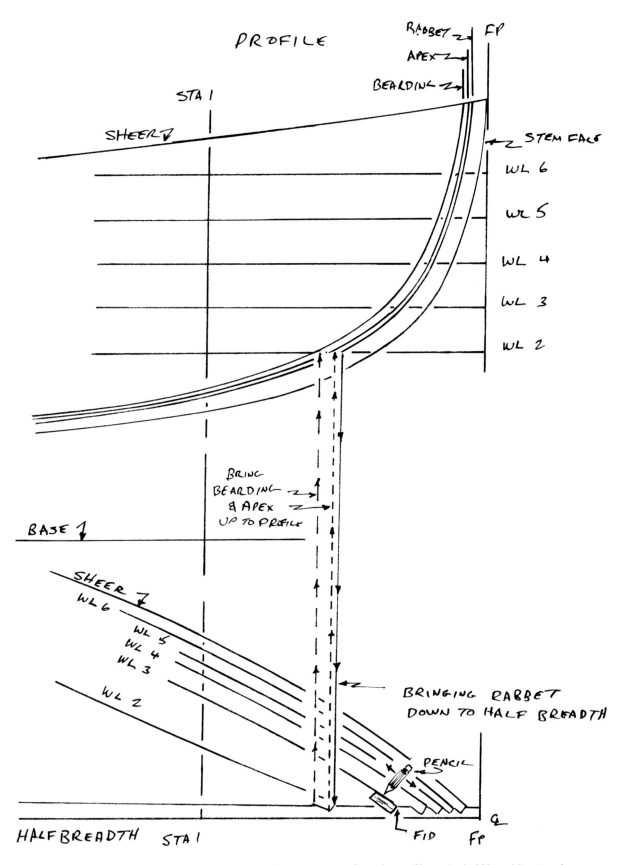

PROFILE

RABBET
APEX
BEARDING
FP

STA 1

SHEER

STEM FACE

WL 6

WL 5

WL 4

WL 3

WL 2

BRING
BEARDING
& APEX
UP TO PROFILE

BASE

SHEER
WL 6
WL 5
WL 4
WL 3
WL 2

BRINGING RABBET
DOWN TO HALF BREADTH

PENCIL

HALFBREADTH   STA 1

FID

FP

Lofting the rabbet, Part A. 1) Bring the waterline/rabbet intersection from the profile to the half-breadths: 2) After water-lines are run in the half-breadth view, place a plank sample on the waterline ending and trace around it (see Part B). 3) Bring the bearding and apex intersections to the profile drawing, spring a light batten, and trace the curve.

196 *Building Techniques*

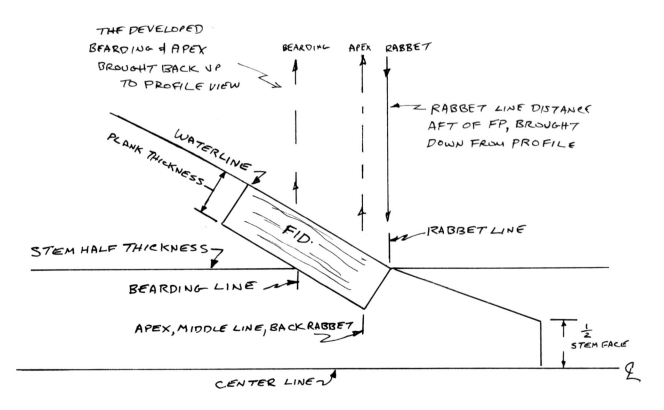

THE DEVELOPED BEARDING & APEX BROUGHT BACK UP TO PROFILE VIEW

BEARDING   APEX   RABBET

RABBET LINE DISTANCE AFT OF FP, BROUGHT DOWN FROM PROFILE

PLANK THICKNESS   WATERLINE

FID.

STEM HALF THICKNESS

BEARDING LINE

RABBET LINE

APEX, MIDDLE LINE, BACK RABBET

½ STEM FACE

CENTER LINE

DETERMINING BEARDING LINE & APEX. LINES TO OUTSIDE OF PLANK

Lofting the rabbet, Part B.

Next, bring the fid to the half-breadth plan. Place the fid on the inside of each waterline as it enters the stem, with the outside edge of the fid touching the rabbet line. Draw around the fid with a pencil. Again, the inner corner of the fid marks the location of the apex, and the intersection of the "inside of plank" face of the fid with the outer face of the keel marks the bearding line. Mark and label both. Pick up the distance aft of the forward perpendicular for the apex and bearding lines with a tick strip tape and transfer them to their respective waterlines on the stem on the profile plan.

That takes care of the upper part of the stem and the length of the keel, but what about the curving forefoot of the stem? That's where the stem section comes in. The stem section is a bit like a station sliced at a near perpendicular to the curve of the forefoot of the stem. The idea of this kind of slice is that we'll be getting crisp right angle information, instead of the less accurate angled, mushy information from the lower waterlines.

The stem section works just like the stations and transom expansion that we have already drawn. There will be a centerline, a grid with waterlines to plot

distances on, and a line drawn parallel to the centerline that represents the side of the stem.

Start by selecting the spot on the curved rabbet on the forefoot that you wish to run this raked station. Draw a straight line that runs tangent to the curve at that point. Then, using a framing square, erect a line that starts at the selected point and is perpendicular to the tangent line. Label this centerline. Then, draw a line that is parallel to that centerline, distant from it by the half-thickness of the stem (as on the half-breadth plan).

Next, use the square to draw lines out from every intersection that this new centerline makes with the profile waterlines. Then draw a square line from the rabbet intersection at the centerline to the parallel side-of-stem line. That will be our rabbet line ending for this section or "station." We now have a completed grid.

Our next job is to pick up the half-breadth widths to plot on our grid. For example: follow our raked section centerline up to where it intersects waterline 15. Draw a line vertically (i.e., parallel to the forward perpendicular and profile stations) up to the centerline in the half-breadth plan. Pick up the distance from the

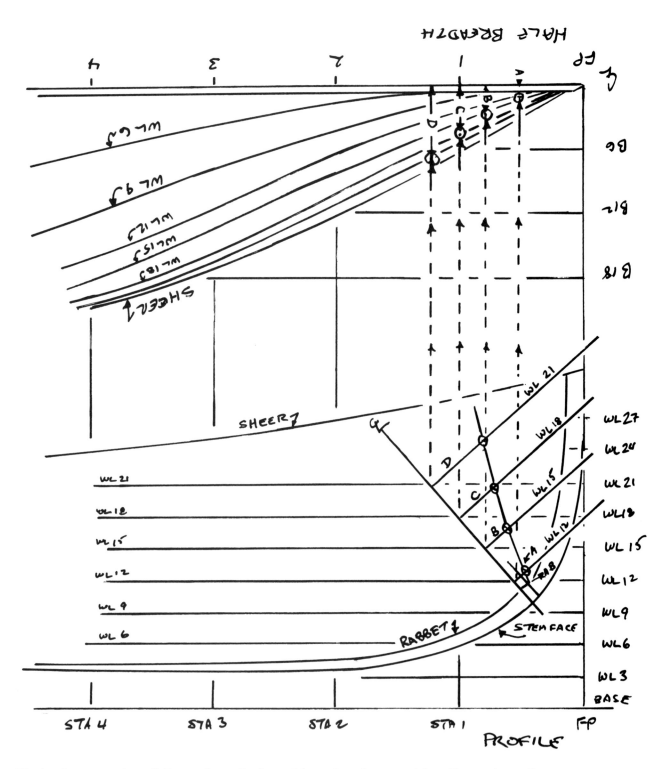

Plotting the stem sections: 1) Draw a "centerline" at a right angle to the curve of the rabbet on the profile. 2) Draw right angles out from this centerline at each intersection with a waterline and the rabbet. This is the stem section "grid." Label these lines with the waterlines to which they correspond. 3) Where the stem section grid waterline intersects the real waterlines, square a line vertically to the half-breadth plan. 4) Using a tick strip, bring the half-breadth distance for each waterline to the stem section grid. 5) After plotting the points for each waterline and the rabbet, connect the points with a flexible batten and trace.

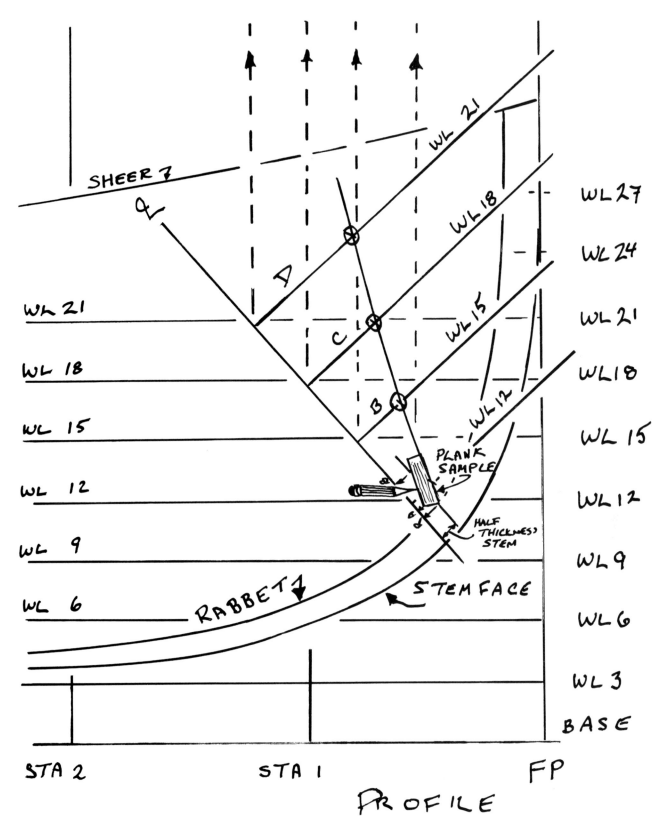

Trace around the "fid" (plank sample) to develop the rabbet, apex, and bearing line. Then square back to the centerline of the stem section grid.

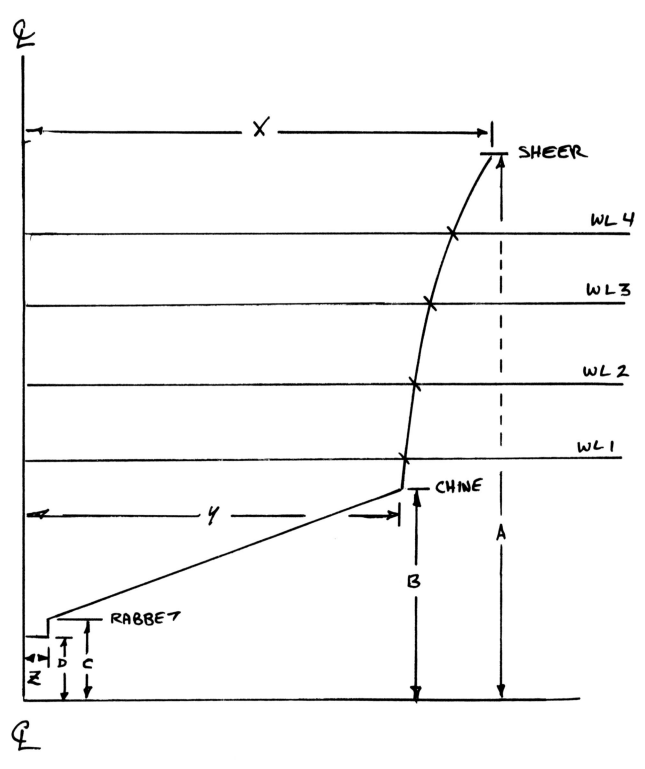

V-hulls with curved topsides must have lofted waterlines. Obtain the heights above base for the sheer, chine, rabbet, and bottom of the keel from the profile. Get the width from centerline for the sheer, chine, rabbet, and outer face of the keel from the half-breadth view. Use the table of offsets for the waterline half breadths.

centerline to waterline 15 in that view with a tick strip. Take that distance and plot it out from the centerline on the waterline 15 line on the stem section grid. Mark it and label it.

Repeat the operation for waterlines 12, 18, and 21. Connect those points with the rabbet on the side of the stem line. *Voila!* You have just drawn the shape of the hull at that slice. Next, place the fid on the inside of the "station" line as we did with the regular stations. Again, the inner corner of the fid makes the apex. Where the inside of the fid hits the outside of the plank is the bearding line. Mark and label both. Square both the apex and bearding back to the section centerline. We now have a very accurate plot of the rabbet at that location. Sections can be run as often as necessary.

For each line—rabbet, apex, and bearding—spring a batten through all the developed points, from the top of the stem to the keel at the stern. With those lines run, the rabbet can be cut.

Deducting the Planking Thickness

One last thing. The lines on this boat were drawn to the outside of the plank. To use the lines to actually build the boat, we must deduct the thickness of the planking from the molds and the transom. On a lightly planked hull (up to ⅝" plank thickness) we can simply use a series of compass arcs, or even just a planking sample as a spacer to make a series of reference points

inside of our drawn stations and transom that we can then connect with a batten to give us the inside of plank shape.

THE V-BOTTOMED HULL

Finally, we come to V-shaped hulls. Flat or "slab sided" V-bottomed hulls are lofted in a very similar fashion to the flat-bottomed hard-chined boat. Usually there are just three main reference points: the sheer, the chine, and the side of the keel (rabbet or apex). The keel will be plotted in much the same way as in the round-bottomed hull. The stem, if two-piece, will be like that in the flat-bottomed sharpie or the semi-dory. If the stem is rabbeted, it can be dealt with in a manner similar to the round-bottomed example.

When the sides sport a curve or flare (as often appears in the topsides above the chine), things can get a bit more complicated. To portray the curved side accurately, we need to have a few more reference lines. Like with the round-bottomed hull, on the profile and half-breadth view, a number of waterlines are drawn parallel to the load waterline. These are used in the same way as the waterlines in the round-bottomed hull. Offsets are given and curved waterlines are drawn in the half-breadth view. Other builders have run shallow diagonals through the curved topsides. The result is the same—to give the builder enough reference points to draw and build a fair and smooth hull.

· 25 ·

Construction Setup

With the lofting under our belts, we can proceed with the setup of the construction jig.

Before getting underway, a decision has to be made as to whether to build right-side up or upside down. Both styles have their place. At first blush, the upright faction would seem to have the edge. There is no need for any of the elaborate permanent assembly that is sometimes required for upside-down construction, you can have ready access to the interior (good for riveting), as the vessel is already upright, there's no need to turn the boat over later, and it looks like a boat. On the other hand, a boat (even one under construction) is like an upside-down pyramid, with all the weight on top of a very small base.

Gravity is also working against you when you are planking. Instead of the weight of the plank working with you, you end up having to push it up into place. The plank, clamps, and glues are always threatening to fall on your head as you work below. Lining out of planks, installing seam battens, strip planking, caulking, and fairing the completed hull is all easier when the hull is upside down. But, yes, after planking, you do need to turn the boat right-side up.

If you are building right-side up, the keel will need to be supported by blocks, timbers, or a narrow rail-like strongback, or construction frame, that will allow you access to the underside of the hull.

If building upside down, the choice is whether to set up directly on the floor or on a strongback. Although the setup and construction techniques of both methods

are the same, the strongback method has the edge for overall practicality. The on-the-floor approach requires the molds and jigs to be fastened directly to the floor (or to sleepers that are fastened to the floor). That's not a

Right-side-up construction. (Photo: Emily Herman)

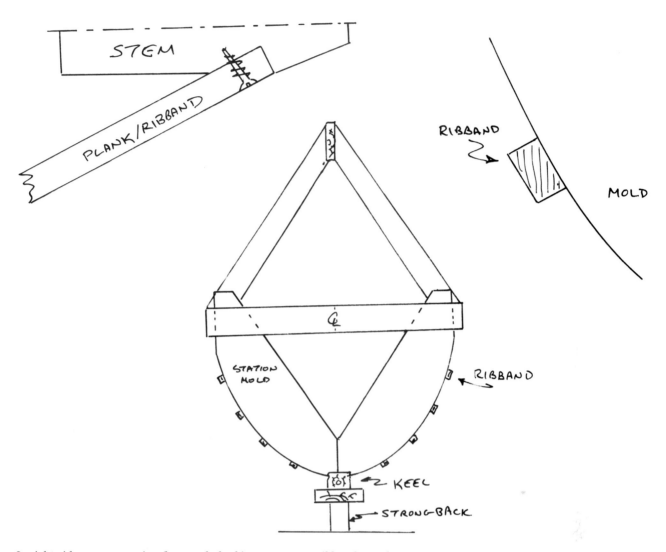

In right-side-up construction for carvel planking, temporary ribbands are fastened to the outside of the molds and transom and into the stem rabbet. Frames are then bent into the ribbands, which are replaced by planking.

big deal, if your floor is wood and in your shop or garage. It is a big deal, however, if the floor is in your den or it is concrete. Also, unless the surface is dead level, you may have to do considerable shimming and truing. Lastly, once you have set up the jig, you've got it for the duration (or at least until you are planked up, at which time you can disassemble the affair).

Using the strongback, it is quite easy to level the base with a few shims, and if it needs to be anchored, it will only take a few fastenings. The molds can then be permanently fastened to the strongback. Once the jig is constructed, it is totally portable (albeit heavy). If you need the space in a hurry, you can remove a few screws and out she goes. Setting it back in place is just as easy. And of course there is no need to disassemble the rig when you are done. Save your patterns, set the whole

business outside under a tarp, and it's ready to go when you decide to expand your fleet. As an added bonus, construction height is readily adjusted with the addition of blocks under the strongback.

BUILDING A LADDER-FRAME STRONGBACK

You can easily build a strongback from everyday materials. One popular method is the ladder frame (so named due to its appearance). It consists of two rails of house framing stock connected with "rungs" made of the same material and a centerline board that is let in flush with the tops of the rungs. This board not only gives you a good base to establish the centerline, but also inhibits the strongback from racking. All that is

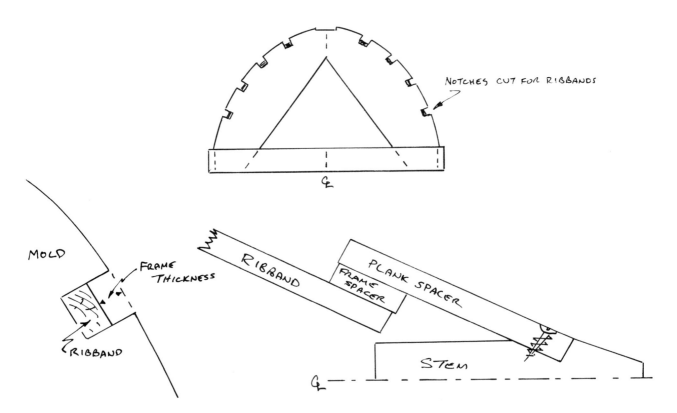

NOTCHES CUT FOR RIBBANDS

MOLD

FRAME THICKNESS

RIBBAND

RIBBAND

PLANK SPACER

FRAME SPACER

STEM

For upside-down carvel construction, the molds are notched for the combined thickness of the ribband and frame. This will allow the outside of the frames to be flush with the station molds. Spacers are used at the stem and transom.

Setting up molds on a strongback. Note the robust bracing.

Setting up sawn frames directly on the lofting board, which is raised to a convenient height.

required for materials is three pieces of common house framing stock (usually 2″ × 6″ or 2″ × 8″) that are slightly longer than your boat, one 1″ × 6″ board of the same length, and some drywall screws. Common lumberyard stuff needs to be double checked before purchase. Eyeball the pieces for warp, twist, bow, and other eccentricities. Also ascertain that the length and width are as advertised. Good alternatives are the new laminated floor joists that are sold in the same dimensions as the natural stuff. Essentially long, thick pieces of plywood, these tend to be very straight and true.

Begin by cutting one of the 2X timbers into pieces roughly 2′ long. The actual finished length of the cross pieces is less important than having them all be equal to one another. Clamp the pieces together side-by-side and mark a centerline across the top with a framing square. Then mark the width of the centerline board onto the top. (Half the width on each side of the centerline.) Now you can mortise out a "channel" in these pieces for the centerline board all at once. There are a number of ways to do this. One of the easiest is to set a circular saw to the thickness of the centerline board

Construction details of a ladder-frame strongback. Put some effort into making it flat, straight, and true.

and cut a series of kerfs in the region and use a chisel to knock out the waste.

Clamp the two remaining 2′ pieces together, mark the rung locations, and the strongback is ready to be assembled. Stand all the 2X pieces up on edge where they belong and hold the assembly together with pipe clamps. Then screw the whole business together with the drywall screws. Prior to installing the centerline board, check to see that the frame is indeed square. You can do this easily by using a tape measure diagonally from the lower left corner to the upper right. Then check the corners diagonally in the opposite direction. If the frame is square, the tape should read the same. If it isn't, rack the frame until the numbers match up. Then screw down the centerline board and you are in business.

The Straight and Level

Since the strongback is our foundation, it's worth taking a moment to get this right, as it will make all the rest of the setup a breeze. Begin by leveling the strongback athwartships, shimming (and twisting) where necessary. Then fasten it down to the floor, fore and aft.

We now need to check for any disconcerting humps or hollows. The easiest, low-tech approach is the same trusty nail and block routine we used to get the centerline on the lofting. All that is required is a string (a chalk line will do) and three small wooden blocks the same size. Begin by driving a nail at the end of each long rail and then stretching a string humming tight between the nails. Slide a block under the string at each nail to elevate the string. Slide the third block under the string at several places along the length of the rail. If it just slides under, it means the rail is dead level. If, on the other hand, the string is lower than the top of the block, it means the rail has an upward bow. If there is a gap between the string and the block, this indicates a hollow. How much is enough to worry about? If there is just $1/16''$ either way, it's small potatoes. If it is a $1/8''$ or more, however, it's worth shimming the strongback into straightness. You'll be glad you did (at least later).

After truing up the strongback, you can establish a construction centerline on the centerline board in pencil. Then, using either a paper tape or long stick, capture the locations of the stations, stem, and bottom of the angled transom mounting bracket from the lofting, and bring them to the centerline of the strongback. Transfer the marks directly to the centerline with a pencil. This method is a lot faster (and more accurate) than using a tape rule. Square out the station lines and check them for accuracy with a 3-4-5 triangle.

A GOOD BASE

Like life, boatbuilding can be good if you have a base to work from. For guidance in such matters, let's go back to the mother of all knowledge: the lofting board. The lofting is the full size blueprint of what you'll be seeing after the boat has been set up for construction. There will be all the parts and pieces: in the profile, there will be the stem, keel, side view of the transom, station spacing, and lots more. On the body plan there will be the shapes of the stations, the rabbet line, bottom of the keel, and sheer line. You have gone to a lot of trouble to get all this drawn so that it interrelates and fits together on the lofting board. The next step is to translate it to 3-D and make it all work.

The reason that the lofting works together is that all the pieces are indexed to a three-dimensional grid. There is a common base that works for both the profile view and the body plan. There are station lines that are common to both the profile and half-breadth views. You can be certain the stations drawn on the body plan will work at their advertised locations on the other views.

So if we make our pieces just like they are on the lofting and join them at the proper locations, we're in business—as long as we keep using the grid to double check what we are doing.

Start by making the pieces exactly as they are drawn on the lofting board. Then, if possible, use the lofting board as an assembly jig. You'll know the boat is exactly the right length, that the rabbet is in the correct location, that the keel is of the proper depth for the molds or frames to sit on, and more. Then, while the parts are sitting on the board, mark the station lines onto the keel. You have to do it anyway. Now is the easiest time. And while you're at it, if the lofting has waterlines, mark them on the stem and stern assemblies as well. It doesn't hurt to have more reference lines.

And speaking of reference lines, you need to establish a construction reference line on the lofting board. This line will be the moral equivalent of the baseline, in that it will keep everything at the right elevation relative to one another.

If you are building upright, you need to draw a line that is parallel to the base that is as close to the sheer amidships as possible. This line will be marked on both the stem and stern assemblies. The line will also be drawn on the body plan. For each station or frame built there is a side-to-side brace called a "cross spall" (or just "spall") that ties the two sides together. This spall will be affixed to the station (or frame) with its top edge aligned with that construction line and the centerline will be marked onto the spall.

Then, when setting up, you can stabilize the keel assembly on its strongback or blocks so that it is plumb, and then raise or lower one end so that the construction line is level fore and aft. Affix a string, or better yet a piano wire and turnbuckle, to the screw eyes at left in both the stem and stern. Tighten the wire and you have the same line that was drawn on the lofting. Bring the middle mold/frame over to the keel and set it up on its respective station line. Brace it temporarily so that it can be plumbed. The wire makes a centerline that can be matched to the centerline drawn on the spall. The wire will also tell you if the mold is high or low and needs to be shimmed or shaved at the bottom. A level can be put on the cross spall and the mold squared to the centerline. Then the mold/frame can be permanently (metaphorically speaking) braced. Then working fore and aft, install the rest of them and cross brace.

If you are building upside down, your construction line will again be drawn parallel to the baseline onto the lofting. This time it runs above both the sheer and the top of the stem. That line is the same as the top of the construction strongback. On the profile view, continue from the top of the stem out past the sheer to the new construction line. The boat's stem will be fashioned so that it ends at that line. (After the boat is off the jig, you can trim the waste wood off the stem back to the original length.) While you are in the drawing business, you can also design a jig to hold the transom that is built to that construction line. Again, draw this line onto the body plan. From the sheer line at each station, square a line to the construction base. The edge of the cross spall will again connect the two sides of the mold/frames at the construction line. With that done you can proceed to make the molds or frames, as described below.

Before setting up, you need to establish the centerline and transfer the station spacing and forward and aft perpendiculars from the lofting board to the strongback or construction floor. The easiest way to capture the station spacing is to lay a long batten or a paper tape onto the base of the profile and scribe the station lines onto it. Bring the batten or tape to the strongback and record the spacings onto the centerline. It's fun and easy, and you don't need to use a measuring tape. Square the stations out onto the floor or to the edges of the strongback.

Then, set the molds up so that the centerlines of the molds line up with the centerline of the strongback. Anchor them in place and angle brace them so they are square to the strongback. Then brace them to one another.

Preparing for the Ends

All that remains is to prepare for the stem and transom. The forward edge of the stem has already been transferred by tape to the jig. Mark the half-breadth of the stem on either side of the centerline. At those lines, install a few brackets to hold the stem.

For the transom, pick up the pattern for the holding bracket that you designed (you did, didn't you?) on the lofting. The location where it sits should have already been brought over by tape from the lofting. Cut, assemble, and install the bracket. The notch that holds the transom top should be exactly the same height above the construction base as it is on the lofting. Also check that it is level. And don't forget to mark a centerline.

Now just bring the backbone assembly over and drop it into place and anchor it.

Hold the transom firmly in place with a bracket designed from the lofting.

MAKING THE MOLDS

Now, with all that under your belt, you need to get into the business of mold making. (We'll talk about sawn frames in a moment.) Going back to the body plan on the lofting, you will see that you have at least half of the story (or at least half of each station) portrayed.

You now need to draw in the other half. In the same fashion as you drew the first half, pick up the heights above base for the sheer, planks, and bottom for each station from the profile and mark them on the body plan centerline. (They may already be there from when you drew the initial half stations.) Then, using your framing square, square out and plot the half-breadth points that were obtained from the half-breadth plan. As before, connect the dots to obtain the shape of the transom. Finally, from the sheer of each station, square down to the construction base and trace with a pencil. With the drawing completed, you are ready to build the molds.

Cut a 1″ × 2″ piece of stock longer than your widest mold. Then tack it down to the far side of the construction base. This is your mold construction stop that like the ledge on a drafting table, will aid in keeping everything square, aligned, and generally right where it ought to be.

The easiest way to assure that the molds are symmetrical is to cut the pieces out in pairs and then join them to make a whole. (This is the Saint Valentine Theory of Symmetry in which early greeting card purveyors discovered that it is much easier to come up with a good-looking heart for your Valentine card if you first fold the paper in half and cut out half a heart and then unfold it.)

Begin the job by roughly determining the size of the pieces that you will be using. Using two tapes, hold the end of one tape at the top (sheer side) location and the end of the other tape at the centerline of the keel. Stretch the tapes out toward each other until they cross. Swing them in or out until they just touch the station shape at one point. The point at which the two tapes overlap will give you the rough length of your stock. Cut two of each.

Next, roughly lay out your pieces on top of the drawn station line. The far ends of the stock will run out to the construction line on one end and over the centerline on the other. The other ends of the stock will overlap each other, about halfway around the mold.

Roughly bisect the angle formed by the overlapped pieces and draw that line onto the top piece. Okay?

Then it's off to the band saw to cut each on the drawn line. Bring the pieces back to the body plan, aligning the cut ends with the centerline and construction line and the angle-cut piece on top of the uncut piece. Trace that angle onto the uncut piece. Take the uncut piece to the saw and slice on the drawn line. Bring it back to the body plan. The two pieces should come together with a tight butt joint in the middle and meet the construction line at the end. Then transfer the centerline onto the pieces and trim it off with the band saw. Now you have the meets and bounds of your mold. Next, temporarily tack one piece in place with a couple of nails.

Getting the Shape

The next job is to transfer the information from your body plan exactly onto the mold stock. The easiest way to do this is the tried and true "bed o' nails" technique. Lift up the unfastened piece and lay down a series of 3d box nails with their heads right on the flats along the edge of the station. Gently lower the piece of mold stock back in place on top of the station. Then squash the piece into the nail heads. Cautiously stepping on it is one good method, as is kneeling on it. Avoid pounding on it with a hammer, as the vibration causes the nails to scatter and give false readings.

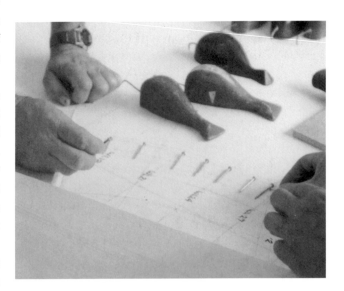

To get the station shapes, lay a row of nails on the lofting with the heads aligned on the station line and the points facing the centerline. Carefully lay a piece of mold stock over the nails and then press hard. Remove the board, connect the indentations made by the nail heads with a batten, and trace the curve.

Make molds and sawn frames directly on the body plan. Make the pieces in pairs.

Lift the piece and you will see that you have a whole series of dents and/or nails in the wood. Use a straightedge to connect the points and give you the shape. Lay it on the second piece you cut for the opposite side at that location and tack them together. Take the pair of them to the band saw, and cut the shape for both and cut the ends off of the new piece. Return them to the body plan and see how close the cut shape fits the drawn one. Touch them up with a plane and anchor them to the body plan with nails to keep them from shifting. Repeat the exercise for the second pair. After fitting, anchor them in place as well.

Assembly

You can now install the plywood gussets that will join the two pieces. First attach the gusset to the top side of the pairs while they are still tacked to the body plan. Drywall screws work well for this job. (Many builders like to add a dollop of carpenters glue under the gusset as well.) After one side has been joined, the two pairs can be pried loose of the body plan (but leave the two sides tacked together). Then glue and screw the second gusset to the other side of the pair.

Separate the molds. One side is lined back up with the drawn station and temporarily anchored into place with nails. The other mirror-image side mates up to it—butting up on the centerline and against the construction line batten while following your newly drawn (second) half station line. Tack the second half in place.

After giving the whole business one more check for accuracy, attach the joining gusset at the bottom with screws and a shot of carpenters glue. In the same manner, affix the aforementioned cross spall at its appropriate location. Don't forget to mark the centerline on the cross spall. Lift it off and repeat the process for the next mold.

Sawn Frames

The technique for developing sawn frames is nearly the same as the one used to build the station molds. One notable difference is that there will eventually be a bevel worked into the frame. This bevel can be developed on the lofting or be worked in with battens and a block plane after the boat has been set up. (Note: prebeveling the frames can speed the fairing process but it is often safer to only partially bevel the frame at first, and then finish the beveling after setup. It is easier to take wood off than to put it back on.) In any case, the initial shape of the frame at the station remains the same as drawn on the body plan. The station will be just one edge of the frame and all the bevels will be worked in from that edge. As the frames remain in the boat forever, attention needs to be paid

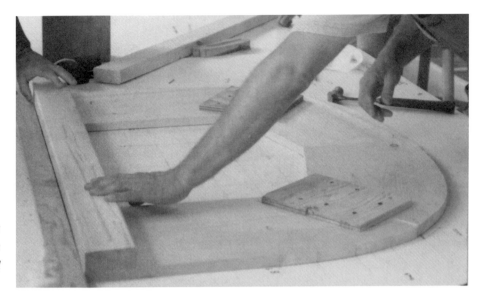

After aligning the mold sections on the lofting board, connect them with good strong gussets, fastened with screws and glue.

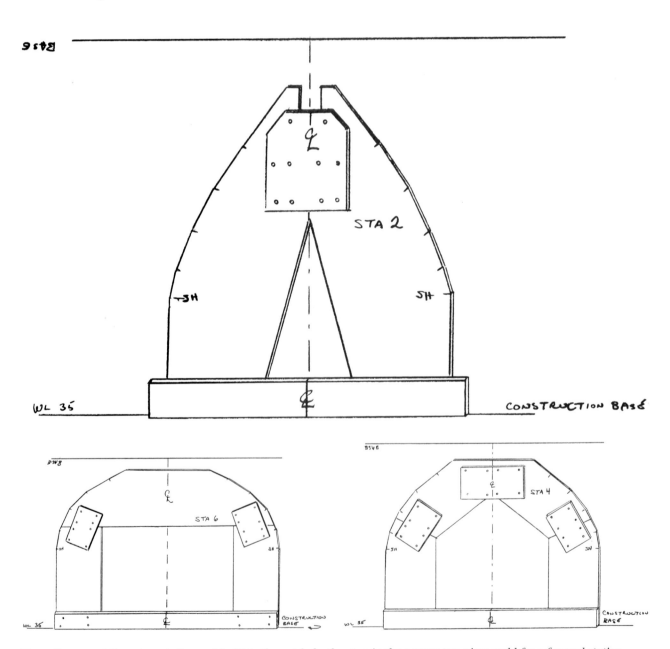

Two-, three-, and four-piece station molds. Note the notch for the stem in the narrow two-piece mold for a forward station.

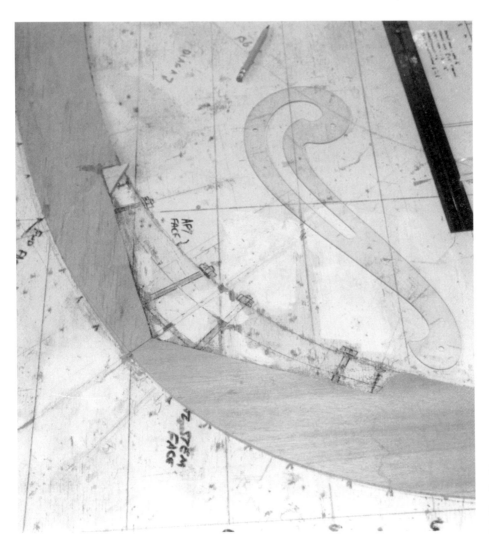

Make sure that stem patterns match the lofting precisely, and pay attention to the placement of fastenings, stopwaters, and such.

to the thickness and width of the stock. Having the depth of the frames the same as called for on the plans can make installing interior structures a lot easier. Also, on some hard-chined boats, the frame may be part of a bulkhead that has specific demands. Again, check the plans.

Picking Up the Patterns

While you still have your nails and stomping boots out, use the same technique to make the patterns for all the miscellaneous components: stem, backbone, transom, skeg, what have you. If your stem is to be made up of two or three pieces, make separate patterns for each piece.

SETTING UP THE MOLDS

After your molds are completed, it's time to set them up at their proper locations. Whether building right-side up or upside down, the theory is the same: the molds must line up on the station lines drawn on the strongback. The question is, which side of the station line, fore or aft? Does it make a difference? Common sense might lead the builder to install the molds in the same fashion as setting up studs when framing a wall in a house, keeping the molds all lined up with a constant distance between each unit, all on one side of the stations as they march from stem to stern. Unfortunately, if that technique is used, one end of the boat will end up being too full.

Just as the battens did in the lofting, your planks will be wrapping around those two-dimensional, paper-thin entities called stations. The station itself is only one face of the built-up mold or frame.

The structure of a mold is there only to support the station. This means that the plank will only be contacting one edge of the mold. So, as a general rule for molds, up forward, from the stem to the widest part of the boat,

Assemble the stem directly on the lofting board.

A nicely gotten out stem, glued and through-bolted together.

set up the molds on the *aft* side of the station line. From the widest part of the boat to the transom, set the molds on the *forward* side of the station line.

On a frame, due to the bevel, the situation is reversed. So up forward, from the stem to the widest part of the boat, set up the frames on the *forward* side of the station line. From the widest part of the boat to the transom, set the molds on the *aft* side of the station line.

Fairing the Assembly

Finally, after everything has been set up in its proper location for construction there is one last step: fairing with a fairing batten so that your planking will wrap smoothly around the hull. The long batten pulled tightly around the assembly should touch all the relevant surfaces of the frames or molds, transom, and stem, simulating what the planking will do. Pulling tightly is the operating word, as a good batten lightly or limply held will naturally tend to make a natural, regular parabola and can imply the setup is unfair when it is not. To get an accurate idea of what's going on, you need to anchor one end (or have someone hold the other end) and haul it around the hull, almost as though you were in a "tug o' war" at the state fair.

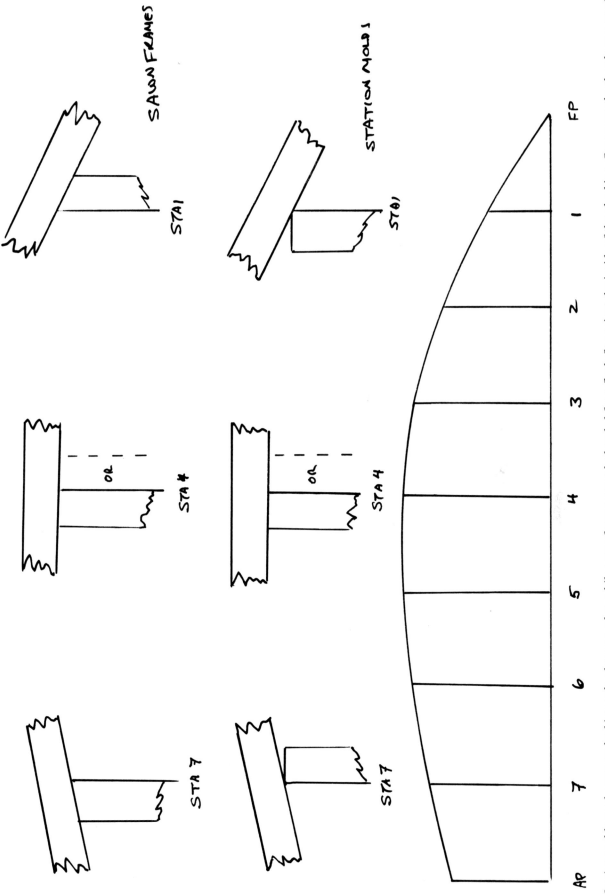

SAWN FRAMES

STA 1

STA 4

OR

STA 7

STATION MOLDS

STA 1

STA 4

OR

STA 7

AP
7
6
5
4
3
2
1
FP

Station molds need contact planking only along an edge, while sawn frames must be beveled for a flush fit against the inside of the planking. Consequently, the placement of molds and sawn frames differs during setup. Molds are set on the inner edge of the station lines, while sawn frames are set on the outer edges.

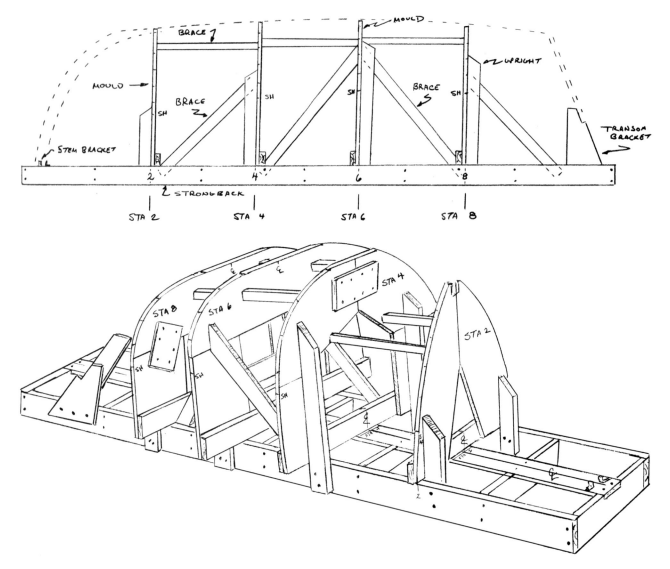

The completed jig, showing ladder frame, molds, bracing, transom, and stem brackets. All waterlines, stations, and centerlines are marked and labeled.

This will cause the batten to bind tightly around the setup. The batten should be run in several different locations and directions.

What you are looking for are anomalies—for example, high spots in the setup frames or molds that may need to be tuned with a fine-set spokeshave or block plane. Hollow areas may need to be shimmed. If the boat has sawn-frame construction, the compound bevel on the frames may need to be corrected. The bevels on the stem and transom may need to be adjusted.

After the setup has been faired, you can line out plank locations and, depending on the construction style, install ribbands or seam battens.

26

The Backbone

Unless you're going to be building a stitch-and-glue hull or a board-bottomed hull such as a dory or wherry, you will need to consider the construction of the keel. The most popular sorts are the built-up keel, fashioned and fitted from sawn pieces and bolted together; the bent keel to which a stem, stern knee, and skeg will be attached; and the "fusion" style keel that may have a bent keelson mated to sawn and fitted pieces. Each approach has its strong points. The bent or sprung keel is lighter, tends to have fewer pieces that have to be made,

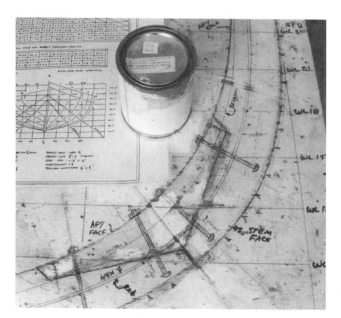

The locations for stem bolts can be established on the lofting long before construction starts.

and has the strength of an arch or bow. The multipieced sawn keel has mass and strength unto itself, without depending on the bow and the rest of the structure to reinforce it. What all the methods have in common is that they must be well fashioned and fitted. Cheat here and the boat is likely to be forever a leaker.

Once again, the place to start is at the lofting board or, if you are working with them, full-size paper templates that act as a surrogate lofting board. The full-size loft is, hands down, the better deal. It is stable, is easy to transfer accurate patterns from, and can be used as an assembly jig. Also, because you have lofted the lines and drawn the pieces, you know that they will work. As for the paper patterns, who knows where they've been? All you can do is hope they are correct and be flexible to modify them if you need to. As a bonus, not only do your drawn lines show you an accurate rendering of the side view of all the sawn parts, the joints, where the stopwaters are, the bolt lengths and locations and such, but they also can give you the accurate length of the bent keel.

THE BUILT-UP KEEL ASSEMBLY

The built-up keel is probably the most complicated. On a small pulling boat or a catboat, the keel might consist of a symphony of components, including the heavy timber that is called the keel, the wedge shaped timbering called the deadwood, and a vertical sternpost at the very end of the keel that will support and reinforce the transom. In some cases, as in a Whitehall,

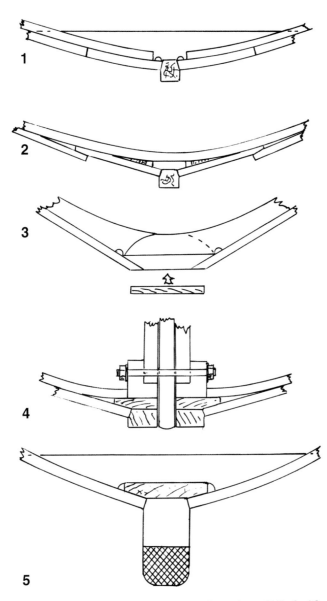

1

2

3

4

5

A few of many possible keel/bottom configurations. 1) Keel with floor on a carvel-planked Whitehall. 2) Keel and keelson on a lapstrake hull. 3) Wherry or dory with a plank bottom, overlapping sawn frames, and an optional chafing or false keel. 4) Centerboard trunk with rabbeted logs. 5) Ballast keel.

these days of high-tech glues, the entire assembly will generally be held together with bolts and drift pins, with the joints filled with a bedding compound. This is because the pieces of wood are relatively heavy and aligned at different angles to one another. The pieces will move at different rates relative to one another and the joints, like those on a cement highway or a bridge, will allow for this movement without breakage. Glue them all together and stress can build up that can cause problems elsewhere.

The Rabbet

An L-shaped channel or rabbet is cut into the keel, into which the planking will be fastened. The location of the rabbet (and the amount of compound bevel it has) is transferred from the lofting to the keel and cut in with a chisel and finished out with a rabbet plane.

Stopwaters

We have been talking about a plethora of joints. The first time the boat is launched, the keel will be pretty tight. But over time, wood can shrink or move. Every joint that is underwater has the potential to leak—even if the planking is well caulked. This is because the water can sneak up between the joints of the keel assembly and pass between the port and starboard planking and soon you have water weeping into the boat. The solution is to bore a hole and install a stopwater where the deepest part of the rabbet (the apex or middle line) crosses the keel joint. The stopwater runs from the apex of the rabbet on one side to the other, and its purpose is to lie in waiting until the day that water hits it. Why does it work? Consider what happens if you hit a piece of pine with a hammer and it makes a dimple. If you put water on the dent, the wood will swell back out. So it is with the stopwater. It will swell and tightly conform to the bored hole and staunch the flow of water.

To make a softwood dowel for a stopwater, bore a hole the same diameter as the stopwater hole into a piece of scrap hardwood. Cut a square-sided strip of softwood (pine or cedar) that is slightly larger in dimension than the diameter of the hole. Roughly round the strip with a penknife. Insert the strip into the bored hole in the scrap wood and rive it through with a mallet. A perfectly round, compressed softwood dowel will emerge from the other side. Cut it off and install it into the stopwater location dry, with no glue or point.

the keel itself might be fairly thin in section and just be beveled to accept planks butting up to it. There may, in addition, be an internal keel structure called a keelson fastened atop the keel. This is wider but thinner than the keel proper, making a "T" shape in cross-section to provide additional strength and support for the planking. To help keep everything aligned, there may be a mortise and tenon joint from the bottom of the sternpost into the keel. It's an interesting jigsaw of joinery and the use of well-made patterns can be a time and stock saver. And even in

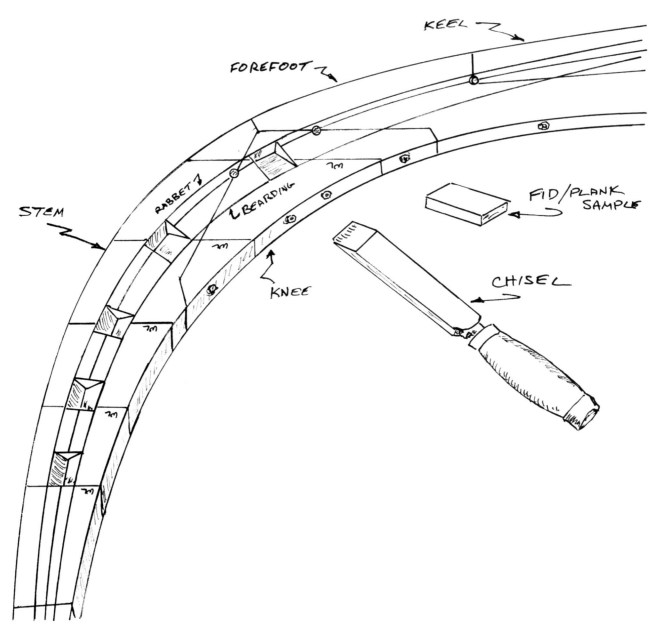

Cutting the stem rabbet.

A BENT KEEL

Let's now consider a simple bent keel, like the one found on the Catspaw dinghy, Joel White's version of Nat Herreshoff's Columbia dinghy. In this case, the keel is fabricated from a single oak plank. It is wider than it is thick. The keel, looking along the bottom, starts off narrow where it meets the stem, then moving aft, it swells—gets wider to accommodate a centerboard trunk. Then it gets narrower again as it moves toward the transom. In this case, there is no added keelson to support the planking (although there could have been). Instead the plans call for roughing out a step along both

sides of the keel with a table saw or router. The resulting rabbeted or "T" shape is nearly the same as if we had taken a narrower keel and jointed it to a wider keelson. Up forward, we'll attach the stem. At this point, the keel is ready to be bent into place over the construction jig.

Bending the Wood

Even fairly heavy wood, like our oak keel, will bend if there is enough length. It will bend like a very heavy batten. In this case, however, as the keel tucks up quickly at the end to get the transom out of the water, cold bending will not be enough. So the end of the keel

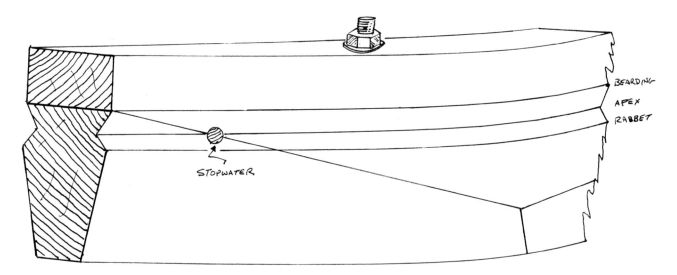

Labels in illustration: BEARDING, APEX, RABBET, STOPWATER

Don't forget the stopwaters!

will be steamed to make it limber enough to bend to shape (see Chapter 27). Back aft, instead of a sternpost to support the transom, we'll use a stern knee that has been fastened to the inside of the keel. A skeg is fashioned, fit, and attached to the outside of the keel and through-bolted to the stern knee. On this particular keel, the rabbet can be planed in after the keel has been bent, rather chiseling it in. There is less need for stopwaters on this keel since there is just the one joint where the keel meets the stem.

OTHER KEELS

Some hulls have much simpler arrangements for their keels. A V-shaped pram might just have a beveled keel batten running from stem to stern and bent over the setup frames. Port and starboard planking is then run over the batten and fastened. Later, the planking is flattened at the centerline and an outer keel is added. Finally, a skeg would be added over the outer keel.

Perhaps the easiest "keel" is that of the cross-planked dinghy, on which the planks simply run crosswise, from chine to chine, over a flat-board keelson. After planking and caulking, an outer keel is added and a skeg is affixed aft.

STEMS

Stems come in two versions: the conventional rabbeted type, and the dory or two-part stem. The rabbeted stem is similar to the rabbeted keel described previously. The location and compound angles of the cut rabbet are derived from the rabbet and bearding line on the lofting

and plotted onto the sides of the stem. As with the keel, the rabbet is cut in with a chisel. After the hull is planked up, the stem forward of the rabbet is beveled into a cutwater.

The earliest stems were likely made from naturally grown crooks. The curve of the grain will follow the shape of the stem, assuring maximum strength, and there will be no joints to leak or weaken the structure. A pattern can be placed atop the stock and the stem can simply be cut out, shaped, and rabbeted.

Fabricated Built-Up Stems

When natural curving stock became too difficult or expensive to obtain, other methods needed to be used. It was impossible to saw a curved stem out of straight-grained stock, even if you could find a plank wide enough, because there would be too much weak "short" grain that could easily break off at the ends of the curve. Instead, a number of straight-grained pieces, well fitted at an angle and interlocking, were used to come around a curve. These would be bedded and bolted. A popular configuration for small craft is the three-piece version consisting of a near vertical portion called the stem. This is fitted to a horizontal piece known as the forefoot or gripe. Reinforcing and joining these two at an angle like a keystone is a third piece called the knee. These are all bolted and bedded together and the entire assemblage is called the stem. The rabbet is again plotted on the sides of the stem and cut out. As with the keel, stopwaters are added at the joints.

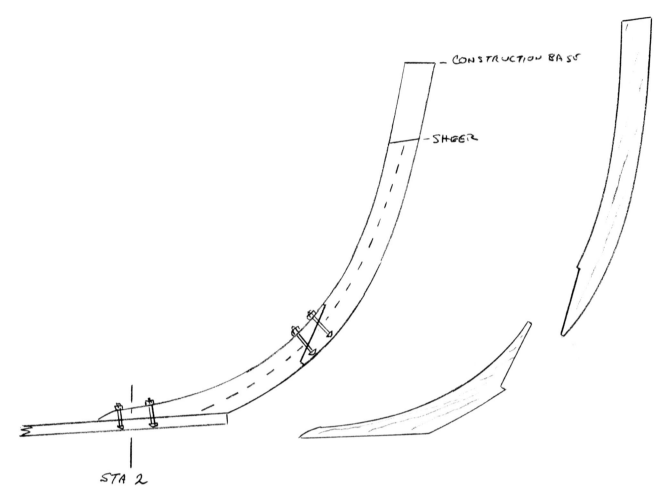

A two-piece stem for a dory.

Laminated Stems

A glued-up stem is a good option for those who lack access to naturally grown stock, are concerned about demanding joinery and potential joint leaks, or are incurable adhesivophiles.

The place to start is with the construction of the bending and lamination jig. The easiest way to do this is to build the jig directly over the stem drawn on the lofting board. Start by drawing the complete finished stem in profile on the board and then laying a piece of clear plastic over the top. Assemble the bending jig, which is just a series of blocks (as tall as the stem is thick) fastened to the line made by the face of the inner stem. Don't forget to cover the faces of the blocks with nonstick plastic.

Next, fabricate your laminates out of stock that will glue up reliably. Mahogany works well. Despite the hassle of gluing multiple laminations (similar to clamping a slithering squid), more thin laminates are better than fewer thick ones, as the potential for "spring-back" or recoil of the laminated stem is reduced. Be sure that you have enough laminations to achieve the full depth of the false stem. The false stem can be glued up at the same time as the "real stem." Just put plastic in between the two sets of laminates.

It's a good idea to steam or boil your laminate strips and bend them around the jig and clamp them into place to convince them that they are going to spend the rest of their lives curved. Then disassemble the strips, butter them up with resorcinol or thickened epoxy, and clamp them back into the jig. After curing, the stem can be faired and treated like a grown knee.

FALSE (STEM) OPTIONS

A false stem is just another term for the forward part of a two-piece dory-type stem. The two-piece stem, used as an alternative to the conventional rabbeted stem, is found on a great number of hulls. With a two-piece stem, the planking runs past the beveled inner or "real stem" and is fastened to it. Then the planking is trimmed and planed square to the face of the stem. The false stem is then fastened to the forward (square) side of the "real" stem and shaped.

Adding a Straight False Stem

The easiest type of false stem to fit is the dead straight sort often found on sharpies and skiffs. Indeed, it is just a matter of fitting two straight pieces together (with bedding in between) and either screwing, or better yet, bolting them together. If bolts are used, it is often best to prebore those bolt holes in the inner stem before it ever is attached to the boat or sees a plank. Those holes can be bored straight and true on the drill press.

Later on, after the boat has been planked up, all that needs to be done is to clamp the false stem into place and (after crawling inside) run a long twist bit through the predrilled holes into and through the false stem. The predrilled holes will act like a doweling jig and the bores in the false stem will end up dead on. Unclamp the false stem, anoint the joint with bedding, replace the stem, add the bolts, and you're ready for shaping.

Adding a Curved False Stem

This is a different kettle of fish. The curve on the face is usually irregular and can be persnickety to fit. Fortunately, there are a number of techniques that work well and can make the job easier to deal with.

Probably the easiest way to fit the inner and outer stem pieces is to cut them out together from a natural knee. Start by making a pattern from the lofting that follows the shape of the inner and outer stem combined. Trace the shape from the pattern onto the knee stock and cut it out with a band saw. Smooth the inner and outer faces of the combined stem. Then, using a marking gauge or combination square set to the dimension of the false, outer stem, draw a line that will become the joint between the two stems.

Use the band saw to cut directly on the drawn line, dividing the stem into two pieces. Set the false stem aside. Bevel the inner stem as per the lofting and attach it to the keel assembly. Plank the hull and trim the planks flush to the face of the inner stem. Then mate the outer stem to the inner. It should fit perfectly. Bed it and fasten.

Another approach is to laminate or steam bend a false stem. Whichever way you choose, first check the curve of the stem on the boat with a light batten for any unfairness. Remove any unwanted lumps, hollows, or crown with a hand plane.

If you didn't glue up a false stem at the same time that you laminated the real stem, or if you have a natural inner stem to which you want to add a laminated false one, now's the time. As described previously, a bending jig can be made on the lofting board that follows the outer face of the real stem. The false stem can be laid up and glued. After the assembly has cured, remove it from the jig, clean up the sides, and fit it to the inner stem. Bed and fasten it in place and do your final shaping.

Steam Bending a False Stem

If you choose to steam bend, remember that the secret to success is preparation. The stock selected should be straight-grained and without defects: no knots, cracks, or sapwood. Saw and plane it to the proper dimensions and be sure it has extra length. Go through a dry run to preclude any surprises. As always, there are a number of approaches.

You can use a bending jig similar to the one used for laminating: just blocks screwed down to the lofting board. No plastic is necessary this time. To compensate for the possibility that the heavy steam-bent wood will spring back, many builders will increase the amount of curve a bit. While there are likely to be scientific formulae for this sort of thing, chances are you will come pretty close by simply taking a light plastic batten and anchoring it halfway along the outer face of the inner stem's length. After that point, just pull a little more curvature into the batten. Trace the shape onto the lofting and fasten your blocks to the traced line.

With the inside of the curve accounted for, the next job is to fasten a second set of blocks that are spaced the thickness of the false stem away from the original set of blocks. This will be the outside face of the stem.

Next steam and bend the stock in the jig and leave it to cool. Then take the false stem off and fit it to the boat.

Alternately, you can bend the false stem directly onto the boat. After the travails of the laminated and jig-bent methods, this one will seem like a cakewalk (sort of). And yet again, we've got more than one method. The first one assumes that you have a friend.

Round up that good buddy who owes you one, the screws that will be used to fasten the false stem (don't forget to wax 'em), an electric drill and bit sized for

Using a come-along to bend an outer stem. Watch where you stand, in case the C-clamp slips!

the screws, and a brace and bit. Mark a centerline and screw spacing onto the outside face of the false stem.

Steam the stock until limber. Then bring the stock to the boat, line it up, and clamp it to the stem above the sheer line of the planking. (Don't forget to use a wooden pad or "button" under the clamp to avoid crushing the hot wood.) Begin pulling the curve into the stock. When the stock contacts the stem at the first fastening mark, stop, drill, and install a screw. Then continue pulling in the curve until the next fastening mark touches. Again, stop and install a screw. Continue pulling in the curve and intermittently fastening.

What's the deal with this incremental approach? If we simply pulled the entire curve in a single swoop, the false stem would act like an extra-heavy-duty batten and produce a very nice parabola. But chances are your stem is not a perfect parabola and there would be plenty of gap generated in the joint between the two pieces that would be very difficult (if not impossible) to correct after the wood had cooled. The slow and steady approach assures that the false stem's shape will

follow the inner stem's shape. You'll need a helper for this method to get the piece bent, clamped, and fastened quickly, while it's still hot and limber.

After the stem has cooled, the screws can be removed and the false stem can be taken off and bedding can be applied to the face of the inner stem. The false stem can then be reattached and shaped to taste.

If you're doing it alone, you will need a little mechanical assistance in the form of a ratchet hoist or "come-along." Begin by firmly clamping an overlength piece of false stem stock to the boat's stem, down near the base. Attach another clamp to the top of the near vertical false stem stock. To that clamp, hook the come-along and run the cable aft to a rope that runs over the transom to the base of the construction jig. Remove as much slack as possible. Then disconnect the stock and pop it into the steam box. After steaming, quickly reclamp the false stem to the boat's stem and reattach the come-along tackle. Then start cranking. The puller will draw the false stem flush to the curve. After cooling, it can be removed, bedded, fastened, and faired.

· 27 ·

Steaming Frames and Planks

For those who have never seen it done, the notion of steaming and/or boiling wood and torturing it into shape seems at best intimidating. Yet in practice, it's quick, straightforward, and considerably easier and less messy than lamination. The key to success is preparation.

TOOLS OF THE TRADE

The first job is to assemble the necessary munitions to do the job: a steam box, a steamer, and a plethora of clamps.

The steam box needs to be long and wide enough to accommodate the stock. But it certainly doesn't need to be fancy. A perfectly serviceable model can be cobbled from utility grade pine boards, spiked together to form a long box. A piece of wood is nailed across one end and the other end has a simple door made from another piece of wood, hung with cheap hinges and having a screen door hook to hold it closed. One can make an interior rack that will allow steam to circulate around the stock by drilling a series of holes (through both sides) at an equal height along the length of the box and inserting dowels or bronze rod. Avoid using iron rod in close proximity to steamed oak as it will blacken it instantaneously. (If you were wondering how to ebonize your frames, this will do the trick.) To finish the unit off, drill a hole in the bottom of the box that is large enough to accommodate a length of automobile heater hose.

When bending narrow, straight stock such as frames or rails, you can use a length of plastic sewer pipe to make a good steam box. The heavy-duty version (schedule 80) works best but the lighter wall stuff works fine as well. PVC is the most common and is the cheapest. It is not intended for hot work but is fine for occasional steaming if supported below by a reinforcing piece of wood. CPVC (chlorinated polyvinyl chloride) pipe is rated for considerably higher temperatures. Pipe has a lot going for it. It's relatively light, it's easy to extend with off-the-shelf couplers, there are stock components that work for attaching the steam pipe, and there is even a screw-in plug that will act as a door. And best of all, a plastic steam box will heat up much faster than a wooden one so you can get to work sooner. Perhaps

A sewer-pipe steam box.

222

Board steam box with a beer-keg steam generator.

the greatest potential drawback with a pipe box is that it's too tight. A wooden box will leak merrily, and that is a good thing. We aren't looking for pressure. You want to have a continuous influx of really hot steam, which means you want to get rid of the old cold stuff. Make sure that you drill ample breather and drain holes (to get rid of condensed water), and as with the wooden box, add dowels or rod for a rack. Did I mention that large-scale steaming is best not done in the kitchen?

Next on the agenda is getting the steamer together. You'll need plenty of volume here. A good gas-fired stove is a must. A prime choice is one of those 130,000 BTU outdoor stoves (popular for Cajun catfish cooking and the deep-fat frying of turkeys). A 5-gallon kerosene can or a beer keg makes a fine steamer tank. Just add a length of automobile heater hose to connect it to the steam box and you are in business. When setting up the hose, be sure it has a straight run from the boiler to the steam box. If the hose has a low loop, condensed water will settle into it (like the drainpipe trap under the bathroom sink) and block the flow of steam.

Round up as many clamps as possible (and then some) before starting work. C-clamps work well. They are slow acting, however, so should be adjusted to approximate size before steaming begins. The sliding bar clamp is a good choice as the bar tends to be thinner

than the C-clamp, enabling it to get into tight openings easier, and adjustment is fast.

Also necessary are clamping pads or buttons. These are simply softwood or plywood squares that can be inserted between the clamp and the steamed wood to prevent crushing the heat-softened fibers.

BENDING STOCK

The best framing stock is straight-grained, free of blemishes (i.e., rot, knots, checks), and if possible, air dried. The stock should be well smoothed, as saw marks can be a starting point for breaks. And, especially with framing stock, the edges should be gently radiused.

White oak works quite well for bending stock. Ash bends well but is nondurable. Elm is very elastic. It's hard to find, however. Oak is a good choice for steam-bent keels. Options include mahogany and yellow pine, but these are considerably stiffer. Coamings are often made of oak or mahogany. Care must be taken to select the highest-quality stock for coamings, since they not only have considerable bend, but are complicated to make and the stock is expensive. It's one thing to break a frame when you have plenty of backup pieces. It's another to break a coaming that has taken hours to make and is the only one you have.

For success when steaming, think asparagus. Not steamed enough and it's tough and inflexible. Steamed too long and it's mush. What we're looking for here is cooking just enough—sort of an arboreal *al dente*. Interestingly, some builders paint or varnish their frames before steaming. This is believed to retard the cooling process caused by evaporation and reduce surface checking. A general rule for steaming time is roughly one half hour for every ½" of thickness. The steam should be running full tilt, with steam roiling, before inserting the wood. To avoid overcooking, put only a few frames in the box to start and then continue to "take one out, put a new one in." Keep the stock in rotation. Also, round up help to do the job and get people there ahead of time to practice.

FRAMING

Steam-bent frames are light, and well-heated wood can be quite limber and amenable to bending. That said, a lot is asked of a bent frame in that it must be twisted and bent on three different axes (as in x, y and z) to make it fit tightly against the hull. Hence, successful steaming does call for a bit of preparation. One old-timer said the formula for success was 90% getting ready to bend and 10% actually doing the bending.

The place to begin is the layout of the frame locations. From the plans, mark the frame spacing onto the ribbands or planking, the sheer, and the keel or keelson. If installing the frames into planking, run the lines continuously for the whole length. It's a good idea to use a spacer block the same width as the frames to record the location of both sides of the frame, fore and aft. Although this second line may seem redundant, it eliminates any doubt of which side of the line the hot frame should be on. It's always good to try a dry run with something like a flexible batten to get an idea what challenges lie ahead. How many clamps will be needed? How much overbend will be necessary? Should there be more than one drill motor? And so on.

Bending Frames Over an Upside-Down Setup

All things considered, it is almost always easier to bend wood around the outside of a curve (such as a building jig) than to push or force it into the inside of a curve (such as the inside of a planked hull). On a round-bottomed hull, this is done by wrapping the frames around a series of fore and aft ribbands (similar to battens) that have been set into notches cut into the setup molds. The notches are spaced regularly from

Bending frames over a jig.

keel to sheer and are cut deep enough into the edges of the molds so that after the frames have been bent over the ribbands, the outside face of the frames is flush with the inside of the planks.

It is always best to start framing in the center, amidships, as the curves are easier and they will require less twisting. It allows you to warm up the job (so to speak). Unless you're bending continuous frames, from sheer to sheer, work side-to-side as you go fore and aft. The idea is to keep the boat in balance without building in stress.

Rather than making the curve in a single bend, you will have to work the frames down against the hull and clamp them incrementally. This is because a steamed frame will act like a fairing batten and it wants to produce a natural, parabola-like curve. That's nice but it's probably not what the boat's bottom is like. It's more likely to be a flat curve near the keel, make a sharp bend at the turn of the bilge, and then transition to an easy curve or maybe a flare as it approaches the sheer. Use as many clamps as necessary to hold the frames to the hull.

Bending Frames into a Right-Side-Up Hull

If you are building the boat right-side up and the frames have to be in place before planking (as in carvel construction), the first job is to attach ribbands that run fore and aft around the hull. This time, the ribbands are attached to the outside of the molds and are fastened into the rabbet (or stem bevel) and the edge of the transom. The frames will be bent to the inside of the ribbands and clamped. The inside faces of the ribbands are thus in the same place that the inside faces of the planks will be after the frames are in place and the ribbands removed. Quite often, the technique will require someone to be inside the boat during the bending process. To avoid untimely capsize, make sure the assembly is well braced. As mentioned previously, the frames will have to be worked against the ribbands—this time by giving them an overbend as they are being forced against the ribbands and then clamped. Again, to keep the framing in balance, start at the center and work toward the ends.

Bending Frames into a Planked Hull

This method, used for lapstrake, dory-plank, and strip planking, is similar to bending into the right-side up hull as above, but this time there are no ribbands to

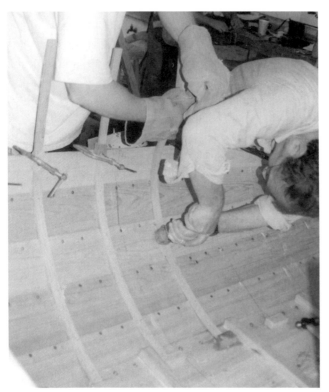

Bending frames unto a hull.

clamp onto. Some builders will premark the frame locations on the inside faces of the planks and drill undersized index holes for the fastenings from the inside to the outside. Then after the frame has been bent into place, the hole for the fastening can be bored from the outside, through the index hole and into the frame.

Start framing at the center where the bends are the easiest. Remove the frame from the steam box, and after giving it a slight overbend, insert it between the location marks. Anchor the foot of the frame with a fastening and temporarily clamp it at the sheer. Then unclamp the sheer and work the frame down against the hull by overbending. Starting at the bottom, drill back through the index holes, and drive in the fastening. Continue up until you hit the sheer. Then move on to the rest of the frames, alternating from side to side and fore and aft to keep the stresses balanced. Rivets (if used) can be heated up during breaks in the steaming. Leave the frames long above the sheer. They will be trimmed after the inwales or sheer clamps have been installed.

A FRAME FIT TO BE TIED

Steam bending typically requires a whole lot of clamps, and clamps can get expensive. Some builders simply hand-wire the frames to the ribbands and hope they don't go adrift. Others, looking for a more reliable fix, will bore undersize holes in the frames and drive temporary nails into the ribbands. If one doesn't mind a few holes (and remembers to remove the nails prior to planking), this method can be quite efficacious. If one has some extra cash, heavy-duty plastic electrical wire ties are effective. Yet another (and cheaper) way to go is the potato bag/rebar tie-up tool.

The humble tie-up tool is a standard agricultural/ construction item that is used to cinch up the wire closures on the necks of produce bags or bind lengths of reinforcing bar together. The design of the device is simple: merely a hook on a shaft that freely spins in a wooden handle. Simply insert the hook through the prefabricated "eyes" of the malleable metal tie that has been looped around the frame and ribband. Pull a slight strain on the wire, and then give the tool a

The rebar wire tie-up tool is a quick way to bring steam-bend frames under control.

quick turn of the wrist as though you were winding up an old-time Victrola. That's all there is to it. Instantly the tie will draw tight, biting slightly into the wood and anchoring the frame firmly in place. To release the frame prior to planking, simply nip the tie with a wire cutter. Simplicity is a wonderful thing.

BENDING PLANKING

The hood end of the garboard and the other lower planks often have quite a bit of twist and need to be heat softened into submission. Although steaming is an option, it does require a considerable amount of organization, as the plank needs to be steamed to perfection, taken from the box, clamped to the stem, wrapped around the hull, and clamped into place, all before it cools. Help is definitely required and all the clamps, pads, and strategy must be readied ahead of time.

Another, less stressful approach that often works is the boil-in-a-bag, hot compress technique. On most boats (except double-enders) the mid-to-after part of the plank has an easy curve that one can bend in without the aid of heat. It's just the forward end that needs some extra help. So what you can do is topically add heat where it is needed to soften the plank for bending.

Start by clamping the mid to aft part of the plank in place and wrap the hood end in rags. Slide a piece of plastic sheet between the boat and the plank. Boil some water and pour some onto the rags. Wrap the plastic around them and clamp it into place to keep the heat in. Every 5 minutes or so, unwrap and repeat the drill. After the usual time schedule ($\frac{1}{2}$ hour for every $\frac{1}{2}''$ of thickness), remove the sodden steaming swaddle, bend the plank easily into place, and clamp. 'Tis a crude, but effective, technique. Just remember to use caution and your hot mitts!

· 28 ·

Scarfs

Dealing with too-short lumber has been a boat-building challenge since Noah was in knee pants.

Years ago, the only way to join long pieces of stock was to use mechanical fastenings. The choice was either to fashion the pieces with interlocking joints with fastenings to hold them in place, or to use backing gussets (or butt blocks) at the joints that, again, would be secured with fastenings. Either tried-and-true method still works fine in many applications today. There is a drawback, however, in that the separate pieces still tend to act independently. This isn't a difficulty with a built-up keel, but it can be problematic with planking, as the short butt blocks can cause "hard" or unfair spots if they are not properly installed. And with spars, butt blocks are clearly unacceptable, and a completely smooth, fair joint is highly desirable.

Since the invention of waterproof glues, builders have another option—the beveled, glued scarf—to produce this essentially seamless joint. So accept both the old and the new, and use the appropriate scarf for the job.

MECHANICAL SCARFS

The mechanical scarf joint is composed of a pair of mating or lapping beveled pieces of wood that, when joined, form a continuous piece. Scarfs can be used on keels, keelsons, cap-rails, sheer clamps, or just about anywhere extra length is desired. There are numerous kinds of scarf joints that can be used to join wood. Charles Desmond's 1919 tome *Wooden Ship-Building*

illustrated a veritable gaggle of scarfs, ranging from simple mating wedges to an esoteric interlocking maze. By the time the Department of the Navy got around to describing the technique in its 1962 *Manual for the Use of Wood as a Ship Building Material*, it had winnowed down the number to just four: the plain (nibbed or stopped) scarf, the hooked scarf, the key-locked scarf, and the key-locked hook scarf.

All of these feature obliquely cut joints that have nibbed ends. A nib is simply a square-cut lip made across the wedge-end or feather-end of a tapering piece of wood. If the wedge were allowed to continue to a point, the very thin (and structurally weak) end would just flare away from the joined pieces of wood. Some old-time scarf designs would use a through-bolted plate on the outside of the timber to contain the featheredge. The very simple mating beveled scarf joint (sans nib) is the easiest to make, but it isn't dependable without very rugged adhesives such as resorcinol or epoxy.

Types of Scarfs

Plain Scarf. This scarf is easy to make. The angled joints are simply lapped (with nibbed ends), joined, and through-bolted. The strength of this joint lies mainly in its bolts. This version is often used for clamps (e.g., sheer clamps), cap-rails, and traditional lapstrake (i.e., nonglued) planks.

Hooked Scarf. This scarf is more difficult to make, as the beveled mating faces are stepped. When viewed from the side, the joint zigzags up at the bottom nib, across at an angle, and then halfway along the bevel there is a downward cut, after which the bevel continues until nearly the top where again there is another nib. The joint is bolted. This resists tension much better than the plain scarf because of the interlocking jogs in the joint. This scarf is often used in the backbone assembly.

Key-Locked Scarf. Also called a coaked scarf, this is very similar to the plain scarf, but in this case, mating slots or cross channels have been added midway, cut into the beveled faces of the joint. When the two pieces are put together, the slots form a four-sided keyway into which a tightly fitted, durable hardwood key (or coak) or opposing wedges can be inserted. The joint is bolted together. Like the hooked scarf, the key-locked scarf is locked from moving forward or aft with a wooden "parking brake." Again, it's used in backbone assembly.

Key-Locked Hooked Scarf. This is the combination of the above two scarfs. Again, the joint is through-bolted. This deluxe version is used in situations where there is a lot of extra shop time available.

The reference books offer a general guide to proportions of a mechanical scarf. For example, if the vertical depth of your stock equals d, then the length of the scarf measured horizontally (nib to nib) would be $6d$. The depth of the nibs and the cross-section of the keys would be about 25% of d. Another way to look at it is that the oblique cut of the scarf should not cross the grain of the timber at an angle greater than 5°, which gives you something like a 10:1 slope.

Assembly

As with dovetail joints cut in a cabinet, the strength of the assembly is dependent on the quality of the workmanship. So take the time to do it right. The place to start is to make a pattern of the shape of the joint. Light plywood such as ¼" lauan is dandy for this purpose; patterns are great for working efficiently.

Full-size templates or patterns for the scarf joints in a keel can be lifted directly from the scarf drawn on the lofting. (This information is typically noted on the construction plans by the designer.) If the location of the scarf on the lofting doesn't match the actual lengths of wood that you're working with, this is the time to make the necessary modifications. Take care, when laying out the scarf on the lofting, that the bolts that secure your scarf will not be in the way of the subsequent floors, ballast bolts, and the like.

Accuracy is important. Neither the wood nor your time is cheap enough to justify doing it twice. Tack your pattern to the flat of the keel stock and trace around it with a sharp pencil. To avoid that doleful lament that the newly scarfed piece is now too short after fitting, let the stock run a little long rather than cutting it exactly to length; it can always be cut to proper length during final fitting.

On a keel scarf, as with any heavy dimensioned wood joinery, it is critical that your joints be cut dead square. After tracing the scarf pattern onto one side of your stock, square down the ends of the nibs so you can accurately locate and trace the pattern on the opposite face of your stock. Then either cut the scarf all at once with a saw or make a series of close-together saw cuts and remove the waste with a chisel and mallet. In either case, the angled face of the joint should be cleaned up with edge tools down to the drawn lines. Remember to keep checking the joint with a square, and watch for any crown or camber on your joint faces, as these might cause a poor fit.

When both halves have been cut, it's time to assemble the two pieces to check whether the joint has gaps and to see if the combined pieces are perfectly straight lengthwise. (Even a slight deviation of a degree or two in the cut bevel can cause a dogleg when the two are tightly clamped together.)

If possible, this test fit should be done on a perfectly flat surface. If this is a keel scarf, a great place to do this task is right over the lofting. It will not only insure that your assembly is straight, and the right shape, but it will let you know if the newly spliced keel is long enough. If the width of the stock allows it, mill the pieces to be scarfed slightly larger than the dimensions traced from the patterns.

Then, if after cutting the joint you find there is a slight dogleg, you'll likely have enough extra width in the stock to adjust the pieces to correct the situation. Again, clamp up the assembly and check it for any vexatious gaps.

If there are gaps, try using a technique similar to what dentists use when looking for a high spot on your new filling: Take apart the joint, rub a little carpenters chalk on one surface, and clamp it back up. Then take it apart. The chalk will likely have transferred to the high point on the opposite surface. That high point can be planed down and the process repeated. After the joint has been fully fitted, the

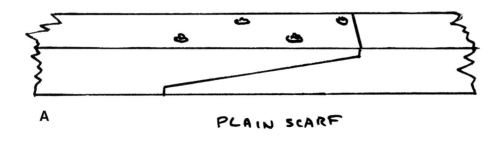

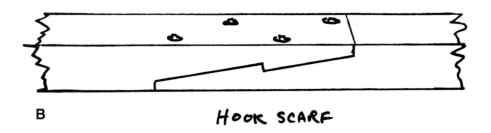

A

PLAIN SCARF

B

HOOK SCARF

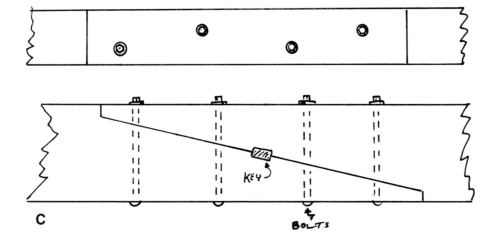

C

BOLTS

D

KEY LOCK HOOK SCARF

A. Plain scarf. B. Hooked scarf. C. Key-locked scarf. D. Key-locked hooked scarf.

chalk dust can then be scraped off the mating faces of the joint.

Reclamp tightly and lay out the location of the bolts as per the plans (or lofting). The holes should be drilled at least square to the angle of the scarf—not square to the stock's face. Some builders like to slant their bolts to help draw the scarf together. If the stock is thick enough, the boltholes should be staggered a bit on either side of the centerline; stock that is more than, say, 5″ thick will likely require two rows of bolts side by side. The joint requires holes of exactly the proper caliber so the bolts fit tightly. So, before boring the real thing, drill a test hole or two in a piece of scrap and check the fit with your bolts. Check your clamps and the alignment of the assembly one more time, and then bore the holes.

Finally, take the joint apart one more time to apply bedding. The old-timers used a number of different products here to exclude water from the joint: tar, white lead, paint. While these potions will work, this is one area that is a good candidate for one of the modern flexible adhesives that come in a tube. Not only does the adhesive add strength, but also the goop's flexible qualities will allow it to stretch and flex with any movement of the wood without opening and allowing water to enter. Clamp up the joint for the final time and insert the bolts. Add the nuts and washers to the bolts, and tighten up the clamps. Then, crank down those nuts, clean up the bedding squeeze-out, and remove the clamps.

GLUED SCARF JOINTS

Modern adhesives permit two or more pieces of wood to be spliced into one continuous piece that behaves like a natural plank or timber, resisting breakage at the joint and bending naturally. Two steps must be performed properly to make this technique work.

First is the joinery. The ends of the two pieces to be joined should be planed to wedge shapes that are exactly the same angle and dead flat, with no crowns or hollows to keep the joint from closing. The angle is important. Matching bevels that are cut at a 12:1 ratio will provide plenty of gluing surfaces and will allow the joined pieces to bend naturally while still being easy to fashion.

The second step is proper gluing. Whether using resorcinol or epoxy, one must be sure that the joint is not contaminated, that the mix is correct, that there is enough glue in the joint to do the job, and that the joint has had enough time to properly cure before it is stressed. One only has to experience one failed glue joint on a scarfed plank or spar to become a true believer in caution.

Making Straight Joints

Despite the foreboding preamble, making straight scarf joints such as might be used for spars, battens, strip planking, or plywood hull panels or planks is

straightforward and easy. All that needs to be done is to stack the stock in a pile that is staggered at a 12:1 ratio and plane a bevel or ramp into it.

For example: We want to make an 18' spar that will be 3" thick at its thickest. We have four pieces of 1½" thick wood: two pieces 8' long and two pieces 12' long. We need to make four scarf joints that are at the same angle so that we will end up with two joined planks that can be laminated together to produce the 3" desired thickness. All we need to do is layer the pieces

To bevel several planks simultaneously for scarfing, line them up and set each back the length of the scarf behind the previous one. Clamp them down so they won't move. Knock off the big edges with a power plane if you have one, then finish up with a long, hand-powered jointer plane. (Photos: Ford Reid)

The completed scarfs will make a continuous ramp, dead straight.

one on top of the other, each one staggered back from the one below like regular stair steps at the proper ratio. Using the 12:1 ratio on our 1½" stock puts the amount of setback for each plank at 18". After squaring up the stock, clamp the sandwiched pile to a good base. Then take a power plane and knock off the corners of the steps and gradually plane in a long ramp. Check the ramp regularly with a reliable straightedge.

The appearance of the individual plies makes it relatively easy to get good results when planing plywood scarfs.

Finish out the job with a sharp jointer plane, removing any dips, hollows, or crowns. That's all there is to it: four pieces beveled exactly the same. When they are glued together, we'll have two planks 18½' long.

The operation is the same for plywood, but even easier, since the laminations act as a "tell tale." As you plane down, the layers of the plies are revealed. As long as they run straight and true from edge to edge, you have a smooth bevel. If they wobble, there is an imperfection on the bevel that needs to be corrected.

Scarfing Planks

Planks change shape considerably as they come around the hull. Swoops, curves, and S shapes are par for the course. One of the many reasons why builders appreciate flitch-sawn (i.e., live-edged) cedar is that the tree grows naturally in curves. If one has enough cedar in stock, eventually just the right plank can be found that matches the curve generated by the spiling batten. The grain will follow the curve, providing a very strong plank. In some localities, great wide (but straight) boards can still be purchased. Some builders will lay out their seriously scimitar-shaped strakes on this wide stock and cut them out and call it good. The problem with this scenario is that at the ends of the plank—the region where there is often the most twist—the plank will be at its weakest as the grain will cross a corner of the plank at an angle.

Traditionally, the way to deal with this problem was to butt-joint two pieces together at an angle with a butt block. You can do the same with an angled scarf joint.

Select two overlength pieces of planking stock. If your plank is to be 1" thick, the combined stock will have to be at least 1' overlength, and preferably more. Lay the two pieces on the floor or bench at approximately the angle of curve shown by the spiling batten. Then lay the spiling batten on top of the cedar and adjust the boards so that the batten covers them properly and the plank will be into good sound wood.

Next, you need to bisect the angle at which the two boards are to meet one another, and trim the meeting butt ends at that angle. After trimming, the two boards should be able to butt together tightly and maintain the angle indicated by the spiling batten. Then overlap the planks by one foot and label the two sides touching one another "scarf me." Label the opposite sides something such as "No!" or "Nyet!" After all this work, what you don't want to do is put the bevel on the wrong side of the plank.

To plane in your angled bevel you'll need to make a scarfing jig. While there are a number of ways to do this, the easiest way is to manufacture two long wooden wedges—that just happen to be cut at a 12:1 ratio. Screw them down onto a rectangular wide board, with the sides of the wedges flush to opposites edges of the board and the tips of the wedges even with the end of the board. Screw the jig down to the end of the bench with the featheredge of the wedges pointing off the bench. That's all there is to it. High-tech, no. Accurate, yes.

Insert the first board with the "scarf me" side up. Align the angled butt end with the edge of the board. This means the board will be entering the jig at an angle. Clamp or screw the board down so that it doesn't move. Now you are ready to cut the bevel.

The tool of choice here is a hand plane. Initially, some of the stock can be roughed out with a power plane, slick, backing out plane, or drawknife. But only do a portion. The rest of the job will be done with a long hand plane that will ride on the top of the wedges. (No long plane? See the sidebar, "The 10-Minute Jointer Conversion," below.) The plane is used at an angle, shaving off the wood at the 12:1 ratio. When the plane stops cutting, it's time to stop cutting as the scarf has been cut to perfection. Insert the second plank and repeat the process.

With both bevels done, the planks can be glued together. Anchor one side down and then, after lining up the second piece, double check with the spiling batten that the angle made by the two legs of the plank is correct. Collect your clamps, clamping pads, and glue and, after doing a dry run, glue it together. Oh yes, don't forget to lay some plastic film on the bench plastic under the glue joint.

THE 10-MINUTE JOINTER CONVERSION

The proliferation of (relatively) low-cost electric standing jointers and handheld planes has led to near abandonment by boat shops of the once-popular cast-iron jointer plane. In the past, the long-bodied (22") planes built by Stanley and Record were commonly used to true up pieces for transoms, centerboards, and decks. They were also useful for scarfing, spar making, oar making, and myriad demanding edge-to-edge applications.

The jointer plane is a tool of nuance, with its long frame assuring that only the subtle high imperfections in the work are removed as fine shavings. For small jobs this cordless implement can be as handy, swiftly finishing the task before its electric cousin even gets plugged in. It is definitely a useful addition to the tool kit—if you can find one. Unfortunately, most hardware emporia these days shy away from stocking hand planes and if they carry one at all, it will be the humble jack plane. What to do? Take that jack and give it the 10-minute jointer conversion.

Start by milling a piece of hardwood stock roughly 1½" thick, 24" long, and exactly the width of the sole of your jack plane (probably about 2⅜" wide). Place and align the plane atop the stock at its midpoint and trace the curves of the tool's leading and trailing edges onto the wood. Cut the curves out of the stock and keep the front and rear pieces. Next, mill out pieces 1" × 2" × 24" for the side rails. Clamp the front and rear pieces and the jack plane between the side rails and check for fit. The jack plane should be held snugly with no bowing in or out of the side rails.

A jointer plane is a good tool for cutting long, accurate scarfs.

(continued on next page)

THE 10-MINUTE JOINTER CONVERSION (CONT.)

Place the entire assembly on a level surface covered with plastic sheeting (a table saw works well). Mix up a batch of 5-minute epoxy and coat the joining wood surfaces, leaving the wood-to-jack plane interfaces dry. Check that all the pieces and the plane are dead flat against the surface, and then clamp the assembly.

After curing, trim the fore and aft edges of the assembly with the band saw. And that's about it. For added security, holes can be drilled through the wood into the iron jack-plane frame for bolts. Insert the bolts, wax the bottom, and the new jointer is ready for action. To convert back to a jack, just remove the bolts and push the plane out of the wooden frame. The best of both worlds, and at a bargain price!

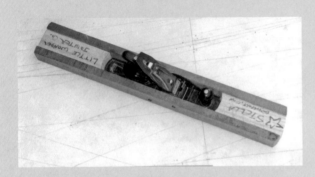

A good, serviceable jointer plane can be fabricated from a jack plane, a few bits of hardwood, and a couple fasteners.

29

Steam-Bent Coaming

After delving into the techniques and pitfalls of heating and bending wood, not to mention the importance of spiling, pattern making and quality joinery, let's take a blow-by-blow look at an operation that combines them all: the steam-bent coaming.

Seen on catboats, steam launches, sharpies, and sloops, the traditional steamed oval coaming bespeaks a bygone maritime grace. Popularized in a period when yachtsmen wore straw boaters and packed picnic hampers with crystal wineglasses, the spar-varnished oak coaming proved that functional design could be elegant. Unfortunately, few items appear quite so daunting for the home boatbuilder. Yet with a bit of preparation, pattern making, and a prodigious pile of clamps, this straightforward technique will produce a finished product that would not look out of place in a posh Victorian regatta.

STARTING BLOCKS

The patient for this operation is a replica of a circa-1880 New Haven oystering sharpie.

The deck framing already is in place. The deck beams, stub beams, and relatively straight-running fore-and-aft carlins have been faired and tuned up relative to one another using edge tools and a heavy but flexible batten. The next job is to check the artful, sharp curves both fore and aft to see whether the coaming is merely a gleam in the draftsman's eye or if it will actually make the bend.

From the drawing, scale the points where the coaming begins its tight bend from the bent carlin to the deck beam, fore and aft, port and starboard. Record these points on the deck framing of the boat. Then take a light but stiff batten and spring it through the forward curve. Check to see if the batten makes it without breaking and remains fair. Then tinker with the batten so that the curve is equal on both port and starboard. Stabilize the batten with spring clamps or small nails. Stand back and eyeball the curve. Still look good? Then slide a light piece of plywood under the batten and, using a pencil, scribe the port and starboard curves onto the top and the lines of the carlins and deck beam on the bottom. Remove the plywood and band saw out the drawn shapes. This will be the pattern for the filler blocks for the sharp turns in the forward curve. Next, repeat the procedure for the aft portion of the coaming.

The filler blocks can then be cut and fit to the deck framing. The blocks should be cut from roughly the same caliber stock as the deck beam and carlins. When the curved filler block seems about right, temporarily fix it in place with screws. Then, using a thin piece of plywood on edge to simulate the coaming, check to see that the angle cut into the curve of the filler block will allow the coaming to make a good transition from the carlin to the deck beam. The plywood should spring easily into the curve cut into the filler block. Touch up any rough spots on the filler block, bed it, and install it with screws. Repeat with the other blocks to complete the deck framing.

A DECK PATTERN

Our deck is to be made of ⅜" (9mm) marine plywood. With the cockpit opening still unencumbered, this is a great time to make the patterns for the deck. The pattern stock can just be floppy el cheapo ⅛" lauan plywood. This limber stuff will easily form to the camber of the deck. After being fit to either the transom or the stem, it can be tacked in place along the centerline and sheer line of the deck beams. Then you can trace the curve of the cockpit opening and the sheer of the deck onto the plywood. Cut the drawn curves out on the band saw, put the pattern back onto the deck framing for final tune-up, and *c'est finis*!

The true (expensive) plywood deck can be roughed out at this point, if desired, but wait until after the coaming has been bent for final deck installation. There will be enough to do when wrestling a hot piece of oak into submission without having to fumble around under a deck looking for places to clamp to.

MAKING THE COAMING PATTERN

The coaming for this boat is made in two pieces—a long forward section and a shorter aft section. The two pieces will have to join perfectly with butt blocks approximately two-thirds of the way back in the cockpit. Like the hull planking, the stock for the coaming tends to be, well, strange looking. This probably should be expected as the wood needs to follow the sweep of the sheer vertically, then turn inward to pick up the crown of the deck, and then turn and follow the sheer in the reverse direction. When cut out, the two pieces are

somewhat reminiscent of two rather long, 4" wide wooden handlebar mustaches.

To avoid any shape-distorting edge-setting or warping of the pattern, the best stock to use is plywood that's just limber enough to replicate the steam-bent curve. For a lightweight coaming such as ours (⅜"), the same ⅛" lauan that we used for the deck patterns will do the trick. The goal is to replicate not only the shape of the two-part coaming, but also its exact length.

Start by tacking overwidth pieces for the coaming pattern into place onto the carlins and beams. The exact length of the individual pieces is unimportant, as eventually they will all be joined with glued gussets that will connect all the separate pieces into one long pattern. Don't worry about the final shape of the top and bottom edges, yet. As long as the pieces are overwidth, you are in good shape. The gussets can be held in place with carpenters glue or 5-minute epoxy.

For better or worse, the coaming is an accent item and everything will show up. So, if at all possible, make sure the joints between the fore-and-aft pieces are directly opposite to one another on the port and starboard sides. Mark the joint locations onto the carlin. Also make index marks at the mid (or center) point of the curve on both the patterns. This index point will be transferred to the actual coaming stock, which will help you get the steaming hot coaming properly centered and clamped into place.

With the rough pattern in place, it's time to trace the actual shape onto it. First do the bottom edge. The plans call for the bottom edge to extend ¼" below the

Spiling batten in place.

carlin. Make a ¼" spacer and using a pencil trace the bottom edge onto the pattern. (It'll be lumpy here and there but that can be cleaned up with a batten after the pattern is off the boat.) For the top edge, the plans call for the coaming to extend 2" above the deck. Again we'll use a spacer block. The deck will be ⅜" plywood, so make a block 2⅜". With that done, remove the patterns and cut the top and bottom edges with the band saw.

SELECTING AND CUTTING THE STOCK

Just as when you are choosing stock for steam-bent frames, the terms *clear stock, straight-grained,* and *defect-free* are the order of the day. Plain-sawn lumber with these qualities is tough enough to find these days; searching for quarter-sawn might set the project back for years. Oak was probably the most common for classic hulls, though occasionally ash or mahogany was used. (Mahogany is tough to bend and has a considerable amount of spring-back.)

After the wood has been selected and planed down, clamp your pattern to the stock and trace it with a pencil. Be sure to carry over the center alignment mark from the pattern to the stock.

When cutting out the stock, leave yourself a little extra length and width as insurance against any miscues when fitting. Final trimming can be done with a plane after the coaming has been installed. "Break" or round the edges of the coaming with a plane or router. This not only makes the piece easier to handle but also seems to discourage cracking. Now we are ready to bend—almost.

BENDING THE WOOD

Generally there are two ways to bend a coaming— either outside of the boat over a custom bending frame (known as a *trap*) or directly into the boat. Both methods have their advantages (and drawbacks).

In some ways, bending over the trap is easier as you have a lot more control and the clamping is a more leisurely pursuit. But it does require the building of a custom frame that has the proper amount of spring-back calculated into it. If one were going to bend the same coaming on a regular basis, the bending frame would definitely be the way to go.

For "one off" bending like we are doing, probably the most practical route to go is to bend directly into the boat. This does require a bit of planning and at least another pair of hands. It is definitely the more aerobic alternative. But the upside is that when you bend and fit the coaming directly into the boat, you know for sure that it is going to fit correctly.

There is only a very short window of time that the steamed wood remains plastic so the key to success is to work out your modus operandi by doing a dry run of all the procedures. Begin by setting up the steam box and place the longer of the patterns inside. Can it be withdrawn easily and quickly?

Next, fit the pattern into the boat. Grab both ends and, in a slow deliberate motion, draw the ends together as though you were trying to make a loop. Place the midpoint of the curve into the forward center part of the cockpit opening, line up the penciled index marks, and clamp it into place. Then, with your assistant, begin working the pattern into the curve, alternately clamping on the port side and then the starboard. Use a wooden mallet to adjust the coaming up or down. Be sure to use the wooden pads between the metal of the clamp and the pattern. Keep working until the entire length is clamped into position. The ends of the pattern should be nearly dead on the butt marks scribed in the carlin. By this time you'll have a pretty good idea whether you have enough clamps and pads and whether they are placed correctly. With this dress rehearsal under your belt, you are ready to go.

Fire up the steamer. The steam box should be thoroughly hot, with steam roiling out, before the coaming stock is inserted. Roughly, the recipe for steaming requires half an hour for every ½" of stock thickness. After steaming the proper length of time, don the leather gauntlets and pull the limber coaming from the box. Then quickly, as before, pull the coaming into a loop, place it into the cockpit, and begin clamping. (Don't forget the plywood pads!) Keep working until the coaming is tightly clamped to the carlin. Watch for gaps developing where the coaming makes the tight turns. If necessary, use bar and pipe clamps to pull the coaming into the curved filler blocks. Use the wooden mallet to tap the coaming up and down into position. Then, after the piece has been cajoled into place, let it set to take its shape, overnight if possible.

After the forward section of the coaming has taken a set, we are ready to bend the aft piece. But with so many clamps holding down the forward one, it is unlikely that there are enough left for the aft piece. Hence, this is the

The after section of the coaming, steamed, bent, and clamped in place.

perfect opportunity to drill and temporarily screw the forward piece in place.

As with the butt block placement, the placement of the screws is a big deal. If they follow a straight line and are equally spaced, they can look great. If they are placed willy-nilly, they are pretty grim. So, take a moment to draw a guide-line and "walk" off the screw locations with a pair of dividers. Drill and install all the screws—with the exception of those closest to the butt joint. The clamps can then be removed.

We are now ready to bend in the after section. The technique is the same, almost. This time we will be tucking the butt ends of the aft coaming under the butt ends of the forward coaming (that's why the screws were left out). Remember, we left both fore and aft coaming pieces a little long. Having a little overlap will now pay off by allowing for the inevitable slight miscalculations, either in the bending or in the length of the pattern. After the aft coaming has cooled, the fore and aft pieces can be trimmed to fit tightly to one another at the butt. Sneak up on this. This operation is a lot like the fitting of the inwales of a small open boat, and it is easy in a moment of irrational exuberance to go one saw cut too far. After the final fitting, the aft piece can have its screw locations walked off and bored.

FINISHING UP

With the coaming bent and stabilized we can get back to the deck installation. There are a couple of ways to do this. The ⅜" plywood can simply be fit to the screwed-in coaming and installed or the coaming can be removed, the deck fit to the cockpit opening and installed, and

then the coaming reinstalled. If choosing the latter course, precautions should be made to keep the coaming from losing its bend either by using cross spalls or at least a "Spanish windlass" to pull the ends together.

After the deck is in place and the coaming is reinstalled (or vice versa), you can give the top of the coaming a final trim. As you did when making the pattern, fashion a scribing block that is 2" high. Again, place a pencil on top and scribe a new trim line around the entire circumference of the coaming. Using a block plane, trim the top of the coaming. Chamfer or round the top. Sand the coaming and give it a few sealer coats of finish.

The decks going on, carefully scribed and trimmed to the curve of the coaming.

There is just one job left: the butt blocks. Tradition calls for wooden butt blocks on either the inside or outside of the coaming. One method is probably as good as the other and which to use depends on the eye of the builder and what was used traditionally on that particular design of hull. As with their colleagues on the hull planking, there is more to butt blocks than simply fastening a flat plate of wood to the coaming. As the coaming has a curve (however slight), that curve must be hand worked into the butt block. The outside edges should be rounded or chamfered. The inside face should be sealed, and bedding added before fastening. The block can be fastened with either screws or rivets.

On some designs, however, the wooden butt block just looks heavy and clunky. In such a situation there is a third way—a brass butt block. For our coaming, a piece of $\frac{1}{8}$" brass fits the bill nicely. Not only does the brass conform to the curve of the coaming, but it also adds a certain air of *savoir faire*. Holes are bored and countersunk for rivets. The butt plate is clamped to the joint and holes are bored through the coaming. Remove the plate and bed, and reclamp. The plate is then riveted into place.

All that remains to finish up the job is to finish coat the wood and trim the coaming-to-deck joint with either a quarter-round wooden molding or a bead of colored synthetic caulk.

Now where'd I put that straw boater?

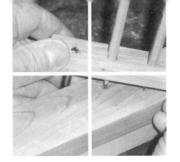

· 30 ·

Oars and Spars

Oar and spar making are quite similar—both are rather easy, and the materials are not expensive. Making spars is one of the tasks inherent to building your own sailboat, while oars can be purchased at the chandlery. There are, however, good reasons to make your own oars. The ones available in stores are usually awful, clubby things—too heavy, poorly balanced, little or no spring, and ugly to boot. A well-designed, well-made pair, on the other hand, is a joy to use.

BUILDING OARS

A good place to begin is by deciding how long the oars should be. Oars that are too short will provide inadequate leverage and efficiency, yet sweeps that are too long may leave you feeling as though you have a steady propulsion position on a trireme. One Maine boatbuilder wrote that the oars that worked best were those that entered the water at roughly a 20° angle and, when held amidships, the ends of the handles were about 3″ apart. Using this approach, the builder could sketch the body of the boat and oars in scale and measure the desired length.

Meanwhile, for the mathematically inclined, the American National Red Cross offers the following formula: The inboard length of the loom (x) should equal one half the span between the rowlocks plus 2″. Miss that? Here it is again:

$$x = span/2 + 2''$$

A solid spar under sail.

The total length of oar should equal one-seventh of the inboard length multiplied by 25, or:

$$length = x/7 \times 25$$

Using that formula on a pulling boat with a 4' beam, you would end up with oars that were 7.7' long. Pretty much in the ballpark. Anyway, the formula continues: The oar should balance within 12" of the button (located at distance x in from the butt of the handle).

Of course, this does not take into account variables such as freeboard, whether the oars will stow properly in the boat, or the conditions in which the vessel will be used. Nor does it account for style, technique, and individual preferences. That being said, either method will give you a good starting place to start experimenting, by borrowing oars of roughly appropriate length until the correct size is revealed by trial and error. It's now time to break out the plans.

Plans

Generally speaking, printed plans are a scarce commodity. (An exception is the availability of some Pete Culler designs at Mystic Seaport. See Appendix B.) Patterns are even scarcer. So why not develop your own? Start with an oar that seems to work for you and make modifications that will make it better. Increase the size of the blade if you wish, make it 3" longer if it suits the boat better, or change the shape of the handle to make it more comfortable. Some builders prefer to leave the loom square for a short way just below the handle to add a bit of weight to counterbalance the outboard portion of the oar. Others will shave a bit of hollow on either side of the ridge of the blade to reduce weight.

At any rate, a good place to begin is to measure the original oar and establish a pair of parallel center-lines and a forward perpendicular on a piece of ¼" plywood. Then line up the prototype oar over the center-line for each of the two views (flat and skinny) and trace the shape in pencil. Make the design changes on the plywood. Then establish your stations. One-foot stations work well for most of the way, with a shorter spacing in the blade and handle regions. Measure the half-breadths at the stations and commit them either to paper for scale drawing or to a grid on plywood for cleaned-up, full-size patterns.

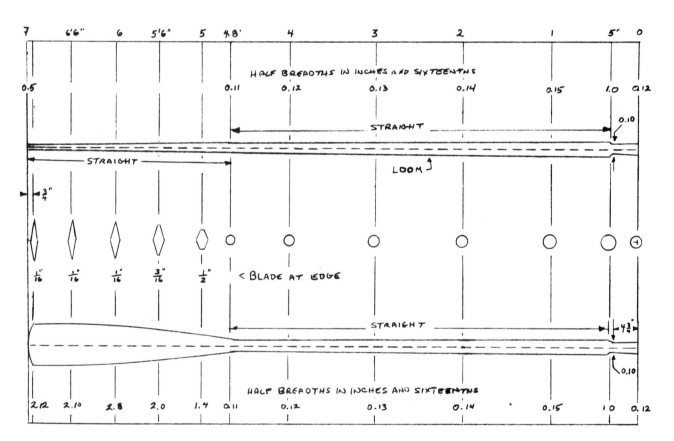

7' oars designed by George Kiefer, drawn by the author.

Laminating an oar (or two) from four boards.

After the offsets have been transferred to the ply-wood and the drawing has been faired with a straight-edge and a flexible curve, it can be cut out with a band saw. Then, after a bit of tuning with a block plane, you are ready to trace it onto the stock.

Good Wood

When shopping for wood for oars, look for stock that is stable, straight grained, without twist, and as clear as possible. The way the grain runs can be an important consideration as well. Flat grain that runs parallel tends to produce an oar that is more limber than one made from vertical-grained stock. If laminating stock for your oar blank, taking the time to align the pieces so that they are not in opposition to one another will save considerable consternation when shaping with hand tools.

For workboat oars, the traditional favorite is ash, although fir or even maple would do in a pinch. For lighter-weight pleasure boats, Sitka spruce is widely favored, while alternatives include other spruces, white cedar, and even pine. Good quality spruce can sometimes be obtained at your local home improvement center, but it may be in the racks cohabitating with fir and pine and amorphously labeled "white wood." Bring a wood sample with you to compare.

Most oars can easily be gotten out of rough (but full thickness) 2" stock. Indeed, with careful picking, it is possible for two oars to be gotten out of a single 2" × 8" piece. If your local lumber merchant only deals with dressed lumber, however, the so-called 2" stock will be a mere 1½" thick. Which brings us to lamination. That anorexic 1½" piece of spruce that isn't thick enough to accommodate the upper part of the loom can become so by simply gluing cheek pieces to the sides.

Oars and spars can be easily fabricated from two, three, or four pieces of wood, allowing the builder the added benefit of working the run of the grain to advantage or even combining different kinds of wood. Using high-quality, truly waterproof glue such as resorcinol or epoxy will prevent delamination. When laminating, weigh the stock before laminating to assure the oars will weigh nearly the same.

Drawing and Cutting

Align your patterns onto the stock to take advantage of the grain and make sure you have enough wood in both dimensions. If you are laminating your blank, cut the pieces generously oversize to allow for slippage during clamping. (Be sure to use plenty of clamps and watch that you don't build a bow or crook into the stock.)

Next, trace the flat of the oar onto the stock in pencil. After checking that the table is dead square to the blade *and* that the blade is sharp (and preferably, new), saw out the flat with the band saw outside the scribed line. Take the blank to the bench and finish shaping to the line with hand tools. Check that the run of the loom is straight and that the edges are square.

After planing, draw a centerline on the newly sawn-out edge. Then place the side pattern on the stock and trace its shape. The taper can now be cut into the blank with the band saw. Use caution to keep the vertical blank square to the saw and again, leave the line. After

Shaping the oar blade on the bandsaw.

sawing, return the oar to the bench to finish planing the taper to the lines. In cross section, the loom and handle are square, and the blade is rectangular.

If you don't have a band saw, or the one you have doesn't have enough depth to cut the taper, you can plane it in with a handheld power planer. Check often with a square and straightedge. The shape of the flat side of the oar can be cut with a good quality saber saw. Leave a bit more distance from the line, however, to allow for possible faux pas.

Shaping the Blade

Since the previous centerlines have been cut off, the next job is to establish new centerlines on the flats of the blade and on its sides. The blade of this oar tapers from the centerline on the flat to an established width measured out from the centerline on the edge of the blade, while the thickness of the edge goes from $\frac{1}{16}$" at the end to $\frac{1}{2}$" when fairing into the rounding of the loom. Mark the offsets from the plan onto the side of the blade, connect the points with a flexible batten, and draw the line. Then clamp the oar to the bench (don't forget the clamp pads!) and shave with a spokeshave and plane the four facets from the center of the blade to the edge. When the job is just about done, it can be given the coup de grace with a cabinet scraper.

Rounding the Loom

Now it is time to round the loom and the handle. This part of the business is simply spar making in miniature. We'll be going from four sides to eight, then roughly knocking off the edges to give us 16, then rounding and sanding. Easy. But first we need to go from four to eight. Begin by making a mini version of the spar-making gauge. The gauge is a devise that will proportionally scribe lines on the flat faces of the four-sided loom that, when connected by planing, will give us an octagonal cross section. The gauge consists of a slip of hardwood roughly 5" long with two short $\frac{1}{4}$" bronze pins and two short pencils installed at a 7-10-7 ratio. To make this little gem, drill a $\frac{1}{4}$" hole dead vertical through the piece of hardwood about $\frac{1}{2}$" in from the end, and insert a pin. Then, measuring over $\frac{7}{8}$" from the side of the pin, drill a pencil-sized hole in the wood. Insert a pencil. From the center of the first pencil hole measure over $1\frac{1}{4}$" and drill another hole and insert a pencil. Lastly, from the center of the second pencil hole measure over $\frac{7}{8}$" and add $\frac{1}{8}$" (total = 1").

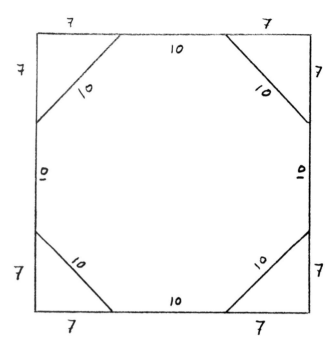

How the oar- or spar-making gauge accurately marks a square timber for eight-siding. To get that hypotenuse right, just apply the Pythagorean theorem: $7^2 + 7^2 \sim 10^2$.

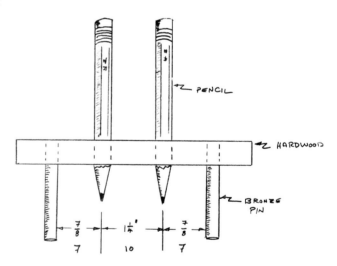

Oar-making gauge.

Drill another $\frac{1}{4}$" hole and insert the second pin. Now, we're in business.

To use the tool, place it over the tapered loom and cock it at an angle so that the pins are pressed against the opposite sides of the loom. As you draw it down the length of the loom, the spar-making gauge will automatically divide and scribe the planed face of the loom

To use the oar gauge, cock it at an angle so that the brass pins bear along the sides of the stock and draw it down the length of the timber.

into the 7-10-7 ratio. Repeat the process on the remaining three sides. Then, using a spokeshave, a block plane, and Pythagoras's theorem, you can commence to round the loom. Planing from a line seven units in from one edge to a line that is seven units in on an adjacent face will generate a facet that can be thought of as a hypotenuse of a right triangle. And as the Great Man said (to paraphrase), "If you square the lengths of the two sides and add 'em together you come up with the square of the hypotenuse"—which is, in this case, 98, the square root of which is mighty close to 10! Hence, when you are done planing to the lines, you will end up with an octagon with faces of roughly 10 units apiece. Setting and clamping the loom into padded blocks that have a "V" cut into them will aid the shaping process. Remember to check your planing with a straightedge as you work.

After the loom and handle have been octagonalized, commence with the rounding. Some builders use a hollow-bottomed spar plane for this task, but equally good results (with probably less chance of tearing out grain) can be had with a low angle block plane. First, working along the length of the loom, roughly knock off the edges, making it sixteen-sided. Then, still working fore-and-aft, use the plane in a rolling or corkscrew fashion around the loom. If the iron is set fine, there is little chance of pulling grain. Fair the loom to the blade. After you have gotten close with the plane, try working with a flat file and use it in

Rough out the handle with a chisel, then switch to more subtle tools such as a file and spokeshave.

The handle is finished. The oar loom has been eight-sided, and awaiting sixteen-siding and final smoothing.

The author with the varnished and leathered oar.

the same fashion. (The file, spokeshave, and rat-tail file work well to shape the handle.) Then switch to coarse sandpaper. Gradually introduce finer paper and return to working straight with the grain to reduce scratching.

With the sanding finished, all that needs to be done is to tack the surface and add a few coats of varnish and the leathers (see Chapter 31), and you're ready to go!

SPARS

For most traditional small craft, solid, round spars are the way to go, even if they are heavier than their hollow brethren. They are easy to manufacture, repair, or replace with little in the way of special jigs or assembly tables. The technology is exactly the same as for making oars, but is in many ways easier.

The Wood

Once again, lightness and strength are of prime concern and the spruces are top candidates. If you have the extra cash, mail ordering Sitka spruce would be a good investment. For most of us, however, the most practical option is a trip to the local wood emporium.

It wasn't that long ago that you could go to the lumber yard and, in a short time of picking, have all the stock you needed for your spars—often in full thickness timbers. That's a pretty rare occurrence these days. And, unless you go to a local sawmill, chances are that the greatest stock thickness will be a nominal 2″ (actually $1^1/_2$″). That means you will end up laminating stock and scarfing planks together to give you the proper thickness and length (see Chapter 28).

Fortunately, both laminating and scarfing are straightforward work and the glues, especially epoxy, are easy (albeit messy) to use and very reliable. The upside of lamination is that you can give the spar a metaphorical "CAT scan" as it is assembled. You will know for sure that there will be very few defects, rot pockets, funky knots, and such buried inside of the stock. With solid wood, you never know for sure what is inside. With that in mind, examine your stock closely. Look for clear straight grain and no sapwood in the region that you are working in. This can be a challenge. The large mills are sawing just about anything that is a shade larger than Christmas trees these days. It not unusual to find 2″ × 4″ studs with bark on each edge. Prudence calls for purchasing planks that are considerably wider than you think you might need just to make sure that there will be enough good wood to work with. Select stock that is straight and without warp or twist.

When laminating, keep in mind that glues cure at different speeds (see Chapter 15). Coating the laminates, then aligning and clamping them can take a considerable amount of time. When working with epoxy, temperature and hardener can affect the rate of cure greatly. Using too fast a hardener on a hot summer day can literally leave you stuck, prematurely. Always check the manufacturer's recommendations as to which hardener to use and when in doubt, opt for the version that offers the slower cure.

If you happen to locate solid stock of a large enough caliber to make the spar, there are a few other things to check out as well. First don't be put off by a few small tight knots. They pose very little problem. Check the butt ends to see if the heart or center of the tree is present. It is best to have the heart present on both ends or not have the heart at all, meaning that the timber was cut to one side of the center of the tree, rather than the heart at one end only. (More on this in a moment.) Watch for deep checks or cracks and for rot.

Laying Out and Cutting the Spar

Designers use a range of presentations when illustrating a spar plan on blueprints. Some offer elaborate depictions of the spar, with wood grained illustrations portraying each and every section with specifications offered in minutiae. On the other end of the scale are the minimalists who offer a small-scale drawing with a just handful of somewhat grudging measurements or offsets. In the end, it is all the same—a centerline with stations given with offsets to be measured out in two directions from the centerline at each station. A batten is then sprung through the given points to produce the taper of the spar.

Begin by laying down a centerline on the widest face of your stock—either sawn or laminated. The line can be cheated one way or the other to avoid defects in the face of the stock. If you are using a sawn timber where an obvious center or heart of the tree is present, it's important to have your centerline follow the heart as close as possible by squaring up from the heart on both butt ends to the face of the timber and connecting the points. Keeping the center of the tree in the center of the spar will keep the stick balanced and help prevent it from warping after it is sawn out.

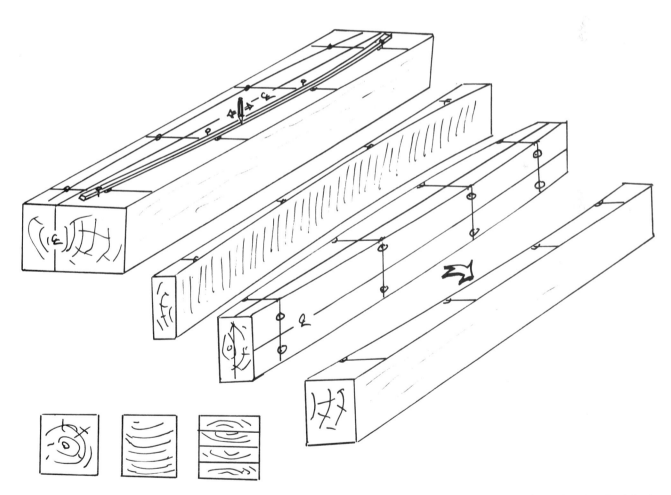

Laying out a spar. You can keep the heart of the timber in the center all the way through, or avoid it altogether, but don't let it wander from the center at one end to off-center at the other. Another approach is to laminate the timber from flat-sawn boards, making sure to reverse the direction of the grain for each one to equalize any propensity toward cupping or warping.

Carefully level the table before laminating spar stock, using shims to provide a dead-flat surface. Use plenty of clamps for even clamping pressure.

After establishing the centerline, record the stations and square them out to the edges of the stock. Measuring out from the centerline, record the offsets onto the stock, spring a batten through them, and scribe the line. Then, take the stock to the band saw and, cutting almost to the line, take a slab off each side. Smooth the cuts down to the line with a hand or power plane.

Next, square the station lines over onto the newly planed side. Establish a new centerline onto the curved face of the stock. Repeat the layout of the offsets and spring a batten through them as before. Then it's back to the band saw to saw a slab off both sides. Next, smooth sides 3 and 4 with the plane.

Fashion a larger version of the "7-10-7" spar maker's gauge described above and scribe the lines for 8-siding the stock. Then, using a power or hand plane, take down the stock until the spar is octagonal in section. The next stop is to make the spar roughly 16-sided by eye, using a long hand plane to flatten the edges of the octagon.

The spar can now be rounded and faired, again using the plane in the same rolling or corkscrew fashion around the spar. Some builders will round the spar by cutting a belt-sander belt so that it lies flat, and adding handles on either end. The coarse sanding belt can be worked "shoe-shine-rag" fashion around the spar.

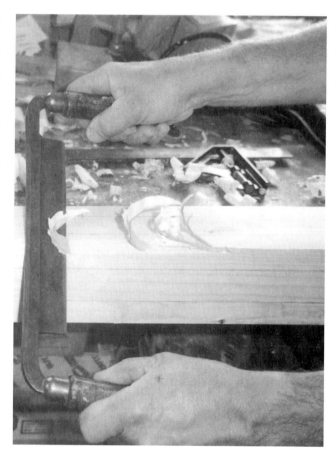

Roughing out the stock with a drawknife. A power plane is another option. Either one will be followed by a hand plane to bring it down to eight sides.

Eight-siding the spar with a jointer plane.

Then the spar can be fine-tuned with a sandpaper long-board, applied corkscrew-fashion.

After the spar has been sanded to perfection (or as close to it as you can stand), it can be coated. As with oars, clear coating with varnish or a similar clear product is the way to go. The woods used in spar making tend to be nondurable, and a clear finish will allow for easy, regular inspection.

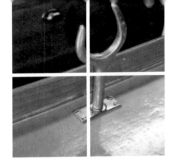

· 31 ·

Oarlocks, Pads, and Leathers

Like the other propulsion systems of power and sail, the business of rowing often needs a bit of tinkering to get it just right. It's worth taking the trouble, however, as a properly set up pair of oars and all their appurtenances make rowing the pleasure it's supposed to be.

OARLOCK PLACEMENT

The proper placement of the oarlocks (aka row-locks) involves a combination of factors that include the height of the rail above the rowing thwart, the width of the vessel, whether the boat has coamings, and even the height and arm length of the rower. Probably the best way to check out oarlock location is to find a boat of the same model as yours and take it out for a spin. Chances are, the owner has already worked out most of the bugs and you'll get a good idea of what to expect.

Oarlock, socket, and pad.

If no prototype is available, check out the blueprints. Generally, the location of the oarlocks is given on the construction plan. If the location of the oarlocks is not specified, a good default (or at least a starting) position for the center of an oarlock is 12″ aft of the after edge of the thwart. The actual location is negotiable to suit the comfort of the oarsman.

Then, there is the matter of oarlock height at the rail relative to the top of the seat. This again is a matter of personal preference in powering propulsion. Pete Culler wrote that he favored the grips of the oars to come just about under his rib cage. Inasmuch as the seat height in the boat has likely already been established, any adjustments of the seat-to-oarlock height can be made by using experimental pads of varying thickness to raise the oarlock to the estimated desired elevation. The dummy pads (with provisionally attached sockets) can be clamped to the rail. Then, after bracing the boat properly, set up your oars and locks and sit in the boat and see how it feels. (This is probably best done when there is no one else around to inquire what on earth are you doing.)

A surprising amount of the efficiency in the business of rowing comes from having a solid place to anchor your feet. In many traditional hulls, a fixture such as a frame will do the job. In newer construction such as plywood or strip, such amenities may be missing. In such cases, incorporating foot braces or stretchers can give you a little extra horsepower when rowing. They can be in the form of chocks fastened to the deck

A removable stretcher set up for the boat's owner. Additional brackets or "keepers" could be added to accommodate rowers of different length of leg.

Begin by stretching the tape from the oarlock center on the starboard side to a point on the centerline of the stem. Pick up the distance (x) and record it. Then, holding the second tape on the stem centerline, swing the other end of the tape until distance (x) strikes the port side and mark it. You've just created an Isosceles triangle—hence, the portside mark is now dead square across from the oarlock center on the starboard. As the great man said, "Here's to Euclid."

OARLOCK HARDWARE

Simple, standard, flat, top-mount sockets are probably the most commonly used. The casting can be best described as a flat rectangular plate with a central tapered cylindrical socket affixed. In recent years, mass produced oarlock socket castings have become progressively coarser, funky and asymmetrical. If possible, buy where you can match up the sockets for appearance and check the fit to the oarlocks.

More elegant patent swivel rowlocks were used primarily in the years before World War II. The rowlock, which can be fastened either to the top of the rail or onto a pad, requires a base measuring roughly 1½" × 4¾". Unlike socket-type oarlocks, the "patent swivel" casting has a center pin surrounded by a slotted T-flange that mates with and engages the round, bored base of the oarlock, preventing the lock from jumping off the gunwale in moments of poor oarsmanship. It's just the ticket for restorations and replicas, and it does not require a hole to be bored through the pad or deck. Its drawback is that it is incompatible with the standard oarlock.

or planking or even a removable wooden bar that is set into a pair of keepers.

Squaring Things Up

After you have determined fairly closely where the oarlock centers should be, it's time to check that they are truly symmetrically located in the boat. It isn't enough to just assume that the oarlock centers are correct because both port and starboard sides are 2″ aft of frame 12. Quite a few boats have asymmetrical frames. But chances are, the boat itself is pretty symmetrical. So break out your old high school geometry book, a couple of tape measures, and a pencil and we'll get to work.

Horned oarlocks and matching sockets.

Swivel oarlocks won't jump out of the socket. (Rostand Manufacturing Company)

Some other options include:

- **Edge mount.** Available in fancy and utilitarian versions, these socket are cast in an "L" shape that fits to the side of the rail and allows for both vertical and horizontal screw fastening.

- **Side mount.** This casting has a single, flat-mounting plate with a socket affixed that allows for attachment on the side of a rail.

- **"Davis" drop pattern.** This has an attached fold-down rowlock. When not in use the oarlock drops down out of the way but can't slip out. This design is rugged albeit a bit clunky. Not bad for working craft or for situations where oarlocks might have the tendency to walk away.

- **"Outrigger" oarlock brackets.** The socket is at the end of an arm that's hinged at the gunwale. When extended, these brackets allow an oar approximately 1' longer to be used, and when they are folded back inboard, the boat is more convenient for traveling and storage. Handy for narrow high-performance pulling boats.

MAKING OARLOCK PADS

Although utilitarian in nature, a well-executed oarlock pad can be a handsome design feature. Many builders standardize their oarlock pads on all their boats as part of their signature. The design should be practical while still looking good. Generally the top of the pad is beveled, tapering down from the oarlock socket in the center towards the ends.

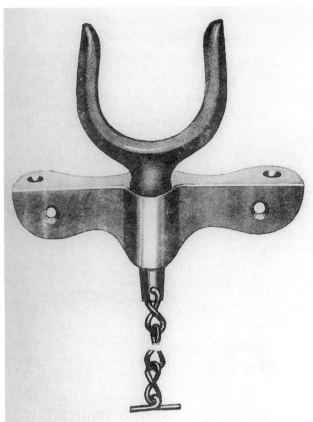

Edge-mount or Boston-pattern oarlocks screw into the rail both horizontally and vertically. (Rostand Manufacturing Company)

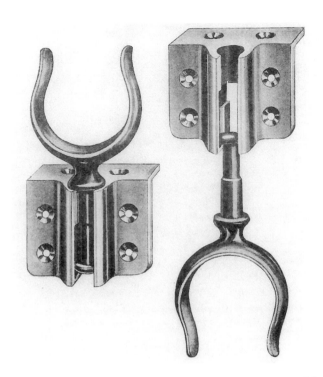

"Davis" or drop-pattern oarlocks can be tucked nicely out of the way and never get lost. (Rostand Manufacturing Company)

Pads on Rails

For a gunwale-mounted oarlock pad, start by devising a tastefully symmetrical pattern and trace it on the sides of a rectangular hardwood blank. Oak, mahogany, and locust all work well, and 10" to 12" are popular lengths.

Next, lay out and drill center holes for the cylinder of the oarlock sockets (chances are the holes will need to be slightly tapered). Due to the aforementioned casting anomalies, it will likely require a custom fit of the socket to the blank, especially if you wish to mortise the top of the pad for the top plate of the socket. Using a block plane, fit the bottom of the blank to the upsweeping curve of the sheer. Rough-cut the top bevels in with a band saw and plane them to perfection.

Then place the blank in its proper location and (if possible) align the bored hole over the gap between the strake and inwale. Trace the curve of the inwale onto the bottom of the blank. This is where a bit of artistry and nuance comes in. Many builders like to run their inboard edge of the pad just a trifle away from (but parallel to) the curve of the inwale. On the outboard side, the curve of the pad runs parallel to the inwale, balancing the appearance of the plate of the socket on top. Cut the desired curve with a band saw and plane to shape. For extra strength, many builders like to include a filler block between the inwale and plank underneath the oarlock pad.

Drill holes for the hold-down screws or bolts. These can be countersunk if the depth of the pad allows. The center hole may need to be chased into the rails to allow the socket to land. Paint the bottom of the pad. Clamp the pad in place on the rails and bore, bed, and fasten.

Coamings and Decks

Small boats with decks and coamings present their own set of challenges. How do you install an oarlock system that works well and still looks good? Some builders simply leave them off their sailboats, opting to rely on a stowed paddle to get them back when the wind fails. Sounds good, until the day you actually have to do it. Oars are better.

Tall oarlock pads are a good option to get the oars over the coaming and further out on the deck to allow the use of longer oars. The approach to making tall deck-mounted pads is similar to that of their less lofty brethren. Start with a blank and a pattern. As with short pads, care needs to be taken to have them look symmetrical in shape and placement. A side-draining limber should be incorporated into the design. The underside

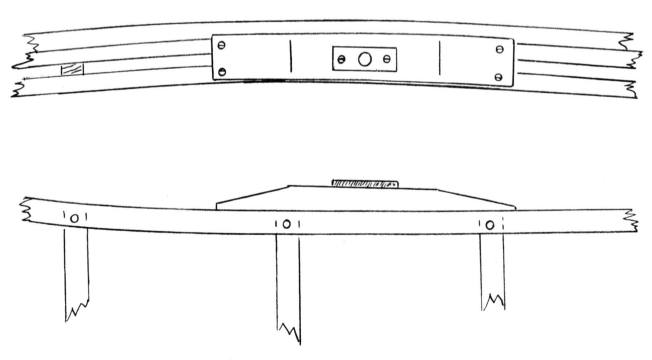

To look right, the oarlock pad should follow the curve of the sheer in both directions.

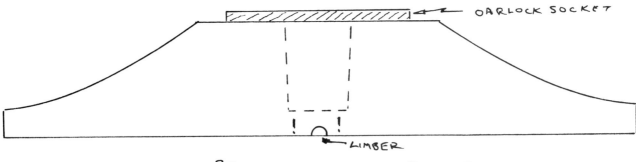

PROFILE OAR LOCK PAD TALL

Remember to cut a limber (drain) hole in tall pads.

of the deck should be reinforced to accommodate the added stress and fastenings. Marine plywood bedded in a flexible adhesive works well for this. Paint the bottom of the pad and bed. Bronze machine screws and nuts make a good pad-to-deck fastener.

Coaming-mounted pads are another solution. Fabricated of the same wood as the coaming, the classic rounded (lozenge) shape assures that there is nothing standing proud on the deck to foul lines. Joinery of these blocks can be a bit finicky, however, as they must fit the curvature of the coaming and the camber and fore and aft curves of the deck. Caution calls for doing those tricky fits first for all the pad blanks and then cutting and shaping the decorative outboard curve. The pad can then be bored for the socket. The pads can be fastened to both the deck and coaming. Remember the bedding and the limbers. Too much trouble? Bronze vertical oarlock holders (similar to those used on the Herreshoff 12½

and Fish Class boats) are available for direct coaming mounting.

Finally, there is the flush-mounted oarlock socket on deck that uses a tall shank "Connecticut River" or "raised" oarlock to carry the oar over the coaming. In this situation, a rugged oarlock socket is set into the reinforced deck. When not in use, the oarlocks are stowed out of the way and the socket opening can be plugged with a rubber cork. Just the ticket for a lightweight daysailer.

The pad has been fitted to the coaming and deck, and is ready to accept the hardware.

Tall oarlocks are another solution for reaching over a coaming or outboard of a wide deck.

OAR LEATHERS

Adding leathers to your oars not only protects the loom of the oar from chafing from the oarlocks, but also adds a touch of utilitarian elegance. Leathers can either be tacked or sewn on. I prefer stitching the leathers. Like sewing a baseball or tying your shoes, sewing will snug the leather up nicely. The application can last for years.

Leather kits are available commercially that provide enough leather for two oars, two leather button straps, tack, waxed twine, and a pair of blunt, "egg eye" leather needles. But scraps from your local leather shop or tannery (avoid variegated patent leather and faux lizard skin), common waxed sail twine, a couple of curved sail needles, and some canoe tacks will do the job as well. Leathers generally run from 7" to 12" long and are wide enough to wrap around the oar. Locate a pair of gloves to protect the hands while sewing.

Begin by scribing a starting pencil line parallel to the run of the loom (shaft) of the oar and in line with the blade edge (see location chart on the following page). To reduce chafing of the sewing twine on spoon-bladed oars, which always face the same direction, place the seam on the aft side of the loom (i.e., the same side as the concave surface of the blade).

Next, measure around the circumference of the loom at the leather location and trim the leather's width ¼" to ⅜" short to allow for pulling the leather tight with the twine.

After placing the leather on a sacrificial board, punch a series of complementary holes with an awl (or bore them with a small-caliber drill bit) approximately ¼" in from the mating leather edges and ⅜" apart. It's best to lay the holes out and mark them ahead of time.

To keep the leather from migrating while you are sewing, apply a line of glue on the inner side of the leather. Waterproof 5-minute epoxy is a good choice. Align the leather with the drawn line on the loom and temporarily hold it in place with a couple of stainless steel hose clamps. Having glue under the leather has an additional benefit. Over time, oar leather tends to loosen up. The jury is still out as to whether the wood beneath becomes compressed or the leather stretches. Nonetheless, glue will keep everything anchored where it should be.

Then cut a piece of waxed twine 6' to 8' long and attach a needle on both ends and begin stitching through the prepunched holes like lacing up a shoe. (Here's where the gloves come in.) Draw the leather together as you work. There should be enough twine when you reach the other end to double back and reinforce your first set of stitches. When finished, knot the twine and tuck it underneath the leather.

While not absolutely necessary, a ring-like stop or "button" applied to the upper end of your oar leather can make the difference as to whether your unattended oar slides through the oarlock and into the water or not. A strip of heavy leather (½" wide or so) wrapped around the applied leathers will do the trick. Wrap the button leather around the oar, allowing for an overlap of ½" or so. With a sharp knife, cut complementary beveled scarf joints into the ends of the leather strip so that when the joints are overlapped, the strips will form a continuous ring. Then butter up the inside of the button with glue, set it in place on the oar leather, and clamp it with an adjustable hose clamp overnight. The next morning clean up any squeeze-out of the glue. Although not absolutely necessary, some like to

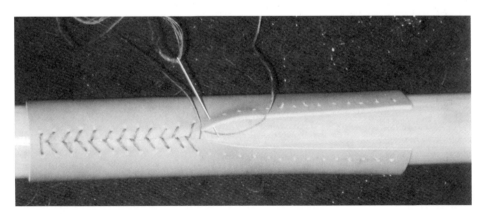

Sewing an oar leather.

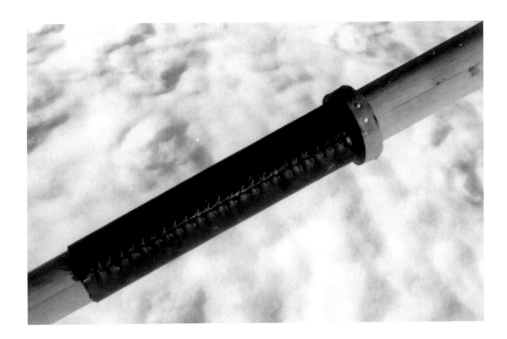

A finished leather and button.

add a line of nicely spaced brass tacks through the button into the wood.

Like treating your boots, lubricating the oar leathers will promote their longevity and make them water-repellent. It will also make rowing easier. There are many recipes to use, including tallow and grease. One that works well is plain old boot dressing made from pine tar and beeswax. It smells great and can even smarten up the finish on the oar.

OAR INSURANCE

Growing up on Staten Island, much of our cruising was done in a heavily planked fishing skiff. Although an irascible Mercury outboard was part of the package,

more often then not, the capricious machine was out of action and we were left to explore the murky, industrial waters of Raritan Bay and the Arthur Kill by oar. Actually, it wasn't too bad a deal, and with four of us toiling at the ash sweeps we could make the old barge move along at a decent clip. Indeed, as our youthful confidence grew, we began to push the envelope some and would challenge ourselves to match our speed to cross the river with a tugboat's ability to run us over. We almost always won these contests.

There was one day, however, when in the heat of the race, an oar broke, sending one of us flying into the bow. With no spare oar to throw into the breach, our horsepower decreased immediately by roughly 50%. This naturally threw our finely honed calculations into disarray. We dodged the bullet that time. And there was a lesson learned: oars (and oarlocks) can break at the least opportune of times.

Nowadays, I always bring along an extra set of oars and a spare pair of locks. It's a great comfort to know that if either oar or lock breaks, I'll be able to keep going and if the conditions get bad, I might even be able to dragoon a passenger into the other rowing station.

An equally vexatious situation is the loss of an oarlock overboard. There are two usual methods of loss prevention. One is the use of a store-bought brass chain and keeper that is attached to an eye at the bottom of the pin of the oarlock. This is an effective deterrent but it has the unhandy drawback of having to feed the chain down through the socket when installing the lock and reversing the process when removing the lock. A more convenient method is to run a lanyard or a stout piece of twine tied from a frame or thwart riser to a cast eye on the horn of the oarlock. If there is no cast eye, a small hole can be safely bored in the lower portion of the oarlock.

Here's a look at a few more oarlock types, including their loss-prevention features:

- **Thole pins.** These are an early form of oarlock and are still in use. Most commonly seen on dories, thole pins are (generally) turned wooden pins that fit into bored holes in the rail. The pins act like the horns on a conventional oarlock, keeping the oars where they ought to be and giving you fulcrum to pull against. All tholes should have lanyards to keep them from disappearing.

- **Round oarlock.** These handsome locks are a boon for those who have problems with oars jumping out of horned oarlocks. They can be slipped over the handle end of the oar, and if a leather stop button is added, the oar cannot slip out of the lock. Unlike the pinned North River locks, the round socket does allow the oar to be feathered.

- **Horn.** Sometimes called ribbed or Boston oarlocks, these are the most common type used today. They occasionally have an eye for a lanyard. (If they do not have an eye, consider drilling a hole for a lanyard—see below.) They generally do have an eye at the bottom of the pin for a safety chain. Oars can easily be removed without pulling the oarlocks.

- **North River.** These oarlocks have a pin that goes through the oars. They are traditional for Adirondack guide boats and have an advantage when you are fishing as the oars won't escape when your mind is on other matters. They do prevent the oars from being feathered, however.

·32·

Bitts and Pieces

A study in symmetry beneath your feet. Small holes for finger lifts; larger holes for a bilge pump hose. All board seams running parallel to the boat's centerline, and the outside edges parallel to the waterline curve of the hull.

Building a boat is a seemingly never-ending jigsaw-puzzle assembly of parts and pieces. Even when the vessel is complete, there always seem to be a few forgotten items that need to be made or acquired. And while some of these last-minute add-ons can be purchased at the local marine emporium, it's hard to beat the look that custom gear adds.

FLOORBOARDS

Floorboards, duckboards, bottom boards, gratings, burdens—whatever you call them, they are intended to protect the bottom planking in a small boat and keep your feet dry. In some ways, the plebeian, workaday floorboard can be viewed like a sacrificial anode, destined to be replaced in the future. Nonetheless, the appearance of these seemingly simple units can make or break the interior of a small boat. A well-laid-out floorboard assembly has a lot in common with well-lined-out planking on a hull. Properly done, the floorboards will complement the rest of the boat's interior with a subtle elegance.

Common Traits

There are many different styles of floorboards to choose from, ranging from simple fore and aft slats screwed to cleats, to elaborate removable curved assemblies that are sprung into place and held down with turn buttons. What most (if not all) floorboards have in common is that they are laid out symmetrically (the centerline or centerboard trunk makes a good starting point) and at least some of them are removable. Removable sections are important to allow access to sponge out the bilge, or clean out the inevitable detritus such as tools and bottle caps that finds its way underneath. Removable sections are generally held together with wooden cross-cleats. Hold-down turn buttons can be made of either brass half round or wood.

Wood for floorboards should be light, relatively durable, and rot resistant, to stand up to frequent immersion. Cedar is a good choice, although pine, fir, or even sassafras works as well. The floorboards take a beating and the edges are prone to wear unevenly. Planing a slight chamfer or rounding the edges of the boards will preclude a prematurely worn appearance.

Unless the floorboards are massive, the screws can be mounted with their heads flush rather than counterbored and plugged. A nice screw pattern will enhance the looks of the assembly. Not only will the flush-fastened floorboard be stronger and easier to disassemble when that time comes, but you'll also avoid the dreary task of dealing with all those bungs.

Floorboard Design

At first blush, the floorboard looks so simple it might appear that it can be casually assembled on the bench in a few minutes and dropped into place. Alas, it cannot. The length and width of the individual pieces, accommodating the curvature of the hull at the margin of the assembly, and accounting for frames and centerboard trunk are just a few of the considerations when laying out a flat floorboard. Let's take a look at just a few configurations.

Totally removable floorboards are typical in boats such as flatiron skiffs. Commonly, the individual pieces are made of straight stock of equal width and are held together with cleats that rest on the bottom planking.

To prevent your removable floorboards from unintentionally being fused into place, cut any frame notches amply enough to accommodate swelling. How much gap should there be along the side of the frame? Fit all the frame notches for all the floorboards. See the widest gap? Unless it is outrageously large, make all the rest of the notches to match it. Voila!

Straight Flat Layout

Straight floorboards are common in many small craft. Built of stock of equal width, they rest on and are fastened to the top of true and level floors or cross-cleats.

The outermost or margin board will likely fit to the curve of the hull, and there will be a removable cleanout section. Floorboards can also be sprung fore and aft to roughly follow the curvature of the rocker of the hull. Again, floorboards can be screwed down to the floors or cleats with a sprung access section held down with turn buttons.

Curved Flat Layout

A well-lined-off curved flat floorboard built of mathematically divided or diminished banana-shaped slats will look almost as if the increasingly sweeping boards are of equal width all along their length. Occasionally, it may be impossible to get enough curved stock to make all of the slats with that size ratio. To avoid the optically funky look of a narrow board being sandwiched between two wider ones, lay out the change in the width of the slats (relative to one another) in a graduated fashion. That way, each successive plank will get progressively (and tastefully) narrower.

Curved Hull Hugging Floorboards

Yet another option is a curved floor that follows the interior of bent frames—sort of like an underfoot ceiling (marine terminology is interesting). In this case, the assembly has a (semi) permanently affixed centerboard and port and starboard margin boards or stringers. Running between these fixtures is a removable, sprung, multiboard panel fastened to steam-bent cleats that follow the curve of the hull. Again, the individual boards should be diminished as above and spiled to fit. The section is held in place with a few elegant turn buttons.

A Few Useful Holes

For a bit of customizing, consider including some ample finger holes for lifting out removable sections. They should be carefully laid out to complement the assembly without weakening it. One inch is a good common size but drill a test hole in some scrap and see how your fingers fit.

Another nice touch (if your floorboard slats are wide enough) is to include a hole large enough to accommodate inserting your favorite hand pump so that you need not remove the floorboards to bail. A 2″ diameter hole will accommodate most hand pumps, and if the hole is bored at the joint between two slats (placing half of the hole in one board and half in the other), the hole is unlikely to weaken the assembly.

Mind the Gap

To be visually pleasing, gaps between the boards should be of equal width. Many builders like to match the spacing of the gaps in other visible structures such as those found in a stern seat. Rather than using a ruler, the easiest way to maintain your gaps (and your sanity) is to insert a couple of wooden spacers of the proper thickness between each of the floorboard pieces being fastened down. No time-consuming and error-prone measuring, just perfect spaces every time. The width of the gap is determined in part by how large a piece of debris you can tolerate falling into the bilge.

When You're Spiling . . .

Generally, the outermost edge of the floorboard should fit the curve of the hull. In many cases, you can capture the shape of the curve by scribing with a block, dividers, or a ruler directly onto the stock. You can also spile the curve onto a pattern, aka a spiling batten. This method is particularly advantageous if your outmost board is wide and the curve is long and sweeping.

One sure-fire approach to spiling the curve is to use the glued feeler gauge method. Begin by tacking rough-cut pattern stock, such as 1/4" plywood, to the bottom cleats or floors as close to the curve as possible. Make up a bunch of long, thin pieces of stock. These will eventually be placed on top of the pattern and slid outward until they contact the hull. If a piece of pattern stock is glued to the bottom of the stick where it contacts the hull, the bottom of the stick will then be in the same plane as the bottom of the pattern. Slide the sticks out until they contact, and glue them down with

5-minute epoxy or a hot-glue gun. Take the pattern out of the boat and place it atop your floorboard stock, mark the ends of your pointer sticks, and connect them with a flexible batten. Draw the line and cut.

If you have sawn frames, the margin of the floorboards will need to be notched around the frames to allow it to reach the side of the hull. This can be trickier than it sounds, as the wide frames intersect the board at an angle. If this angle is not accounted for when spiling, the cut notch can end up moving the board fore or aft or making it not fit at all. An easy way to get the right fit is to take a small pattern with the notch already cut into it and slide it into place around the frame. Then attach it to the rest of your spiling batten. Later, when you are recording the rest of the data from your spiling batten onto your stock, simply trace around the notch. It has to come out right. If making a pattern doesn't appeal, then experiment with your scribing technique on a piece of scrap rather than on that difficult-to-find curved stock. To get an even tighter fit to the curve of the hull, under-bevel the floorboard where it contacts the frame.

In Praise of Paint

Floorboards take a beating and have to suffer many indignities, such as sand-embedded boat-shoe treads, hobnail-booted brothers-in-law, effusive Labrador retrievers, and thoughtlessly parked anchors. Most varnishes simply are not formulated to stand up to such abuse. Paints are much tougher. Using paint equates into more time boating instead of sanding. There is something to be said for that.

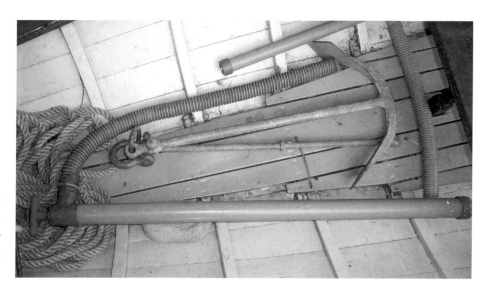

Varnish doesn't always look good, especially on floorboards that take a beating. You'll worry less and may enjoy the boat more if you use good old paint.

CURVED GAFF JAWS

For their size, gaff jaws offer plenty of interesting challenges for the mechanic. These curvaceous units have to be properly designed to be strong, have sufficient clearance for the mast, and be well fabricated so that they stand the test of time. One must make a decision as to whether or not to have a pivoting tumbler. And then there is the intriguing question of how best to get the curve.

As usual, there are options: one can use a grown crook, steam bend the curved shape, or laminate it. Today, the latter two options are probably the more practical.

First lay out a jaw pattern (a flexible ⅛″ piece of plywood works well) either scaled up from the plans or traced from an existing set of jaws. A pattern should also be made of the curve of the jaw as viewed from the side. If you are making a repair set of jaws, it's a good idea to analyze whether the original ones were adequate in strength and design in the first place. Was the failure due to rot or poor construction technique, or was the original design simply too wimpy? If possible, it's a good idea to locate a similar boat and rig with operational jaws that can be replicated.

Steam-Bent Jaws

With the curve captured, proceed to manufacturing the bending jig. Perhaps the easiest way to produce a form that is strong enough for bending solid stock is to fashion it from a large softwood block. It is much easier to bend a longer piece of wood than a short one, so select a block considerably longer than the length of the finished jaws.

The curve of the jaw can then be traced onto the side of the jig block. To accommodate the inevitable "spring back" of the bent wood, you can build a bit of extra curve into the jig. While there are formulae to help predict the amount of recoil, merely placing a light batten along the drawn curve and giving it a bit more of a bow "by eye" should do the job. (Check to see that you have maintained the straight run where the jaw contacts the gaff.)

Then, after checking the band saw blade for squareness to the table, cut out the curve. To ease clamping, cut notches or flats on the bottom side of the block. Anchor the jig securely to a sawhorse or bench.

The best steaming stock should be considerably longer than the length of the finished jaw, be as freshly cut as possible, and have no sapwood or defects. The grain running along the narrow side should be as flat as possible. Use the pattern to find the orientation on the flat side that will follow the curve of the mast to afford the greatest strength. Also, it is good insurance to have a backup piece of stock ready to go into the steamer in case the unthinkable happens. (Having a spare almost always guarantees success with the first piece.) Assemble the necessary clamps and pads and do a "dry-run" of your bending routine.

Insert your offering into a piping hot steam box and heat thoroughly. After donning the requisite hot mitts, pull the stock from the box. Affix the wood to the side of the jig, placing a wide hardwood or plywood block between the stock and the clamps. The curve can then be slowly but steadily pulled into the wood until it contacts the entirety of the jig. Let the stock cool.

This heavy board, soon to be a pair of gaff jaws, was steamed before being bent to a jig.

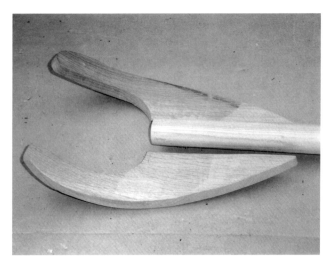

Fitting the jaws to the gaff.

After the bent wood has set, it can be removed from the jig. There will be a small amount of spring back. Take your jaw pattern and lay out two mirror images, side-by-side, using the natural curve in the grain of the stock. Cut out with a band saw and shape to suit.

Laminated Jaws

You would rather have a laminated jaw? No problem. For bending laminates, you can use a lighter weight jig consisting of L-shaped wooden brackets screwed down to a curve drawn on the floor. Trace the curve of the jaw onto the floor (or bench) and screw down the blocks at right angles to the curve. If thinner laminates are used, there will be less stress in the wood and less spring back can be expected. Heavier laminates can be steamed and prebent on the jig.

As with solid stock, grain selection is critical, because "short" grain can still break easily during lamination. Before bending, cover the jig with plastic sheeting. For a bit of additional strength when laminating, some builders add reinforcing fabric (such as fiberglass cloth) between the plies. If gluing oak, it is a good idea to use either resorcinol or a specially formulated epoxy. After the glue has cured, the jaws can be laid out and shaped like their steamed colleagues.

Natural Jaws

For the deluxe version, it is difficult to beat jaws fashioned from a naturally grown knee. Strong and elegant, a properly selected crook with grown curvature to the grain precludes any potential stresses that may be imposed in a steam-bent jaw and eliminates any concerns about the lamination coming off. And, of course, you don't need to build a bending jig.

That said, there are drawbacks, the primary one being where to get the stock. One good option for a small vessel is apple wood. Often neglected these days, apple crooks are light and strong (consider an apple branch covered with fruit and an early snow) and grow in a plethora of shapes. The wood can often be gathered for free at orchards that are eliminating their standard trees in favor of semidwarf varieties. The wood must be well

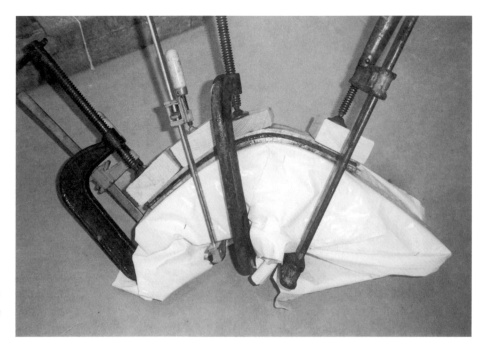

Laminating jaws over a jig, considerately covered with plastic to avoid sticking.

The finished laminated jaws fastened to the gaff and with a "tumbler" attached to bear against the mast.

seasoned, since it shrinks a lot while drying. You'll need a lot of specimens to pick through to find one that is the right shape with the proper quality of wood.

Another good choice is Eastern larch (aka tamarack or hackmatack). These tenacious roots are well known for doing yeoman duty as knees and stems. The wood (when well selected) also works fine for bent jaws. Even though you don't need much length, you will need a piece thick enough to accommodate the curve of the jaw, and this can make larch an expensive option. One way to get around this is to use scraps left over from other jobs. After you've sawed out the blank, lay out the side curve. Cut it out and smooth the surface, then lay out the "around the spar" curve and cut, smooth, and shape to taste. (See Chapter 14 for important safety advice concerning band-saw cutting of natural crooks.)

Final shaping comes next. The contact faces of the jaws should be well rounded so they cannot chafe the mast. Provisions can then be made for a throat halyard attachment and a pivoting tumbler that adjusts for any change in the angle between the jaws and the mast. Leather for the jaws can be cut and fit at this time. Holes can be bored for the parrel. (The parrel is a collar that holds the gaff to the mast while allowing it to be raised or lowered and swivel around the mast. Rope parrels are commonly threaded through balls of wood, to ease hoisting on the mast.)

The jaws can now be test fit to the spar and their locations can be marked. Admittedly, getting a good square fit of the two halves directly opposite from one another can be a bit of a challenge. What is called for here is a homemade alignment tool. Just take a short piece of 2″ × 4″ lumber and cut a notch into it large enough to fit around the spar. The wide, flat sides of the jaws rest on this "keep level" device while the notch allows the end of the gaff to be adjusted into place.

With everything in alignment, the jaw halves can be clamped to the spar and checked for fit. To get an even better landing for the jaws, flatten the marked sides of the spar with a block plane.

After fitting, drill through-holes for the rivets or bolts either by eye *in situ* or with a drill press. Clamp the entire assembly into place on the spar and check all fits again. Bore the holes in the spar. Unclamp and add bedding to taste. After bedding, all the pieces can be reassembled, clamped, and fastened. Then add a bit of finish, fasten on the leather and parrel, and you're good to go.

Gaff Saddle

An alternative to gaff jaws is the store-bought gaff saddle, a curved plate affixed to the bottom end of the gaff that bears against the mast. The saddle pivots on its mounting bracket, which takes the form of a pair of metal straps that fasten to either side of the gaff. The device is usually outfitted with a loop to attach to the throat halyard. And as with gaff jaws, parrels are used.

LOOPED GRAB RAILS

Stout grab rails go a long way toward enhancing safety. Rugged, balanced rails can also add a dash of pragmatic elegance. Curiously, while the fashioning of a single rail can be tedious to get right, making a matched pair is a cinch.

The theory is as follows: lay out a centerline down the length of the stock. Along this line, bore a series of holes with a large forstner bit or a hole saw. These holes will form the circular ends of the loops of the grab rail or bar. Separate the two pieces at the centerline, draw lines to connect the tops of the half circles, use a band saw to cut along the drawn lines, and voilà, you have a series of symmetrical loops.

A good place to begin the operation is with the selection of the stock. The major considerations are strength, length, and how big your fingers are. The

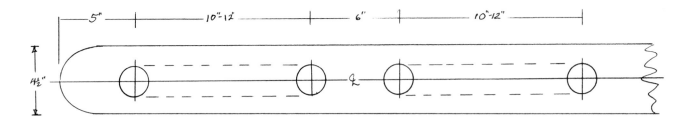

LOOPED HAND RAIL - STOCK 1⅛"-1¼" THICK - HOLES 1¾"-2¼"

Plans for hand rails. They don't look much like rails yet, but they will when the stock is cut in two.

rails are best made of a good quality hardwood 1⅛″ to 1¼″ thick.

The pair of rails can be fashioned from a single piece of wood or made by clamping two halves together, edge to edge. If using the single piece, it should be roughly 4½″ wide, while the separate pieces would run (you guessed it) 2½″. All stock should be well jointed.

The next step is the layout. If using the single piece, lay out a centerline for marking the centers of the circles. If using two pieces, the joint will be the centerline. A good spacing between the centers of the hand loopholes is 10″ to 12″. The length of the solid support portions between the loops is roughly 6″ while at the ends it is 5″. The bored holes can range from 1¾″ to 2¼″ in diameter. Bigger holes will accommodate bigger fingers. The ends of the rail should be artfully curved.

Drilling can be done with a press or by hand. If doing the job by hand, preboring pilot holes is useful to prevent unpleasant skidding of the bit. After boring, separate the two pieces by either unclamping the two halves or ripping the single piece into two on the table saw. Connect the tops of the bored holes to make the loops and saw them out with a band saw. A router with a quarter round bit makes short work of shaping up the edges. Then all you need to do is carve a slight radius cut into bottom edge, apply the finish, and install.

CLEATS

Cleats are also good candidates for do-it-yourself construction. While many chandlers still stock well-made metal units, their sizes and shapes are limited. Also, there is something about the refined lines of a wooden

Use a hole saw to cut what will become the ends of the handhold loops.

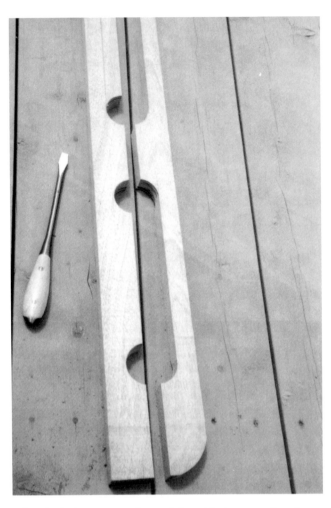

After the holes are cut, the stock is cut in two on a band saw, the half-holes are connected to make loops, and the ends are shaped to smooth curves.

cleat that can impart an air of *savoir faire* to a small boat. Plus cleats are a lot of fun to make.

Once again, the place to start is with a pattern. Copy one of your favorites or develop one of your own fancy. Symmetry is important, and one way to help guarantee that quality is to use half-patterns that you flip over on the stock to make a mirror image.

Your construction material should be a rugged, defect-free, tight-grained hardwood such as oak or locust. After selecting your stock and planing it to dim-ension, align the pattern to optimize the grain pattern, and trace the shape. Drill holes for the tight radius turn where the "horns" meet the base. This is most easily done with a drill press, but careful eyeballing with a handheld drill works fine. Cut the profile shape into the still rectangular stock with a band saw. The result-ing cleat-shaped cut can be trued up with a spoke-shave, rasp, and file. Scribe a centerline across the top edge of the cleat and lay out the hole location for the fastenings (symmetrically, of course). Bore these out and countersink.

The bottom-to-top taper is the next thing to be work in. On the top edge, draw two lines that are equi-distant from and parallel to the centerline. Use a block plan to work from the lines to the full cleat thickness at the bottom of the base. Then aesthetically round the edges of the horns with a rasp and file. Work in the relief under the horns (where the line wraps around) with a rat-tail file, and sand to taste.

A finished hand rail. Sure beats store-bought!

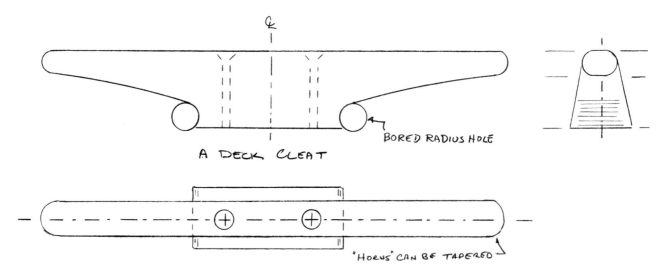

C̵

BORED RADIUS HOLE

A DECK CLEAT

"HORNS" CAN BE TAPERED

A good-looking deck cleat, scalable to just about any size.

As with the handrails, you'll save time when making cleats by planning ahead. It's a lot easier to drill the tight-radius curves where the horns meet the base than to cut them with a saw. Might as well drill the mounting holes now too, while the block is still wide and stable.

Saw the tapered sides, smooth the edges with a rasp or file, sand, and finish.

Part Four

BOATS TO BUILD

*T*he business of selecting the right boat to build can be as complicated or nuanced as deciding what kind of car to buy—perhaps more so. There is always the balance between utility, efficiency, performance, construction technique, materials, and simply what looks good. In the following chapters we'll take a look at a number of designs for oar, sail, and power, and we'll do a bit of comparison shopping.

· 33 ·

Pulling Boats

When getting around by oars, it's hard to surpass the traditional round-bottomed pulling boat. Much like the stone worn smooth by running water, these boats have had years of practical use that has removed any inefficiencies of the design, and their kindly waterlines enable them to excel in most conditions. These are elegant boats, but their elegance was born of practicality in an age when there was a job to be done with no means other than arms, back, and legs for propulsion. Sail occasionally could be used to advantage, but by and large these were "power" boats that needed to go whether there was a breeze or not, and their efficiency and seaworthiness remain valuable in their new role as recreational craft. These race-horses in disguise can be built using just about any sort of construction method, including carvel, lapstrake, strip, glued lap, stitch-and-glue, LapStitch, and cold molded—not to mention fiberglass (please!).

Considerations such as speed and stability are affected by subtle differences in shape, and these can be compared when looking at different line plans while selecting a design for building. For example, when comparing the waterlines in half-breadth view, a full or rounder bow tends to make for good load capacity and buoyancy, while a fine or hollow entrance makes for easy rowing and easy planking. Notice that whether the boat has a transom or not, at the load waterline all these boats are double-enders (or very nearly so), with their transoms hoisted clear of the water to keep the flow around the boat as smooth as possible.

Looking at the body plan, high-performance boats tend to have a narrow beam at the load waterline, with a round or slack turn of the bilge amidships. The surface area of the hull in contact with the water, known as the *wetted surface*, equates to frictional resistance, and boats with less wetted surface are obviously faster. The angle at which the bottom meets the keel is known as *deadrise*, and hulls with a lot of deadrise (or *rise of floor*) have less wetted surface than flatter-bottomed designs. Even with their narrow bottoms, these boats are often

(Photo: Joe Provey, Chesapeake Light Craft)

267

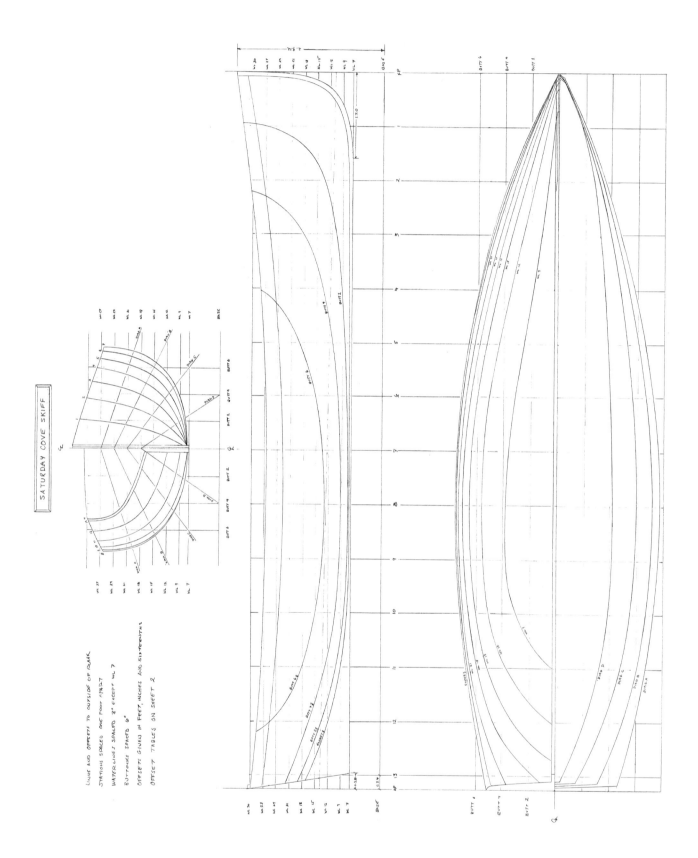

SATURDAY COVE SKIFF

LINES AND OFFSETS TO OUTSIDE OF PLANK

STATIONS SPACED ONE FOOT APART

WATERLINES SPACED 3" EXCEPT WL 7

BUTTOCKS SPACED 6"

OFFSETS GIVEN IN FEET, INCHES AND SIXTEENTHS

OFFSET TABLES ON SHEET 2

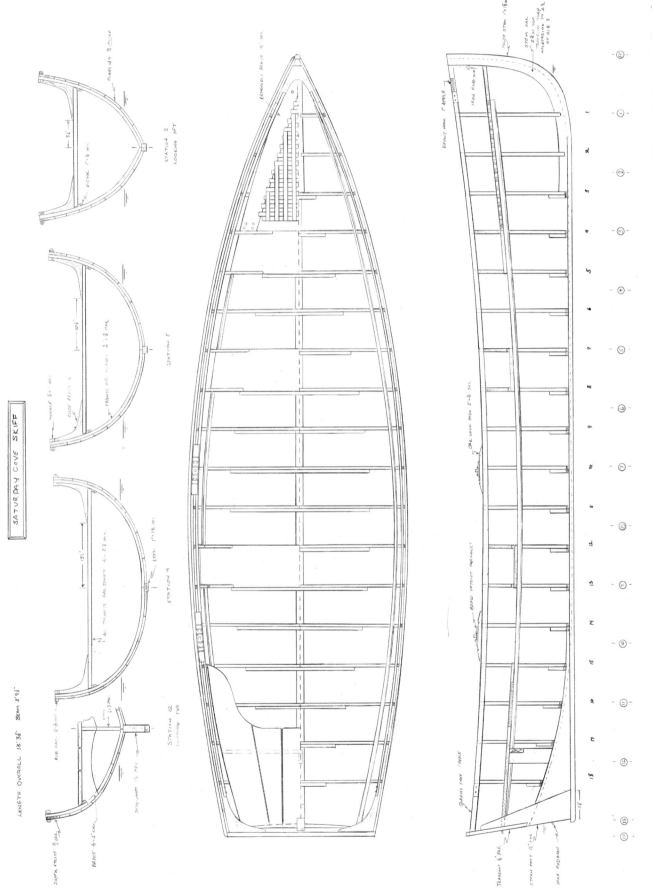

Note the following design and construction features that contribute to the sweet-rowing performance of the Saturday Cove Skiff: Very round bottom; hollow waterlines forward; plumb stem with modest cutaway at the forefoot; tucked-up transom; very lightweight keel; light frames fairly far apart; and sizeable skeg.

There's nothing "fancy" about the carvel-planked Saturday Cove Skiff—and that makes it perfectly elegant.

fairly beamy at the sheer, which promotes the use of longer oars. Narrow-bottomed hulls also have easier curves, which mean less complicated planking.

The drawback of these sleek whippet-like boats is that they have less initial stability than their chubbier colleagues. They can feel tippy or unstable when you get in and can become interestingly lively if you travel with an enthusiastic Labrador retriever.

A more stable hull, one that is capable of carrying heavier loads, will have a lower angle of slope coming out from the keel, and then there will be a quick turn of the bilge with the topsides almost vertical. There will be a bit more wetted surface with this hull so that it will not be quite so slippery in the water. But it can still be a fine rowing boat and will have a great all-around quality that can make the difference in whether anyone else will want to go rowing with you.

A long straight keel (as found on Whitehalls) assists tracking and keeps the boat "on rails." When crossing open water, bucking the wind on your beam, or shooting under narrow bridges, this is a real plus. The cost is in maneuverability. You may feel you have to jack the boat around with the oars to change course or have to at least plan ahead. If you want to be able to turn a boat quickly, a good choice might be one with a cambered or "rockered" keel that curves downward amidships and then sweeps up toward the stern. These keels are often steam bent. A flat-board keel will allow the boat to ground out and sit upright.

Size matters, at least in boats. As boat historian Ben Fuller notes:

> Many people pick a small [boat], say a 14–15 footer, and figure that they will have a good time rowing it

with two. They don't. Or they get a boat that is laid out for one with a passenger and then wonder why it gripes rowing solo. A single person rowing maxes out around 16 feet in length. On the other hand, boats for two rowing generally need to be at least 16 feet—depending on type.

BOAT CHOICES

There are hundreds of good pulling boat designs out there; many of them are by renowned designers, and others are examples of well-known "types" that evolved over time. And there are other equally good boat designs whose lights are hidden under various barrels. These may be the work of individual designers who never got good PR, or ones that were overshadowed, for whatever reason, by more widely distributed models. Poking around in archives can yield some fine designs—and some less so—and in the absence of first-person reports, it takes a practiced eye to know the difference from a set of plans. The following categories, on the other hand, are all widely acknowledged as "good" types or designs, and you won't go wrong if you decide to build one of these.

The Whitehall Type

The Whitehall style is perhaps the most familiar of the pulling boat types. This nineteenth-century design was common to coastal harbor cities such as New York, Boston, and San Francisco. Handsome, stable, and efficient, the Whitehall was used in livery and ship-to-shore transportation of people and goods. Indeed, the swift commercial "pickup truck and taxi" was a popular choice for businesses ranging from ship chandlers to the crimps engaged in San Francisco's flourishing Shanghaiing trade.

The swift, classic Whitehall is amenable to a variety of planking methods, including carvel, strip, and lapstrake, as in this example. (Photo: David Stotzer)

Today the style still shines as an everyday great rowing boat. It is fast, seaworthy, and good in a lake or harbor chop, where it slices through the water when more modern powerboats pound. The keel is deep enough to keep the vessel on course but not so deep as to preclude gunk holing or landing easily on a beach. It can be sailed, although it certainly isn't a barn burner under sail—there are better choices. The transom will accept a small outboard—either gas or, better yet, a small electric motor, which will push the boat effortlessly with silent savoir-faire. It doesn't tow easily because the deep forefoot can "catch" the water, causing the boat to yaw. If it must be towed, a shouldered eyebolt should be installed low on the stem to lift the forefoot when underway.

The hull shape of the Whitehall has much in common with the workaday schooners it served. The lines of the hull allow for good cargo capacity while still moving through the water easily. The signature wineglass-shaped transom is tucked up out of the water, virtually eliminating drag even when loaded. For efficiency the boats are narrow. No matter what the length, be it 12' or 20', a Whitehall rarely has a greater beam than 5'.

As on many classic pulling boats, the sheer plank of the Whitehall is robust. It's often made of a hardwood, such as oak, and is generally slightly thicker than the rest of the (softwood) planking. If all the planking is carvel, the thickness difference is fairly obvious. One way to compensate for this is to cut a continuous bead along the lower edge of the sheer plank. This not only adds an air of elegance, but also optically eases the transition between the different thicknesses of plank.

Another way to deal with the transition is to fashion the sheer plank as either a lapstrake or a dory lap plank. The interior of the boat is classic and eye turning. There are commonly two rowing stations and distinctive horseshoe-shaped stern sheets. The thwarts are rugged and often tapered or beaded along their visible edges to optically reduce thickness. The thwarts also sport substantial knees and vertical turned stanchions (posts) between the bottom of the thwart and the keel—an elegant and practical touch, since Whitehalls have rather lightweight backbones. The keel has no strength-imparting arch or keelson and is often only 1½" square. The seat-supporting stanchions work to counter the Whitehall's tendency to "hog" over time—to develop an upward curve in the middle of the keel.

Peapods

Before the familiar, inboard-powered Maine lobster-boat, there was the "double-ender" or peapod. This able, seagoing vessel was once ubiquitous on the Maine Coast. While the jury is still out as to when the Peapod was developed, many believe it originated in Penobscot Bay in the mid- to late nineteenth century. The design made for a nimble craft that could easily work around ledges and shallow waters. Fishermen could row them facing forward or aft, sitting or standing, and their stability and carrying capacity made them a natural for the lobster industry. The boats and the people who built and used them are an important piece of the rich tapestry of Maine coastal tradition. Howard Chapelle used a heavy fisherman's peapod as a tender and on the open water. He said he preferred a pod to any other small skiff he had ever seen.

Peapods are true double-enders with both ends often being the same. They have been built in many different styles and materials—from traditional plank-on-frame in carvel and lapstrake to stitch-and-glue. The design is quite a malleable and elastic one that can be modified for the conditions in which it is used and the work that it is intended to do. The boat can have a traditional keel (sometimes quite deep for sailing) or, for better landing on a beach, a board keel. The forefoot can have a sharp turn to it like the traditional Whitehall, or it can be rounded or "cut away" for better maneuverability. Some designs have straight keels, while others have considerable rocker or curve. The amount of deadrise too was customized for use. The common length for a working boat was 15′, with enough stability so you could stand in it, roll it gunwale-down, and lean back to pull up a trap. Today, 13′ overall is a common size suitable for general recreation or use as a yacht tender.

Peapods do make for great rowing and able sailing but one should do a bit of research before purchasing the "standard peapod" plan, as there really is no such thing. A good place to begin is with John Gardner's essay on peapods in *Building Small Craft* and Howard Chapelle's in *American Small Sailing Craft*.

Wherries

The term wherry means different things depending on where you are. If you are in the Norfolk Broads in England, it might mean a clinker-planked double-ended cargo vessel with the mast stepped well forward and a single gaff sail. Quite different are the Thames wherries: wide, stable rowing boats with long raking bows that were used as water taxis by intrepid Thames watermen. For many, a wherry might be any svelte, round-bottomed rowing boat, lapstrake or carvel, that didn't seem quite like a Whitehall.

With blue-collar roots in the salmon fishing trade, the Maine-coast or Lincolnville wherry performs ably, as you'd expect. Distinct from all of the wherries mentioned above construction-wise, it appears to be a closer cousin to the dory, but in performance, it is more akin to the round-bottomed Whitehall. While some American wherries had a Whitehall-like stick keel, the vast majority had relatively narrow, rockered board keels—just the ticket for working off the beach. When dried out the boat would stand upright, protecting the lapping planks, and if reinforced with a replaceable chafing shoe, the wherry could be dragged (or put on rollers) to and from the water.

The traditional Lincolnville wherry ranged in length from 12′ to 18′. The boats have a rounded dory-shaped stem and a high, tucked-up, cocktail glass shaped transom, the top of which is nearly as high as the stem head. In the underwater section, the boat is a near double-ender. With more buoyancy down low than a Whitehall, it is seaworthy and able both close to shore and offshore in a following sea. The old-timers were often built with sawn frames; newer versions are likely to have steam-bent ones. Wherries can be built with traditional cedar lapstrake planks or with plywood.

According to Lincolnville, Maine boatbuilder Walt Simmons, who has built many wherries over the years,

The multi-chine Wineglass Wherry is available as a stitch-and-glue kit from Pygmy Boats. It features a dramatically curved sheer, double-ended waterline, a flat bottom panel, and a remarkably clean interior, with no internal structure other than the seats and their supports. She can also be set up for sail. (Photo: Pygmy Boats)

these boats do have equals, but one won't find a better traditional pulling boat anywhere.

Freshwater Boats

Names such as the Rangley Lake Boat, Adirondack Guide Boat, and St. Lawrence River Skiff, and J. Henry Rushton's pulling boats all evoke a Victorian-era feeling of style, travel, and appreciation of nature.

There are some similarities between brine and sweet-water vessels. Like the coastal boats, the lines of these inland vessels are remarkably smooth and efficient. They tend to be stable, with the amount of deadrise varying with the intended use. Some are double-enders such as the peapod or the native canoe. Others sport a high transom not unlike the Whitehall or the wherry. As in dory construction, many of the boats have two-piece stems, allowing the planking to run over the inner stem and be trimmed off after fastening.

Rushton's lovely, lightweight lapstrake "Pleasure Boat #109" design was modified for a bit more depth by builder Koji Matano for use on Japan's sizeable Lake Biwa. (Photo: Koji Matano)

The outer stem is applied later. Many sport the thin board keel reminiscent of the wherry.

There are differences as well. Since these boats were once hand-carried, and were not expected to carry a ton or more of cargo, lightness was a key consideration, and their construction was more like that of wooden aircraft than say, post-and-beam barns. Where saltwater boats have chunky sawn-oak frames, or a small number of heavy steamed ones spaced fairly far apart, freshwater models use either sawn frames of lightweight spruce knees or a plethora of small caliber frames, rounded on the outside (like split dowels) and often made of steamed elm to take almost impossible bends. Planking is quite light, often $^3/_{16}$", $^1/_4$" or perhaps an industrial strength $^5/_{16}$". Due to the thin stock, the heads of the fastenings (often copper or brass nails) are left flush with the outside of the planking.

In many ways these traditionally built pulling boats were feats of lightweight engineering, and for weight and performance they compare favorably with their modern colleagues built in strip, stitch-and-glue, or LapStitch. Of course, the difference here is in construction time, cost, and availability of materials. That said, if one desires an efficient, crowd-pleasing boat for inland use, these old-time designs are certainly worth considering.

Dinghies

The humble dinghy is a tough boat to get right. Boat-owners want everything from their tender—it should row well, take an outboard motor, and sail. It needs to look great, have tremendous carrying capacity, be stable, and tow well. It must be light enough to pull up on deck and heavy enough to plow through the waves. It certainly should require little or no maintenance. And for many, no matter how much money is spent for the mother ship, the dinghy must cost nearly nothing. Some overwhelmed boat owners simply throw in the towel and purchase an inflatable or an overgrown margarine tub.

There's no question about it: the diminutive boats are a challenge. Their short length precludes the narrow beam-to-length ratio that makes the pulling boats so efficient. Proportionally shrink a pulling boat or a dory to dinghy caliber and you'll achieve a very unstable design. The beam of a 12' Whitehall is, by necessity, nearly as great as one that is 18' long. That sort of chubby shape is hard to work a good-looking sheer line into. All that said, there are still handsome and practical designs out there to be built.

For many, the round-bottomed tender is ideal—a well-turned-out mini-yacht of the likes of Nathanael Herreshoff's Columbia dinghy. Writing in *The Common Sense of Yacht Design*, his son, L. Francis Herreshoff, noted that prior to 1890, his father based his tenders on the Whitehall. But "Captain Nat" felt that while the Whitehall rowed well, it did not tow well and was only a fair sea boat. This eventually led to the development of the Columbia. These boats had a rockered keel, with a nicely rounded forefoot. L. Francis said it was the best model for a tender he had ever seen. It rowed well, sailed well, and was a good dry sea boat that would tow through anything. Joel White's Catspaw dinghy is based on the Herreshoff Columbia model dinghies and at 12'8", it represents a 10% expansion.

The best dinghies tend to be full bodied for stability and carrying capacity, have good freeboard, and have fine underwater lines with their transoms carried up out of the water (at least when lightly loaded). Transoms are often rounded rather than wineglass-shaped, so they gain buoyancy when loaded. Compared to Whitehalls, the bows are fuller, and there is more rocker in the keel, which makes for better towing, maneuverability, and sailing performance.

A drawback of the traditionally built dinghy is that it can be as complicated and time-consuming to build as a boat twice its size. Depending on its use, the dinghy may spend a good deal of its working life out of the water, being dragged up onboard and then lounging upside down on deck. Carvel planking would be a poor choice for this kind of lifestyle, as it is too heavy and the seams would soon open in the sun. Outfits such as Old Town once offered smooth, canvas-covered hulls (like their canoes) that eliminated the open seam conundrum. Lapstrake then became a more popular way to achieve a lighter and tighter hull.

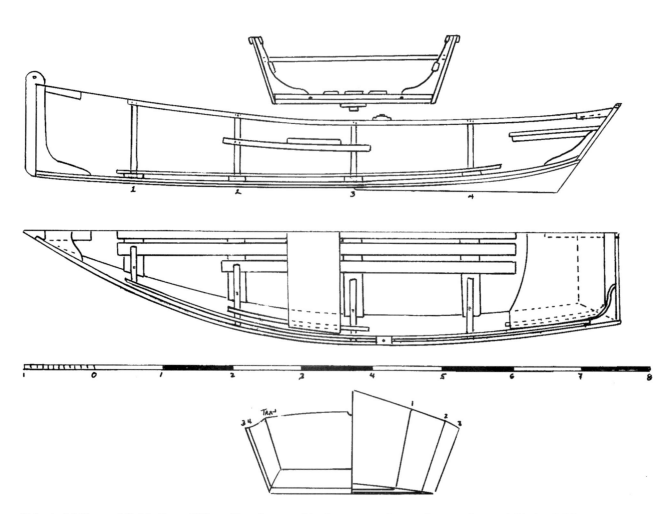

This straightforward flat-bottom skiff would make a good tender or general messabout craft, especially for children.

Glued plywood lap technology has been a boon for modern round-bottomed dinghy design—many of the boats are based on the classic yacht tender with some modifications. They tend to have a fine entry, full bilges, and a bigger transom to accommodate a small outboard. Overall weight has been reduced. Not only is the planking lighter and durable, but also as the hull gains strength from the glued planks, the need for frames has been greatly reduced. And all those worries of leaks and shrinking and swelling are reduced to a minimum. Drawbacks are that these are still complicated hulls to build and stability is problematic on some designs.

On the other end of the scale is the flat-bottomed skiff. This option is certainly worth consideration. This yeoman style, with a cross-planked or plywood bottom, is relatively simple and inexpensive to build. It is a great shallow water boat, if straight-bottomed, and is fine with a small outboard motor. Flat-bottomed hulls have high initial stability (a boon when loading small children and bouncy dogs). Having sufficient rocker is important for rowing—more back aft to keep the transom clear of the water, less up forward for more carrying capacity. Flaring topsides will add buoyancy and like the keel on the pulling boat, an ample and long skeg will help the boat track. Add a jaunty sheer line and you have a dinghy to be reckoned with.

Small semi-dory type tenders are yet another option. They can feel a bit tender or tippy, especially when boarding. On the other hand, they are strong and easy to build and if well designed, can row and tow very well. Their narrow fore and aft planked flat bottom allows for easy grounding and, unlike a round-bottomed hull, it will sit upright like a duck. L.F. Herreshoff called them fine rowing craft, as they were

With its transom bow, this pram has more buoyancy forward than a pointy-bowed dink, and it will store more easily on the deck of a larger boat.

narrow on the waterline and still wide enough at the gunwales to allow for long oars. These are good candidates for plywood lap or stitch-and-glue construction.

If space, either at the dock or on deck, is a prime concern, the pram or the more exotic sampan is certainly worth serious consideration. Having transoms both fore and aft, the pram offers excellent carrying capacity in a minimum overall length. As with the flat-bottomed skiff, having the proper amount of rocker in the bottom is important to keep the transoms out of the water. Without it, the boat would row like a washing machine shipping crate. The hulls are relatively easy to build in multichined, V-, and flat-bottomed versions.

Whatever the style, for a dinghy to tow well, the bow eye should be located low on the stem to lift the bow out of the water when underway.

· 34 ·

Canoes and Kayaks

The canoe and the kayak are further examples of working craft that have been fine-tuned over the centuries. Whether the boats were built of hide or bark or carved totally of wood, the styles were highly evolved to use the best materials available and to perform their jobs efficiently and safely.

For canoes, one must consider the same sort of displacement-hull design factors used in the pulling boats. For example, the "crooked" canoe built by the Cree had an exaggerated rocker or curve to the bottom of the hull that diminished load carrying capacity but at the same time allowed it to ably jink and dodge in rapids. Other hulls had considerably less rocker and lower deadrise or flatter bottoms that permitted greater cargos on cross-lake transits. East Coast canoes often exhibited longer hull length, more tumblehome (rolling inward of the topsides), and a higher sheer amidships for rough open-water travel.

Very flat bottoms feel stable initially and allow the boat to turn quickly but can be unsafe in rough water. A round bottom is fast, as it has less wetted surface, but is quite tippy. A good compromise is the shallow arched (semi-elliptical shape) hull. The shape helps stiffen the hull, tracks well, and offers decent initial and final stability.

Kayaks also varied in design, depending on the location and how they were used. The traditional kayak was foremost an arctic hunting machine that had to perform safely in demanding and difficult sea conditions. Fewer and fewer kayakers these days, however, are dodging icebergs and pursuing seals, walrus, and narwhals. But even for recreational purposes, the boat's intended use determines what qualities are desirable, and this influences the design features. The nature photographer or bird watcher in a Minnesota marsh might crave a short maneuverable boat with great initial stability. The serious sea kayaker might desire greater length and the ability to roll and recover. Our man in the marsh might be just as happy if the boat never even thought of rolling. What he probably needs is a double paddle canoe.

Building a traditional wood-and-canvas canoe requires a big time investment and an elaborate building jig, but such a boat is suffused with soul that no other construction method can match. Plans for this 17-foot, 1908 B.N. Morris model are available from Northwoods Canoe Co. (Photo: Rollin Thurlow)

As when selecting any other kind of boat, consider how and where you want to use it, and its carrying capacity, comfort, and weight. A wood and canvas 18' guide canoe with a keel is great for crossing open water with heavy loads—a fine lake canoe for fishing or extended camping trips, but definitely not the right boat for whitewater rivers or wilderness trips that require a lot of portaging.

Most boat-plan catalogs do a pretty fair job describing a design's specifications and strengths—although they may not be quite so forthcoming about the weaknesses. When you've identified a likely prospect, check the specs to see how well they suit your needs and contact the designer or kit manufacturer to ask about the design's performance. Good boats get a lot of good word-of-mouth, and their designers and kit makers tend to sell a lot of plans, so there should be a good base of information. If not, you might want to look elsewhere. If possible, find a boat like the one you wish to build and take it out for a spin.

CONSTRUCTION CHOICES

The earliest canoes and kayaks were built by eye by skilled native craftsmen. By the mid-nineteenth century, canoes were being mass-produced over standardized solid construction forms. While over the years there were many subtle permutations in planking and framing schemes, perhaps the most successful was the cedar-canvas canoe. The process involved building the hull on a heavy strip-planked production jig and then stretching a canvas skin over the boat, tacking it into place, filling the weave of the fabric, and painting the boat the color desired by the customer. The result was an economical hull that was strong, durable, easy to maintain, and relatively light. This technique is used both commercially and by home boatbuilders today. The drawback of this method of "one off" construction is the serious investment of time and materials required to build the jig.

Strip construction is a faster way to build a canoe or kayak. It also requires a construction mold, but it is not nearly as complicated as the one required for the cedar and canvas canoe. The jig is a setup series of molds much like those used in standard plank-in-frame construction. Time does need to be taken to get the assembly plumb, true, and accurate. The time is well spent, however, as with a good jig the assembly will go like clockwork, while a funky jig will be a constant cause of heartburn. Strip planking can produce a very handsome boat with a minimum of time, tools, and materials.

Durable, lightweight, beautiful kayaks can be built from thin-strip planking, encapsulated with layers of fiberglass and epoxy on both sides. Nick Schade designed and built this beautiful 17' Petrel with ³⁄₁₆" thick western red cedar. Plans are available from Guillemot Kayaks. (Photo: Guillemot Kayaks)

Open canoes, such as this 17'6" Redbird, also lend themselves to wood-strip construction, with no less beautiful results. (Photo: Dick Persson, Courtesy Bear Mountain Boat Shop)

Stitch-and-glue kits are another good way to build a kayak or canoe. Nowadays, kit manufacturers are offering a wide array of kayaks for every occasion in both hard-chined and multi-chined versions. According to the catalog of Pygmy Boats, one of the largest kit providers, the performance and stability of the two kinds of hulls are similar. With less wetted surface, the multi-chined hull is slightly faster at cruising speeds, while the hard-chined hull has a tighter leaned turn. The canoe kits give the boat a look that is reminiscent of lapstrake. Stitch-and-glue kits can be built without much in the way of a construction jig, but a few molds and a strongback are a quick way to gain an additional degree of control and help guarantee a top-notch product. Glued plywood lapstrake is another option to produce a strong, lightweight, and durable canoe.

Last but not least, you might consider a wooden framed "skin on frame" kayak. Although these boats are less popular than they once were, the plans and components are still available. In many ways, the boats hearken back to the kayaks of antiquity, with very tough Hypalon-coated nylon or canvas replacing hide stretched over the frame. Most builders use sawn stems

and frames connected by fore and aft stringers, while others are using bent frames. In both cases, the finished boat is flexible and relatively light. Maine inventor Platt Monfort took the principle yet a step further with his Geodesic Airolite construction method, in which a super lightweight epoxy-glued wooden framework is reinforced by Kevlar roving strands and covered by a heat-shrunk Dacron skin, for a boat that can weigh as little as 8 pounds.

Decked and Double-Paddle Canoes

One of the earliest promoters of personal watercraft was the London barrister John MacGregor. In the mid-1800s, MacGregor began his tours of the waterways of Europe and beyond in a professionally built 15' wooden decked lapstrake canoe/kayak called the Rob Roy. Over the years he had a number of these able little vessels built and published accounts of his peripatetic travels from the Baltic to the Levant. The outdoor-loving public eagerly followed his travels. Over on our side of the pond, business-savvy builders noticed the trend. Soon, Staten Island builder W.P. Stephens began manufacturing MacGregor-influenced decked cruising canoes, as did Canton, New York builder John Henry Rushton. Lightweight, portable, and easy to paddle, the boats caught on, and until the early 1900s, American recreational canoeing was dominated by the "double-paddle" canoe—i.e., one designed to be propelled by a single paddle with blades on both ends, like a kayak paddle.

Fast forward a century, and once again the notion of solo backwater exploration in double-paddle canoes—some decked, others not—has caught the public's fancy. For example, "Mac" MacCarthy's 11½' strip-planked Wee Lassie weighs a bit more than 20 pounds, while at 13', Bear Mountain Boat Shop's slightly larger

Magic, a long (18'2") fast sea kayak, is available as a kit for stitch-and-glue construction. (Photo: Ted Moores, Bear Mountain Boat Shop)

Double-paddle canoes are similar to kayaks, but generally have more open cockpits and are intended for use in more protected waters. Designs exist for building in lapstrake, stitch-and-glue, skin-on-frame, and (as here) strip planking. (Photo: Guillemot Kayaks)

Rob Roy comes in at 25 to 40 pounds. Tom Hill, working in ultralight glued plywood lapstrake construction, also offers plans for boats built in the Rushton tradition, including a 15' coming in at 39 pounds. As all these lightweight craft are so easily cartopped and portaged, they make a good choice for instant exploration whether it be in the backwaters of the Okefenokee Swamp or in remote mountain lakes.

So has the introduction of high-tech wood composites, epoxy resin, and glass-cloth rendered traditional wood construction obsolete for the home kayak builder? Not according to New Brunswick boatbuilder Harry Bryan. He says it's just a matter of simplifying design. Harry builds and offers plans for his decked Fiddlehead canoe, which is again based on a Rushton design. Planked and decked with lightweight northern white cedar, and with frames and stems of spruce and coamings of oak or ash, the diminutive craft tips the scales at a respectable 42 pounds. Harry adapted Rushton's design to light dory construction, with wide lapped planks, sawn frames, and a flat bottom, which he says results in a huge reduction of labor. And contrary to the Fiddlehead's contemporary brethren, there is little in the way of high-tech glues and resins—just seams sealed with polyurethane adhesive, and epoxy to seal the underside of the deck and the end grain of the wood. The deck and interior are finished bright and the hull is painted—all with conventional marine finishes.

While Harry says he didn't design it as an amateur boat, it has worked out well. It's small and has very few pieces and it's simple enough to be used in school shop classes. As to the matter of wood, he says, some of the Fiddleheads have been built with plywood, but he prefers the look and feel of natural wood.

· 35 ·

Dories

Historians have traced the dory's North American ancestors back to at least the early 1700s. There are newspaper reports that note a "doree" was in use in Massachusetts in 1726. It is likely that the hull style was based on one that European forebears brought to this side of the Atlantic for the fisheries. The French developed a river dory (or batteau) for commerce on the St. Lawrence River that is quite recognizable as a close relative of today's dory. A version of the batteau was used for log drives in Maine.

The familiar Banks dory developed in the mid-nineteenth century with the growth of the fishing schooner fleet. The mass-produced fishing dories were standardized and ruggedly built to handle continuous service, as well as regular hoisting and lowering from the schooner decks. The thwarts and pen boards were removable so that the boats could be nested like egg cartons on deck.

While the style has continued to evolve, and modern materials have in some cases replaced the old, the look and utility of the dory remain the same.

TRADITIONAL CONSTRUCTION

Dory construction has some notable differences from other small craft. Let's start at the bottom. Instead of a cut or bent oak keel, the bottom is softwood planking running fore and aft, and reinforced with cleats that run athwartships. The bottom tapers to a point at the stem for all styles, and for dories with the traditional tombstone transom, it tapers to a point at the stern as well. Other than the occasional skeg or oak-chafing strip to protect the garboard, the dory bottom is dead flat from side to side. Fore and aft, however, there can be quite a bit of shape.

The swoop-curved stem was originally fashioned from a single timber—a tricky business as the long curve could leave one with a weak short grain if the stem was cut from straight stock. Therefore, a grown

A working dory from Grand Manan Island, New Brunswick, Canada. Note how the traditionally arched top of the transom has been cut down square to accept a small outboard motor.

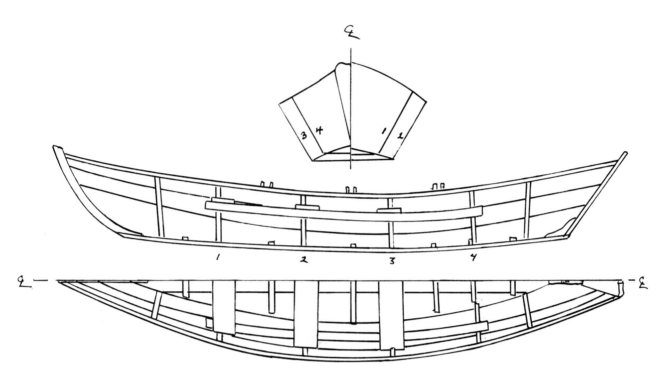

Like all dories, the straightforward, straight-sided Banks dory has no backbone.

knee would often be used to provide a lot of strength. If that was unavailable, the stem could be made up of two pieces mechanically scarfed together halfway up. Or a reinforcing knee could be added to the foot of the stem where it was bolted to the bottom. Nowadays, a laminated stem can provide most of the superior qualities of the grown stem, except maybe the aesthetics. The stem is bolted to the plank bottom and instead of a cut rabbet, the forward end of the stem is beveled on both sides to accept the planks running by. The planks are fastened to the bevel and trimmed flush with the forward edge of the stem. A false or outer stem is added later.

The dory transom tends to have a strong rake. On a wide-sterned semi-dory, the transom is built in the conventional fashion with horizontal boards. The Bank dory "tombstone" transom is a different kettle of fish. This unique transom is made of vertical stock and is V-shaped with an inside cross-cleat at the sheer. The transom is fastened to the board bottom with a substantial stern knee. The high and narrow tombstone transom tends to keep following seas from swamping the boat.

Dories are nearly always built with sawn frames. During construction, the frames do double duty as they act as the construction molds. As with the stem, old-time builders used naturally grown knees when they could, and overlapped them in the center of the boat. A paucity of knee stock led to the use of multi-piece frames that were joined together with steel clips or plywood gussets. Here, too, a lamination would make sense, producing a rugged frame.

The stem, transom, and frames are usually attached to the plank bottom while it still looks like an industrial strength surfboard. Next, we need to deal with the curve of the bottom.

The bottom of the boat can have considerable rocker or curve bent built into it. That means the builder has to come up with a way to force that shape into the bottom before planking can commence. Like most boats, dories can be built either right-side up or upside down. Right-side up construction allows for easier riveting and clench nailing, while upside down construction permits much easier beveling of the bottom prior to planking. Generally, the garboard runs over and is attached to a bevel planed into the outer edge of the bottom (see Chapter 4). Banks dories have fairly steep sides, which means the bevel in the bottom is relatively easy to plane in. Some Swampscott and semi-dory designs, however, have garboards that rise at a low angle amidships, and this translates into a long, low bevel that needs to be planed into the bottom. Also the garboard will have a good deal of twist as it comes into the stem. Both tasks are better done when the boat is upside down. Whatever your persuasion, check the lofting board for the proper amount of rocker.

If building right-side up, place and fasten blocking or a short sawhorse (perhaps a saw-burro?) fore and aft, under the completed bottom board assembly. Amidships, place a shorter spacer block that reflects the amount of rocker you want to put in the bottom. Then, using props to an overhead ridgepole or ceiling, force the curve into the bottom until it lands on the midship spacer block. Level, plumb, and brace the assembly and you are ready to go.

For upside-down construction, consult the lofting to build a custom-made strongback that has been cut to the curve of the inner side of the plank bottom, or a bending frame similar to a conventional setup of construction molds. Bend the assembly over the jig (brace from the ceiling if possible), anchor down the ends, and you are ready to plank.

MODERN CONSTRUCTION AMENDMENTS

On boats with simple curvature to the sides, like the Banks dory, plywood can be used. Batten seam construction has been used as an alternative to the traditional dory lap. On Swampscott dories, battens are let into the frames at each knuckle. Plywood planking can be used. The ply planking is butted and glued to both the frames and battens with epoxy. For a deluxe version, the exterior joints and bottom can be covered with epoxy and fiberglass cloth. The resulting hull exterior has a look quite similar to one built in stitch-and-glue. And speaking of stitch-and-glue, plans are offered for that construction method as well.

Because dory garboards are so wide in the ends, checking can be a serious problem. One way to overcome this is to use plywood garboards, with conventional planking the rest of the way.

The introduction of scarfed sheet plywood has also allowed a few changes in how the boat is framed. New designs often have chines either made of wood (added after the sides have been bent around a construction jig) or virtual ones in the form of epoxy fillets reinforced with fiberglass cloth. The strength of the plywood allows a reduction of the number of frames.

DORY STYLES

There are lots of good dory designs, ranging from heavy, strictly traditional fishing boats to sleek circa-1900 racing models, to lightweight stitch-and-glue designs that can be put together in a couple of weekends. Whether the intent is for oar, sail, or power, the following styles are all worthy of the mechanic's consideration.

The Banks Dory

The original Banks fishing dory was roomy, had deep straight sides, and was heavily constructed and designed to handle well when you were butt-high in fish and gear. When used recreationally, sans cod et al, this

Sam Devlin's 17'2" stitch-and-glue Oarling is designed for sliding-seat rowing. Devlin has another dory design, the 19'3" Seaswift, for sail. (Photo: Sam Devlin)

style is less satisfactory and rather tiddly. More modern designs sport shallower sides and more flare that make for a much better performing boat. Good examples of this sort are the Coast Guard dory described in John Gardner's *The Dory Book* and Phil Bolger's Gloucester Light Dory.

Swampscott Dory

It has been said that the Swampscott Dory was developed to meet the needs of local fishermen who fished "off the beach" and needed a boat that could both row and sail well. Hailing from the north shore of Massachusetts, this unique style is a bit of a hybrid between the chunky Banks dory and a classic round-bottomed hull. Like the Banks dory, it had a narrow fore-and-aft planked flat bottom that allowed the boat to land upright and be moved with rollers. It retained the tombstone transom and dory stem. It even had the same kind of planking. Where it differed was that instead of the sides being straight (or slab sided), they were round—almost. In reality the frames had facets or flats cut into them that the planks wrapped around. These "knuckles" tended to improve sailing qualities while giving the boat more of a round-bottomed hull feel. John Gardner referred to the Swampscott boats as the "aristocrats of the dory clan." As pulling boats or centerboard sailors, these boats are relatively inexpensive to build, tough and seaworthy, good handlers, and salty as can be.

The Semi-Dory

For many, the search for a proper all-round boat is a quixotic one at best. To combine quality, performance, ease of construction, and a maybe even a dash of elegance is a tall order indeed. Few boatowners can afford to invest the capital to buy a professionally constructed classic round-bottomed wooden boat, and fewer still have the time to build one. Standard flat-bottomed construction is easy and economical but might not fill the bill. For many, the semi-dory or dory skiff is an elegant compromise.

As an able, affordable, seaworthy, and low-maintenance design, the semi-dory draws on the heritage of various New England working craft. It is really a variation on a number of themes. It shares with its distant cousin, the familiar Banks dory, the fore and aft bottom planking, the swooping stem, and the dory-lap planking style, but differs from it with its nearly round sides.

Not all dories are straight-sided. This nearly round hull is a sailing version of the capable little Chaisson semi-dory that we lofted in Chapter 24.

It is similar to the round-sided, but flat-bottomed, colonial wherries and the Swampscot dory, but it has a wider bottom aft and a broader, more conventional transom and usable stern seats. The style has been used for a variety of craft, ranging from the Chaisson tender (highly regarded by its owners for its handling characteristics, carrying capacity, and ease in towing) to rugged fishing skiffs that require little horsepower and can handle a sloppy bay with a good load aboard, and even as general purpose sailing knockabouts.

The St. Pierre Dory

The St. Bernard of the dory breeds, the St. Pierre is another variant of the Banks dory. Native to the French islands of St. Pierre and Miquelon (south of Newfoundland), it is a bit like a banks dory on steroids—larger, with a tremendous sheer and highly rockered bottom. The large size and shape of these dories have contributed to the outstanding sea qualities of this unique design.

The Power Dory

The seaworthiness and cargo carrying capacity of the dory has long made it a good choice for economical, low horsepower power. Choices include an outboard mounted on a transom or in a well, an inboard engine installed in the conventional fashion, and—for boats operating in shallow waters—an inboard engine with a tunnel stern. For boats that are beached often, like the St. Pierre working dories, a universal joint in the shaft allows it to be pulled up into a box in the hull.

· 36 ·

Sailboats

Boats have been built for sail since at least the days of Pharaonic Egypt. Indeed (for better or worse), sailing craft have helped to change the map of the world. Interestingly, this truly ancient sort of conveyance is also, in many ways, the most progressive sort of transportation available today. Using free, non-polluting, renewable energy, one can transport passengers and vast amounts of cargo to the four corners of the globe. When oil runs out, someone will still be plying the oceans propelled by wind.

As with power and paddle, designs for the home boatbuilder can be selected to fit both the waters and type of sailing desired—from leisurely day trips to white-knuckle high performance. As always, hull design is the key.

KEELS

Sailboats need some sort of underwater appendage to resist sideslipping and enable them to sail into the wind. A full keel with either interior or external ballast is perhaps one of the older approaches. With the keel on the outside of the hull, you have more room inside than you would with the adjustable centerboard. Ballast can make the boat stiffer and adds stability and momentum.

Designer Paul Gartside's Swan-song. (Photo: Paul Gartside)

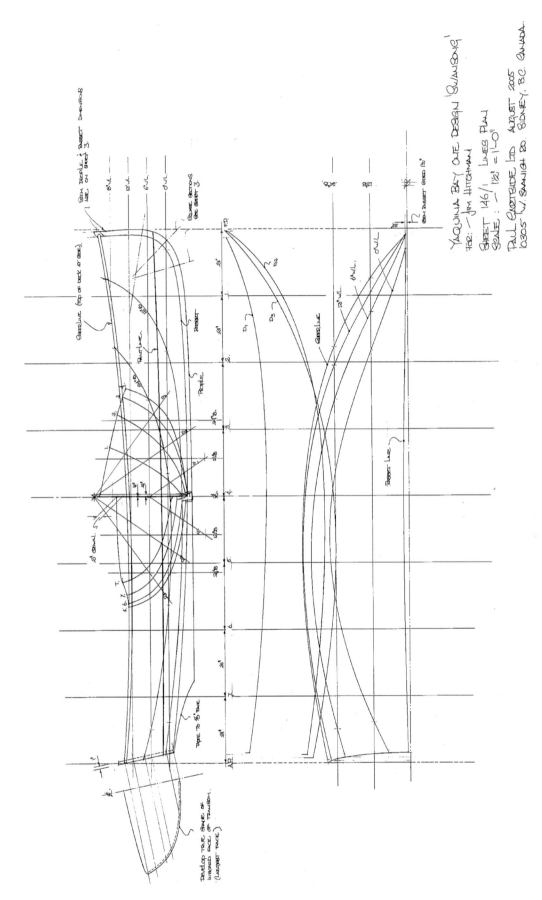

Swansong's lateral plane comes from its long and fairly straight keel and modest skeg.

Lead and You: A Caveat

In a word, molten lead is dangerous. It is extremely hot (boatyards have been burnt down by escaping molten lead), it is explosive in contact with any moisture, and the fumes are toxic. Hence, a good deal of preparation and caution are called for, even if you are just casting ballast for a centerboard. Anyone around the job should be properly clothed with welders gauntlets and heavy shoes. A leather apron is a good idea as well. A face shield and respirator are also recommended. If possible, work with the breeze at your back and never work in the presence of water or rain. And keep a fire extinguisher handy.

Whether for cost or just convention, external ballast seems to be more popular in yacht construction. Lead is often used because it is dense and relatively easily cast—a good option for those with limited access to a Bessemer forge. Although less dense than lead, iron or steel will also work, and it is relatively easy to bolt on sheet or plate stock.

Interior ballast is seen more on workboat-influenced hulls. The ballast can range from moveable rock or lead "pigs" to more permanent poured concrete filled with sundry boiler punchings or sash weights. Some builders like to stack moveable ballast on fixed boards in the bilge that span the frames and/or floors so that the weight isn't bearing directly on the planking. Some boats use a combination of fixed external ballast and movable internal weight that can be used to trim the boat at will.

Ballasted deep keels are not often seen on sailboats less than 20'. They preclude the ability to sail close to shore in shoal waters, and this represents the preferred form of sailing for many. They also make daysailing from a trailer far more complex and difficult. Indeed, depth of keel can make all the difference in whether you can haul the boat yourself or need a boatyard to do it.

Centerboards, Daggerboards, Leeboards

The centerboard is an alternative to the full depth keel. It can be considered sort of a movable or retractable keel (that pivots or swings around a pin), which can be adjusted to increase the size of the lateral plane. A pivoting centerboard can also be used to move the center of lateral resistance aft to match a change in sail plan. The board itself can be made of metal or of ballasted wood.

There's a lot to be said for a centerboard. For example, you don't need to have a massive and deep ballast keel. This is a boon for sailing in bays, lakes, and other shoal waters. The trunk and board assembly, while sometimes a bit complex, is still straightforward carpentry. Being able to tuck your keel up into the hull means that the boat will be a lot easier to load onto a trailer—something to consider if the boat is not going to live on a mooring. A centerboard-equipped boat can get you into shallow waters that the full keel sailor would never venture into—especially if the boat also has a pivoting rudder.

There are some downsides as well. The trunk does take up a lot of space in the interior of the boat. The long centerboard trunk in a sharpie is like having a freestanding partition running down the center of the boat. A centerboard alone doesn't add much in the way of stability. If you run aground with the board up, shells or mud can stick in the slot and cause the board to jam.

Then there is the matter of leaks and warped and/or hung-up centerboards—usually caused by the construction of the board and trunk having been given short shrift. Here's the deal: the slot for the centerboard is a whole lot like a long hole in the bottom of the boat. There is also a lot of sideways action putting pressure onto the board and the case or trunk that contains it. If the trunk just has a few screws or pins holding it to the keel (and some plans call for just that) and if the trunk is not properly braced, sooner of later it is going to leak. A much better approach is to fasten the trunk sides to a rabbeted log or base that can then be bolted down to the keel. A metal centerboard is one way to avoid warps. Another way is to laminate a board of high-quality plywood and, adding a bronze bushing for the pin, cover it with dynel and epoxy. A chunk of lead can be cast and faired right into the centerboard to help the board drop down on its pivot when desired.

An alternative is the combination centerboard/ballast keel, which provides positive stability at all sailing angles, plus the ability to enter shoal waters. The boat is more easily towed and launched than a full-keel design, because the centerboard retracts into the hull through a slot in the cast lead keel. Keel/centerboard hulls open up many shoal draft destinations while maintaining full-keel type performance.

A daggerboard is another kind of centerboard that instead of swinging on a pivot, lifts vertically, sliding like a dagger into a scabbard. It is often longer and thinner (fore and aft) than a centerboard; hence its slot in the bottom of the boat is much shorter. Daggerboards are usually found in small craft such as daysailers, where a single person can handle their size.

A leeboard is a swinging foil (much like a centerboard) that is located on the outboard leeward side of the boat. Generally leeboards are mounted in pairs, one for either side of the boat. While not very common in the United States, they can be seen on Dutch and Thames sailing barges. Having the boards on the outside of the hull offers shallow water operation while keeping interior space unobstructed, and there are no holes in the hull to leak. These qualities make leeboards worth considering for a sharpie.

Portable and removable leeboards are an option that can quickly convert an open boat built for paddle into a sailboat. Indeed, the Folbot folding kayak company used to offer an optional sailing package with a removable leeboard rig that you just clamped into place. All you had to do was insert the mast and rudder and you were in business.

SPARS

There is much to be said for simplicity. For traditional rigs of low aspect ratio, solid round wooden spars have stood the test of time. Masts, booms, sprits, gaffs, gaff jaws, and sundry "hardware" can be made of (relatively)

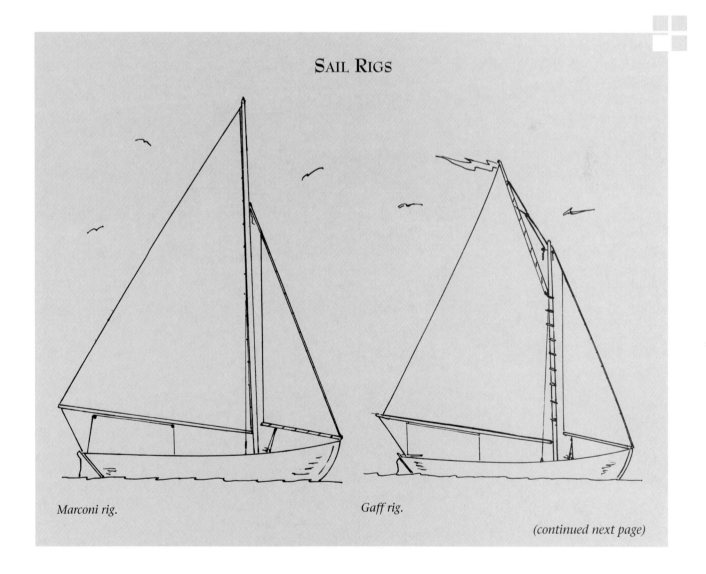

SAIL RIGS

Marconi rig.

Gaff rig.

(continued next page)

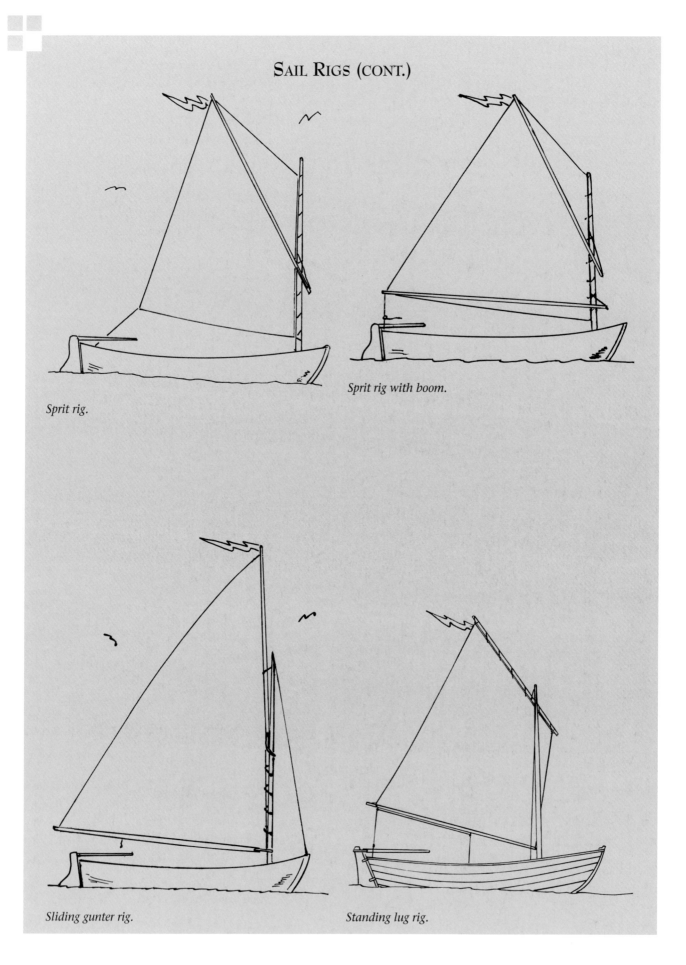

Sprit rig.

Sprit rig with boom.

Sliding gunter rig.

Standing lug rig.

SAIL RIGS (CONT.)

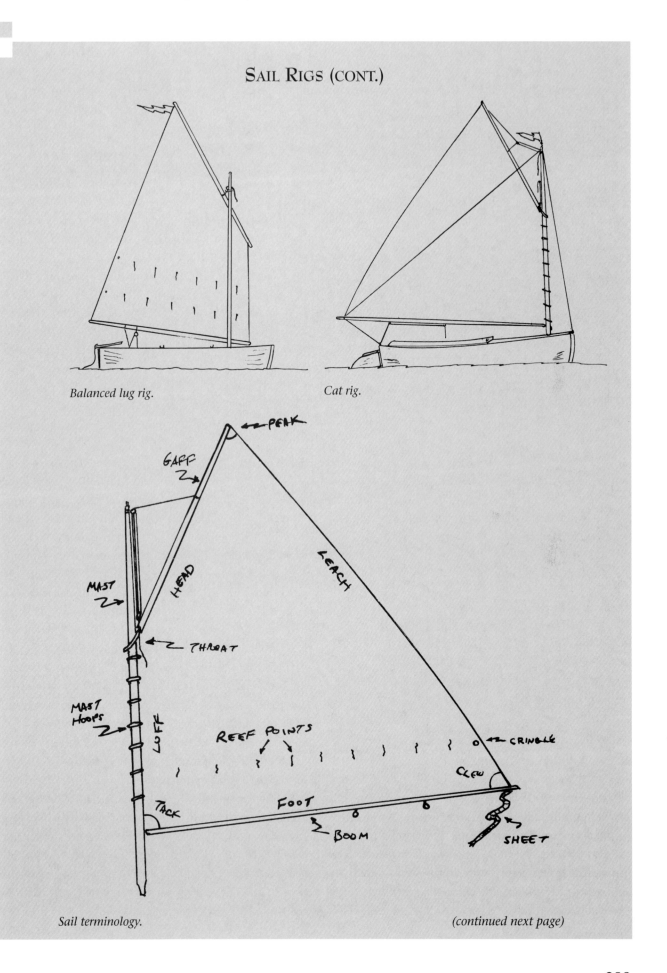

Balanced lug rig.

Cat rig.

Sail terminology.

(continued next page)

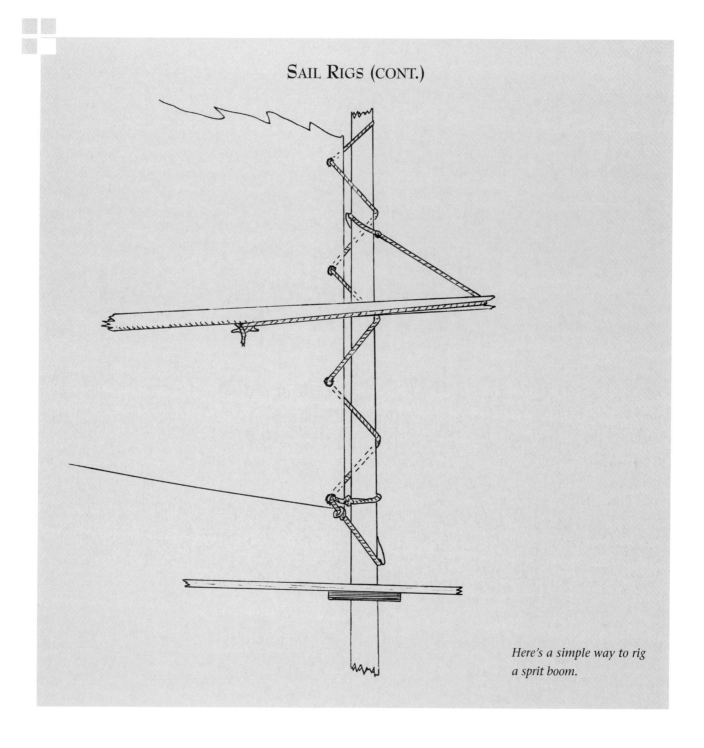

Here's a simple way to rig a sprit boom.

easy to find lumber and common fastenings. The layout of the spar is easy and no special jigs or spar assembly table is necessary. Repairs are easier and materials can be found in remote locations. A spar gauge can be manufactured in a jiffy and all the tools necessary can be rounded up in a minimal workshop. If the stock does need to be laminated, even the clamps can be quickly and cheaply assembled using hardwood, some threaded rod, and a few nuts and washers. And there is that traditional look. What's not to like?

AUXILIARY POWER

Consideration should be given to the notion of some sort of auxiliary power such as oars. Old-time designs often had provision for either oarlocks or a skulling oar. Even ballast keelboats with a coaming can be rowed. Oarlock sockets can be mounted on the coaming or on blocks outside of the coaming on the washboards (side decks), or a socket can be let into the side deck and an extra tall oarlock can be used. Trying to get your ballast keel sloop home just using a canoe paddle after the wind has died and the sun has set is less romantic than it sounds.

SAILBOAT CHOICES

As with paddle and power, there are a multitude of possibilities in sailing boat design and method of construction. Let's consider just a few representative samples starting with round bottoms.

The Herreshoff 12½ and Its Progeny

For the deluxe in sailing it is hard to do better than the Haven 12½ or the larger Flatfish—both from the pen of Joel White. These boats are shoal draft variants of Nathanael Herreshoff's much admired 12½ and Fish Class with a combination lead ballasted keel and centerboard substituting for the deeper fixed keel of the origi-

nals. Many consider these boats the best daysailers ever designed. These little yachts have been built in traditional carvel fashion and cold molded, and there is even a glued lap version designed by John Brooks. There's a lot that goes into the building of a Haven or Flatfish—from the complex construction jig, to the casting of the slotted lead keel, building the centerboard trunk, the fashioning of the signature molded sheerstrakes, and the elegant curved coamings. The work and time is well worth it.

Catboat

Perhaps even the modified keel of the Haven is too deep for your waters, however. Then the classic round-bottomed catboat might be worth serious consideration. Built in carvel or lapstrake (and nowadays even plywood), these distinctive centerboard craft, with

Joel White's Haven 12½ is a shoal-draft version of the (Nathanael) Herreshoff 12½. Traditionally built carvel-fashion with a lead ballast keel and centerboard, it's a lot of boat on a 12½-foot waterline. (Photo: Rich Hilsinger, WoodenBoat)

their workboat heritage, always look great under sail or at anchor. Length considered, the broad-beamed catboat provides commodious accommodations for the buck. The boat's single sail and unstayed mast is a boon for those who prefer a simple sail rig without a lot of fuss. And the boat's shallow draft is great for coastal cruising and getting into those shallow bays and bights where deep-water vessels dare not venture.

For traditional round-bottomed construction, one might look to the designs of Fenwick Williams, Fred Goeller, Jr., William Hand, Ted Brewer, William and Jan Atkin, or Baker Boat Works. For those who prefer V-hulls, V-hulls are what they are called! Phil Bolger offers one for conventional plank-on-frame construction. If you are a trailer sailor, you might look at Charles Wittolz's 17' V-hulled cat built over sawn frames. Although planked with plywood, it has a very traditional profile. For stitch-and-glue construction, consider Bolger's 12'3" Bobcat (also known as Dynamite Payson's "Instant Catboat") as a daysailer. For cruising, look at Bolger's 15'1½" Catfish and Sam Devlin's 20'2" Wompus Cat.

Round-Bottomed Dinghies

Perhaps a traditional lapstrake dinghy is more to your style. Designer and builder Paul Gartside, of Sidney,

British Columbia, has penned a handsome 14' sailing dinghy called Swansong. With a beamy (4'10"), stable hull, an ample lug rig (99 square feet), and a half deck for extra seaworthiness, it was designed for single-handed sailing in open water but will take up to four (well-behaved) adults. The hull is built of ³⁄₈" western red cedar on bent oak frames, ten strakes per side, all copper fastened. Decks are double skin cedar with a light glass overlay. The centerboard was designed for ¼" galvanized steel plate but a wood board weighted with lead could be substituted if preferred.

Paul notes that the hull shape is not a difficult one to plank as the forefoot is the only place where there is any real twist. The first four pairs of planks are best installed steamed; the rest can go on cold.

A boat need not be large to be enjoyable. A smaller boat that might work as a dinghy can do double duty for recreational sailing, as in picnic trips to a nearby island, nature exploration in shallows, a sporty sail in afternoon breezes, or a relaxing sunset cruise. One

Phil Bolger's Bobcat is a stitch-and-glue interpretation of the famous Beetle Cat catboat. (Photo: Dynamite Payson)

Frances, a glued-lap design by John Brooks. (Photo: John Brooks)

The stitch-and-glue 18'1" John's Sharpie has a flat bottom bow to stern, an unstayed cat-ketch rig, and weighs only about 200 pounds, rigged. (Photo: Chesapeake Light Craft)

might consider a nineteenth-century carvel dinghy in the 12' to 14' range with a centerboard and sprit rig. Or for a rugged and seaworthy approach, a sailing peapod in carvel, lapstrake, or even glued lapped plywood might fill the bill. If a trailer is to be your mooring, a glued-lap pulling boat or a double-ender rigged for sail can get you out onto the water quickly and leak-free.

Sharpies

On the other end of the spectrum are the flat-bottomed sharpies. The earliest sharpies were developed in the mid-nineteenth century as the ideal boats for the oyster fishery of the Connecticut shore. They provided a stable platform to work from, their shoal draft was perfect for operating in shallow waters, and they were fast. Perhaps the greatest promoter of the type was Commodore Ralph Munroe, who brought his adaptation of the New Haven sharpie, the 28' cat-ketch *Egret*, to Biscayne Bay in southern Florida. The swift boat proved most seaworthy (for her type) with abilities to handle both the shallows of the bay and the deeper waters offshore, run a breaking bar, and land upright on a beach. This led to a succession of high performing sharpie-based hulls that became world famous.

The sharpie is long, lean, and fast. The flat-bottomed boats have lots of initial stability, are stiff (stand up to their sails), have less wetted surface, and are fast. They can also capsize easily if heeled too far. Having flared sides adds reserve stability. Some sharpies also carry ballast to increase stability.

The straight-sided sharpie-style hull is easily constructed. As the boat is essentially a big, long skiff, it is lofted quickly with just a few lines. The construction jig is simple and straightforward. The boats can have either a built-up interior keel or bent keelson onto which a centerboard trunk can be installed. Traditional flat-bottomed sharpies have but a few really wide side planks and cross-planked bottoms. The design also lends itself to standard plywood construction as well as stitch-and-glue.

V-Shaped Hulls

Howard Chapelle noted that the rise of popularity of V-bottomed boats came in the late nineteenth century. Since that time, hard-chined, V-hulled sailing craft have been a favorite for the home boatbuilder—showing up often in boating and do-it-yourself type magazines. Sawn-frame construction has a lot of appeal, as it eliminates many of the requirements of round-bottomed carvel construction, such as steaming frames, hollowing the inside faces of the planking and much of the beveling, and building construction molds. The boats can be built using conventional carvel (some with herringbone cross-planking on the bottom) and batten seam methods and in plywood, including stitch-and-glue. (Due to limitations in how much twist sheet plywood can handle, however, not all V-shaped hull designs can be translated into plywood sheet construction.) Some are even built in a modified cold-molded fashion, with laminations laid atop strip planking.

There is a vast array of designs and sizes of craft from which to choose. For something with a workboat flavor, consider the traditional-built, shoal draft "flattie" crabbing skiffs of the Chesapeake, with their distinctive "stick up" headsail, plumb stem, and a bottom that starts off flat and transitions to a V as it approaches the transom. A modern variant is Karl Stambaugh's sharpie-inspired Windward 17, with a plywood V-bottom, raked stem, simple sprit boom rig, centerboard, and side decks with coaming. These boats have a simple salty elegance.

The sporty and fun-to-sail Comet has lots of appeal. It first appeared in a 1932 article in *Yachting* magazine titled "A Younger Brother of the Star for the Chesapeake Bay." At 16′ overall, the Comet combines a hard-chined planing hull with a classic sloop rig and a large mainsail that allows it to plane in 10- to 15-knot winds. It was designed so that someone with modest boatbuilding skills could build it at home. Other close cousins include the Penguin, Star, Lightning, Bluejay, Rhodes Bantam, and Windmill. There have been numerous V-hulled cruising boats designed for the home boatbuilder. Over a century ago Thomas Fleming Day (then editor of *The Rudder*) introduced the Sea Bird yawl as "a cruising boat for the common man." Enlisting Charles Mower to draw up a set of plans to his specifications, he designed the 25′7″ centerboard hull to be capable of long-term cruising with shoal draft, and of straightforward construction suitable to building on a tight budget. Fleming was so impressed by the capabilities of the boat that in the summer of 1911 he sailed across the Atlantic to Europe with a crew of two. These boats have been built all over the world.

One of Day's regrets about the Sea Bird, however, was the presence of a rather large centerboard trunk that usurped much of the cabin space. This problem was largely solved in the plywood-over-sawn-frame version designed by Charles MacGregor. The lines are essentially the same as the original boat, but with increased depth because of the lead ballasted keel. The reduced size of the centerboard means more room for cabin accommodations.

In 1923 John Hanna designed the popular 27′ Gulfweed for backyard construction. The plans offer three separate keel configurations: centerboard, intermediate, and deep keel. As compared with Sea Bird, Gulfweed has a little deeper V-bottom, a little more flare in the topsides, and a bit higher freeboard.

Also consider the famous 18′ plank-on-frame tabloid cruiser Picaroon by Sam Rabl. Weston Farmer wrote that Picaroon was "a delight to the eyes of every sailorman" and "a little masterpiece." The boat first appeared in a 1925 issue of *MotorBoat* magazine and can be seen in Rabl's book *Boat Building in Your Own Back Yard*. Ernest Hemingway's kid brother Hank built one of these and used it to roam the Spanish Main, driving the Cuban navy to distraction in the process.

Multi-Chined Style

Multi-chined boats, built by many different construction methods, are a great way to get most of the advantages of a round hull quickly and relatively inexpensively. Although multi-chined plywood boats may look complicated, hanging their relatively narrow strakes can be much easier than wresting with large sheets of plywood on many V-hulls.

For getting out on the water in a hurry, the standing-lug-rigged, 11′2″ Shellback dinghy or the 12′10″ Pooduck skiff might be a good choice. Both boats are designed by Joel White for building in glued plywood lap, and are natural evolutions of his famous Nutshell Pram—built in the same fashion, but longer, and with a pointed skiff bow. Both are

The Chaisson semi-dory, once again.

handsome boats (although the Pooduck does have a snazzier sheer) and sail well. The Shellback is designed for a daggerboard, while the larger Pooduck can be equipped with a centerboard.

Even dories get into the act. A semi-dory makes for an excellent sailing dinghy, while the Swampscott sailing dory is actually a high-performance thoroughbred in a traditional mold. Before you say that sailing a dory sounds like prosaic stuff, consider that the safe and seaworthy Swampscotts were once actively raced. John Gardner observed that the Swampscott-style 21' Beachcomber-Alpha dory, "With a full rig, 50 pounds of lead on either side of the centerboard trunk, and a crew of three hiked out on the rail, will draw smartly to windward and handle like a spirited colt." Easy to loft and relatively inexpensive to build, these boats can be planked in with natural wood or plywood in the traditional semi-dory fashion, or with plywood planks laid and glued over seam battens.

· 37 ·

Powerboats

Powerboats have gotten a reputation of being the last bastion of the unrepentant fuel-oholic. Unfortunately, many of the designs sold today are indeed too loud, too fast, giant-wake-producing gas guzzlers that have the fuel economy of an F-16 and all the charm and style of a fiberglass shower enclosure.

Fortunately, it doesn't have to be that way. There are plenty of great designs, both new and old, that offer a good turn of speed, are quite seaworthy, are fuel efficient, and look great. The builder has the option of building in any of the styles—be it plank on frame, plywood, or stitch-and-glue. There are options for inboard, outboard, traditional gas and diesel, or even electric or steam.

Powerboats are a sensible option for many. They afford greater range (or at least getting to that greater range quicker) than hulls powered just by oar and paddle and they still can go when there is no wind. And they might get you into shore when there's a threat of too much wind. For those whose boating depends on what is offered for weather on weekends during a far too short summer, the powerboat is a top-notch choice.

BOATS FOR THE MECHANICALLY INCLINED

A good powerboat may be as simple as a plywood skiff with an outboard, or as elaborate as a heavily built plank-on-frame inboard cruiser. One could start by simply hanging an outboard on the transom of a pulling boat. Heretical as it may sound, a small engine of a single horsepower or so can instantly transform the little vessel into a Victorian launch. Mount an electric motor into the blade of a rudder and you have (virtually) invisible propulsion. Tell onlookers that you have harnessed the mysteries of Brownian movement.

Various dory permutations are worthy of consideration. As mentioned before, a semi-dory skiff is easily and inexpensively built. The shape comes close to round-bottomed performance, yet the flat bottom allows it to plane and be beached on a moment's notice. It requires little in the way of horsepower (maybe 15 or so) and would make a great first boat or a handy bay fishing craft.

Harry Bryan's 21' Handy Billy has traditional good looks and excellent performance with low horsepower. (Photo: Harry Bryan)

John Gardner wrote of the commendable qualities of the grand dories used for the commercial fishery off the French Islands of St. Pierre et Miquelon near the coast of Newfoundland. He noted that these simply built but rugged craft with a dramatic sheerline might be the answer for many in search of a low-cost, seaworthy powerboat. The flat dory bottom made it an ideal vessel for working in shoal water and for beaching, and yet these large dories (typically around 27' overall) were quite seaworthy, working in all weather in rough water and sometimes venturing as much as 20 miles offshore. These workhorses were powered by low horsepower, slow turning, gas inboard engines.

A much smaller craft suitable for use around the working waterfront is the shallow draft, stable, and easily built Garvey. Suitable for either plank-on-frame or plywood construction, these boats would make a great choice for a boatyard skiff, tender, or ferry.

But perhaps you are looking for something more exotic that could be used for either commercial fishing or pleasure? In the book *Fishing Designs*, the Food and Agriculture Organization (FAO), an agency of the United Nations, offers plans for several seaworthy open V-bottomed fishing boats ranging from 16' to 30' and designed for economical construction and operation. Intended for use in developing countries, the boats have plans that are easy to follow and call for construction with either conventional planking stock or plywood over the same jig with the same construction procedure. Emphasis is on using easily obtained local wood, employing only a few frames, and planking with boards of equal width to simplify construction and reduce waste. Best of all, the long and slender craft are miserly with fuel. A 10-horsepower outboard is all that is necessary, although the larger boats can be outfitted with an agricultural one-cylinder diesel engine of 6 to 8 horsepower and a "liftable" drive system developed by the FAO for beach landing on the East Coast of India.

With so many designs floating about (so to speak), one of the best ways to determine whether a boat is right for you is to ask someone who designs, builds, or uses a particular model (or all three). Here's a small sampler of a few more good powerboats.

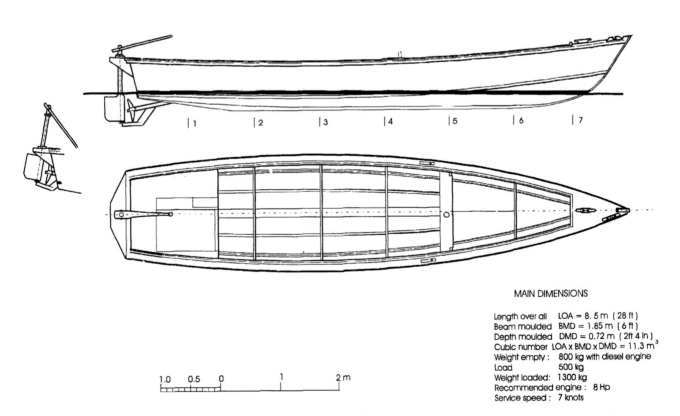

MAIN DIMENSIONS

Length over all   LOA = 8.5 m (28 ft)
Beam moulded   BMD = 1.85 m (6 ft)
Depth moulded   DMD = 0.72 m (2ft 4 in)
Cubic number   LOA x BMD x DMD = 11.3 m³
Weight empty :   800 kg with diesel engine
Load   500 kg
Weight loaded: 1300 kg
Recommended engine :   8 Hp
Service speed :   7 knots

The UN's Food and Agriculture Organization commissioned this fishing boat design for use in developing countries. The slender hull is easily and economically driven by a small, unsophisticated engine, and it can be easily built in just about any available material. (Image Courtesy of United Nations Food and Agriculture Organization)

The tremendously seaworthy *Simmons Sea Skiff*. (Photo: Ellis Rowe)

The Simmons Sea Skiff

Rowe Boats in Orland, Maine is owned by North Carolina native Ellis Rowe. Ellis has been building in traditional, plywood, and cold-molded styles and been doing repair and restoration since 1975.

Ellis says:

> Growing up on the coast of North Carolina in the 50s and early 60's, I saw many outboard boats being used for the various waterborne activities of the region. Barbours and Lymans were good examples of wooden lapstrake hulls.

> The unsinkable Boston Whaler was the popular fiberglass boat for folks who didn't mind being pounded toothless. But the boat that I dearly loved, the boat that serious fishermen used to venture from protected sounds to the open Atlantic, was the Simmons Skiff. Seeing groups of these boats fishing in the Gulf Stream 30 miles offshore was not unusual. I certainly don't advocate venturing that far offshore in such a small boat, but that was the confidence some of these fishermen had in their Simmons Skiffs.

Ellis continues:

> T. N. Simmons was the designer and builder of these boats. From the mid 50's until 1972, the Simmons shop built around 1,000 of the boats. Simmons gave the rights to the plans to the Cape Fear Museum and since then, there have been close to another 1,000 built—some as far away as New Zealand.

The Simmons 18 is a hard-chined outboard-driven skiff with moderate deadrise forward to a very shallow deadrise aft. Incorporating a motor well for the outboard motor enables the boat to have the transom raked at 35°, much better for a following sea than the 10 or 12° transoms of most outboard boats.

Given the high cost of fuel and outboard motors these days, Ellis and others find these boats very economical. A 25-horsepower will have a top speed of around 30 mph and cruise at 22 to 24 mph. Any other boat with the strength and sea-keeping ability of the Simmons would require at least twice the horsepower, he says. Due to the light weight of the Simmons, a lighter weight trailer is also adequate. Given these considerations, Ellis believes that over the life of the boat, the savings in fuel, larger motors, and trailers would easily pay for the boat—especially if it is home built.

The Simmons 18 is a fairly simple boat to build, with a sort of modified shell construction, and no lofting is required. The plans give you a full-size pattern for the stem, and measurements for all floor timbers and the transom-motor-well assembly. Once the jig is set up and the stem and transom-motor-well assembly is in place, the hull's shape is easily determined.

Says Ellis, "I built my Simmons 18 about 12 years ago, and I still believe it's the best all-round outboard in its class. Fast, economical, seaworthy, and salty as all get out. What more could you want?"

Ocean Pointer

South of Orland in Boothbay is Stimson Marine, owned by builder and designer David Stimson. In 1989, he designed the 19½' outboard-powered Ocean Pointer skiff.

Like the Simmons, the Ocean Pointer has blue-collar roots, being inspired by the strip-built, 18' West Pointer lobstering workboat built by Alton Wallace in West Point, Maine for more than 50 years. Like the West Point, the new design has a handsome sweeping sheer line and an old-time tumblehome back aft.

Strip planking has been a longtime favorite for the construction of reliable workboats. The planking material is inexpensive and relatively easy to get. And like carvel you can build round hulls but without the elaborate spiling. It worked well on the West Pointer, and it is used on the Ocean Pointer. Where the newer boat differs from the older one (other than length) is in the introduction of new materials and building techniques to promote longevity and water tightness. Back when the cost of materials was a prime consideration and labor was cheap, strip planking was pine, laid up dry (with no glue or mastic in between the planks) and the planks were edge-nailed to one another with galvanized finish nails. It worked well enough for a boat that was used like a pickup truck with limited life expectancy. But since labor is now more valuable than materials, and both recreational and commercial users have come to value durability, the Ocean Pointer plans call for cedar strips, glued with epoxy and edge-nailed with bronze ring nails. The steam-bent oak frames have been replaced with plywood bulkhead frames. The result is an inter-connected structure that is so stiff that it rings like a bell when it is struck with a mallet, according to David.

The Ocean Pointer is round bilged. Generally speaking, the round-bilged (or bottomed) hull has a bit of an edge over most flat or V-shaped bottoms. It is stronger, has a slower roll and is softer riding than a V-shaped hull. And at displacement speeds, round hulls have less wetted surface than their hard-chined colleagues. The Ocean Pointer's bottom is relatively flat, which gives it good initial stability and also allows it to plane easily (and cheaply) with modest power—indeed the hull is driven easily with a 25-horsepower outboard and will handle as much as 75 horsepower. Add a self-bailing cockpit, surrounded by Styrofoam floatation, and you have a safe and thrifty hull with a Downeast elegance.

The Handy Billy

Just across the border in New Brunswick, Canada, is Harry Bryan's boat shop. For many years, as a builder and designer, Harry had put off the business of powerboats because he says their speed, noise, stench, and the perceived need for ever-increasing power were at odds with his day-to-day life.

Harry was then introduced to the designs of William Hand, whose early-twentieth-century V-hulled

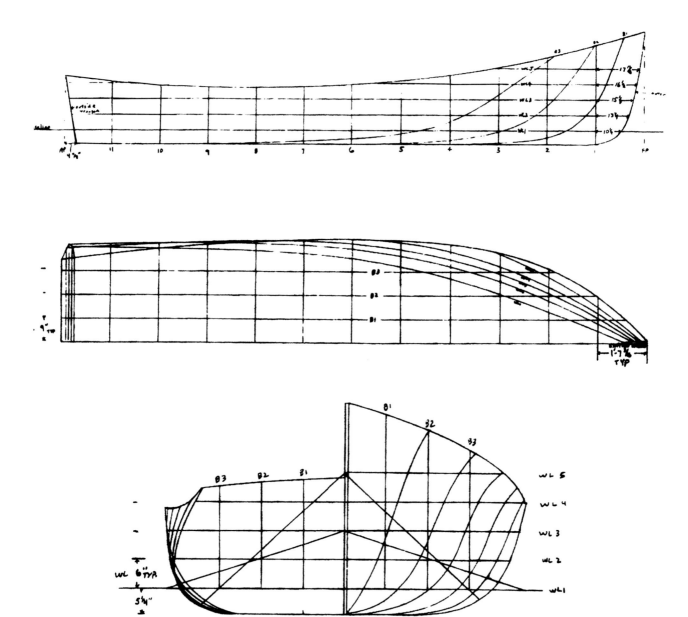

Some features to note in the lines for David Stimson's Ocean Pointer: flared topsides forward; tumblehome art; and the dead-flat bottom with soft chines.

launches were handsome and speedy yet fuel efficient. The key is in the hull shape. As with many low power-boats of that era, the hulls were relatively lean for their length. Another difference is the shape of the bottom (fore and aft) compared to more modern deep-V and round-chined hulls. Commonly, the after part of the bottom runs straight for more than half of the boat's length. That leaves a good amount of transom area immersed at slow speed, producing waves and reducing operating efficiency. The Hand designs have the bottom swoop upward from the midpoint of the hull toward the waterline at the transom. As the bottom curve approaches the transom it becomes straighter. The effect of this is that when the boat is operating at low displacement speeds, the hull is efficient as little of the transom is submerged. As power is increased, the bow lifts and that straight planing surface comes in line with the direction of travel. As one goes faster, less boat is in the water, and the area that is in the water is narrow and straight, making travel efficient.

The 21' Handy Billy was influenced by William Hand's circa-1912 Piute class. The length was shortened a bit, a little width was added, and the transom was widened a little to provide greater buoyancy for a four-stroke outboard set into a sound insulated motor well—an efficient and affordable luxury unavailable in Hand's time. Harry recommends a 25-horsepower outboard, which at full throttle will deliver 16 to 18 mph.

Being that Handy Billy is hard-chined with straight section lines (rather than curved) from rabbet-to-chine and from chine-to-sheer, the boat is quite easy to loft. The construction technique is one that was popular in Hand's era: sawn V-shaped frames with batten seams and cedar planking.

The Surf Scoter

Across the continent in Olympia, Washington, is Devlin Designing Boat Builders. Since 1982, Sam Devlin has been designing and building stitch-and-glue boats at his shop on Puget Sound. Sam was born and raised on the West Coast, which is known for its rugged, island studded waters that run from the Oregon Coast to the Alaska panhandle.

Sam's designs are influenced by this coast's hard-working craft, with their strong sheers, powerful bows, and snug cozy pilothouses (for dealing with the clammy weather that is so common there). The Surf Scoter 22 shows those qualities in its classic workboat look.

The Surf Scoter is a semi-displacement powerboat that will cruise at a respectable speed of 12 to 17 knots. It has a traditional western pilothouse design with a flush deck forward and a self-bailing cockpit aft. Just aft of the stem is a self-bailing recessed well deck. Anchoring and line handling can be done while standing in the hatchway.

The boat is built in stitch-and-glue but in a slightly different fashion than usual (see Chapter 9). There are six plywood bulkheads athwartships that help to define the hull shape (and happen to correspond with a

variety of structural parts of the boat). They are set upside down like molds on a simple backbone framework. There are also two longitudinal bulkheads that form the support and edges for the motor well and help with setup of the transom on the jig. The side panels of precut ½" plywood are wrapped about the bulkheads and stitched together and glued with epoxy and fiberglass cloth tape. Another layer of ¼" marine plywood set in epoxy resin is cold molded over the initial ½" skin. The ¾" thick hull is then sheathed with a layer of Dynel polyester cloth set in epoxy resin. The resulting hull is rugged, nearly maintenance-free, and tougher than a boiled owl.

Sam notes that the Surf Scooter can be powered by an outboard 4-cycle engine that runs in a motor well, or by an inboard diesel engine that steers with an outboard rudder. Speeds vary with the power package, but with a 90-horsepower outboard engine, the top speed is 20 knots, and when cruising at 17 knots the boat has fuel economy of 3.5 gallons of gasoline per hour. With a 30-horsepower 3-cylinder diesel inboard, top speed is 12 knots, cruising speed is 9–10 knots, and fuel consumption is 1.5 gallons per hour. For amenities, there are a couple of berths forward and an optional enclosed head. Add a cabin heater for those edge-of-the-season days and you have a boat capable of running up to Alaska and back, though it is also good just for spending the day on the water.

REGIONAL DECISIONS

As you have probably noticed, there is a pattern developing here. Part of what makes a custom powerboat great is that it can be fine-tuned to the nuances of the region in which it operates and the needs of its owner in a way that no stock boat can. The older regional designs tend to have the edge as they have been proven durable, seaworthy, and able to do the job as efficiently and economically as possible, whether they are built in traditional plank-on-frame, plywood, strip planking, or thoroughly modern stitch-and-glue.

Perhaps the best way to start a search for the right powerboat is to do a little research. Visit a local marine museum, find some old photos of the waterfront in your area, and ask some old-timers what they would use if they were you. Keep an eye (and mind) open for what works locally. To quote Yogi Berra, "You can observe quite a bit by watching."

Built stitch-and-glue, Sam Devlin's Surf Scoter has great traditional good looks. (Photo: Sam Devlin)

· 38 ·

Taking the Lines

S o you say you've spotted the boat you want to own in the back shed of the local marine museum. The elderly one-off had been in doubtful shape and the restoration was lengthy and cost more than estimated, but the result was a grand classic saved from the brink of the burn pile. It would be dandy to be able to build a replica of her—if only there were the blueprints. Alas, as has been the case with so many vessels of the period, the building plans have either disappeared or never existed in the first place, since the boat was built from a model or simply by eye. So the next best route is to take the lines off the old hull and whip up a set of plans.

Lines taking is a method of mapping a hull to develop a working set of construction plans. Foresighted historians such as Howard Chappell and John Gardner have used the technique to save countless classic and historic craft from the dustbin of maritime history. There is still as much call as ever for the documentation of hulls. As fiberglass replaces traditional hulls in distant ports and as the collapse of fisheries obviates the need for fathers to teach their sons how to build their indigenous craft, there will soon be a hole in the historical record.

Boat plans are essentially a topographic map of the vessel. The only real difference is that the marine version is a more complete portrayal, showing three or more views instead of just one. But the mapping process is basically the same—just surveying, recording distances, and drawing contours onto a grid. And

A plumb bob hanging from a stern.

because only one side is generally measured, even damaged hulls can be recorded.

There are a number of techniques that can be used, from quick and dirty to scientific. Which one to use depends on how complete the hull is, the level of detail desired, where the vessel is located, and how long you have to do the job. You may have the luxury of working in a museum storage building; then again the hulk du jour may reside on the beach with the tide on the rise and the owner's surly Rotweiller straining at the chain.

REVERSE LOFTING

For a truly accurate plan, it is hard to beat a complete mapping, which is a bit like reverse lofting where offsets and lines are dropped directly from the outside of the plank of the three-dimensional boat to the two-dimensional lofting board. This method is a good choice for vessels in a wide variety of lengths and boats that are right side up.

If working inside, it is best to set the boat up on a level floor that allows you to establish a full-scale grid onto which you can record your measurements (the floor will be your baseline). If you are outside, look for as level an area as possible that allows you to drive stakes for a string-grid frame (more on this later). The vessel should be elevated and safely braced to allow you to work under it. Sawhorses can work for light craft, while wooden blocks with notches cut to let a centerline string pass though are just the ticket for the heavier models. (Try to place them away from where you expect the stations to be—see below.) To establish the centerline, stretch a string directly beneath the centerline of the keel and transfer it in pencil onto the floor or onto a white-painted plywood lofting board. If possible, shim the boat up so that the painted waterline (or, if the waterline is not painted on the hull, the scumline, or natural waterline) is parallel to the base.

Next, level and check the boat for twist. This can be a bit of a challenge as there is no way to tell how true the vessel was when it was first built and if the sheer was cut symmetrically, thwarts were leveled, and so on. The best that can be done is to plumb the stem with a plumb bob, then brace and anchor it to the floor with clamps. Then place a level across the sheer at the transom. You might be able to gain access to a sternpost or other vertical member to plumb as well. If you

detect a bit of a twist back aft, this can sometimes be temporarily corrected on a small boat by stacking sand or lead-shot filled bags on the "high" sheer at the transom. When leveled, the aft end should be well braced to avoid precipitous capsize of the vessel. (Remember to pad all clamps to avoid injuring the artifact.)

The Drawn Grid

After the patient has been stabilized, erect perpendicular posts that touch the top of the stem and the crown of the transom. Set them so that one edge is on the centerline. These posts will be your fore and aft perpendiculars for the profile view of the plans. Onto these verticals, mark waterline heights above the baseline and square them across the face of the post. Every 3″ to 4″ is a

Setting up the forward perpendicular, with waterlines already marked, on the hull's centerline.

good spacing for small craft; 6″ works for larger vessels. These marks should continue to the top of the stem.

Then come the stations. Stations are those cross-sectional slices through the hull made at regular intervals (similar to slices in a loaf of bread) that are drawn on the floor perpendicular to the centerline. How many you'll need depends on how shapely your hull is. A small boat might need a station every foot, while a larger boat might need one every two or three feet. They are measured back from the forward perpendicular.

Lastly, the buttock grid lines need to be drawn in. Buttocks are vertical fore and aft slices through the hull that run parallel to the centerline. They are generally drawn on the floor 6″ to 8″ out from the centerline. Two or three should be enough.

The String Grid

If you are working outdoors over rough terrain, an alternative to the drawn grid is a string web grid, similar to an old-time wooden rope bed frame. In place of a grid of lines drawn on the floor, you can use stretched strings at the same spacing.

To make the box, start with some straight construction stock (2″ × 4″ stuff is fine). Begin by setting a long piece directly below the keel as a centerline. After making sure that it is dead level and straight, anchor it to the earth with stakes. Set up the fore and aft perpendiculars as previously described and brace them. Then, from where the fore and aft perpendiculars hit the 2 × 4 centerline piece, horizontally fasten two pieces of stock out at right angles. That gives you three sides of the box. Make sure they are dead level and square and anchor them to driven posts. To complete the box, fasten a piece of stock to the right angle ones. Just make sure it's out beyond the sheer and parallel to the centerline piece. And, of course, it too will be straight, dead level, and anchored to driven posts. Install a couple of diagonals to keep the frame from racking and you are in business.

To run the strings for the stations, measure (and mark) their locations back from the forward perpendicular on the centerline stock and its parallel. Stretch strings between the points. Then mark the buttocks on the perpendicular pieces. Take buttock strings and weave them over and under the station strings and

If you're taking lines where you can't draw directly on the floor (as in a museum), you can use low-tack masking tape to create the grid. Another option is a string grid.

pull them taut. That's all there is to it. You now have a fretwork of string that will do everything that a drawn grid will.

Recording the Line Data

Many measurements are generated in lines taking. The easiest way to deal with them is to generate a blank table of offsets with spaces in which to log the heights above base and the half-breadths. It's also handy to make a sketch of the profile of the boat, set up with stations, perpendiculars, and so on, so that any measurements that do not easily fit into a table of offsets can be entered graphically.

Surveying the Boundaries

A good place to begin is at the outer boundaries or edges of the hull: the sheer, the face of the stem and the stem rabbet, the rake of the transom, and the keel's bottom, width, and rabbet.

Start with the stem. Record the height where it contacts the forward perpendicular. Then, using a square, record on your sketch the distance aft of the forward perpendicular that the stem face and the rabbet are at the sheer and each waterline. Also record the half-breadth of the stem face and the rabbet. You can get the rabbet width by dropping a plumb bob down from the waterline height to the grid below. Mark the

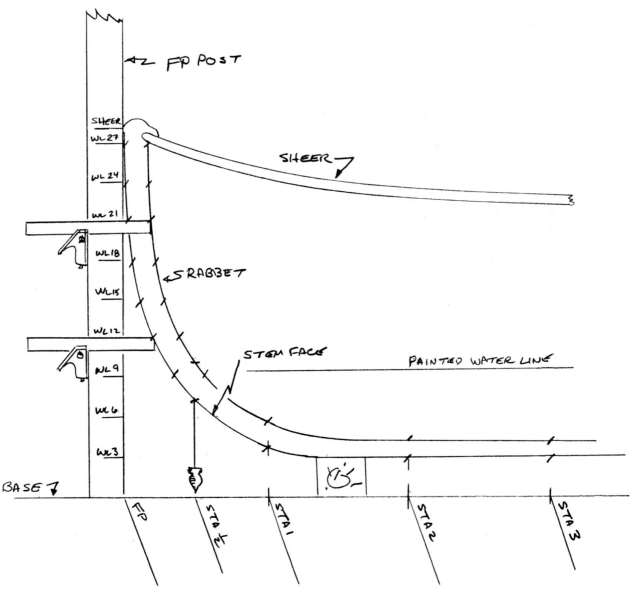

Picking up the stem face, rabbet, and painted waterline.

point and measure out from the centerline; that is the thickness or half-breadth of the rabbet.

Moving along to the bottom of the keel, at each station, use a tape rule to pick up the bottom of the keel and the rabbet line. Again, use the plumb bob to establish the width of the rabbet and keel bottom. These are usually, but not always, the same.

Record the rake of the transom by placing a long straightedge along the rake and mark and record the height where it touches the aft perpendicular and the horizontal centerline of your grid (measured forward of the aft perpendicular). Then, using your trusty tape and plumb bob, record the location of the transom sheer, and the height and width of the bottom of the keel and rabbet.

Finally, the sheer for the remainder of the hull can be captured. Run the plumb-bob string along the sheer until it dangles directly over the station line. Mark that point on the grid and measure in to the centerline for the half-breadth (remember to deduct for the width of the rub rail) and then up for the height. Record the information on the table of offsets and proceed to the next stations. Don't forget to note the height of the painted waterline.

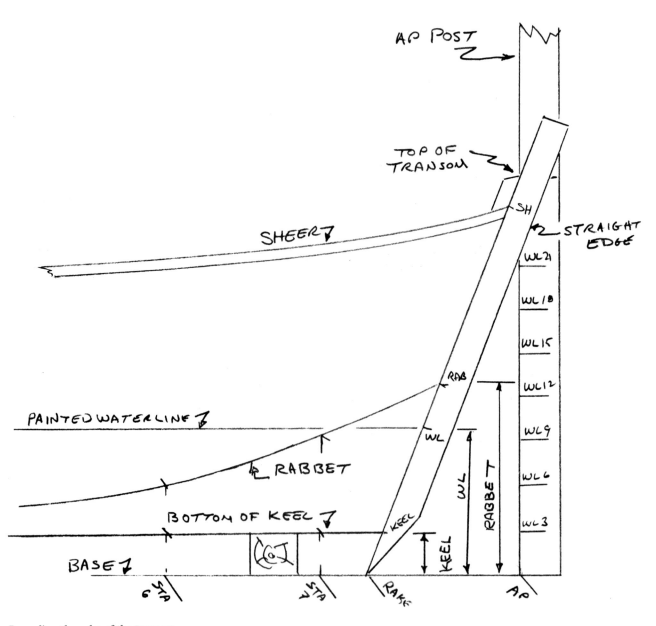

Recording the rake of the transom.

Capturing the Transom

One easy way to record the half-breadths of the transom is to first establish a centerline on the aft face with low-tack masking, or draftsman's tape. Use a combination square to bring the waterline heights over to the taped centerline. Then use a framing square on the transom face to find where the waterline hits the edge of the transom. Capture this width with a tape measure. Repeat for the other waterlines, sheer, and rabbet. The crown of the transom can also be recorded at this time.

Calibrating the Waterlines

You can use two similar methods to plot the half-breadths of the waterlines: the "square and block" method and the "bob-and-line." The former works off the floor and uses a stick or pointer of the proper length (for example, 12″ for waterline 12) that is clamped at a right angle to the end of a squared-off block. The block can then be slid in on a station line until it contacts the hull. Mark that point. Measure to the centerline and record. Proceed to the rest of the stations

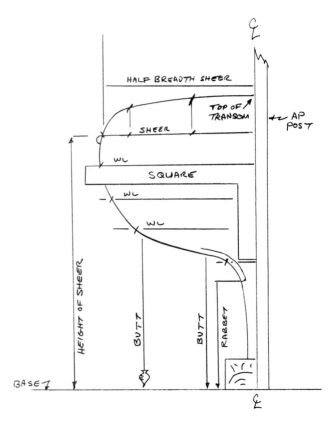

Recording the transom's buttocks and waterlines.

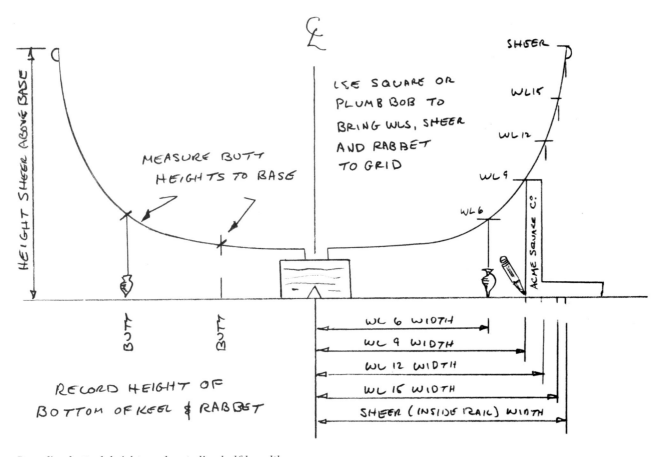

Recording buttock heights and waterline half-breadths.

and the transom. Repeat the operation for the rest of the waterlines.

The "bob-and-line" procedure is the one to use with the string grid. Decidedly low-tech, it requires only that you pinch the string between thumb and forefinger at the given distance from the point of the bob (e.g., 12″ up the string from the point of the bob). Suspend and move the bob along the string station line toward the centerline (with the point touching the line) until the pinched string touches the hull. Mark the string station line and measure to the centerline. Repeat for the other stations and waterlines.

Recording Buttocks

The technique to record the buttock heights is quite similar to the "bob-and-line" method. In this case, place the point of the bob at the intersection of the station and buttock lines on the grid. Then, lifting the bob by the string, let the string pay out between your pinched fingers until it spans the distance from the grid to the hull. Mark that spot on the hull with a piece of tape and measure back down to the grid and record it on the table of offsets. Repeat the operation at the rest of the stations and the transom.

After capturing the buttocks, you are ready to draft up the plans on paper. With all the information derived in your "survey" it will not only be easy to get a set of fair lines, but the lines will also be of top-notch museum quality to boot. They can then be lofted full size and, if desired, remeasured to develop a corrected set of offsets. Just add the construction details from the prototype and you will be in business!

Quite a bit of measuring you say? There is another way.

THE DIRECT HULL MEASURING DEVICE

If the craft is small and stable enough to allow it to be safely turned over, the Direct Hull Measuring Device offers a more graphic approach. This contraption is a moveable recording station with adjustable pointers that can be locked in place—a bit like those multipin contour gauges you've seen at the hardware store. This method is both quick and accurate.

To construct the measuring jig, start by building a strongback that has three board rails laid on the flat: one in the center and the other two set wider than the greatest beam of your hull. Use 1″ × 8″ or 1″ × 10″ boards that are longer than your boat. The middle board contains the centerline. The outer boards support the moveable recording station.

Set the strongback up at a convenient working height so that it is dead level both fore and aft and athwartships. Nothing fancy—sawhorses and shims work fine. This level jig will be the "base" for your drawing.

Draw a centerline on the middle board. On this line, record a forward perpendicular near one end of the jig and the spacing for your stations (1′ intervals are fine). Square these points out onto the outer rails.

Mark a centerline on the transom of the boat and place the boat upside down onto the jig. Center the stem and transom on the centerline and align the face of the stem with the forward perpendicular. Then level the boat the best you can athwartships. Mark on the centerline where the crown of the transom hits and square that point out to the outside rails. This is the aft perpendicular. Brace the boat up, and if necessary, add cleats to the jig to keep the vessel from shifting.

The Moveable Station

Now you can build the moveable station. Again, this U-shaped unit is definitely not fancy. Make it from the same stock as the rails. You need two pieces for the legs that are of the same length and long enough to get you over the top (er, bottom) of the keel, and one piece that is as long as the jig is wide. Butt the top edges of the shorter pieces to the bottom edge of the longer piece, creating a bridge or an upside-down "U." After making sure the station is square, screw and glue the gussets over the two joints on one side only. A light diagonal brace can be added to the same side as the gussets to keep the station from wracking. When stood up, the station should span the boat, and the outside edges of the legs should match the outside edges of the jig rails. Mark a centerline on the top edge of the spanning piece and square it across.

Stand the station frame up and align the bottom edge of the ungusseted side with a station line drawn on the jig rails. Use a framing square or level to make the station frame square to the rails. Temporarily anchor it into place and fasten a diagonal brace to keep it plumb.

Now you need a dozen or so pointers. These can simply be pieces of lath that have one end cut at an angle to form a point. Round up some spring clamps, Sheetrock screws, and a driver and you're ready to go.

Measuring

Start by placing a pointer along the vertical centerline on the station and sliding down to it until it contacts the keel. Clamp it into place. Then go to the sheer of the boat and, holding the lath horizontally, place the point on the sheer and clamp the other end to the station. Then place the rest of the pointers with their points against the side of the hull and radiating out from various points on the hull to the movable station. There should be a pointer every inch or so of the hull. (Be sure to pick up the edge of the keel and the rabbet.) Take a moment to arrange the pointers where you want them and then anchor them in place with the Sheetrock screws. Remove the clamps.

The Body Plan

The next step is to set up the body plan. A light piece of lauan plywood painted flat white works well. Scribe a long baseline parallel to one edge of the plywood. This line is the counterpart to the top of the rails on the measuring jig. At the halfway point on this base line, erect a perpendicular centerline. Next, draw a series of waterlines parallel to the baseline every 3″ or 4″. While you're at it, draw in a few buttocks parallel to

Pointers on the movable bridge are used to capture multiple points along the boat's station. The bridge is set up over each of the boat's stations in turn and the pointers are reset to capture the curve.

the centerline. Every 6″ should do the trick. Finally, screw a strip of wood to the bottom side of the baseline.

Unfasten the braces and remove the station frame from the jig and place it on top of the body plan. The bottoms of the two "legs" should touch the baseline cleat and the centerline on the spanning piece should be in line with the centerline on the body plan. Then bring the points down from the ends of the lath pointers to the body plan. Connect the points with a flexible batten, draw in the keel with a square, and you have captured the station! Repeat the operation with the rest of the stations.

Getting the Ends

Bring the moveable station up to the forward perpendicular, and square and anchor it as before. Then take another board and stand it up vertically, with the bottom edge touching the centerline on the jig and the top of the stem, and the upper edge touching the centerline on the moveable station. Screw or clamp it into place. Then use the pointer laths to pick up the curve of the forward face of the stem. The rabbet can be picked up in similar fashion.

Use the same setup at the aft perpendicular for the rake of the transom. Remember to pick up the bottom of the keel and the bottom of the transom, and square over the height of the sheer at the transom. Label the pointers to prevent confusion.

The Lofting Board

Set up the lofting board as you did the body plan. Establish your baseline and centerline. Using a paper tape or long batten, pick up the station spacing, forward perpendicular, and aft perpendicular from the measuring jig and record them on the lofting board. Square them up. To complete your grid, bring your waterline and buttock spacing over from the body plan and draw those lines in.

Next, bring the board with the stem pointers over to the profile view and align it with the forward perpendicular and the base. Record the points and spring a batten through them. Do the same at the stern to plot the rake of the transom, rabbet, keel, and sheer.

All the rest of the half-breadths and heights above base for each station are brought over by paper tape from the body plan. Fair the lines and you're done—except for making that dreaded table of offsets.

Transferring points from the station curves from the movable station to the lofting board.

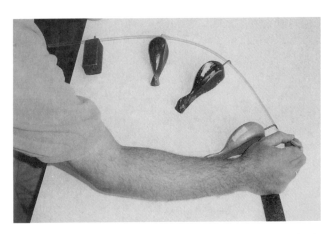

Connect the dots with a thin batten held in place with drafting ducks and trace the curve.

RECORDING CONSTRUCTION DATA

To complete your rendering, you must do a full cataloging of all the components. Necessary tools include a tape rule, a note pad, and a dash of patience. A camera is also invaluable to record oddball items that might be forgotten otherwise. As this might be your only chance, make notes of everything! What was she built of? Capture the caliber of the frames (and their placement

and fasteners). Where were the oarlocks located? Are they mounted on unusual pads? These might be worth sketching. The configuration of the backbone is a must to record. How about the camber of the transom or the placement of the floorboards? Are there any custom castings for the hardware? Perhaps there's an accent sheerstrake. Record the species and the width at each station. And while you're at it, note any unusual wear and tear. That will go a long way toward telling the story of how this boat was used.

Combine all this data into a well-drawn construction plan and you have saved this old girl for all time!

CURATOR'S CAVEAT

There are different approaches to lines taking when recording an old boat moldering next to a burn pile versus an old boat in a museum. The former is just an old boat, while the latter is an artifact and an antiquity. Break out the permanent marker in the gallery and you may find yourself quickly captured and ushered to the exit by uniformed guards.

What to do? First check with the curator. Can the boat be moved? Can the boat be "untwisted"? Is there a problem with a camera flash? Can marks be made on the floor? Can marks be made on the boat? Low-tack masking tape and soft, easily removed chalk are safe alternatives to the ubiquitous "sharpie" pen. Padded clamps are de rigueur. Consider using a laser level to create a waterline on the hull from which to drop your plumb bob. And work with the museum. Lines taking is an interesting business for the public to watch. If you are willing to become "part of the exhibit" for a day, previously closed doors may be opened.

HEAVY METAL FOR TRADITIONALISTS

Yet another casualty of the electronic age and of computer design is the paucity of spline weights, or drafting ducks, on the market today. Purveyors of drafting implements have simply stopped carrying these items due to lack of demand. These solid citizens are essential tools for lofting and drafting ship lines. What's a builder to do? Whip up a batch at home, of course!

Spline weights are basically a lump of lead with a bent rod sticking out of one end that can grab hold of a plastic or wooden drafting spline to anchor it in place. Some have a graceful, whale-like contour, while others are just rectangular blocks. While the ornate versions are a joy to behold (and use), they do involve considerable effort to produce—employing patterns, casting sand, and time. If you can get by with less elegance, there is the quick and dirty, pour-a-slab-and-slice method.

Casting

The casting trough can be made from a piece of 2 × 4 or 2 × 6 common softwood lumber. Decide on the shape your ingot will be (tapered sides work well). The trough need not be exceptionally wide or deep, as one cubic inch of lead equals about 0.4 pound. Commercial ducks run roughly 4 pounds each. The length of the trough is determined by how much lead you can pour at one time. Shorter is better than too long. Most of the work can be done on the table saw. Two bevel cuts into the flat of the wooden block, down the length of the piece, will form the sides of the ingot. You can remove the remainder of the stock in the center with a dado or simply by running a series of saw kerfs that can then be cleaned out with a gouge. Work out the final roughness with a rabbet plane and sandpaper.

Next, add a stopper door on both ends of the trough. This can be just a piece of ½" plywood firmly screwed in place. Then set up the casting form—leveled both fore and aft and athwartships in a protected and well-ventilated location (preferably outdoors).

With the casting form set up, you are ready to melt the lead. But where does one get lead these days? Building supply stores carry it in the form of roof flashing, while auto mechanics and tire stores have barrels of used lead wheel weights available at discount prices.

The setup of the melting operation is straightforward: an iron pot, a ladle, and a hot gas stove. Simple as the tools are, this is not a task to be taken lightly or done in your kitchen. Molten lead is hot, unforgiving stuff. Any moisture can cause it to spatter, with painful

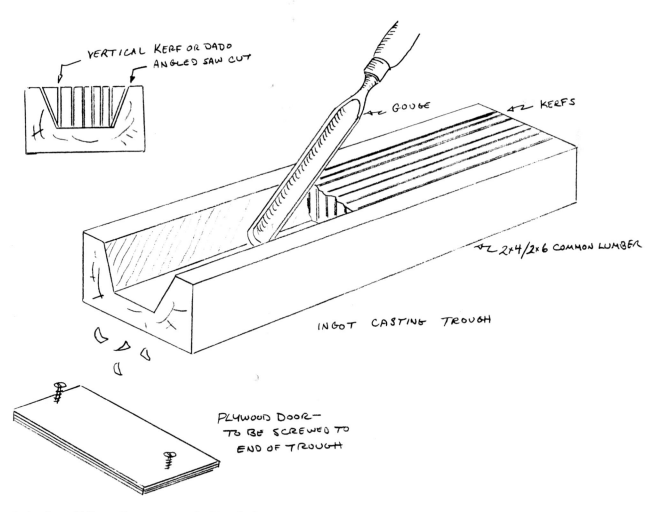

A simple mold for casting your own drafting ducks.

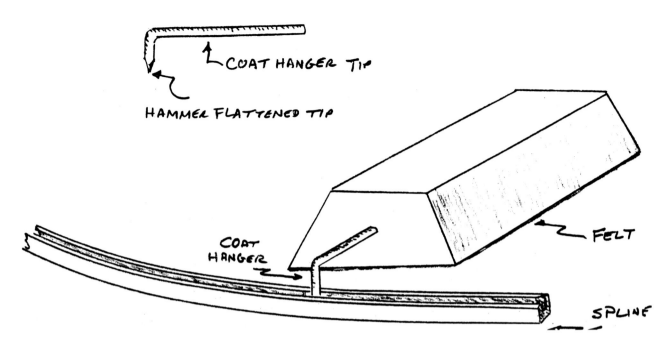

COAT HANGER TIP

HAMMER FLATTENED TIP

COAT HANGER

FELT

SPLINE

Drill the end of the duck and epoxy the hook in place.

results. Work with any breeze at your back. Wear gloves, a protective apron, a face shield, and a proper respirator.

As the lead melts, skim off any dross with a wooden paddle. When you are pouring, the mold should be slightly overfilled to accommodate the lead slumping slightly after cooling. Any imperfections in the casting can be smoothed with hand tools or filled with epoxy putty.

After the lead has cooled, you will have a long bar of lead that can be cut to 4-pound lengths with a hacksaw. Lead can be smoothed and/or beveled with a hand plane.

Finishing

The next question is philosophical: whether to have the narrow side down or up. Having the wider side at the top makes it easier to grab, while having it down gives a greater nonskid base. Either orientation works well.

For the duck's wire hooks, hardware store variety L-shaped threaded hanging hooks work well. Drill a hole in the lead and screw it in. Or simply grab a wire coat hanger from the closet and nip off pieces about 2½″ long. Heat one end of the wire with a torch, insert about ¾″ of it into a vise, and pull a 90° bend into it. Then, using a ball peen hammer, beat a flat into the business end of the hook so that it will fit the spline. Then drill a hole in the ingot about ¾″ up from the bottom and large enough to allow a slight sliding fit for the coat hanger hook. Drip in a little 5-minute epoxy and insert the wire. Align the hook and let it set up. All that remains is to give the duck a stylish paint job, glue some felt on the bottom, and you're all set.

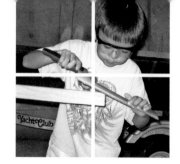

▪ 39 ▪

Young Folks and Boatbuilding

Boats are good things for young people—a great alternative to today's fare of organized activities, "career enhancing" sports endeavors, and the addictive, soul-deadening, digital extravaganzas that consume so much of kids' time and attention. Where else can a young person build a mode of transportation from scratch, customize it, see the results—both good and bad—of their workmanship, and use it, having a lot of fun in the process?

Part of the value of boatbuilding is the confidence that comes from seeing that you can do it—and just about anyone *can* do it, given sufficient motivation and perhaps a little guidance and encouragement. Although some aspects of boatbuilding can be challenging, responding to challenges and overcoming them is really what "it" is all about, whether one is talking about boats or life.

A boatbuilding project can be one of the best experiences you'll ever have with your young one. Kids love to learn practical skills—so much so that they might even forget, temporarily, that you, as an adult, presumably know nothing at all. On the other hand, if you really *do* know nothing about boatbuilding, it'll be a great experience for them to watch an adult tackle the task and end up with a boat—especially if you do it in partnership.

YOUTH BOATBUILDING PROGRAMS

Aside from the personal, one-on-one approach, there are public programs and social and educational organizations working to achieve the benefits to young people of boatbuilding. Youth boatbuilding programs are used to teach math and geometry (required to build a boat); history (how a boat design evolved in the local

Getting a good start. (Photo: Marc Bourassa)

community or a foreign culture); physics (the inclined planes, levers, and vectors that make tools work and boats go); and chemistry (glues, paints, and galvanic action). Learning to navigate involves math, astronomy, and geography, while using the boat can provide a quick study in judgment and responsibility. The list goes on, and I haven't even mentioned the spiritual and aesthetic benefits of getting out on the water and experiencing solitude and nature firsthand.

One of the most popular of the public efforts is the Family Boatbuilding Program, organized by *WoodenBoat* magazine as a way to promote boatbuilding and get families involved in a fun, productive activity. Highly flexible in form and content, the program typically involves several dozen family groups that gather over the course of a weekend to build small boats. While some of the vessels are constructed using traditional methods, others are designed specifically for the program to be quickly and easily built in stitch-and-glue. *WoodenBoat* acts as a facilitator of some 50 to 60 sessions every year, all over the world, while the sessions are sponsored by various organizations such as 4H clubs, maritime museums, nonprofit associations, church groups, and even homeless shelters.

A very different environment exists in the Apprenticeship Program, run by the Alexandria (Virginia) Seaport Foundation, to work with disadvantaged youth in a formal, but unconventional, educational setting. High-school-age kids who go through the six-month program are certified as preapprentices with the local Carpenters Union, learning both woodworking and carpentry trade skills, and work-oriented disciplines and life skills such as showing up for work on time. The program also helps its students obtain their graduate equivalency degree (GED) credentials, and offers driver's education, drug tests, health care, job placement, and follow-up counseling.

Also working with at-risk youth, the San Francisco Maritime National Historical Park runs shorter progams, lasting about two weeks, in which students build San Francisco Bay Pelicans in an intensive learning experience that often represents their first exposure to woodworking tools and boating in any form. Assistant Curator of Small Craft Jason Rucker says that on the first day of Pelican building class the young carpenters are given an introduction to shop safety and shown some precut pieces. Instructors often hear the students whispering to one another things such as "No

way I'm getting in any boat we build." Nine to twelve days later, however, the boat is launched with a crowd of parents, teachers, and friends in attendance. Says Rucker,

> From the students' responses, we can tell that it's the best work they've ever done. Those who began the program disinterested quickly found the excitement of the project overwhelming. Students who didn't want to work with their peers realize they have to if they are to finish the boat. Those who doubted they could build a boat find that with some focus and practice, they too can skillfully use the tools they'd never seen before the class started. It's these realizations that make boatbuilding a powerful experience for these students and make it rewarding for them and the teachers alike.

Not all such educational programs are associated with maritime museums. An independent, nonprofit organization in the Bronx called Rocking the Boat runs after-school and summer programs to teach inner-city high school students traditional boatbuilding skills and expose them to the history and the environment of the waters around New York. Rocking the Boat goes far beyond boatbuilding. Each day, the organization's fleet of Whitehalls is launched from the rocky beaches of upper New York Harbor. Each boat carries a crew of four to six students who learn boat handling and navigation and work on a range of Bronx River restoration scientific projects. Adam Green, one of Rocking the Boat's founders, says he figures that the organization's boats get more daily use than any other traditionally built boat in the country.

Interestingly, the school has moved away from high-tech construction methods and materials to traditional skills and sawn lumber—even adding a forestry component that dovetails with the program's environmental component. Kids saw their own lumber, gaining a deeper understanding of the structure of wood and learning that these resources don't just appear on the racks at a lumberyard.

The shop's repertoire includes traditional craft such as Whitehalls, an oyster skiff, a bateau, a Melonseed skiff, a nineteenth-century Croton River cargo ferry, and a Fiddlehead decked canoe. Through the hands-on vehicle of boat construction, the young builders apply math, carpentry, and organizational skills, and have opportunities to solve problems individually and in teams.

CREATING A YOUTH PROGRAM

There is no set formula for creating a youth boatbuilding program. It can be a formal educational program or one that offers pure fun and recreation, lasting from a weekend to a semester or more. One common factor of successful programs, however, is the existence of defined and attainable goals. While it might be interesting to build a replica of Old Ironsides in Iowa, practicality would suggest something of a smaller scale.

Having the resonance of a historical and/or local component can bring local support and input. (A river-driving bateau might be just the ticket for a program in northern Maine, for example, while a pirogue would do the same for southern Louisiana.) Programs can weave in the greater community—families, businesses, marine museums, and old-timers telling their stories of how they built and used these boats. And of course everyone should have a good time.

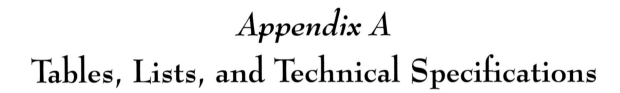

Appendix A
Tables, Lists, and Technical Specifications

IMPERIAL/METRIC CONVERSIONS

INCHES TO MILLIMETERS
CONVERSION: .001″ = .0254 MM

Inch Fraction	Inch Decimal	Millimeters	Inch Fraction	Inch Decimal	Millimeters
1/64	.015625	0.397	33/64	.515625	13.097
1/32	.03125	0.794	17/32	.53125	13.494
3/64	.046875	1.191	35/64	.546875	13.891
2/32	.0625	1.588	9/16	.5625	14.288
5/64	.078125	1.984	37/64	.578125	14.684
3/32	.09375	2.381	19/32	.59375	15.081
7/64	.109375	2.778	39/64	.609375	15.478
1/8	.1250	3.175	5/8	.6250	15.875
9/64	.140625	3.572	41/64	.640625	16.272
5/32	.15625	3.969	21/32	.65625	16.669
11/64	.171875	4.366	43/64	.671875	17.066
3/16	.1875	4.763	11/16	.6875	17.463
13/64	.203125	5.159	45/64	.703125	17.859
7/32	.21875	5.556	23/32	.71875	18.256
15/64	.234375	5.953	47/64	.734375	18.653
1/4	.2500	6.350	3/4	.7500	19.050
17/64	.265625	6.747	49/64	.765625	19.447
9/32	.28125	7.144	25/32	.78125	19.844
19/64	.296875	7.541	51/64	.796875	20.241
5/16	.3125	7.938	13/16	.8125	20.638
21/64	.328125	8.334	52/64	.828125	21.034
11/32	.34375	8.731	27/32	.84375	21.431
23/64	.359375	9.128	55/64	.859375	21.828
3/8	.3750	9.525	7/8	.8750	22.225
25/64	.390625	9.922	57/64	.890625	22.622
13/32	.40625	10.319	29/32	.90625	23.019
27/64	.421875	10.716	59/64	.921875	23.416
7/16	.4375	11.113	15/16	.9375	23.813
29/64	.453125	11.509	61/64	.953125	24.209
15/32	.46875	11.906	31/32	.96875	24.606
31/64	.484375	12.303	63/64	.984375	25.003
1/2	.50000	12.700	1	.1.000	25.400

MILLIMETERS TO INCHES
CONVERSION: 1 MM = .03937″

mm	inches	mm	inches	mm	inches	mm	inches
.1	.0039	20	.7874	48	1.8898	75	2.9528
.2	.0079	21	.8268	49	1.9291	76	2.9921
.3	.0118	22	.8661	50	1.9685	77	3.0315
.4	.0158	23	.9055	51	2.0079	78	3.0709
.5	.0197	24	.9449	52	2.0472	79	3.1102
.6	.0236	25	.9843	53	2.0866	80	3.1496
.7	.0276	26	1.0236	54	2.1260	81	3.1890
.8	.0315	27	1.0630	55	2.1654	82	3.2283
.9	.0354	28	1.1024	56	2.2047	83	3.2677
1	.0394	29	1.1417	57	2.2441	84	3.3071
2	.0787	30	1.1811	58	2.2835	85	3.3465
3	.1181	31	1.2205	59	2.3228	86	3.3858
4	.1575	32	1.2598	60	2.3622	87	3.4252
5	.1969	33	1.2992	61	2.4016	88	3.4646
6	.2362	34	1.3386	62	2.4409	89	3.5039
7	.2756	35	1.3780	63	2.4803	90	3.5433
8	.3150	36	1.4173	64	2.5197	91	3.5827
9	.3543	37	1.4567	65	2.5591	92	3.5220
10	.3937	38	1.4961	66	2.5984	93	3.6614
11	.4331	39	1.5354	67	2.6378	94	3.7008
12	.4724	40	1.5748	68	2.6772	95	3.7402
13	.5118	41	1.6142	69	2.7165	96	3.7795
14	.5512	42	1.6535	70	2.7559	97	3.8189
15	.5906	43	1.6929	71	2.7953	98	3.8583
16	.6299	44	1.7323	72	2.8346	99	3.8976
17	.6693	45	1.7717	73	2.8740	100	3.9370
18	.7087	46	1.8110	74	2.9134		
19	.7480	47	1.8504				

LIQUID MEASURE

1 pint = 0.4732 liter
1 pint = 0.5000 quart
1 quart = 0.9464 liter
1 quart = 0.2500 gallon
1 US gallon = 3.785 liter
1 liter = 2.113 pints
1 liter = 1.057 quart
1 liter = 0.2642 US gallon
1 Imperial gallon = 1.2 US gallon
1 US gallon = 0.833 Imperial gallon

WEIGHT

1 ounce = 28.35 grams
1 gram = 0.03527 ounce
1 pound = 16 ounces
1 pound = 456.6 grams
1 kilogram = 2.2046 pounds

FASTENERS

FLATHEAD SCREWS FOR PLANKING

Plank Thickness	Screw Length and Size
⅜"	¾" × # 7
½"	1" × # 8
⅝"	1¼" × # 8 or 9
¾"	1½" × # 10
⅞"	1¾ × # 12
1"	2" × # 14
1⅛"	2¼" × # 16

RIVETS (U.S.)

BURR TO RIVET FIT

Size Nail	Loose	Drive
15	15	N/A
14	14	N/A
12	12	13
11	12	13
10	9	10
9	8	9
8	7	8
6	5	6

COPPER BURRS

Size	Hole I.D.	Approximate Count/Pound
14	0.093	2050
13	0.106	1350
12	0.124	1240
10	0.138	750
9	0.146	580
8	0.166	465
7	0.176	380
6	0.206	184

Source: Jamestown Distributors

American common nail rivets use washer-like burrs to provide surface area on the end opposite the nail head. Loose-fitting burrs are handy where gravity keeps them in place before the end of the nail is nipped and peened. Many builders prefer to work with tight-fitting burrs that must be driven on with a burr set, because the burr stays put until the end is peened. Some rivet sizes do not have corresponding tight-fitting burrs.

COPPER COMMON NAILS

Penny	Gauge	Length	Shank Diameter	Head Diameter	Approx Count/Lb.
2 D	15	1"	0.072	3/16"	685
3 D	14	1¼"	0.083	3/16"	424
4 D	12	1½"	0.109	¼"	205
5 D	12	1¾"	0.109	¼"	165
6 D	11	2"	0.120	9/32"	133
8 D	10	2½"	0.134	5/16"	86
10 D	9	3"	0.148	5/16"	55
12 D	9	3¼"	0.148	5/16"	52
16 D	8	3½"	0.165	3/8"	40
20 D	6	4"	0.203	7/16"	23
30 D	5	4½"	0.220	½"	18

NOMINAL COMPOSITION OF CORROSION-RESISTANT NAIL MATERIALS

Copper	Silicon Bronze	304 Stainless	316 Stainless	Monel
Cu 99.92%	Cu 96.75%	Fe 71%	Fe 68.5%	Ni 67%
O_2 .08%	Si 3.25%	Cr 19%	Cr 17.0%	Cu 31.6%
		Ni 10%	Ni 12.0%	Fe 1.4%
				Mo 2.5%

Source: Hamilton Marine Catalog

Appendix B
Resources

SOURCES OF INFORMATION ON BOATBUILDING AND DESIGN

After selecting the kind of boat to build, it's time to find out more about it. A good book can not only provide information and inspiration but also save you time and money. This list should be enough to load up your bedside table for a while.

Traditional Plank-on-Frame Construction

Boatbuilding. Chapelle, Howard I. New York, NY: W. W. Norton & Company, 1941.

Boatbuilding Down East. Lowell, Royal. Camden, ME: International Marine, 1977.

Boatbuilding in Your Own Backyard. Rabl, S. S. Cambridge, MD: Cornell Maritime Press, 1947.

Boatbuilding Manual, 4th ed. Steward, Robert M. Camden, ME: International Marine, 1994.

Boats Oars and Rowing. Culler, R. D. Camden, ME: International Marine, 1978.

Building Classic Small Craft. Gardner, John. Camden, ME: International Marine, 1991.

Building Small Boats. Rössel, Greg. Brooklin, ME: WoodenBoat Books, 1998.

Clinker Boatbuilding. Leather, John. Camden, ME: International Marine, 1973.

The Dory Book. Gardner, John. Camden, ME: International Marine, 1978.

Fishing Boat Designs: 2V-bottom boats of planked and plywood construction. Gulbrandsen, Øyvind. Grimstad, Norway: FAO Fisheries Technical Papers, 1997.

Go Build Your Own Boat. Payson, Harold H. "Dynamite." New York: Van Nostrand Reinhold, 1983.

How to Build a Wooden Boat. McIntosh, David C. "Bud." Brooklin, ME: WoodenBoat Publications, 1987.

How to Build the Catspaw Dinghy. Editors of *WoodenBoat* Magazine. Brooklin, ME: WoodenBoat Publications, 1986.

The Sharpie Book. Parker, Reuel B. Camden, ME: International Marine, 1993.

Traditional Boatbuilding Made Easy: A 12 foot Skiff for Oar and Sail. Kolin, Richard. Brooklin, ME: WoodenBoat Publications, 1996.

Wherries. Simmons, Walt. Lincolnville Beach, ME: Duck Trap Press, 2004.

Wood: A Manual for Its Use as a Shipbuilding Material. Department of the Navy, Bureau of Ships. Kingston, MA: Teaparty Books, 1983.

Wooden Boats to Build and Use. Gardner, John. Mystic, CT: Mystic Seaport Museum, 1996.

Traditional Techniques

Boat Carpentry, 2nd ed. Smith, Hervey Garrett. New York: D. Van Nostrand Company, 1965.

Planking & Fastening. Spectre, Peter. Brooklin, ME: WoodenBoat Publications, 1996.

Practical Yacht Joinery. Bingham, Fred. Camden, ME: International Marine, 1983.

Using Epoxy

The Gougeon Brothers on Boat Construction, 5th ed. Gougeon, Meade. Bay City, MI: Gougeon Brothers Inc., 2005.

Plywood and Glued Lap Construction

Building with Plywood. Witt, Glen L. Bellflower, CA: Glen-L Designs, 1989.

Build the New Instant Boats. Payson, Harold "Dynamite." Camden, ME: International Marine, 1984.

Clinker Plywood Boatbuilding Manual. Oughtred, Iain. Brooklin, ME: WoodenBoat Publications, 1988.

How to Build Glued Lapstrake Wooden Boats. Brooks, John, and Ruth Ann Hill. Brooklin, ME: WoodenBoat Books, 2004.

The New Cold-Molded Boatbuilding: From Lofting to Launching. Parker, Reuel B. Brooklin, ME: WoodenBoat Publications, 2005.

Ultralight Boatbuilding. Hill, Tom. Camden, ME: International Marine, 1987.

Strip Planking

Building a Strip Canoe. Gilpatrick, Gil. Yarmouth, ME: DeLorme Mapping, 1993.

CanoeCraft. Moores, Ted. Richmond Hill, Ontario: Firefly Books, 2000.

Featherweight Boatbuilding. McCarthy, Henry "Mac." Brooklin, ME: WoodenBoat Publications, 1996.

How to Build the Ocean Pointer: A Strip-Built 19'6" Outboard Skiff. Stimson, David. Brooklin, ME: WoodenBoat Publications, 2002.

KayakCraft. Moores, Ted Brooklin. ME: WoodenBoat Publications, 1999.

Rip, Strip and Row. Brown, Picket, and Hartsock. Cambridge, MA: Tamal Vista Publications, 1985.

Stitch-and-Glue

Devlin's Boatbuilding: How to Build Any Boat the Stitch-and-Glue Way. Devlin, Samuel. Camden, ME: International Marine, 1996.

Kayaks You Can Build. Moores, Ted and Rossel, Greg. Richmond Hill, Ontario: Firefly Books, 2004.

Stitch-and-Glue Boatbuilding. Kulczycki, Chris. Camden, ME: International Marine, 2005.

Wood and Canvas Canoes

Building the Maine Guide Canoe. Stelmock, Jerry. Camden, ME: International Marine, 1980.

The Canoe: A Living Tradition, Jennings, John, et al. Richmond Hill, Ontario: Firefly Books, 2002.

The Wood and Canvas Canoe: A Complete Guide to Its History, Construction, Restoration, and Maintenance. Stelmock, Jerry and Rollin Thurlow. Gardiner, ME: Tilbury House, 1987.

Lofting and Design

American Small Sailing Craft. Chapelle, Howard I. New York, NY: W. W. Norton & Company, 1951.

Building a Liftable Propulsion System for Small Craft: The BOB Drive. Gulbrandsen, O. and M. R. Andersen. Madras, India: Food and Agriculture Organization of the United Nations, Bay of Bengal Programme, 1993.

Elements of Yacht Design. Skene, Norman L. Dobbs Ferry, NY: Sheridan House, 2001.

From My Old Boatshop: One-Lung Engines, Fantail Launches and Other Marine Delights. Farmer, Weston. Camden, ME: International Marine, 1979.

Lofting. Vaitses, Allen H. Brooklin, ME: WoodenBoat Books, 1999.

Polluting for Pleasure. Mele, Andrew. New York, NY: W. W. Norton & Company, 1993.

Ship and Aircraft Fairing and Development, Rabl, S. S. Centreville, MD: Cornell Maritime Press, 1985.

The Nature of Boats. Gerr, Dave. Camden, ME: International Marine, 1992.

Understanding Boat Design, 4th ed. Brewer, Ted. Camden, ME: International Marine, 1993.

Yacht Design Explained. Killing, Steve. New York, NY: W. W. Norton & Company; 1998.

Yacht Designing and Planning: For Yachtsmen, Students and Amateurs. Chapelle, Howard I. New York, NY: W. W. Norton & Company, 1995.

Watercraft, 2nd ed. Bray, Maynard. Mystic, CT: Mystic Seaport Museum, 1986.

87 Boat Designs: A Catalog of Small Boat Plans from Mystic Museum. Fuller, Ben. Mystic, CT: Mystic Seaport Museum, 2002.

103 Sailing Rigs. Bolger, Phil. Gloucester, MA: Phil Bolger & Friends, Inc., 1998.

U.S. Government

Federal Requirements for Recreational Boats
Navigational Rules
Boatbuilder's Handbook
U.S. Coast Guard
Office of Boating Safety
2100 2nd Street, SW
Washington, D.C. 20593
800-368-5647
http://www.uscgboating.org/

Magazines

Boatbuilder
P.O. Box 112,
Jamestown, RI 02835
401-423-1400

Boat Design Quarterly
P.O. Box 98
Brooklin, ME 04616

Classic Boat
Leon House, 233 High St.
Croydon, Surrey, England. CR9 1HZ
Tel: +44 (0)208 726 8000
Fax: +44 (0)208 726 8195

Messing About in Boats
29 Burley St.
Wenham, MA 01984-1943
978-774-0906

Water Craft
Bridge Shop, Gweek, Cornwall
TR12 6UD Great Britain
Tel: +44 (0)1326 221424

WoodenBoat
Box 78
Naskeag Road
Brooklin, ME 04616
207-359-4651

BOAT PLANS

The Internet has opened up access to many designers who previously had only local followings. Here is a sampling of the myriad plans available.

The cost of plans ranges from dirt cheap to a fairly hefty sum. Generally, unless otherwise stated, the fee will allow you to build only one boat from the plans. What you are getting with a set of plans is the designer's skill and training and a reasonable assurance that the boat you build will work. To avoid a Frankenboat monster, changes in a design should only be done in consultation with the designer. Like buying a car, it's always better to take a copy of a prospective boat out for a spin—or at least talk to someone who has.

Museums are a great source for traditional boat plans. It is worth noting, however, that historical plans don't guarantee performance, only that the prototype vessel is old and has been measured relatively accurately. Caveat Emptor!

Adirondack Museum
Rte 28N
Blue Mountain Lake, NY 12812-0099
518-352-7311
    Adirondack small craft, including guide boats and J.H. Rushton pulling boats and canoes.

The Alexandria Seaport Foundation
P.O. Box 25036
Alexandria, VA 22313 703-549-7078
Fax: 703-549-6715
    Bevins Skiff plans.

Antonio Dias Design
171 Cedar Island Road
Narragansett, RI 02882
401-783-4959
    Traditional small craft.

Arch Davis Design
37 Doak Road,
Belfast, ME 04915
207-930-9873
www.by-the-sea.com/archdavisdesign/
    Kits and plans for traditional plywood and glued-lap construction.

Atkin & Company
P.O. Box Box 3005
Noroton, CT 06820
    More than 200 designs previously published in *MoToR BoatinG*. Sailing dinghies, houseboats, double enders, utilities.

Bear Mountain Boat Shop
P.O. Box 191
Peterborough, Ontario K9J 6Y8 Canada
877-392-8880
    Plans and kits for elegant strip-built and stitch-and-glue canoes and kayaks.

Benford Design Group
605 S. Talbot St, Ste. One R
St. Michaels, MD 21663,
410-745-3235
    A wide range of designs, from lapstrake dinghies to steel trawlers

Brooklin Boat Yard
Brooklin, ME 04616
207-359-2236
Fax: 207-359-8871
  Classic Joel White designs, from small craft to cruising and racing boats up to 74'.

Brooks Boats
HC 64 Box 491
Brooklin, ME 04616
207-359-2491
  Elegant and practical glued lap designs for oar and sail.

Charles W. Wittholz, NA
Mrs. Esselle A. Wittholz
100 Williamsburg Dr.
Silver Spring, MD 20901
301-593-7711
  From plywood catobats to trawler yachts.

Chesapeake Bay Maritime Museum
St Michaels, MD 21633
410-745-2916
  Yet more Chappelle.

Chesapeake Light Craft
1805 George Ave.
Annapolis, MD 21401
410-267-0137
  Plans and kits for stitch-and-glue construction.

Clark Craft
16–98 Aqua Lane
Tonawanda, NY 14150
  Sport powerboats, fishing boats, duck boats, cabin cruisers, house boats, a few plywood dories, hydroplanes, speedboats, kayaks, canoes.

Classic Marine
Lime Kiln Quay, Woodbridge, Suffolk IP12 1BD UK
(From within UK) Tel: 01394 380390 Fax: 01394 388380
(From outside UK) Tel: +44 1394 380390 Fax: +44 1394 388380
  Small boat plans, many glued lap.

Devlin Designing Boat Builders
2424 Gravelly Beach Loop NW
Olympia, WA 98502
360-866-0164
www.devlinboat.com
samd@orcalink.com

Stitch-and-glue designs by Sam Devlin, from dinghies and hunting "sleds" to blue-water cruisers, for oar, sail, and power.

Feather Canoes
3080 North Washington Blvd.
#19 North
Sarasota, FL 34234
941-355-6736
  Plans for Mac McCarthy's double-paddle canoes, designed for lightweight strip building.

George Bueler Yacht Design
P. O. Box 966
Freeland, WA 98249
360-331-5866
  Long-range cruising designs to 102'.

Gerr Marine Inc.
838 West End Ave. - Suite BB
New York, NY 10025
212-864-7030
Fax: 212-932-0872
  New designs, big and small.

Glen-L Marine
Box 1802
Rosecrans Ave
Belleflower, CA 90707-1804
310-630-6258
  Sailboats, canoes, dinghies, work boats, from 7' to 55'.

Guillemot Kayaks
824 Thompson St, Suite I
Glastonbury, CT 06033
860-659-8847
  Plans and kits for strip-built, stitch-and-glue, and hybrid kayaks, plus canoes and other designs.

Harold "Dynamite" Payson
Pleasant Beach Road
South Thomaston, ME 04858
207-594-7587
  Plans for straightforward plywood small craft.

Harry Bryan
329 Mascarene Road Letete
New Brunswick Canada E5C2P6
506-755-2486
  Innovative and fuel-efficient traditionally built small craft.

Hart Nautical Collection
MIT Museum
265 Massachusetts Ave.
Cambridge, MA 02139
617-253-5942
Fax: 617-258-9107
   Works of the old master, N.G. Herreshoff; classics by
   William H. Hand; George Lawley and Son; others.

Iain Oughtred
Struan Cottage—Bernisdale
Isle of Sky
Scotland IV51 9NS Great Britain
Tel: 01470 532732
   Lapstrake rowing and sailing craft.

John Bull
Muriel Short
San Francisco Pelican Boats
203 Hawthorn Ave.
Larkspur, CA 94939
   Pelican boat plans.

John G. Alden Inc.
Donald G. Parrot
89 Commercial Wharf
Boston, MA 02110
617-227-9480
Fax 617-523-5465
   More than 1,000 original plans dating back to the early
   1900s.

L. Francis Herreshoff
LFH Plans—Elizabeth Vaughn
P.O. Box 613
Santa Rosa, CA 95402
   Vessels of L.F. Herreshoff.

Maine Maritime Museum
Washington Street
Bath, ME 04530
   Traditional small craft from the coast of Maine.

The Mariners Museum
100 Museum Drive
Newport News, VA 23006-3759
757-591-7782
www.mariner.org
tmmlib@infi.net

Nearly 50,000 plans on file detail the construction of
modern pleasure craft (including Hacker and Chris
Craft), warships, junks, schooners, sloops, steam-
boats, and much more.

Monfort Associates
50 Haskell Road
Westport, ME 04578
207-882-5504
pmonfort@prexar.com
   Kits and plans for Geodesic AiroLITE skin-on-frame
   boats: canoes, kayaks, sailboats and rowboats.

Museum Watercraft Plans Collection
75 Greenmanville Avenue
Mystic Seaport Museum
P.O. Box 6000
Mystic, CT 06355-0990
860-572-5360
shipsplans@mysticseaport.org
   Historic small craft for the Mystic Seaport collection.
   Also includes plans by Capt. R.D. "Pete" Culler, Elco,
   Henry Devereaux, F.D. Lawley, and William F. Crosby.

Paul Gartside Ltd.
P.O. Box 1575
Shelburne, Nova Scotia
Canada. B0T 1W0
   New, traditional designs in carvel, lapstrake, and strip,
   for sail and power.

Philadelphia Maritime Museum
321 Chestnut St.
Philadelphia, PA 19106
215-925-5439
   Traditional small craft.

Phil Bolger and Friends
P.O. Box 1209
Gloucester, MA 01930
   Innovative designs for all types of boats in every
   construction method.

Pygmy Boats
P.O. Box 1529
Port Townsend, WA 98368
360-385-6143
   Stitch-and-glue kits and plans: kayaks, wherries, and
   canoes, multi-chined and hard-chined.

R.H. Baker Catalog
29 Drift Road
Westport, MA 02790
508-636-3272
    Traditional small craft.

San Francisco Maritime National Historic Park
Historic Documents
Building E, Fort Mason Center
San Francisco, CA 94123
    Plans for traditional and historic Pacific Coast vessels.

Selway Fisher Design
15 King St.
Melksham, Wiltshire, England SN12 6HB
Tel/fax UK 01225 705074
International: +44 1225 705074
    Canoes, daysailers, steam and electric launches.

Smithsonian Institution
Ship Plans
Division of Transportation
National Museum of American History -CBO54/MRC 644
Smithsonian Institution
Washington, D.C. 20560
    Plans from the published works of Howard I. Chapelle
    and Harry V. Sucher.

Solway Dory Sailing Canoes Kirkbride, Carlise
Cumbria, England
CA5 5HX
    Plans for rigs and boats.

Stimson Marine Inc.
261 River Road
Boothbay, ME 04537
207-380-2842
    Small craft plans, including the Ocean Pointer power
    skiff, wherries, skin-on-frame kayaks, and a bow-roof
    greenhouse/shed.

Swallowtailboats
Nant-y-ferwig
Gwbert Rd.
Cardigan, Wales, SA43 1PN U.K.
Tel: 01239 615140 (From outside the UK: 44 1239 615140)
    Classic boat kits.

Thomas J. Hill Design-Build
166 Ferguson Ave.
Burlington, VT 05401-5912
802-658-9150

Light glued lapstrake small craft: canoes, skiffs,
dories.and others.

Uffa Fox Ltd.
Thetis Road
Cowes, Isle of Wight, England
    Uffa Fox designs. Need I say more?

Walter Simmons
Duck Trap Woodworking
P.O. Box 88
Lincolnville Beach, ME 04849
207-789-5363
    Traditional wooden small craft including wherries

Weston Farmer Association
18970 West Azure Road
Wayzata, MN 55391
    23 Weston Farmer designs including "Tahitiana."

Windward Designs
794 Creek View Road
Severna Park, MD 21146
410–544-9553
    Karl Stambaugh designs.

WoodenBoat Store
Box 78
Naskeag Road
Brooklin, ME 04616
207-359-4651
800-273-7447
    Various classic and new designs: kayaks, canoes,
    shells, rowing and sailing small craft in three bound
    study catalogs.

TOOLS
Conant Engineering
P.O. Box 498
Boothbay, ME 04537
207-633-3004
    Planking clamps.

Cumberland General Sore
Route 3, Box 81
Crossville, TN 38551
800-334-3640
    Blacksmithing tools, anvils, forges, bolt rod nuts (nuts
    w/ handle for making homemade clamps), rivet sets.

Garrett Wade Company Inc.
161 Avenue of the Americas
New York, NY 10013
800-221-2942
Hand tools of all sorts.

Highland Hardware
1045 N. Highland Ave. NE
Atlanta, GA 30306
404-872-4466
Hand tools.

Jamestown Supply
28 Narragansett Ave.
P.O. Box 348
Jamestown, RI 02835
800-423-0030
Hand tools, marine supplies.

John Henry Inc.
P.O. Box 7473
Spanish Fort, AL 36577
334-626-2288
A tool to convert planers for scarfing plywood.

Lee Valley Tools Ltd.
1090 Morrison Drive
Ottawa, Ontario, Canada K2H8K7
800-267-8767
or
12 East River St.
Ogdenburg, NY 13669
800-871-8158
800-513-7885 fax
Lots of hand tools.

Lehman's Non-electric Catalog
Lehman Hardware and Appliances Inc.
4779 Kidron Road
P.O. Box 41
Kidron, OH 44636
216-857-5757
Fax 216-857-5785
Blacksmithing tools, lead melting pots and ladles, woodworking tools, gas hot plates.

Professional Graphics
33 Omni Circle
P.O. Box 1327
Auburn, ME 04211
207-783-9132
Fax 207-777-3570
Drafting supplies.

Rutlands Limited.
Deepdale Business Park, Ashford Rd,
Bakewell, Derbyshire DE45 1GT, UK
Tel: 01629 815518
Tools, power and hand.

Sears, Roebuck and Company
Sears Tower
Chicago, IL 60684
Hand and power tools. The catalog is back.

Tools on Sale
Seven Corners Hardware Inc.
216 West 7th
St. Paul, MN 55102
612-224-4859
Discount power tools.

Wag-Aero
1216 North Road
Lyon, WI 53148
800-558-6868
Pneumatic tools: air drill, air hammer and rivet set, bucking bars, and other oddities such as wire twisters, snake drill attachment, and industrial heat gun.

Woodcraft
210 Wood County Industrial Park
P.O. Box 1686
Parkerburg, WV 26102-1686
800-225-1153
Unusual or hard to find hand tools (e.g., spare parts for wood planes) domestic and imported. Also glues, hardware, and a selection of power equipment.

SUPPLIES, GENERAL

American Leather & Hides
Commercial St.
Hartland, ME 04943
207-938-4433
Leather, whole hides for oars, spars, mast partners etc.

Atlas Metal Sales
1401 Umatilla St.
Denver, CO 80204
800-662-0143
Fax: 303-623-3034
Silicon bronze rod, sheet, tube, and bar. Also naval brass.

Bristol Bronze
P.O. Box 101
Tiverton, RI 02878
401-625-5224
    Bronze hardware.

Classic Marine
Lime Kiln Quay
Woodbridge, Suffolk IP12 1BD, UK
(Within UK) Tel: 01394 380390 Fax: 01394 388380
(Outside UK) Tel: +44 1394 380390 Fax: +44 1394 388380
    Traditional marine hardware.

Davey & Co. London Ltd.
1, Chelmsford Road Ind Est.
Great Dunmow CM6 1HD, UK
Tel: 01371 876361
e-mail: 100713.1037@compuserve.com
    Traditional marine hardware, red lead powder, white
    lead paste, LanoCoat waterproofer.

Defender Industries
255 Main St.
P.O. Box 820
New Rochelle, NY 10802-0820
    Dynel cloth and other marine supplies.

duPont Preservation Shipyard
Mystic Seaport Museum
75 Greenmanville Ave.
Mystic, CT 06355
860-572-5343 or 5341
    Genuine, high quality imported tarred hemp oakum.

Fisheries Supply Company
1900 N. Northlake Way
Seattle, WA 98103
800-426-6930
    Paints, compounds, fasteners, abrasives, etc.

George Kirby Paints
153 Mt Vernon St.
New Bedford, MA 02740
617-997-9008
    Great custom and old-time marine paints you thought
    no one made anymore.

Hamilton Marine
Route 1
Searsport, ME 04974
207-548-6302
800-639-2715

Fasteners, paints, glues, hardware, oakum, and other
marine supplies.

H.M. Hillman Brass and Copper Inc.
2345 Maryland Road
Post Office Box "R"
Willow Grove, PA 19090
800-441-5992
Fax: 215-659-0807
    Silicon bronze, copper nickel, naval brass.

Jamestown Distributors
17 Peckham Drive
Bristol, RI 02809
800-497-0010
    Fasteners, paints, hardware, glues, tools including
    Fuller bits.

J.M. Reineck & Sin
9 Willow St.
Hull, MA 02045
781-925-3312
    Traditional bronze hardware, including Herreshoff
    patterns.

Maritime Wood Products Corp.
3361 S.E. Slater Street
Stuart, FL 34997
800-274-8325
    Boatbuilding and repair materials.

Northwoods Canoe Shop
RFD #3
Box 118-2A
Dover-Foxcroft, ME 04426
    Canoe hardware, canoe tacks, canvas, clenching irons,
    plans.

Pert Lowell Co Inc.
Lane's End
Newbury, MA 01951
978-462-7409
    Mast hoops, parrel beads, wood cleats, etc.

Robbins Timber
Brookgate, Ashton Vale Trading Estate
Bristol, BS3 2UN, UK
Tel: 0117 963 3126
Fax 0117 963 7927
    Cedar strips, lumber, marine plywood, fastenings,
    glues and caulk.

Rostand RI Inc.
Box 737
335 Long Entry Road
Chepachet, RI 02814
800-635-0063
    Bronze hardware.

R & W Rope Warehouse
New Bedford, MA 02740
866-577-5505
    Traditional rigging and Davey hardware.

Shaw & Tenney
P.O. Box 213M
Orono, ME 04473
207-866-4867
    Paddles, oars, leathers, oar locks.

Spartan Marine Hardware
340 Robinhood Road
Georgetown, ME 04548
207-371-2542
800-325-3287
Fax: 207-371-2024
    Traditional hardware—fairleads, lift rings, bronze quart knees.

Standard Fastening
800 Mount Pleasant
P.O. Box 51208
New Bedford, MA 02745
800-678-8811
Fax 508-995-3886
    Fasteners, paints, hardware, glues.

Strawberry Banke Inc.
P.O. Box 300 BBM
Portsmouth, NH 03801
603-433-1100
    Copper clench nails.

Traditional Marine Outfitters
P.O. Box 268
Annapolis Royal
Nova Scotia, Canada BOS 1A0
800-363-2628
    Traditional style hardware.

Tremont Nail Company
P.O. Box 111
Wareham, MA 02571
    Hot-galvanized boat nails.

W.H. Keys LTD
Hall End Works
Church Lane
West Bromwich
West Midlands
B71 1BN England
Tel: 0121-553 0206
Fax: 0121-500 5820
    Alfred Jeffery Marine Glue.

GLUES

Aircraft Spruce and Specialty Company
201 W. Truslow Ave.
P.O. Box 424
Fullerton, CA 92632
    Aerolite two-part waterproof glue.

Dynochem
Duxford, Cambs CB2 4QB
England
Tel: 44(0) 1223 837370
    Aerodux resorcinol glue.

Gorilla Glue
The Gorilla Group
P.O. Box 42532
Santa Barbara, CA 93140-2532
    Unique one-part waterproof glue.

Gougeon Brothers,Inc.
P.O. Box 908
Bay City, MI 48707
989-684-7286
    WEST Epoxy and supplies.

Gurit (Newport) LTD.
St. Cross Business Park
Newport
Isle of Wight, P030 5WU
Great Britain
Tel: +44(0) 1983 828 000
    Epoxy.

Industrial Formulators of Canada, Ltd.
3824 William St.
Burnaby, BC Canada
    G2 epoxy (for gluing oily hardwoods) and Cold Cure.

Matrix Adhesive Systems
1501 Sherman Ave.
Pennsauken, NJ 08110
800-398-7556
    Epoxy and supplies.

System Three Resins Inc.
P.O. Box 70436
Seattle, WA 98107
206-782-7976
    Epoxy and supplies.

Wessex Resins
Cupernham House
Cupernham Lane
Romsey, Hants SO51 7LF
England
Tel: +44 (0)1794 521111
    WEST Epoxy and supplies.

SAILMAKERS

Center Harbor Sails
Brooklin, ME 04616

E.S Bohndell & Co.
Route 1
P.O. Box 628
Rockport, ME 04856
207-236-3549

Gambell & Hunter
16 Limerock St.
Camden, ME 04843
207-236-3561

Nathaniel S. Wilson
P.O. Box 71
Lincoln St.

East Boothbay, ME 04544
207-633-5071

Ratsey & Laphorn
42 Medina Road,
Cowes, Isle of Wight, PO31 7BY
Great Britain
Tel: 01983 294051
Fax: 01983 294053

MARINE PLYWOOD & BOAT LUMBER

Boulter Plywood Corp.
25 Broadway
Somerville, MA 02145
617-666-1340
Fax: 617-666-8956

Flounder Bay Boat Lumber Company
1112 18th St.
Anacortes, WA 98221-1503
800-228-4691

Harbor Sales
1000 Harbor Court
Sudlersville, MD 21668-1818
800-45-1712
Fax: 800-868-9257

Maine Coast Lumber
7 White Birch Lane
York, ME 03909
800-899-1664
207-363-7426
Fax: 207-363-8650

M.L. Condon Company Inc.
260 Ferris Ave.
White Plains, NY 10603
914-946-4111
Fax: 914-946-3779

Roberts Plywood
44 North Industry Court
Deer Park, NY 11729
631-586-7700
Outside NY State: 800-422-4944
Fax: 631-586-7009

BEDDING COMPOUNDS

BoatLIFE Life Caulk
BoatLIFE
2081 Bridgeview Drive
P.O. Box 71789
Charleston, SC 29415-1789
800-382-9706
boatlife@boatlife.com
   One-part polysulfide compound.

George Kirby Paints
153 Mt Vernon St.
New Bedford, MA 02740
617-997-9008
Info@KirbyPaint.com
   Red lead primer & white lead paste.

International Paint Inc.
2270 Morris Ave.
Union, NJ 07083
908-686-1300
yacht.us@yachtpaint.com
   Oil-based bedding compounds, including Boatyard
   Bedding Compound #214 Natural (thin with boiled
   linseed oil).

Kop-Coat Specialty Coatings Co.
36 Pine St.
Rockaway, NJ 07866
800-221-4466
973-625-3100
   Dolfinite 2005N Bedding Compound and Pettit 7908
   Bedding Compound Natural.

3M Marine
3M Center, Building 223-6S-06
St. Paul, MN 55144-1000
651-737-6501
877-366-2746
   Polyurethane compounds, including Adhesive
   Sealant "5200", Fast Cure "4200," and one-part polysulfide Marine Sealant "101."

Sika Corporation
30800 Stephenson Highway
Madison Heights, MI 48071
888-832-7452
www.sikaindustry.com
   Polyurethane compounds, including Sika 291, 291
   LOT.

Glossary

Apex—The lowest point in a cut rabbet where the inside face of a plank would end. In profile, it is found between the rabbet and bearding line. Sometimes called the "middle line" or "inner rabbet."

Apron—A structural, backing piece fit behind the stem. Often wider than the stem and set to form the after part of the rabbet.

Athwartships—At right angles to the centerline plane of the hull.

Batten—A thin, flexible length of wood, usually rectangular in shape and usually made of clear, straight-grained softwood. Used to create a smooth, fair line.

Backbone—The full assembly of all the components, including stem, keel and transom, that make up the center section of the hull.

Baseline—The starting point for vertical measurements on a marine blueprint—both profile and body plan.

Beam Mold—A pattern or template used for marking the shape (camber) of deck beams.

Bed Logs—The rabbeted structural members of a centerboard case that run fore and aft next to the centerboard slot. The logs are fastened to the keel with screws or bolts. The rabbets are designed to accept the side panels of the trunk and face inward toward the slot.

Bedding—A nonhardening, elastic putty that is used like a gasket compound between two pieces of wood to exclude water. "Natural" bedding is oil based and nonadhesive. Synthetic (ex. 5200, Sikaflex and Lifecaulk) beddings are adhesive—some to a very high degree.

Bearding Line—The point where the inside face of the planking touches the outside face of the stem as it enters the rabbet.

Beeswax—A plastic, dull-yellow substance secreted by bees for building cells. The stuff is hard when cold, easily molded when warm. It cannot be dissolved in water, and is used for waterproofing and lubrication.

Bevel—An angle or slant planed into a piece of wood, usually to facilitate the joining of that piece of wood to another. Lapstrake planks are beveled on their outside upper edge to allow the next plank to overlap and have a good fit.

Bevel Gauge—A two-bladed gauge used to capture angles.

Breasthook—A triangular structural member fit at the sheer immediately behind the stem. Fitted and fastened to the stem and the adjacent planking, the breasthook acts like a gusset in a truss to add great strength to the upper part of the stem.

Body Plan—The view on a set of lines or lofting portraying the athwartships or transverse view of the stations. Generally only one half of the width of the stations is illustrated. The body plan normally offers a split view, one side illustrating the stations as they would appear if one looked at the boat from the bow, the other as they would appear if viewed from the stern.

Bore—To drill a cylindrical hole.

Broad Strake—The second strake out from the keel, following the garboard.

Bung—A wooden plug used to cover a fastening.

Butt Block—A gusset-like block of wood used to join two parts of a strake together.

Buttock—A fore and aft slice or plane through the hull that runs parallel to the centerline plane.

Camber or Crown—A convex curve found on a deck, cabin top, breasthook, or other transverse member. The term is also used to describe an unwanted curve on a flat-planed bevel.

Carlin—A piece of deck framing that runs fore and aft and forms the inboard edge of the side decks and is connected to and supports the stud beams.

Carvel (planking)—Smooth-sided planking.

Ceiling—The inside planking on a vessel. It adds to structural strength and prevents debris from getting between frame members.

Centerboard—A pivoting keel made of either wood or metal.

Centerline—A line or plane running down the middle of the hull that divides the hull into two equal parts.

Cheeks—Pieces affixed to the side of a structure to strengthen it. Often seen on the inside face of a transom forming a frame and affording more area for fastenings. Another example is on the sides of the upper body of a thin rudder to allow it to accommodate a tiller.

Chine (1) The line that follows the intersection of the sides and bottom on a flat or V-bottomed boat. Chine Log (2) A narrow strip of wood running fore to aft, where the side and bottom legs of the frames join in a flat or V-bottomed boat.

Clench Nail—A square cut nail that can be used in a similar fashion to a rivet. Driven through a predrilled hole, the tip is bent back over itself to form a sort of one-legged staple.

Clinch Ring—A round, dished washer with a hole in the center into which a metal rod can be inserted and peened over, turning it into a drift pin.

Clinker (British)—*See* Lapstrake.

Coaming—A raised vertical wooden guard around a cockpit or hatch to keep water on deck from running in.

Cold Molding—Forming a hull with wood veneers and self-curing glue (usually epoxy) laminated over a form.

Cove and Bead—Concave and convex shapes cut into the edges of strip planks.

Counterbore—A cylindrical hole drilled for the head of a fastening. Usually filled with a bung or putty.

Crook—A naturally grown branch or root on a tree that can be sawn out and used as a structural member—a knee, stem, deck beam, or rib.

Cross Spall—A board (usually installed on a common waterline) that holds the two sides of a mold together. The term is also sometimes used for a temporary spreader placed sheer-to-sheer to hold the shape of a hull until permanent interior bracing is installed.

Deadrise—The angle the bottom of the boat makes with the horizontal plane at the keel.

Deadwood—Solid wood pieces in the middle of the backbone assembly.

Deck Beam—An athwartships structural component that not only supports the deck but also acts like a hull-strengthening tie connecting the port and starboard sides at the sheer. These pieces are manufactured with a convex or cambered shape. They can either be built of natural stock or be laminated.

Diagonal—A diagonal slice drawn through the lines plan when lofting to check the fairness of the hull.

Diminishing Device—An architectural tool used to graphically divide up distances. Often used when lining out strakes equally. It can easily divide different lengths of girth throughout the boat into a given number of planks of equal width.

Dory Lap—A system similar to lapstrake except it uses two complementary bevels in the laps rather than a single bevel.

Drift (or Drift Pin)—A homemade spike often used to blind fasten heavy keel members to one another. Also used to edge fasten rudders, centerboards, and transoms.

Edge Set—The forcing sideways of a plank on the flat. Undesirable for a spiling batten, but sometimes necessary for a plank.

Epoxy—A vernacular term that generally refers to the mixed two-part combination of epoxy resin and hardener.

Fair—A smooth line or curve without any unnatural distortions, lumps, or hollows.

Flitch Sawn—Planks or timbers sawn through and through as two-sided slabs with bark on either side.

Floor (or Floor Timber)—A plank roughly the same width as the rib that is set athwartships that is fitted and fastened to the garboard strake and keel. Floors are key components as they tie one side of the boat to the other.

Forefoot—The lower part of a built-up stem that falls in the region between the stem piece and the keel.

Frame—The nautical equivalent to the stud in a wall. Frames or ribs generally run perpendicular to the keel and are what the planks fasten to. Frames can be sawn or steam bent to shape.

Freeboard—The distance (measured vertically) on the side of a boat from the waterline to the deck.

Gaff Jaws—A pair of curved wooden pieces affixed to the end of the gaff that loosely surrounds the mast.

Garboard—The bottom-most plank closest to the keel.

Gooseneck—Fitting that attaches the boom to the mast, allowing it to move freely.

Green Wood—Newly cut wood with a high moisture content.

Gripe—*See* Forefoot.

Gudgeons—The hinges on which the rudder swings.

Half-Breadth—Distance measured out from the centerline.

Hanging Knees—Knees placed in vertical position below the deck beams.

Harpin—A sawn-to-shape inner backing member at the sheer. Installed horizontally, it is similar to a sheer clamp in use.

(To) Hog—A distortion of the hull in which the fore and aft ends droop lower than the rest of the keel.

Hog Piece—Similar to a keel batten. Used on top of the keel to give better landing for the garboard plank.

Hood End—The forward end of the plank where it fits into the rabbet.

Horn or Horn In—To check the squareness of an athwartships member (thwart, frame, mold) by measuring from a point on the centerline to the outermost edges of the piece being checked—thus forming an isosceles triangle. If both legs of the triangle are the same, the piece is square to the centerline.

"Inside of Plank"—The shape of the boat minus the plank thickness, i.e., outside of the rib or mold.

Inwale—A long piece of wood fastened at the top edge of the inside face of the ribs in an open boat. It generally serves the same purpose as a clamp in a decked boat.

Joining—The mating of one piece of wood to another.

Keel—The main structural member running fore and aft.

Keelson or Keel Batten—A structural member that is wider than and installed parallel to the keel for added strength. Often used to add greater bearing surface for the planking.

Kiln Dried—Wood that has been artificially dried in an oven to a specific percentage.

Knee—A brace or bracket between two adjoining members.

Landing or Lap—The flat bevel planed into the edge of a plank to allow the next plank to lie flush against it.

Lapstrake—A system of planking in which the edges of the strakes overlap one another.

Ledge—Fore and aft vertical ends of the centerboard case.

Limber—Drain hole cut in the lower edge of a floor.

Line Off Planks—To predetermine the location where the planks will be on the hull.

Live Edge—*See* Flitch Sawn.

LOA—Length overall.

Load Waterline or LWL—The theoretical level at which the hull will float when carrying its design weight.

Lodge Knees—Used to prevent deck beams wracking and to strengthen deck framing near the sides of the vessel.

Lofting—To draw the lines of the hull full size and fair them with battens on a large grid. Stations are generated, components are drawn, and measurements are checked. The patterns to build the boat can then be lifted from the grid.

Loom—Part of the oar that reaches from the bottom of the handle to the top of the flat blade.

Mast Partner—Extra framing added around the opening for strength.

Mast Step—Piece used to anchor the heel (bottom) of the mast.

Mold—The mold is the three-dimensional manifestation of the two-dimensional station curves drawn on the lofting.

Molded—*See* Sided.

Nib—A square cut made at the wedge or featheredge end of a piece of wood. Usually used on planking and on the ends of mechanical scarf joints.

Outwale—The chaffing strip on the outside sheer of the boat.

Parrel—A wire or rope collar that holds a yard or gaff to the mast that allows it to be raised or lowered and swivel around the mast. Sometimes beads or rollers are threaded on the collar to reduce friction.

Pine Tar—A heavy, blackish-brown liquid prepared by distilling pinewood and used in marine coatings and preservatives.

Pintles and Gudgeons—Fittings used to hang a rudder on a boat. Generally, the pintle is a downward facing pin mounted on the rudder. The gudgeon is a cast eye mounted on the transom.

Plank—A long, shaped (usually narrow) piece of sawn wood that makes up the boat's shell and is fastened to the outside of the ribs. A strake can be made up of one or more planks.

Plumb—Vertical.

Poppet—A brace for supporting a boat during construction or storage.

Profile—The side view of the vessel as seen at a right angle to the keel or centerline.

Quartersawn—Sometimes called edge-grained or vertical-grained lumber. This is lumber that has been sawed in a manner that the grain runs at right angles to the flat side of the board.

Rabbet—A notch or slice cut in a structural member to allow another piece to fit flush against it. An example would be the rabbet in a stem that the planking fits and is fastened to.

Rake—An angle or inclination (generally aft) from the vertical. Transoms on traditional small craft tend to be raked aft.

Rib—*See* Frame.

Ribband—A temporary batten-like wooden strap bent around the mold to which the steamed ribs are bent. The ribbands not only dictate the shape of the rib but also give the setup of the hull strength and resistance to wracking.

Riser—A fore and aft brace fastened to the inner side of the frames that supports the thwarts.

Rivet—Made from a nail that is driven through a hole drilled through two pieces of wood clamped together. A ring or burr is driven over the nail and the excess of the nail is nipped off with pliers. The stub of the nail is then peened against the ring with a hammer as the head of the rivet is backed up by a heavy iron.

Rocker—The fore and aft curvature in the keel.

Rove—*See* Burr.

Scantlings—Dimensions and sizes of all structural parts used in building a vessel.

Scarf—To join two pieces of wood using long beveled joints. Usually cut in a length-to-width ratio of 12:1, these joints are extraordinarily strong. Scarf joints in keel members are usually fastened with bolts, while for planking, the scarfs are generally glued.

Scribe—To mark a piece of wood for fitting using either a compass or a block of wood and a pencil. The term is also used for the scratching or etching of a line into a piece of wood with a sharp tool.

Shaft Log—A square-sided wooden "tube" that is part of the keel assembly through which the propeller shaft passes. Some shaft logs are made of a single piece of wood with a hole bored all the way through. Others are built of two pieces and bolted together.

Sheer—The uppermost visible line of the hull in profile view, the outermost (usually) in the half-breadth view. This probably has the least to do with how well the boat performs and the most to do with how it looks.

Shutter Plank—The final plank to close up a hull. Usually placed in an area with little shape and/or twist as these units are hard enough to fit as it is without complicating matters.

Sided and Molded—Two terms used to describe the thickness of a given cut part of the structure. The sided dimension is the notation of the constant thickness of a timber. The molded dimension is the varying thickness of the piece as cut.

Skeg—A vertical timber that is fastened to the after end of a small boat that acts like a deep keel and helps the boat to track.

Spall—*See* Cross Spall.

Spar—A round or square wooden shaft, such as a mast, boom, yard, or bowsprit, used to support sails and rigging.

Spile—To make a pattern for an oddly shaped piece, such as a plank, by recording measurements onto another piece of expendable stock. These measurements can then be transferred to the actual stock and connected by battens and drawn in pencil to give the proper shape of the new piece.

Spiling Batten—A long flexible batten made of light stock to record information when spiling a plank.

Spring Back—The degree to which a piece of bent stock, either steamed or laminated, will straighten out when released from its clamps.

Stanchion—A supporting post or pillar. An example might be the vertical brace under a thwart.

Station—A two-dimensional slice at regular intervals through the hull. Think of slices in a loaf of bread.

Staving—In boat interiors, it is the nautical equivalent of wainscoting.

Stealer—A short plank used to fill in an area or straighten out a run of planks.

Stem Band—Protective strip of metal (usually half round or oval) fastened to the face of the stem.

Stern Post—The vertical (or near vertical) backbone member that supports the transom.

Stern Sheet—The area aft with seat and benches.

Stitch-and-Glue—A system of planking that uses plywood planks or panels that are temporarily held in place with wire until they can be glued together. Plank shape determines the shape of the boat and few molds are used.

Stopwater—A softwood dowel placed in a drilled hole where the rabbet crosses an underwater backbone joint. Used to stop water from leaking into the hull; hence the pithy name.

Strake—A continuous run of a hull planking traveling from fore to aft. Can be either a single piece or built up of several planks.

Strip Planking—Planking composed of long, rectangular sectioned strips of wood that are wrapped around the hull and whose edges are fastened to one another with nails or glue.

Stretcher—An adjustable brace running across the boat for a rower to brace their feet against.

Strongback—A frame or horse to support a boat that is under construction.

Stud Beam—A short beam under a side deck.

Template—A pattern made of thin stock for any structural member.

Thole (Pin)—Vertical wooden peg or pin inserted through the sheer rail to form a fulcrum for oars when rowing.

Thwart—A transverse seat in a small boat. It not only provides a place to sit but also ties the boat together.

Toe-rail—A low strip running around the edge of the deck.

Transom—The transverse structure (usually flat) at the aft end of the boat upon which the planks land.

Trunnel—A homemade dowel-like fastening that is driven into a predrilled hole and wedged at either end.

Tumblehome—When viewed in a transverse section through the hull, it is the narrowing or returning inward of the topsides as they approach the sheer. The opposite of flare.

Turn Button—A small button or cleat that can be pivoted to hold doors, panels, or floorboards in place.

Waterline—On a set of plans, it is a regular height of elevation above a base—similar to those found on a topographic map. In profile view, the lines are straight and parallel. In the half-breadth view, they are curved.

Index

Numbers in **bold** refer to pages with illustrations

trash can cyclone lid, 148–49
"Treatise on the Origin, Progress, Prevention and Cure of Dry Rot in Timber, A" (Britton), 133
twisting spanner, 76–**77**
two-piece stems, **219–21**
two-way clamps, **35**, **139**

U
ultimate stability, 8
Understanding Boat Design (Brewer), 84
United Nations Food and Agriculture Organization (FAO), 297
upside down vs. right-side up construction: carvel planking, 34, 35–36, **202**, **203**, **204**; decision about, 25, 34, **202–3**; frames, steam bending, **224**; height of construction jig, 182; strip planking, 74
U.S. Coast Guard, **11**, 322
U.S. government resources, 149, 322

V
vacuums, 148–49
varnish. *See* paint and varnish
V-bottomed hulls: advantages of, 82; building process, **82–83**; catboats, **292**; characteristics, 8–**9**, 293–94; construction methods for, 89, 293–94; deadrise, 83–**84**; FAO de-

signs, **297**; frames, 81–**82**; lofting, 82, **200**, 201; planking material, 83–84; popularity of, 81, 293; power-boats, 81, 82; sailboats, **81**, 82. *See also* hard-chined hulls

W
Wallace, Alton, 299
waterlines: accuracy of, 184; length of, 7; lofting **163**, 186, 188–90, **189**; on plans, 159, **160**; shapes, 6–**7**; taking lines off boats, 306, **307**–8
watertight construction, 66, 71. *See also* caulking
Web sites: National Association of State Boating Law Administrators, 12; U.S. Coast Guard, 11
Wee Lassie, 278
weight: of hulls, 9; of wood species, 101
West Pointer workboat, 299
wetted surface, 267
wherries, **73**, **216**, **272**–73
Whilly Boat, 4–5
White, Joel, 4, 5, 217, 274, 291, 294
Whitehall-style pulling boats: characteristics, 1, 270–**71**, 273–74; construction methods for, **2**, 17, **21**, **271**; hull design, **7**, 271; keels, 215–**16**, 271; lofting, **183**, 184–**99**, 201
wild cherry, 109

Windward 17, 294
Wineglass Wherry, **272**
wire tie-up tool, **224**
Wittolz, Charles, 292
Wompus Cat catboat, 292
wood: for boat bottoms, 64–65; borate preservatives, 133–34; cost of, 99, 107; cupping, 64–65, 102, **103**; defects, 102–3; demands on, 27–28; flitch-sawn vs. quarter-sawn, 102, **103**, 231; moisture content, 100, 103, 114; planking stock, 75; ply-wood vs. sawn lumber, 64; politics and, 103–4; resources, 330–31; seal-ers, 130; selecting, 64, 99, 102–4, **103**; sources of, 99; types of, 99–102; width of planking, 64–65. *See also* plywood
wood dust, 90, 148–49
WoodenBoat magazine, 314
Wooden Ship-Building (Desmond), 227
wood flour, 90
Wood Handbook (Forest Products Laboratory), 64

Y
youth boatbuilding programs, **313**–15

Z
zinc, 123, 124